D0890454

ENCYCLOPEDIA OF
ARKANSAS
MUSIC

EDITED BY

ALI WELKY AND MIKE KECKHAVER

BUTLER
CENTER
BOOKS

The Butler Center for Arkansas Studies
Central Arkansas Library System
100 Rock Street
Little Rock, AR 72201

First printing: September 2013

Project director: Rod Lorenzen
Book and cover design: Mike Keckhaver

Library of Congress Cataloging-in-Publication Data

Encyclopedia of Arkansas music / edited by Ali Welky and Mike Keckhaver.
     pages   cm
Includes index.
 ISBN 978-1-935106-60-9 (pbk. : alk. paper) -- ISBN 978-1-935106-61-6 (e-book)
 1. Music--Arkansas--Encyclopedias. 2. Music--Arkansas--History and criticism.
 I. Welky, Ali, editor of compilation. II. Keckhaver, Mike, editor of compilation.

 ML101.U6E535 2013
 780.9767--dc23

                                                 2013021174

This book is printed on archival-quality paper that meets requirements of the American National Standard for Information Sciences, Permanence of Paper, Printed Library Materials, ANSI Z39.48-1984.

Butler Center Books, the publishing division of the Butler Center for Arkansas Studies, was made possible by the generosity of Dora Johnson Ragsdale and John G. Ragsdale Jr.

Printed in Canada

TABLE OF CONTENTS

About the Encyclopedia of Arkansas History & Culture

The Encyclopedia of Arkansas History & Culture (EOA) is a project of the Butler Center for Arkansas Studies at the Central Arkansas Library System (CALS) in Little Rock, Arkansas. It is the only state encyclopedia in the country to be produced by a library system. The EOA strives to offer a definitive, comprehensive, and accurate record of America's twenty-fifth state. The mission of this free online encyclopedia is to collect and disseminate information on all aspects of the state's history and culture and to provide a comprehensive reference work for historians, teachers, students, and others seeking to understand and appreciate Arkansas's heritage.

The EOA debuted online to the public in May 2006 as a work in progress. At that time, it contained approximately 700 entries and 900 pieces of media; as of 2013, the site offers more than 3,200 entries and more than 4,200 pieces of media.

Users have come from every continent (including Antarctica) and more than 215 countries. During its first month online, the EOA had about 47,000 visits; the EOA now receives more than 1.6 million visits each year.

Major funding for the establishment of the EOA was provided by the Winthrop Rockefeller Foundation. Over the years, the EOA has also received funding from the Department of Arkansas Heritage, the Arkansas General Assembly, the Arkansas Humanities Council, and the National Endowment for the Humanities, as well as donations from individuals, foundations, and organizations. CALS has pledged to keep the EOA in operation in perpetuity.

EOA staff members:
Guy Lancaster, Editor
Mike Keckhaver, Media Editor
Mike Polston, Staff Historian
Ali Welky, Assistant Editor
Kay Bland, Education Coordinator
Jasmine Jobe, Editorial Assistant

Former EOA staff members:
Tom W. Dillard, Founding Editor
Jill Curran, Project Manager
Nathania Sawyer, Senior Editor and Project Manager
Tim Nutt, Special Projects Editor
Steven Teske, Fact Checker
Anna Lancaster, Editorial Assistant
Shirley Schuette, Editorial Assistant

For more information, visit the EOA online at www.encyclopediaofarkansas.net.

PREFACE

There ain't no use in kiddin' myself. I like the way I am. I'm a natural, actual, real authentical, Arkansas lovin' man.

—Johnny Cash, "Arkansas Lovin' Man"

There's a lot to love about Arkansas music—if one can even declare such a broad category of "Arkansas music." Arkansas music is folk music. It's blues music. It's rock, it's jazz, it's classical, it's metal, it's opera. Arkansas music flows like a river, in and out of the state, in and out of decades. Or maybe it flows like a *blood*stream. It has a pulse. Or perhaps it defies such conceits entirely and just shows up, picks up a fiddle or a sax or a microphone or a guitar, and fills the room with melodies old or new or maybe old *and* new.

Putting together this book has been full of surprises ("Wow, I never knew [name of excellent musician] was from Arkansas!"), questions ("Now, when exactly was Sonny Boy Williamson born?"), and logistical puzzles ("Should we categorize Al Green as gospel or R&B?)—but mostly delights. After all these years publishing the Encyclopedia of Arkansas History & Culture (EOA) online, it is a pleasure to give some weight to all these words and pictures. It's like moving from the new-fangled on-the-go mp3 to the vinyl record album playing in the living room; sit down, stay awhile, and immerse yourself in the richness of all this music. There is just something about flipping through a book, enjoying the pictures and the surprise of what the next page may bring. The sheer heft of it in your hands conveys the importance of this subject.

We've been lucky to have so much musical expertise to build on in the EOA's first venture into print, from all our knowledgeable entry authors to Robert Cochran's seminal book on Arkansas music, *Our Own Sweet Sounds*, as well as the radio show *Arkansongs* from Stephen Koch and Keith Merckx. But in putting together this collection of encyclopedia entries and media covering music in Arkansas (some material quite new and some that has been on the EOA site for years), we know we are not capturing everything. We are probably even, despite our best efforts, leaving out some *major* things. Although complete coverage of the topic is a noble goal, we are not attempting to be exhaustive. It is folly. If we know anything from running the online EOA, it is that there is *always* more. Always. Moreover, this encyclopedia is a repository of knowledge about Arkansas music past and present, but leaning more heavily on the past. Many artists performing today, or maybe people just now picking up instruments or opening their mouths to sing, will likely be enshrined in the encyclopedias of the future.

Finally, reading about all these musical legends is marvelous and enlightening, but *listening* is really the thing. May this book inspire you to fill your ears with some of this "natural, actual, real authentical" music from the Natural State. You'll be pleased with what you hear.

Ali Welky
August 2013

Brockwell (Izard County):
• Brockwell Gospel Music School

Bryant (Saline County):
• Crystal Recording Studios

Conway (Faulkner County):
• Soundstage
• Toad Suck Daze

Crossett (Ashley County):
• Jeffress/Phillips Music Company

Eureka Springs (Carroll County):
• Eureka Springs Jazz Festival/Jazz Eureka
• Opera in the Ozarks at Inspiration Point
• Winterwood Recording Studios

Fayetteville (Washington County):
• George's Majestic Lounge
• Rockwood Club*
• Walton Arts Center

Hartford (Sebastian County):
• Hartford Music Company and Hartford Music Institute (now part of Powell, Missouri–based Brumley Music Company)

Helena-West Helena (Phillips County):
• King Biscuit Blues Festival
• *King Biscuit Time* radio program
• KFFA—1360 AM
• Delta Cultural Center

Hope (Hempstead County):
• Klipsch Audio Technologies

Hot Springs (Garland County):
• Hot Springs Music Festival
• Hot Springs Jazz Fest
• Vapors*
• Wilson's Tell-'Em-'Bout-Me Café*

Jonesboro (Craighead County):
• The Forum Theatre

Little Rock (Pulaski County):
• Afterthought
• Anthro-Pop Records*
• *Arkansongs* radio program—KUAR (FM 89.1)
• *Barnyard Frolics* radio program—KLRA FM
• Barton Coliseum
• *Beaker Street* radio program—KAAY (AM 1090)
• Beverly Gardens*
• Cinderella Gardens and Dance Palace*
• Downtown Music
• Dreamland Ballroom (restoration in progress)
• E&M Studios and My Records*

• Jaggars Recording Studio*
• Juanita's
• KABF (FM 88.3)
• KLRE (Classical FM 90.5)
• Mosaic Temple*
• Moses Melody Shop/KALO*
• Opera Theatre at Wildwood Park for the Arts*
• Ray Winder Field*
• Revolution Room
• Riverfest Arts and Music Festival
• Robinson Center Music Hall
• *Steve's Show*
• Verizon Arena (formerly Alltel Arena)
• The Village*
• Vino's
• War Memorial Stadium
• Whitewater Tavern

Newport (Jackson County):
• Silver Moon Club*

North Little Rock (Pulaski County):
• Arkansas Record and CD Exchange
• Hawk's Nest Studio

Mountain View (Stone County):
• Arkansas Folk Festival
• Jimmy Driftwood Barn

Pine Bluff (Jefferson County):
• Trio Club*
• WOK AM*

Pocahontas (Randolph County):
• Skylark Drive-In Theater rooftop*

Springdale (Washington and Benton counties):
• Sundown to Sunup Gospel Sing (later moved to Fayetteville, then Missouri)

Swifton (Jackson County):
• King of Clubs*

Texarkana (Miller County):
• Arkansas Municipal Auditorium (under renovation)

Trumann (Poinsett County):
• Vaden Records*

Tull (Grant County):
• Old Folks' Singing

Walnut Ridge (Lawrence County):
• Stopover of the Beatles/Beatles at the Ridge Festival

West Memphis (Crittenden County):
• 8th Street "Beale Street West"*
• KWEM AM*

* = defunct

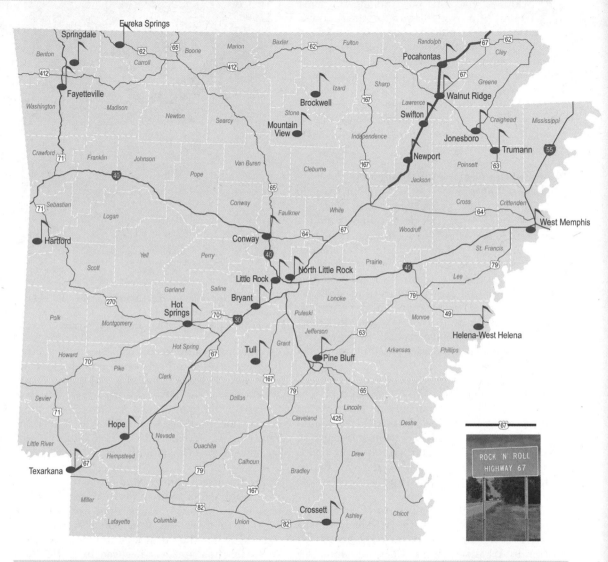

ROCK 'N' ROLL HIGHWAY 67

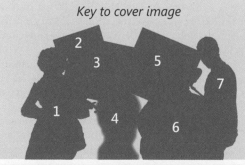

Key to cover image

1. Violet Brumley Hensley
2. Rock 'n' Roll Highway 67
3. "Big Bill" Broonzy
4. Barbara Hendricks
5. Johnny Cash
6. Sleepy LaBeef
7. Ben Nichols of Lucero

INTRODUCTION

Arkansas has long been among the most significant contributors to the nation's musical foundation, serving as fertile ground for the development of multiple genres as well as being native home to some of the best-known and influential musicians, singers, songwriters, and songs that the world has known. Much of this is due to the state's geography—both its diverse landscape and populace and its proximity to key musical hubs and regions in the nation.

Pre-European Exploration through the Nineteenth Century

"From the first, music mattered. You can even see it in what the archaeologists find... fragments of cane flutes and whistles older than Columbus," wrote Robert Cochran in his history of Arkansas music, *Our Own Sweet Sounds: A Celebration of Popular Music in Arkansas.* "But you can't hear this music, and until the first explorers published their accounts in the sixteenth and seventeenth centuries, you couldn't even read about it. The Osage drums, the leg rattles of Caddo dancers, the voices of Quapaws raised in song—all is silence."

Cochran traced what could be the earliest reference to Arkansas music to European explorers encountering Native Americans in the state on multiple occasions in the 1680s. Other accounts are sparse and isolated to settlements such as Arkansas Post, Washington (Hempstead County), and scattered outposts along trade routes such as the Arkansas River and the Southwest Trail.

Perhaps the most famous piece of music from this period referencing the state is "The Arkansas Traveler." The tune may or may not have been written in Arkansas, but, as Cochran wrote, "By 1845 it was known as a fiddle tune and in 1849 it was reported as the name of a race horse and the most popular dance tune in [the resort town of] Hot Springs." The tune eventually spawned a popular dialogue as well as a stage drama of the same name and, later, famous Currier & Ives engravings of two paintings by Arkansas painter Edward P. Washbourne: *The Arkansas Traveler* and *The Turn of the Tune.*

Cochran also noted that there were strong Ozark Mountain folk music and African-Ameri-

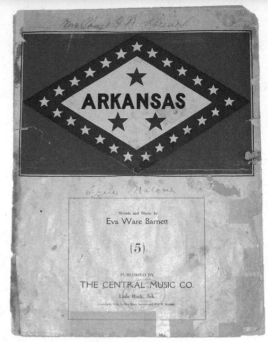

Arkansas's first officially recognized state song, Eva Ware Barnett's "Arkansas."

Courtesy: Old State House Museum Collection

can musical traditions in Arkansas in the 1800s, but very little of either was documented. Exceptions include Emma Dusenbury of Baxter County, who recorded 116 songs with the Library of Congress and sang at the Arkansas centennial celebration in 1936, and vaudeville star Essie Whitman of Osceola (Mississippi County), who was one of the Whitman Sisters.

Early Twentieth Century and Radio

The advent of radio in the 1920s enabled musicians, in Arkansas and around the world, to make their marks far from home. Music was a natural fit for the aural medium, and, by 1925, Arkansas had stations licensed in Little Rock (Pulaski County), Fayetteville (Washington County), Hot Springs (Garland County), and Fort Smith (Sebastian County), joining the original WOK in Pine Bluff (Jefferson County).

Plenty of early talent found fleeting fame on the airwaves of stations that, by the 1930s, were scattered around the state. Programs found on 10,000- to 50,000-watt "clear channel" AM radio stations with far-reaching signals proved most influential on the future artists from Arkansas, often musicians and singers who chose musical performance as a way out of the cotton fields.

The *National Barn Dance* on WLS out of Chicago, Illinois, gave Ruby Blevins (a.k.a. Patsy Montana) of Beaudry (Garland County) her first taste of national fame. WLS would also pick up the *Lum and Abner* program starring comedians Chester Lauck and Norris Goff of Mena (Polk County), and it hosted comedian, radio host, and banjo player Benjamin "Whitey" Ford of Little Rock—perhaps best known as the Duke of Paducah.

Shreveport radio station KWKH's *Louisiana Hayride* served as a showcase for famed Arkansas singers and musicians such as Johnny Cash of Kingsland (Cleveland County), Lefty Frizzell of El Dorado (Union County), and Floyd Cramer of Huttig (Union County), while WSM out of Nashville, Tennessee, broadcast weekly from the Grand Ole Opry.

These and other programs of the day served as something of a model for Arkansas's most famous and longest-standing radio broadcast. In November 1941, Helena (Phillips County) businessman Sam Anderson and a group of business partners put KFFA on the air. They were soon approached by blues musicians Sonny Boy Williamson of Helena and Robert Lockwood Jr. of Turkey Scratch (Phillips County) about the possibility of letting them play live on the air as a way to advertise nightly appearances around the area. Anderson told them they would need a sponsor and put them in touch with Interstate Grocery Company owner Max Moore, who had been considering an advertising campaign for one of his products, King Biscuit Flour.

The fifteen-minute *King Biscuit Time* program aired live from the Floyd Truck Lines building with Lockwood, Williamson, and a rotating cast of musicians performing as the King Biscuit Entertainers. The program was so popular that Moore soon re-branded another product as Sonny Boy Cornmeal. As of 2013, the program airs daily from the Delta Cultural Center in Helena-West Helena (Phillips County) on KFFA with longtime host "Sunshine" Sonny Payne.

Later in the 1940s, Williamson briefly migrated upriver to KWEM in West Memphis (Crittenden County), a station that hosted musicians who would pay to play live in the studio. The exposure worked to boost the careers of many musicians, including James Cotton of West Helena (Phillips County), Pat Hare of Cherry Valley (Cross County), and Robert Nighthawk of Helena. The station also influenced future trends. Noted figures from Elvis Presley to the Memphis Horns' Wayne Jackson of West Memphis to Albert King of Osceola have said that the music they heard on KWEM influenced their own careers.

The blues music that was a staple for these and many other radio stations around the Mississippi Delta region was highly influential and helped define the sounds of other genres. These include rhythm and blues (R&B), rock and roll, and country music, all of which would frequently borrow the song structure and phrasing of early Delta blues heard on recordings by the likes of Peetie Wheatstraw of Cotton Plant (Woodruff County)—best remembered for his direct influence on Robert Johnson, who, in turn, served as a musical mentor to Robert Lockwood Jr. when Johnson lived with Lockwood's mother near Helena, which served as the de facto capital of blues music in the Delta for roughly three decades, beginning in the 1920s.

Gospel also had an impact on these genres of music, and it is the style in which "Sister Rosetta" Tharpe of Cotton Plant got her start. She was four years old when she began performing as a singer and guitarist alongside her mandolin-playing mother at tent revivals around the South. It was only after moving north that she began to play blues, jazz, and R&B publicly. Her 1945 hit "Strange Things Happening Every Day" is often cited as the first rock and roll record. The song was later covered by Johnny Cash, who said Tharpe was his favorite singer when he was a child.

By this time, one of the most important figures in the history of Arkansas music was in New York paying his dues. Songwriter, musician, band leader, and jump blues pioneer Louis

Jordan of Brinkley (Monroe County) was born in 1908 into a musical household and studied at Arkansas Baptist College in Little Rock before he left the state to pursue a career that—for nearly a decade beginning in 1942—would see him dominate the R&B charts as the "King of the Jukebox."

With his 1943 hit "Ration Blues," Jordan became the first black musician to achieve "mainstream" crossover success on both the pop and country charts. Jordan's influence was as broad as it was deep. He has been called the "Father of Rhythm & Blues" and the "Grandfather of Rock 'n' Roll" by the Rock and Roll Hall of Fame (he was inducted in 1987) and has been cited as a key influence by fellow musical legends including Chuck Berry, B. B. King, Bob Dylan, and James Brown.

Popular Music in the Post–World War II Era

The roughly three decades following World War II became the most important period for music in Arkansas, both in terms of the number of artists and other musical figures hailing from the state as well as the music they produced during this time.

Journalist and Arkansas music historian Stephen Koch, host of the NPR-affiliated radio program *Arkansongs*, wrote, "It's literally impossible to overstate the significance of this period—both in terms of the product of our fellow Arkansawyers as well as the deep and lasting marks they left—on the music world. The number of important players in the music industry rivaled that of nearly any other state, and their impact and significance may exceed it. The global influence that they had is truly staggering, especially when one considers how little credit the state

Sonny Burgess and the Pacers; circa 1957. (Left to right): Kern Kennedy, piano; Sonny Burgess, electric guitar and lead vocals; Russ Smith, drums; Jack Nance, trumpet; Joe Lewis, acoustic guitar; and Johnny Ray Hubbard, double bass.
Courtesy: Sonny Burgess

has traditionally gotten. It cannot be denied that Arkansas has had a tangible and disparate role in shaping the record collection of almost anyone who has one."

It was across the Mississippi River in Memphis, Tennessee, that artists began building upon the foundation of Tharpe's early work, laying the groundwork for rock and roll. Much of this was done at Sun Records, where artists like Cash, Billy Lee Riley of Pocahontas (Randolph County), and Sonny Burgess of Newport (Jackson County) found a home, however briefly. Riley and Burgess continued to perform rockabilly music, often in venues along a storied stretch of Arkansas highway now known as Rock 'n' Roll Highway 67.

Cash, who had moved to Dyess (Mississippi County) with his family as a young boy, joined fellow Memphis-based Sun Records alumni Charlie Rich of Colt (St. Francis County) and Conway Twitty of Helena (who had already sat atop the rock and pop charts) in pursuing their ambitions in Nashville, Tennessee, as country singers. All three achieved legendary status, while Cash transcended boundaries to become a cross-cultural icon to his generation and those to come. He was the recipient of twenty Grammy Awards (most coming late in his career and some awarded posthumously), Kennedy Center honors, and the National Medal of Arts. He is a member of the Country Music, Rockabilly, Gospel, Rock and Roll, and Songwriters Halls of Fame; as of 2013, he is the only person ever inducted into all five.

Given its largely rural population during this period, Arkansas had no shortage of native musicians who decided to pursue country music. In the early part of the postwar era, the trade publications referred to the music of rural America as "folk," while the music industry used the "hillbilly" label. Either moniker would have been embraced by Jimmy Driftwood of Timbo (Stone County), who used his grandfather's homemade guitar in the process of penning literally thousands of songs over the course of his life. Driftwood's chosen career was as a teacher, and after earning his degree in education from Arkansas State Teachers College (which later became the University of Central Arkansas), he began writing songs as a way to make learning more interesting for his students. Driftwood's greatest success as a songwriter and musician came relatively late in life. He became a member of the Grand Ole Opry in the 1950s and was in his fifties when he charted six songs simultaneously on the pop and country charts in 1959. Five Driftwood songs would eventually earn Grammy Awards, including "The Battle of New Orleans"—a song written in 1936 as a lesson for his students—which was named Song of the Year in 1959.

Conway Twitty (born Harold Lloyd Jenkins) was one of the top country artists of the twentieth century. In 1943, when he was about ten, his family moved to Helena from Louisiana. He formed his own band, the Phillips County Ramblers, and, after serving in the military, went to Memphis to pursue his music career. It was here that he took his stage name by combining Conway, Arkansas, and Twitty, Texas. By 1958, his rock and roll recording "It's Only Make Believe" was number one. But even with his success as a rock and roll performer, Twitty preferred country music. By 1965, he had changed genres. His 1968 recording "Next in Line" became his first country number-one single. Twitty released dozens of top-rated singles in his rock and country careers, recording some 110 albums. In the 1970s, Twitty and fellow country star Loretta Lynn collaborated on a number of highly successful duet recordings. He was inducted into the Country Music Hall of Fame in 1999.

Future country legend Glen Campbell of Billstown (Pike County) hailed from southwestern Arkansas, meaning that a migration to Memphis and then Nashville was less natural. He picked up the guitar as a youth, and, in the mid-1950s, moved to Albuquerque, New Mexico, to play in a band with his uncle; he later formed his own band. While honing his skills, Campbell became friends with fellow Arkansas expatriate and guitarist Louie Shelton of Little Rock, and then moved to Hollywood, California, in 1960 to work as a session musician. Campbell was quickly recognized as a formidable guitar player and found plenty of work (along with Shelton) as part of the renowned Wrecking Crew group of studio players. During this period, he played on records for a varied list of artists that included Frank Sinatra, Elvis Presley, Merle Haggard, Jan and Dean, and Nat King Cole. For a time, he was also a key component of producer Phil Spector's famed Wall of Sound. Campbell's session work was also heard on the Beach Boys' landmark *Pet Sounds* album, and, for a period in the mid-1960s, Campbell was a touring member of the Beach Boys, filling in for Brian Wilson, who had tired of the road.

Campbell also worked to launch his own solo career and struck gold in 1967 with "Gentle on My Mind" and "By the Time I Get to Phoenix"—performances that earned him five of his nine Grammy Awards. Eventually, Campbell's listener-friendly brand of country pop topped the charts nine times on the way to his 2005 induction into the Country Music Hall of Fame.

Campbell is just a single example of an influential musical artist from Arkansas for whom the lines between country and rock were blurred. This was also the case with Levon Helm of Elaine (Phillips County), who picked up the guitar at an early age and performed in talent shows around Helena with his sister. What he described as the "hambone" elements of their act may have played a role in Helm's fascination with the drums. It was the drumming that led to his hiring on as a teenager with rockabilly singer Ronnie Hawkins of Huntsville (Madison County), known for his wild stage antics. It was through Hawkins and his connections north of the border in Canada that Helm would meet the members of the group of multi-instrumentalists and singers that eventually became known simply as the Band. Often credited as being the progenitors of the Americana genre, the Band was adored by fans and critics alike, and Helm became one of the most respected drummers of the era. The Band's active period with its original lineup began in 1967 and ended less than a decade later amid differences in creative vision between Helm and singer/guitarist Robbie Robertson. Their final concert in their original configuration was chronicled in the acclaimed Martin Scorsese documentary *The Last Waltz*—a project that Helm never truly embraced due to creative and logistical conflicts, again, with Robertson. The remaining members of the group reunited in 1983, releasing several studio albums, touring intermittently, and playing at their induction into the Rock and Roll Hall of Fame in 1994—all without Robertson. The Band called it quits for good in 1999 following the death of Helm's dear friend—bass player and singer Rick Danko. Helm was already battling throat cancer by this time, which severely marred his distinctive singing voice. He played several years with his own band, leaving the vocal duties to others, including his daughter Amy Helm. By 2004, he was singing again and later released two studio albums and one live album, all of which won Grammy Awards. Helm died of cancer in 2012.

Straightforward, "Southern-fried" rock and roll was the style of Black Oak Arkansas (BOA), led by the flamboyant front man "Jim Dandy" Mangrum of Black Oak (Craighead County). His onstage mannerisms and vocal trademarks were unabashedly copied by David Lee Roth of the more successful Van Halen (with Mangrum's evident but unsolicited approval). All of the members of BOA originally hailed from Craighead County but spent some time based in New Orleans, Louisiana, and Memphis, where they signed with the mostly R&B-oriented Stax Records as the Knowbody Else. The band finally signed with Atlantic subsidiary Atco and settled at a compound in the Ozark Mountains, where many of their antics were chronicled by manager and future central Arkansas concert promoter Butch Stone. BOA was prolific, releasing fourteen live and studio records between 1971 and 1978. The band's popularity had peaked by that time, as the record-buying public became more enamored of the disco and "urban cowboy" fads. Still, BOA continued to release albums despite frequent personnel changes, even involving Mangrum. As of 2013, the group was still playing occasional concerts as Jim Dandy's Black Oak Arkansas.

The disco craze would prove to be the high point in the already distinguished career of Johnnie Taylor of Crawfordsville (Crittenden County). Even though he was well established as a respected blues, soul, gospel, and R&B singer and one of the biggest artists charting hits for Stax, Taylor was perhaps best known for his 1976 hit "Disco Lady," which spent four weeks at the top of the pop chart and was the first single ever certified platinum by the Recording Industry Association of America for sales of two million copies. Much of Taylor's tenure at Stax was spent while the label was being run by

"I'll Take You There"

Al Bell recalled writing the song "I'll Take You There" while sitting on the hood of an old school bus that was rusting in his family's back yard in North Little Rock. "We were prepared to go into Muscle Shoals and record the Staple Singers when I got word that my brother was dead," Bell said. After the funeral, Bell said that he did not want to be in the house where everyone was gathered. "I went back there and sat on the hood of that bus thinking about all that was happening and all of a sudden I heard this music in my head. And I heard these lyrics: 'I know a place ain't nobody worried, ain't nobody crying and ain't no smiling faces lying to the races. I'll take you there.'"

Al Bell of Brinkley, who made Taylor a marquee artist at the label along with icons like Isaac Hayes and the Staple Singers. Bell is the writer of "I'll Take You There," arguably the Staples' signature song.

The R&B talent from Arkansas was prodigious. "Little Willie" John of Cullendale (Ouachita County) had a short but extraordinary career as an R&B artist. He was the first to cut the song "Fever," which went on to be recorded numerous times by Peggy Lee, Barry Gibb, and Madonna, to name a few. The John recording, produced by Henry Glover of Hot Springs (who was also a trusted friend of Levon Helm throughout his career), hit the top of the R&B chart in 1956. John's personal demons caused his star to fade, and he charted his last hit in 1961. He died in prison in 1968, but the significance of his contributions did not go unrecognized; he was inducted into the Rock and Roll Hall of Fame in 1996.

Al Green of Forrest City (St. Francis County) was one of the world's brightest musical stars in the early 1970s when he released a string of number-one albums, until a domestic incident with a girlfriend at his Memphis home pushed him into the ministry. While preaching, Green found middling success exclusively as a gospel singer but gravitated back to R&B in the late 1980s and went on to release a number of secular albums that did well but never achieved the success he enjoyed at the peak of his career.

The blues continued to thrive in Arkansas in the postwar years in the hands of such musicians as Williamson, Lockwood, and Nighthawk. It was with the latter that a young Frank "Son" Seals of Osceola got his start as a drummer. He soon picked up the guitar and began tearing up the Chicago blues scene. His contemporary, Luther Allison of Widener (St. Francis County), taught himself to play guitar and went on to share the stage with the likes of Howlin' Wolf and Freddie King.

Jazz, Opera, and Classical Music in the Modern Era

Arkansas is not commonly associated with jazz, opera, or classical music even though recognition is warranted. Pharoah Sanders, born in Little Rock, worked as a sideman for John Coltrane and Don Cherry before setting out on his own. He became one of the most admired saxophone players in jazz, moving from avant-garde to hard bop and post-bop. He became a free jazz pioneer, eventually influencing his former mentor, Coltrane, with his dissonant style. Sanders earned a Grammy Award in 1988 for his part in a collaborative tribute to Coltrane.

Cool jazz and bebop pianist and singer Bob Dorough of Cherry Hill (Polk County) became an influential figure, first achieving success in the 1950s. His biggest influence may have been as the composer and singer for many of ABC's Saturday morning *Schoolhouse Rock!* cartoons produced in the 1970s and 1980s.

Singer and actress Gretha Boston of Crossett (Ashley County) is the first Arkansan to win a Tony Award. The mezzo-soprano was recognized in 1995 as the Best Featured Actress in a Musical for her role as Queenie in the Broadway revival of *Show Boat.*

Some of the most prominent names in American opera are among the alumni of Opera in the Ozarks at Inspiration Point, a training program and festival located on a mountainside overlooking the White River west of Eureka Springs (Carroll County).

Barbara Hendricks of Stephens (Ouachita County) is one of the biggest stars in opera, as well as a noted humanitarian. Known for her interpretations of French and Scandinavian composers over the usual German and Italian fare, the soprano won competitions in New York, Switzerland, and France—and all prior to her graduation from Juilliard and her Paris, France, recital debut in 1973. In 2001, Hendricks performed at the Nobel Peace Prize concert in Oslo, Norway. In 2006, she started her own record label.

Robert McFerrin of Marianna (Lee County) received international acclaim as a baritone opera singer and a music teacher—and for fathering a subsequent generation of musicians, including Grammy Award–winning pop vocalist Bobby McFerrin. He moved to New York City in 1948 and made his operatic debut the following year in Verdi's *Rigoletto.* McFerrin also sang in the world premiere of *Troubled Island* at the City Center of Music and Drama in New York City in 1949.

Drugstore in Alma (Crawford County); circa 1909. At the time, there was an opera house above the drugstore.
Courtesy: Butler Center for Arkansas Studies, Central Arkansas Library System

Troubled Island happened to be one of more than 150 pieces written by William Grant Still, who grew up in Little Rock. In 1931, Still became the first black composer to have his work performed by a major symphony orchestra in the United States, when the Rochester Philharmonic performed his *Afro-American Symphony.* The same symphony was performed by the New York Philharmonic at Carnegie Hall in 1935. In 1936, Still became the first African American to conduct a major symphony orchestra when he directed the Los Angeles Philharmonic during a performance of his own work at the Hollywood Bowl. Still's body of work transcended racial barriers, however, and he is widely regarded as one of the most important and influential American-born composers.

Arkansas State University (ASU) professor Michael Dougan noted in his book *Arkansas Odyssey* that Scott Joplin, born in Texas and raised in Texarkana (Miller County), was the first major musical figure to hail from Arkansas and the first African American to gain acclaim in American musical history. "Born in 1868 near the present site of Texarkana, he studied with his violinist father and played piano in honky-tonks and brothels," wrote Dougan. "By the turn of the century, he had become the preeminent figure in an essentially black musical idiom known as Ragtime of which he was the accomplished king. Joplin's own piano playing was preserved on piano rolls, and he composed perhaps the first opera by a black composer, *Treemonisha.* Set in Reconstruction Arkansas to libretto of his own devising, the opera celebrated the victory of education over superstition and ignorance." The work is said to be influenced by both Joplin's mother, Florence, and his second wife, Freddie, whom he married in her hometown of Little Rock just weeks before her death in 1904 from pneumonia at the age of twenty.

The prolific composer Francis McBeth, who lived most of his life in Arkadelphia (Clark County), was a native Texan who found his home in Arkansas when he accepted the position of band director at what is now Ouachita Baptist University (OBU) in 1957, where he would remain as a distinguished professor and resident composer until his retirement in 1996. McBeth served as conductor of the Arkansas Symphony Orchestra from 1971 to 1973 and is credited with making the ensemble a viable and financially stable entity with its own permanent venue and professional musicians. In 1975, McBeth was named composer laureate of Arkansas—the first composer laureate in the United States.

Late Twentieth Century and Looking Forward

The 1980s saw far less Arkansas music finding national attention; the careers of the postwar luminaries were either slumping or in permanent decline. Little Rock's Ho-Hum flirted with mainstream rock and roll success, even seeing a song of theirs used in an episode of the popular television program *Melrose Place*. Little Rock band Ashtray Babyhead found some interest from major labels with its brand of hook-laden power-pop but ultimately never achieved success as a group even after re-branding themselves with the radio-friendly moniker the Kicks. Member Jeff Matika eventually joined Arkansas native Jason White of North Little Rock (Pulaski County) in the ranks of popular rock band Green Day as a touring member.

The future of Arkansas music remains bright, however. For example, Trout Fishing in America of Prairie Grove (Benton County) combined keen talent, hard work, and high-mileage vehicles in building a loyal audience stretching from coast to coast. Between 1979 and 2010, the duo, consisting of bassist Keith Grimwood and guitarist Ezra Idlet, released nearly two dozen albums—most on their own Trout Music label—as well as two books and at least two full-length concert videos. Almost half of the albums were marketed as "family" releases because of their kid-friendly content. As a result, many of the dates on their full touring schedule consist of daytime concerts for families, followed the same evening by more adult-oriented concerts in clubs. The band has been nominated for four Grammy Awards.

Multi-platinum-selling rock band Evanescence of Little Rock won Grammy Awards for Best New Artist and Best Hard Rock Performance in 2004 while being nominated for three others, including Album of the Year. The group, led by singer and multi-instrumentalist Amy

Lee, is still producing music and touring as of 2013 despite numerous personnel changes.

Country singer Joe Nichols of Rogers (Benton County) signed his first record deal at age nineteen and, between 2003 and 2011, became a Music Row veteran with eight studio albums including a greatest hits compilation that included three number-one singles.

Shaffer Smith of Camden (Ouachita County), better known by his stage name Ne-Yo, is a singer/songwriter, producer, and actor known for collaborations with some of the biggest names in R&B and hip-hop music. As of 2013, he has been nominated for thirteen Grammy Awards and has won three.

Memphis-based Americana and southern alt-country-rock band Lucero, fronted by Ben Nichols of Little Rock, was formed in 1998 and, by 2013, had released nine studio albums on at least five labels, including *Nobody's Darlings*, which was produced by legendary pioneer of the "Memphis Sound" Jim Dickinson of Little Rock and released in 2005 on their own Liberty & Lament label, as well as *1372 Overton Park* (2009) and *Women & Work* (2012).

A line can be drawn from Arkansas artists such as Louis Jordan and even comedian Rudy Ray Moore of Fort Smith to hip-hop and rap music. Jordan made copious use of the spoken word

Lucero frontman Ben Nichols at the 2012 Arkansas Sounds music festival in Little Rock.

Photo: Mike Keckhaver

16

in his work, and his music is seen by many as a forerunner to rap and hip-hop. Arkansas's own rap/hip-hop scene began bubbling under the surface in the 1980s and is active in the twenty-first century with a substantial number of prolific artists. No Arkansas rappers, however, have yet managed to gain the notoriety of their counterparts in other southern cities such as Memphis, New Orleans, and Houston, Texas.

The talent pool of Arkansas musicians is seemingly not as wide nor deep as it was during the postwar heyday, but the soil has been turned, and the influential seeds of the pantheon of Arkansas music are planted in fertile ground, leaving a rich legacy for those who will come after.

For additional information:

Arkansongs. http://www.ualr.edu/kuar/arkansongs/ (accessed December 19, 2012).

Cochran, Robert. *Our Own Sweet Sounds: A Celebration of Popular Music in Arkansas*. 2nd ed. Fayetteville: University of Arkansas Press, 2005.

Dougan, Michael B. *Arkansas Odyssey: The Saga of Arkansas from Prehistoric Times to the Present*. Little Rock: Rose Publishing Co., 1995.

George-Warren, Holly, and Patricia Romanowski, eds. *The Rolling Stone Encyclopedia of Rock & Roll*. New York: Rolling Stone Press, 2001.

Kingsbury, Paul, ed. *The Encyclopedia of Country Music*. New York: Oxford University Press, 1998.

Palmer, Robert. *Deep Blues*. New York: Viking Press, 1981.

Keith Merckx

BLUES / R&B

The origins of the blues are murky, but the state of Arkansas seems to have hosted the music and its creators since its beginnings in North America and helped spread it worldwide. Blues is acknowledged as the root from which sprang jazz, rhythm and blues (R&B), rock and roll, and hip-hop; in addition, it has informed the genres of country and western, gospel, and bluegrass. Blues and its offspring have long since crossed the globe, but its standard-bearers are largely confined to the Mississippi River Delta, especially eastern Arkansas and western Mississippi.

Emerging in part from call-and-response "field hollers" dating from the slavery era, blues had practitioners originally belonging to many different groups with their own musical styles. Most scholars believe that commercial blues was born around the start of the twentieth century and popularized by bandleader/songwriter W. C. Handy. Traveling medicine shows played the region, and blues stars were among the first to test 78 rpm recording technology. The genre gained momentum in the 1920s with female vocalists such as Ma Rainey and Bessie Smith and with stage shows and brass bands. This style largely faded with the Great Depression. Handy's own description of how he first heard what became known as blues was more the standard image— blues tunes played by a nondescript solo male street performer.

In the 1930s, William Bunch, known as Peetie Wheatstraw, of Cotton Plant (Woodruff County), Roosevelt Sykes of Elmar (Phillips County), and Robert "Washboard Sam" Brown of Walnut Ridge (Lawrence County) were among the era's most popular and prolific blues performers. Washboard Sam, best known for the song "Mama Don't Allow," also recorded under the names Ham Gravy and Shufflin' Sam—and sometimes performed with his half-brother "Big Bill" Broonzy, who was raised in Langdale (Jefferson County). Casey Bill Weldon, born in Pine Bluff (Jefferson County), had a mid-1930s hit, "Somebody Changed the Lock on My Door," and recorded as a member of the Memphis Jug Band, the Hokum Kings, and the Washboard Rhythm Kings.

Locally, Marianna (Lee County), Forrest City (St. Francis County), Brinkley (Monroe County), Osceola (Mississippi County), and many other Arkansas cities were brimming with homegrown and transplanted talent, and patrons packed clubs with names like the Dipsy Doodle, White Swan, Blue Flame, and Wilson's Tell-'Em-'Bout-Me Cafe.

In 1941, a blues music radio program, *King Biscuit Time*, began broadcasting five days a week on KFFA 1360 AM out of Helena (Phillips County). For the first time in its birthplace, blues was heard regularly live over the airwaves, a medium that knew no color line, and recognition of both *King Biscuit Time* and the blues widened. "Sunshine" Sonny Payne was employed at KFFA at the inception of *King Biscuit Time* in the 1940s and has hosted the Peabody Award–

winning program into the twenty-first century, interrupted only by his World War II service. Host to Elmore James, Johnny Shines, Muddy Waters, Little Walter, Robert Johnson, and countless others, Helena-West Helena (as it is now called) was already a bustling music town with a lively nightlife. With the success of *King Biscuit Time*, still more bluesmen were attracted to the region. Others, like James Cotton, "Forrest City" Joe Pugh, Fred Below, and Willie "Big Eyes" Smith, did not have as far to travel to catch the zeitgeist. In addition to the ever-growing audience, the program helped launch a number of performers. *King Biscuit Time* made a star of the show's originator, Aleck "Rice" Miller (a.k.a. Sonny Boy Williamson), a decade before he ever cut a record. Williamson was even honored with his own brand of corn meal, bags of which displayed him atop a giant corncob. Robert Lockwood Jr., Houston Stackhouse, Joe Willie Wilkins, Robert "Dudlow" Taylor, and James "Peck" Curtis, who had played on Blytheville (Mississippi County) radio in the mid-1930s, all took their turns as King Biscuit Boys on *King Biscuit Time*, as did many others.

Bluesman CeDell Davis performing at the White Water Tavern in Little Rock; circa 2008.
Courtesy: Dotty Oliver/*Little Rock Free Press*

Some heard their first electric guitar on the show, an experience signaling a new era, courtesy of Lockwood, the de facto stepson of performer Robert Johnson (who spent likely the most settled period of his life in Helena). After two years on *King Biscuit Time*, Lockwood, born in Turkey Scratch (Phillips County), had his own show promoting Mother's Best Flour. By 1943, Chester Arthur Burnett (known as Howlin' Wolf), a farmer in the region, did a show promoting Hadacol elixir on KWEM in West Memphis (Crittenden County). These shows' popularity helped spread blues beyond its core rural black constituency.

As black southerners migrated north to catch the industrial revolution, so did the music. Although the solo acoustic performer remained a staple, blues increasingly featured drums and plugged-in instruments. Howlin' Wolf, who moved to Chicago, Illinois, and embodied the louder, more aggressive sound until his 1976 death, named this style for the town where he created it—the West Memphis style. It is more popularly known as Chicago blues.

Meanwhile in the 1940s, Louis Jordan of Brinkley trademarked the popular, more urbane jump blues. In the midst of the big band era, Jordan's stripped-down blues- and jazz-based Tympany Five set the prototype in style and substance for R&B and rock combos to come. In addition to his incredible chart success, he influenced such musicians as Chuck Berry, B. B. King, James Brown, and Ray Charles.

Around the same time, "Sister Rosetta" Tharpe of Cotton Plant exploded a myriad of taboos with her wild, bluesy electric guitar stylings in a black gospel setting; Isaac Hayes and Johnny Cash both claim her as an influence. Jimmy Witherspoon of Gurdon (Clark County) had a 1949 big band hit with a remake of Bessie Smith's 1923 song "Ain't Nobody's Business." Guitarist Auburn "Pat" Hare, born in Cherry Valley (Cross County), experimented with distortion. Little Rock (Pulaski County) native author/producer Robert Palmer dubs Hare "the power-chord king" in his *Rock & Roll: An Unruly History*, crediting Hare with cutting "the first heavy metal record" in 1954.

Although he had long performed in combos, "Big Bill" Broonzy subsequently exploited the nostalgia for "authentic" blues performers, often portraying himself as just off the farm. With several tours in the 1950s, Broonzy helped spark European interest in blues. American blues performers proved to be the inspirational source of the early 1960s British Invasion of the American charts: the Rolling Stones recorded with and appeared with Howlin' Wolf on TV, and both the Yardbirds and the Animals recorded with Sonny Boy Williamson.

Albert King, who played a right-handed, flying-V guitar left-handed, is probably the most imitated blues guitarist today, with Eric Clapton and Stevie Ray Vaughan being just two of King's acolytes. King, who settled in Crittenden County, is buried in Edmondson (Crittenden County). Like King, guitarists/vocalists "Son" Seals of Osceola, Larry "Totsy" Davis of Little Rock, Willie Cobbs of Smale (Monroe County), and Luther Allison of Widener (St. Francis County) forged successful blues careers during the sometimes lean 1960s and 1970s, as did lesser-knowns such as Elmon "Driftin' Slim" Mickle of Keo (Monroe County), as well as Claude "Blue Smitty" Smith and Floyd Jones, both guitarist/vocalists from Marianna who recorded for Chess.

Robert Palmer's 1981 book *Deep Blues* helped raise scholarly awareness of blues. In the early 1990s, Palmer further helped spark renewed interest in what many saw as an antiquated musical form by producing vibrant albums by the Jelly Roll Kings, with Sam Carr of Marvell (Phillips County) and Frank Frost of Auvergne (Jackson County), along with R. L. Burnside, Junior Kimbrough, and Helena-born CeDell Davis for the Fat Possum label of Oxford, Mississippi, which Palmer helped found. Davis cut a 2002 album produced by Little Rock native Joe Cripps with rock-star power from R.E.M.'s Peter Buck and others. The 1986 inception of Helena's King Biscuit Blues Festival also helped repopularize blues in its cradle. Worldwide appetite for American blues made international stars of Luther Allison, Eb Davis of Elaine (Phillips County)—both of whom moved to Europe—John Weston of Smale, Michael Burks of Camden (Ouachita County), and other Arkansans who may be better known around the world than in their hometowns.

Blues laid the foundation for the entirety of the modern American sound and has influenced generations. Arkansas produced much of the original class of rock and rollers—Sonny Burgess and the Pacers, Billy Lee Riley and His Little Green Men, Roland Janes, cousins Ronnie and Dale Hawkins, Charlie Rich, Johnny Cash, Conway Twitty, Roy Buchanan, and Levon Helm. All were heavily influenced by blues. R&B acts are equally indebted to blues, and many Arkansans contributed to the sound: musician/songwriter/producer Henry Glover, born in Hot Springs (Garland County); Cullendale (Ouachita County) native Little Willie John; Junior Walker, who was born in Blytheville (Mississippi County); Johnnie Taylor of Crawfordsville (Crittenden County); Osceola's Harvey Scales; Al Green of St. Francis and Lee counties; Lenny Williams of Little Rock; Brinkley-born producer/songwriter Al Bell; and Ne-Yo of Camden, among others.

Though other popular musical strains have caught on over the decades, at their core is blues. "I think blues will never die," said Helena-born slide guitar great Robert Lee "Nighthawk" Mc-

Collum. "You can always come up with something else, but when you wind up, you wind up with the blues every time. It's just something you can't get rid of."

The Delta Cultural Center, part of the Department of Arkansas Heritage, opened in 1990 on Helena's historic Cherry Street. Around the corner is a street named for harmonicist Frank Frost. Once the music of societal outsiders, blues is now celebrated around the world, and, at last, in its birthplace.

For additional information:

Cheseborough, Steve. *Blues Traveling*. Oxford: University Press of Mississippi, 2000.

Chilton, John. *Let the Good Times Roll: The Story of Louis Jordan and His Music*. Ann Arbor: University of Michigan Press, 1997.

Helm, Levon, with Stephen Davis. *This Wheel's on Fire: Levon Helm and the Story of the Band*. 2nd. ed. Chicago: Chicago Review Press, 2000.

Koch, Stephen. "Big Bill Broonzy." *Arkansas Times*, December 2, 2004, p. 26.

———. "King Biscuit: Recipe for Rock Rises From Arkansas Delta." *Arkansas Business*, March 15, 2004, pp. 74–80.

———. "Robert Nighthawk." *Arkansas Times*, December 23, 2004, p. 24.

Lomax, Alan. *The Land Where the Blues Began*. New York: Pantheon, 1993.

Palmer, Robert. *Deep Blues*. New York: Viking Press, 1981.

———. *Rock & Roll: An Unruly History*. New York: Harmony Books, 1995.

Riesman, Bob. *I Feel So Good: The Life and Times of Big Bill Broonzy*. Chicago: University of Chicago Press, 2011.

Stephen Koch

Timeline

- 1902 – Peetie Wheatstraw was born.

- 1908 – Louis Jordan was born.

- 1928 – Chester Arthur Burnett's father bought him a guitar. The electric blues guitar and powerful voice of Howlin' Wolf helped shape rock and roll.

- 1938 – "Big Bill" Broonzy filled in for Robert Johnson, who had died unexpectedly, at the Spirituals to Swing Concert at Carnegie Hall, helping to establish Broonzy as a key figure in Chicago blues.

- 1938 – "Sister Rosetta" Tharpe was signed to Decca Records.

- 1941 – *King Biscuit Time* began broadcasting on the radio five days a week on KFFA 1360 AM out of Helena (Phillips County).

- 1981 – Ethnomusicologist Robert Palmer helped raise scholarly awareness of the blues with his book *Deep Blues*.

- 1986 – Inception of Helena's King Biscuit Blues Festival helped repopularize blues locally.

CLASSICAL / OPERA

Although Arkansas is generally better known for its blues, gospel, folk, country, and rock and roll performers, classical and opera music have deep roots in Arkansas history and culture, often appearing in interesting ways in unusual places.

Internationally famous Arkansan composers of classical music include Scott Joplin, Florence Beatrice Smith Price, William Grant Still, and Conlon Nancarrow. Sarah Caldwell, who grew up in Fayetteville (Washington County), was a longtime opera director in Boston, Massachusetts, and the first woman to conduct an opera at the Metropolitan Opera House in New York City. Arkansas has been home to opera singers Mary Lewis, Barbara Hendricks, Susan Dunn, Marjorie Lawrence, Mary McCormic, Robert McFerrin Sr., and William Warfield. Classical music figures prominently in academic music degree programs at the state's universities, and Arkansans have at various times held regular opera performances at the Opera Theatre at Wildwood Park for the Arts in Little Rock (Pulaski County) and at Opera in the Ozarks at Inspiration Point in Eureka Springs (Carroll County). The Arkansas Symphony Orchestra in Little Rock is one of ten symphony orchestras in the state.

Classical Music: Early Arkansas History

Music figured prominently in early Arkansas history, with traveler Washington Irving identifying French *chansons* being sung at Arkansas Post in 1832. Early American pioneers brought their own music with them. This folk music was transmitted orally well into the twentieth century and fell into categories such as ballads, religious hymns, and even scatological songs. Familiar tunes usually provided by one or more fiddle players accompanied dancing. Early Arkansans also brought along pianos and sheet music. Surviving sheet music collections contain popular songs as well as non-vocal compositions, including polkas, waltzes, marches, and transcriptions of opera arias. The most "refined" were the parlor songs, while others more suited to the porch than the parlor, such as "Juanita," were performed outdoors.

Church music fell into denominational camps: those who used organs, pianos, or other instrumental combinations and those who did not and depended on singing schools to teach the "shape note" singing tradition. Training in church music remains an important part of the curriculum at Ouachita Baptist University (OBU) in Arkadelphia (Clark County) and Harding University in Searcy (White County).

The first recorded formal concert in Arkansas was held at Arkansas Post in 1821 by a Mr. Fries. Before the Civil War, Batesville (Independence County) residents put on a performance of Joseph Haydn's *The Creation*, which requires an orchestra, chorus, and soloists. After 1853, H. G. Hollenberg's Great Southwest Music House out of Memphis, Tennessee, was the major source for both sheet music—which Hollenberg started publishing himself—and musical instruments. Hollenberg's Little Rock branch was long the capital city's leading supplier. Moses Melody Shop in Little Rock followed later. Violinist Ferdinand Zellner gave an Arkansas-related title to his "Fayetteville Polka" in 1856. Benjamin Franklin Scull, son of a pioneering Arkansas County family, composed music for minstrel troupes while studying medicine in Philadelphia, Pennsylvania. His "I Am Near to Thee," with words by Little Rock newspaperman John E. Knight and dedicated to Mary E. Woodruff, was published in 1858.

Since Arkansas has for a long time occupied a distinctive position in the American imagination, the tune, story, and visual image of "The Arkansas Traveler" attracted international attention. The Arkansas-based version of the Trav-

Arkansas Symphony Orchestra strings and woodwinds.
Courtesy: Arkansas Symphony Orchestra

eler story is said to have begun in 1840. Sandford C. (Sandy) Faulkner—for whom Faulkner County would later be named—got lost in rural Arkansas and asked for directions at a humble log home. Faulkner, a natural performer, turned the experience into an entertaining presentation in which the Traveler was greeted by the Squatter at the log cabin with humorously evasive responses to his questions. Finally, the Traveler offered to play the second half, or "turn," of the fiddle tune the Squatter was playing. The tune was the "Arkansas Traveler." In his happiness at hearing the turn, the Squatter mustered all of the hospitality of his household for the Traveler. When the Traveler again asked directions, the Squatter offered them but suggested that the Traveler would be lucky to make it back to the cottage "whar you kin cum and play on thara'r tune as long as you please."

Following the publication of the story, both Mose Case—an entertainer from Buffalo, New York—and Cincinnati violinist Jose Tasso produced sheet music versions of the tune (the Case version was published in 1863 and distributed widely), and violinist Henri Vieuxtemps played an elaborate set of variations of it, as well as including it in his *American Bouquet* (No. 6) series. Twentieth-century composer David W. Guion in 1929 wrote a difficult piano concert transcription based on the tune, and Harl McDonald's *The Legend of the Arkansas Traveler* was recorded by Leopold Stokowski and the Philadelphia Orchestra in 1939. An arrangement was also recorded by the Boston Pops Orchestra. Finally, this fiddle tune, improbably supplied with words by a committee, was legislated into becoming Arkansas's official state song between 1949 and 1963. It is now the state's official historical song.

Classical Music:
Civil War through the Gilded Age

Many backwoods soldiers received an expanded musical education during the war. The tune "Wait for the Wagon" was fitted with pro-secession and anti-secession lyrics in the spring of 1861, and Harry MacCarthy, "the Arkansas Comedian," authored the South's first highly popular song, "The Bonnie Blue Flag." Civil War brass bands, with their own special music but also transcriptions of newly popular songs, performed on the Fourth of July and other occasions. "Dixie" was rendered by bands during and after the war. The popular song "Lorena" was

Timeline

• 1821 – The first formal concert recorded in Arkansas was held at Arkansas Post.

• 1856 – Violinist Ferdinand Zellner titled one of his compositions "Fayetteville Polka."

• 1872 – Wolf Detleff Carl Botefuhr became the founding director of music at the University of Arkansas.

• 1930 – William Grant Still completed his *Afro-American Symphony*, which became the first symphony written by an African American to be performed by a major orchestra.

• 1960 – Following the disbanding of the Little Rock Civic Symphony, the current Arkansas Symphony Orchestra was formed.

• 1976 – University of Arkansas graduate Sarah Caldwell became the first woman to conduct an opera at the Metropolitan Opera House.

• 1979 – The Arkansas Chamber Singers formed.

• 1997 – Opera star Gretha Boston, the first Arkansan to receive a Tony Award, was inducted into the Arkansas Black Hall of Fame.

the only tune one southern Arkansas band knew.

After the war, town bands became popular; Bradford (White County) had an ensemble that included women. Academic institutions, at first academies and then colleges, supplied music education and offered performances. Little Rock's St. Johns' College and Arkansas Industrial University (now the University of Arkansas) in Fayetteville were music centers. UA's founding director of music in 1872 was Wolf Detleff Carl Botefuhr; *Moonlight on the Poteau* was one of his many compositions. Botefuhr moved to Fort Smith (Sebastian County) in 1881, where he opened his own conservatory and taught the young William Worth Bailey, a talented blind violinist called "the American Paganini." In 1923, Bailey became the concertmaster of the Fort Smith Symphony; his wife, Katherine Price Bailey, was the conductor and remained in that position for many years.

Opera: Post Civil War through the Gilded Age

The late nineteenth and early twentieth century saw a rise in the popularity of classical music, especially opera—considered a "higher" form of music by the educated elite. In 1870, Little Rock's first visiting opera company, headed by the famed tenor Pasquilino Brignoli, came by steamboat and presented six operas in a shabby setting, and Little Rock responded by erecting a $50,000 opera house in 1873. Many other communities, including Fort Smith, Hot Springs (Garland County), Clarendon (Monroe County), Cotton Plant (Woodruff County), Van Buren (Crawford County), and St. Joe (Searcy County) built what were styled "opera houses." These structures were used as venues for all kinds of local performances and school events as well as for major national companies passing through by train. However, plays and minstrel shows were more common than opera companies.

Classical Music: Twentieth Century

During the early part of the twentieth century, music clubs around the state, as well as individual music supporters, began pushing for music education for the young and for quality musical performances for the enjoyment of the citizenry.

The music club movement was central to organized culture. Little Rock's Musical Coterie, founded in 1893, was one of the first groups preceding the Arkansas Federation of Music Clubs formed in 1908. By 1940, there were forty senior and thirty junior clubs around the state. Music was not neglected at the state's colleges; Frederick Harwood worked from 1913 to 1946 building a music program at what is now Henderson State University in Arkadelphia.

For about a decade starting in 1912, Little Rock held May festivals that imported outside orchestras and performers. The Community Concerts organization was active for more than ten years in Little Rock and in other communities in the 1950s. Famous twentieth-century violinist Jascha Heifetz came to El Dorado (Union County) during the oil-boom days. Colleges and high school auditoriums or basketball courts were used for concerts. Radio stations regularly broadcast classical music, including Saturday matinees live from the Metropolitan Opera in New York.

In 1933, the Little Rock Civic Symphony, precursor of the Arkansas Symphony Orchestra, was organized and directed by Laurence Powell of the music department at Little Rock Junior College (now the University of Arkansas at Little Rock) as part of the school's music program. Powell had already organized an orchestra in Fayetteville. Low pay led him to leave Little Rock in 1939, and the group folded. The State Symphony Orchestra and the Arkansas Philharmonic Society followed, but the current Arkansas Symphony Orchestra was not established

until 1960. By 2013, it was the only symphonic body in the state with some salaried players; all other orchestras operate completely on a per-service basis. Paul W. Klipsch, who began manufacturing high-end high-fidelity speakers in Hope (Hempstead County) in 1946, was an important symphony supporter.

Signs of renewed interest in classical music emerged in the mid-1950s. In 1966, the Arkansas Arts Council, which received funding from the National Endowment for the Arts, was created to advance the arts in Arkansas, including classical music. New regional orchestras appeared in the mid-twentieth century. The Jonesboro Symphony Orchestra became successively the Northeast Arkansas Symphony Orchestra and then the Delta Symphony Orchestra. Aided by Arkansas Arts Council grants, these orchestras organized youth concerts, held competitions, and expanded their outreach. By 2013, symphony orchestras could be found in Conway (Faulkner County), Fort Smith, Pine Bluff (Jefferson County), El Dorado, Texarkana (Miller County), Fayetteville, Mountain Home (Baxter County), Bentonville (Benton County), and Jonesboro (Craighead County). Children's concerts, pop concerts, and salutes to the military were featured prominently in regional orchestras.

The Arkansas Symphony was praised by the music critic of the *Washington Post* for its 1976 Bicentennial concert in the national's capital, and the Fort Smith Symphony made three recordings of William Grant Still compositions for the Naxos label. These various orchestras were not without problems, however. The North Arkansas Symphony, which had made a commercial recording, had to cancel its last concert in 2008 and shut down. The Symphony of Northwest Arkansas started up two years later. Band music, aside from its connection with high school and college football games, declined in popularity, and only one semi-professional band remained active in the state.

What is now the Diamond State Chorus, a men's barbershop singing group, started in 1955, with the women's group, now called Top of the Rock Chorus, starting in 1961. The Arkansas Chamber Singers, founded in 1979, became the premier volunteer chamber chorus in the state.

A musical series, Artspree, succeeded in bringing a variety of individuals and groups to Little Rock, and the Chamber Music Society of Little Rock, founded in 1952, brought in notable ensembles and individuals. In Helena (Phillips County), the Warfield Concerts provided free admission; classical music figured prominently in the offerings. Phillips County's Lily Peter brought the Philadelphia Orchestra at her own expense to play in Little Rock in 1969. The Hot Springs Music Festival started in 1995 and paired students with professionals to offer public concerts.

Opera: Twentieth Century

Opera did not fare as well as classical music in the twentieth century, although there were some successes. Beginning in 1941, Hot Springs was home to retired opera star and professor Marjorie Lawrence. She held summer opera coaching sessions at her ranch, Harmony Hills, which advanced the cause of classical and opera music in Arkansas. A nationally famous program supported by the music clubs dating back to 1950, Opera in the Ozarks at Inspiration Point, includes internationally known tenor Chris Merritt among its alumni. Former Metropolitan Opera star Blanche Thebom came to Little Rock in 1973 and founded the Arkansas Opera Theatre. After she left in 1989, it became the Opera Theatre at Wildwood under the direction of Ann Chotard. Following Chotard's retirement, the board chose to expand the park's vision, and opera productions have not resumed. Operas were also produced at the state's universities. An Arkansas State University music teacher, soprano Julia Langford, who performed with City Opera of New York and many regional companies, frequently featured her students in campus productions. Mezzo-soprano Mignon Dunn of Tyronza (Poinsett County), who appeared 653 times at the Metropolitan Opera, was the wife of Kurt Klippstatter, who conducted the Arkansas Symphony in the 1970s.

Trailblazers in Classical and Opera Music

Classical and opera music may not have achieved the recognition granted more specialized popular forms, but especially notable are the many trailblazers in classical music and opera who have been associated with Arkansas—especially African Americans. Scott Joplin, renowned for his ragtime compositions, wrote his single surviving opera, *Treemonisha*, with a plot set in Arkansas. William Grant Still of Little Rock completed his *Afro-American Symphony* in 1930. First performed in 1931 by the Roches-

ter Philharmonic Orchestra and still performed today, it is Still's most well-known composition and was the first symphony composed by an African American that was performed by a major orchestra. Florence Beatrice Smith Price, a graduate of the New England Conservatory of Music who taught at Cotton Plant Academy and Shorter College in Little Rock but was denied membership in the Arkansas State Music Teachers Association, became the first black female composer to have a work performed by a major American symphony when the Chicago Symphony Orchestra performed her *Symphony in E Minor* on June 15, 1933.

Robert McFerrin Sr. of Marianna (Lee County), father of singer and conductor Bobby McFerrin, was a baritone opera and concert singer who was the first black male to appear in an opera at the Metropolitan Opera House; his debut came less than

William Grant Still of Little Rock; circa 1920.

Courtesy: Special Collections, University of Arkansas Libraries, Fayetteville

a month after the well-publicized breaking of the color barrier by contralto Marian Anderson. More recently, opera mezzo-soprano Gretha Boston of Crossett (Ashley County), who was inducted into the Arkansas Black Hall of Fame in 1997, debuted at Carnegie Hall in May 1991 with Mozart's *Coronation Mass*. The first Arkansan to receive a Tony Award, she won the 1995 Tony for Best Featured Actress in a Musical for her role as Queenie in the Broadway revival of *Show Boat*. Juilliard-trained soprano Barbara Hendricks from Stephens (Ouachita County) had an international career in opera and film and performed at jazz festivals. She also has been noted for her work with refugees and for other humanitarian causes. She also performed at a gala for President Bill Clinton's 1993 inauguration. Soprano Georgia Ann Laster grew up in Arkansas; a branch of the National Association of Negro Musicians is named after her.

Other Arkansan classical and opera musicians who have achieved fame include Mary Lewis of Hot Springs, who made her way to grand opera via vaudeville and operetta. Her career included radio performances and recordings with His Master's Voice (HMV), Victor, and RCA. Celebrity status was accorded to Mary McCormic—born Mamie Harris in Belleville (Yell County). A graduate of what is now OBU, she sang in Paris, France, and in Chicago, Illinois, and left behind a recorded legacy.

Frances Greer of Piggott (Clayton County) and Helena had an extensive vocal career that included *The Frances Greer Show* on radio, performances with the Metropolitan and Philadelphia Opera companies, and work in operetta and radio. Susan Dunn of Malvern (Hot Spring County), a Hendrix College graduate, was a prominent soprano during the 1980s and 1990s. One of the important names nationally in opera production was UA graduate Sarah Caldwell, who brought opera back to Boston and became the first woman to conduct an opera at the Metropolitan Opera House, on January 13, 1976. Also making a name for herself in opera is soprano Kristin Lewis of Little Rock, who began her vocal studies at the University of Central Arkansas in Conway and performs around the world.

Some other notable Arkansas classical composers, performers, and directors are player-piano composer Conlon Nancarrow of Texarkana; world-renowned composer and conductor Francis McBeth, who was professor and resident composer at OBU and also conducted the Arkansas Symphony for many years; Jeff Hitt, an outfitter at Yellowstone National Park who composed *Yellowstone for Violin and Orchestra*; composer John S. Hilliard of Hot Springs, who is especially known for his piano compositions; the Grammy-nominated New York Philharmonic Orchestra English horn player Thomas Stacy, who grew up in Augusta (Woodruff County); and Buryl Red of Little Rock, who is the musical director and conductor of the CenturyMen choral group. UA professor Bruce Benward wrote the bestselling two-volume book *Music In Theory and Practice* (1963), which has long been the standard in the field.

For additional information:

Barnwell, RyeAnn. "Frederick Harwood and Henderson State Teacher's College: A History." PhD diss., University of Oklahoma, 1987.

Cochran, Robert. *Our Own Sweet Sounds: A Celebration of Popular Music in Arkansas.* 2nd ed. Fayetteville: University of Arkansas Press, 2005.

Dougan, Michael B. "Bravo Brignoli! The First Opera Season in Arkansas." *Pulaski County Historical Review* 30 (Winter 1982): 74–80.

Hudgins, Mary. "Composer Laurence Powell in Arkansas." *Arkansas Historical Quarterly* 31 (Summer 1972): 181–188.

Michael Dougan

COUNTRY

While the precise origins of country and western music are not entirely clear, it is thought to have its roots in traditional folk music of the British Isles. Once this particular sound was brought by British immigrants to the United States, country music began to change as it was blended with the music of immigrants from other places, as well as with traditional religious hymns and the music of African slaves predominantly residing in the southern United States. Arkansas has had a firm place in the history of country music from its very beginnings in the United States, and the state has been the birthplace of many well-known country artists, as well as particular style variations of country music.

While the folk music of the British Isles was more focused on topics of love and romance, the early forms of country within the United States were centered on practical topics as well as tragic ones, which can still be heard in the music of popular country artists. Country music was not performed on the radio until 1922, when the music industry decided to broaden the options of available genres. During the 1920s, the instrumental style of what was then known as "hillbilly" music did not stray far from homemade banjos and fiddles. Dr. Smith's Champion Hoss Hair Pullers were very influential during this time period; they were one of the most popular string bands in Arkansas between 1926 and 1929 and even recorded a few songs at Victor Records in 1928. They proved to be a boon to the public perception of Arkansas music.

The 1930s brought a new era and style of country music, as the "hillbilly" fiddle band sound was beginning to fade out and be replaced by "country/western," inspired by Jimmie Rodgers of Mississippi, who many consider to be the "Father of Country Music." This music featured lyrics of grand, romantic ideals of life in the western states and was performed in western cowboy apparel, which is still a common style in country music today. Yodeling also became a popular performance mode in country music. Patsy Montana, born Ruby Blevins, of Garland County was influenced by this new style of country music and wore a typical western get-up, including a cowboy hat and a gun and holster. She was discovered on *The National Barn Dance* on the radio station WLS from Chicago, Illinois, and her 1935 release "I Want to Be a Cowboy's Sweetheart" was the first record by a female country/western singer to sell over one million copies. Elton Britt of Zack (Searcy County) and Carolina Cotton (born Helen Hagstrom) of Cash (Craighead County) were also heavily influenced by Rodgers's yodeling style throughout their music careers in the 1940s. Jimmy Wakely of Mineola (Howard County) was one of the last country musicians to fully embrace the classic image of a "singing cowboy." He achieved a great deal of national success, appearing in several films with Gene Autry.

Two other Arkansas country artists of the 1930s and 1940s, Lonnie Glosson of Judsonia (White County) and Wayne Raney of Wolf Bayou (Cleburne County), popularized the harmonica throughout the United States. Together, Glosson and Raney established a highly successful mail-order harmonica company. Both musicians had somewhat of a "hillbilly boogie" sound; their hit single "Why Don't You Haul Off and Love Me" was number one on the country music charts in 1949. Glosson's solo career was also quite successful; his 1936 song "Arkansas Hard Luck Blues" is considered by the Country Music Hall of Fame to be a precedent to the talking blues style of both Bob Dylan and Woody Guthrie.

The 1940s also brought a new variation of country music called honky-tonk, which is a type of country music with strong beats and lyrics that bemoan misfortune. Several Arkansas country musicians influenced, participated in, and contributed to this mode. T. Texas Tyler of Mena (Polk County), born David Luke Myrick, used honky-tonk instrumentation in his music and combined it with a nearly spoken vocal style. His 1948 hit "Deck of Cards" reached the top of

Timeline

• 1922 – John Carson recorded two "hillbilly" songs in Atlanta, considered to be the founding moment for country music in the United States. Arkansas's own Dr. Smith's Champion Hoss Hair Pullers, Lonnie Glosson, and Wayne Raney performed in the hillbilly style.

• 1932 – Johnny Cash was born. The most famous musical artist to emerge from Arkansas, he was inducted into the Country Music, Rockabilly, Gospel Music, Rock and Roll, and Songwriters Halls of Fame and earned numerous Grammys.

• 1933 – Harold Lloyd Jenkins, later known as Conway Twitty, was born. He was inducted into the Country Music Hall of Fame in 1999.

• 1935 – Patsy Montana released "I Want to Be a Cowboy's Sweetheart," which was the first record by a female country singer to sell over one million copies.

• 1943 – Louis Jordan became the first African-American male to succeed in both the country and pop charts with his single "Ration Blues."

• 1948 – "Lefty" Frizell's "Deck of Cards" reached the top of the country music charts.

• 1950 – "Arkie" Shibley recorded the original version of "Hot Rod Race," which would later be covered by several major country as well as rock and roll artists.

• 1953 – Ronnie Dunn was born in Coleman, Texas; he spent most of his childhood in El Dorado. He and Kix Brooks became Brooks & Dunn, who have won more awards than any other duo in country music history.

• 1987 – K. T. Oslin became the first female country artist to win the Country Music Song of the Year award, for her single "80's Ladies."

• 1987 – Wayland Holyfield's "Arkansas (You Run Deep in Me)" was adopted as an official Arkansas state song. Holyfield wrote songs for major country artists such as Conway Twitty, George Strait, and Brooks & Dunn.

• 2009 – Justin Moore from Poyen (Grant County) released his first album, *Justin Moore*, which quickly achieved gold status, as did his 2011 album *Outlaws Like Me*.

the country music charts, and its storytelling style was widely imitated. "Lefty" Frizell, who was born in Texas but grew up in Arkansas, debuting as a singer in El Dorado (Union County), also performed country in the honky-tonk style. Willie Nelson has claimed that he and many current artists have been influenced by this style. Considered to be one of the most influential artists in the history of country music, Frizell released several chart-topping honky-tonk hits, including "If You've Got the Money, Honey, I've

Sheet music for Patsy Montana's "I Want to Be a Cowboy's Sweetheart." Courtesy: Old State House Museum Collection

Got the Time" (1950), "I Love You a Thousand Ways" (1950), and "Saginaw, Michigan" (1964). He was inducted into the Country Music Hall of Fame in 1982.

Country music, throughout its history, has tended to blur the lines between genres. Almost all country music borrows elements of song structure from early Delta blues music, so it is unsurprising that several country artists have crossed over into the rhythm and blues (R&B) genre. The Browns of Sparkman (Dallas County) succeeded in straddling the line between country and R&B with their hit "The Three Bells" in 1959. The Browns were also important in developing the smoother, more elegant "Nashville sound" of country that would further develop and become popular in the 1990s. Country artist Floyd Cramer, who grew up in Huttig (Union County), also influenced the Nashville sound with his smooth piano playing in songs like "Last Date," which hit number two on the *Billboard* charts. Cramer is widely considered to be the most influential pianist in the history of country music due to de-

veloping the bluesy "slip-note" style that influenced many pianists who would follow him.

Country music was beginning to cross over into rock and roll during the 1950s as well. Crawford County native Jesse Lee "Arkie" Shibley's 1950 recording of "Hot Rod Race," which hit number five on the country charts, is considered to be influential to the origination of rock and roll as a genre. He also influenced the genre of blues with the talking blues style that he incorporated into many of his songs. Conway Twitty, born Harold Lloyd Jenkins, was also influential in both the country and rock genres. Growing up in Helena (Phillips County), Twitty began as a rock artist and was hugely successful, releasing several singles that hit number one on the pop charts, such as "It's Only Make Believe" in 1958. However, as the years passed, he played more in the country style. He released several singles that reached number one on the country charts, such as "Next in Line" in 1968. He was inducted into the Country Music Hall of Fame in 1999 and is still one of the most successful musical acts to emerge from Arkansas. Levon Helm of Marvell (Phillips County) also blurred the lines between the country and rock genres; in the late 1960s, he was a leading member of the early Americana group the Band.

Several country artists also ventured into the pop genre and influenced modern country with a more pop-like sound. Jimmy Driftwood of Timbo (Stone County), who was a member of the Grand Ole Opry in the 1950s, released six singles that made the country and pop charts simultaneously in 1959. Glen Campbell of Pike County, a renowned country guitarist, played guitar on records for popular artists such as Elvis Presley, Merle Haggard, and Nat King Cole. He also toured as a member of the Beach Boys for several months during the 1960s and won several Grammys for his contributions to both country and pop music.

Charlie Rich of Colt (St. Francis County), a popular country musician from the late 1950s to the 1970s, ventured into several different genres, including pop, gospel, blues, and rockabilly. His single "The Most Beautiful Girl" topped both the country and pop charts, and he was influential to the lush, pop-like "countrypolitan" sound that is popular in Las Vegas, Nevada, and other large cities. Narvel Felts of Keiser (Mississippi County), a country musician of the 1970s, also worked within the rockabilly genre and is in the

Rockabilly Hall of Fame. The Cate Brothers of Washington County, although they were never as widely successful as Rich or Felts, were also well respected in their musical crossovers from country into the rockabilly and rock genres.

The country artist who experimented with the most genres throughout his career, as well as arguably the most famous musical artist to emerge from Arkansas, was Johnny Cash. Born in Kingsland (Cleveland County), Cash explored country, gospel, blues, pop, and rock and roll. He had several singles, such as "Ring of Fire" and "Understand Your Man," that topped both the country and pop charts. He is also the only musician ever to be inducted into the Country Music, Rockabilly, Gospel Music, Rock and Roll, and Songwriters Halls of Fame. He also garnered several Grammys throughout his musical career.

While many country artists were gaining success through venturing into other genres, the Wilburn Brothers of Hardy (Sharp County) were taking advantage of listeners' appreciation for a more classic form of country. Performing from the late 1950s into the 1970s, this sibling duo performed at the Grand Ole Opry and received the only "lifetime recording contract" ever made by Decca Records. They helped launch the careers of several more modern country artists, such as Loretta Lynn, Patty Loveless, and the Osborne Brothers.

Modern Arkansas country music has moved somewhat back into a more traditional mode, although it often still crosses over into pop music. Some recent Arkansas musicians have had a great deal of success within Arkansas as well as nationally. Wayland Holyfield of Mallett Town (Conway County) is an excellent example of this more modern yet homely country sound; his single "Arkansas (You Run Deep in Me)" was adopted by the Arkansas General Assembly as an official state song in 1987. He has also been inducted into the Arkansas Entertainers Hall of Fame and written/co-written songs for artists such as Conway Twitty, George Strait, and Brooks & Dunn. Ronnie Dunn, born in Texas, was raised in El Dorado (Union County). Dunn was a member of the wildly successful and internationally famous country duo Brooks & Dunn and has been performing since the 1970s. K. T. Oslin of Crossett (Ashley County) was the first female artist to win the Country Music Song of the Year, for her hit single "80's Ladies," and has also garnered several Grammy Awards. Tra-cy Lawrence of Foreman (Little River County), who, like Dunn, was born in Texas and raised in Arkansas, released several chart-topping singles during the early 1990s, such as "Texas Tornado," "Time Marches On," and "I See It Now." Collin Raye of De Queen (Sevier County) has had multiple hit singles, such as "Little Rock" and "Every Second," and has garnered multiple Country Music Award nominations. Joe Nichols of Rogers (Benton County) released several hugely successful studio albums between 1996 and 2013 and has had several number-one hit singles. Justin Moore of Poyen (Grant County) is one of the most recent acts from Arkansas to gain success within the world of country music; both of his records, *Justin Moore* (2009) and *Outlaws Like Me* (2011), have achieved gold status.

Throughout the years, country music has transformed from a somewhat down-home genre to one that is popular in cities and cosmopolitan areas as well. However, throughout all of country's changes in sound, as well as country artists' evolutions in style, it has retained its solidly American sensibility and its themes of love and loss, family, and practical struggles of the working class.

For additional information:

Blevins, Brooks. *Arkansas/Arkansaw: How Bear Hunters, Hillbillies, and Good Ol' Boys Defined a State*. Fayetteville: University of Arkansas Press, 2009.

Brown, Maxine. *Looking Back to See: A Country Music Memoir*. Fayetteville: University of Arkansas Press, 2005.

Bufwack, Mary A., and Robert K. Oermann. *Finding Her Voice: The Saga of Women in Country Music*. New York: Crown Publishers, 1993.

Cochran, Robert. *Our Own Sweet Sounds: A Celebration of Popular Music in Arkansas*. 2nd ed. Fayetteville: University of Arkansas Press, 2005.

Cross, Wilbur, and Michael Kosser. *The Conway Twitty Story*. New York: Doubleday, 1986.

Edwards, Leigh H. *Johnny Cash and the Paradox of American Identity*. Bloomington: Indiana University Press, 2009.

Hemphill, Paul. *The Nashville Sound: Bright Lights and Country Music*. New York: Simon and Schuster, 1970.

Horstman, Dorothy. *Sing Your Heart Out, Country Boy*. Nashville: Country Music Foundation Press, 1996.

Kingsbury, Paul, ed. *The Encyclopedia of Country Music*. New York: Oxford University Press, 1998.

Lindley, Helen C. "The Hoss Hair Pullers and Hill-Billy Quartet." *Izard County Historian* 5 (April 1974): 9–13.

Wolfe, Charles K. *Classic Country: Legends of Country Music*. New York: Routledge, 2001.

Darby Burdine

FOLK

Folk music is part of what may be called a society's "unofficial culture," much of which is passed on through face-to-face contact among close-knit people. Early folk music in Arkansas falls into two broad categories: folksongs (which do not present a narrative) and ballads (which tell a story). Folksong collectors sought to record and preserve this traditional music in the twentieth century, with Vance Randolph, John Quincy Wolf, and others working in Arkansas. The lyric folksong form of the blues developed in the Arkansas and Mississippi Delta regions in the late nineteenth century among the first generation of African Americans to come of age after slavery. Protest music of the early to mid-twentieth century, dealing with labor and social conditions—as well as war, civil rights, and politics—took on the folk style and sensibility, contributing to the renewed interest in traditional folk music, termed the folk revival, of the 1950s and 1960s. The mid-to-late twentieth century brought the contemporary/popular folk style into prominence, with the singer/songwriter at the center.

Most commentators identify verbal material as folklore on the basis of its oral dissemination, its performance taking place in situations where speaker or singer and audience are in immediate contact. Because verbal folklore, including folk songs, circulates among individuals in oral interactions, it lacks the permanence that writing or other communicative media might produce and is variable. Each performance of a song evinces some distinctive elements, although some performance features—such as diction, style, and theme—remain relatively constant. (It is this unique nature of the traditionally performed folksongs that later folksong collectors sought to capture before modernizing forces caused these songs to be lost and forgotten as the singers who served as the keepers of the traditions died.)

Arkansas's Image in the Folk Music Tradition

Early European and Euro-American impressions of Arkansas often drew upon folk traditions. Stories about the state's remarkable fruitfulness, for example, incorporated elements from similar boasts in Europe: crops that would grow up overnight and produce gargantuan yields, game and fish both plentiful and compliant, and an environment so healthy that the very water had medicinal properties. When Arkansas failed to live up to its billing, negative folklore and folksongs developed that exaggerated its failings—again using traditional images and patterns. The song usually known as "The State of Arkansaw," which probably dates from the 1890s, articulates the state's anti-image that developed. The song's narrator arrives in Arkansas full of hope that fortune awaits him. He is soon disabused of this illusion when an unkempt, unhealthy-looking Arkansawyer offers him a job draining swampland. After weeks of hard labor on mean rations, the narrator laments, "I never knew what misery was till I came to Arkansas."

An emblem of the image of frontier Arkansas, the Arkansas Traveler—a tune, dialogue, and painting from the mid-nineteenth century—became a catch-all phrase for almost anything or anyone from Arkansas and had positive or negative connotations depending on the presentation. Dealing with the interactions between a traveler and a fiddle-playing squatter in a log cabin, the Arkansas-based version of the Traveler story is said to have begun in 1840. While this version of the dialogue or song portrayed tensions based upon differences among people from Arkansas—such as urban versus rural or wealthy versus poor—most other versions told the story from the Traveler-as-outsider perspective, taking an uncomplimentary view of the state. The sheet music to the tune was first published in Cincinnati,

Currier & Ives print of Edward Payson Washbourne's painting Arkansas Traveler; *circa 1870.*
Courtesy: Butler Center for Arkansas Studies, Central Arkansas Library System

Ohio, in 1847 as "The Arkansas Traveller and Rackinsac Waltz," arranged by William Cumming; no one was credited with the composition. If not from the folk tradition, the tune was most likely written by Jose Tosso. Several others, including Sandy Faulkner and Mose Case, have also been credited with its composition. Over the years, "The Arkansas Traveler" has become one of the most recorded tunes in American history. The 1922 version of the song by native Arkansan "Eck" Robertson was among the first fifty recordings named to the National Recording Registry of the Library of Congress, and the tune has appeared in jazz and symphonic arrangement.

Offering a fanciful, modernized, and somewhat more positive take on the image of Arkansas, "The Rock Island Line" is a world-famous song—recorded by the likes of Johnny Cash, Harry Belafonte, and Grandpa Jones—the earliest known performances of which are two 1934 versions recorded in Arkansas prisons by teacher and folksong collector John Lomax and musician Huddie Ledbetter (who would later be famous as Leadbelly). A tall tale in rhyme, the song's subject is a train so fast that it arrives at its destination in Little Rock (Pulaski County) before its departure from Memphis, Tennessee. Inmate Kelly Pace of Camden (Ouachita County) sang on the recording of the second version; Pace eventually contributed more than thirty performances to the Library of Congress archives. The song remains a staple of the American folk music repertoire, although its Arkansas roots have mostly been forgotten. Cash, who had earlier recorded the song for Sun and other labels, performed it at Cummins Prison in 1969, renewing its fame.

In both positive and negative manifestations, Arkansas's image is far from unique, as many geographic areas could not live up to settlers' hopes for them. Similar negative images in American folksong have attached to the "dreary Black Hills" of the Dakotas, "Nebraska land," and the abode of the "Lane County Bachelor."

Blues and Gospel in the Folk Tradition

The blues may be the most widely known folklore form associated with the Arkansas flatlands. Influenced by the field hollers and worksongs that accompanied agricultural labor and by religious music—especially the gospel music that was emerging with it—the blues operates as a commentary on the everyday life of its performers and audience. Although its most frequent topic is the tensions associated with male-female relations, the blues may deal with virtually any concern in the community. It does so succinctly, usually in three-line stanzas in which the first two lines are virtually identical. Blues imagery is concrete and relies extensively on metaphors, which often have sexual connotations. Traditional performance settings for blues have included barbecues, fish fries, and other community celebrations; juke joints—unlicensed clubs run by black proprietors and usually located in rural situations; and street corners. A blues performance in one of these venues is an extemporaneous combination of stanzas. The song itself may not be traditional, but the stanzas that compose it usually come from the store of material that blues performers have been developing for more than a century. Commercial recording of the blues began in the 1920s, and performers associated with Arkansas such as Peetie Wheatstraw (William Bunch), who grew up in Cotton Plant

Timeline

• 1847 – "The Arkansas Traveller and Rackinsac Waltz," arranged by William Cumming, was first published in Cincinnati, Ohio.

• 1910 – Famed folklorist and political songwriter Zilphia Horton was born.

• 1934 – John Lomax and Huddie Ledbetter recorded the earliest-known performances of "The Rock Island Line" in Arkansas prisons.

• 1946–1950 – *Ozark Folksongs*, a comprehensive collection detailing folksongs from the northern Arkansas and southern Missouri region, was published in four volumes.

• 1959 – Jimmy Driftwood began to gain popularity when Johnny Horton recorded his song "The Battle of New Orleans."

• 1963 – The Rackensack Folklore Society was organized to perpetuate traditional Arkansas folk music.

• 1963 – Mountain View (Stone County) hosted the first Arkansas Folk Festival.

• 1969 – Johnny Cash recorded another version of "The Rock Island Line" at Cummins Prison, bringing it back into popularity.

• 1973 – The Ozark Folk Center State Park opened in Mountain View.

• 1998 – Lucinda Williams, a singer/songwriter with strong Arkansas ties, won the Grammy for Best Contemporary Folk Album for *Car Wheels on a Gravel Road*.

Jimmy Driftwood was a prolific folk singer/songwriter from Mountain View.

Artists: Patterson and Barnes / From the Old State House Museum Collection

(Woodruff County), and "Big Bill" Broonzy (William Lee Conley), who lived in Pine Bluff (Jefferson County), were appearing on recordings within the next decade. Many traditional blues performers, though, were never recorded at all.

Religious music—including hymns from the late eighteenth century (called "Dr. Watts," for composer Isaac Watts, in black folk speech), spirituals that developed during slavery times, and gospel music performed by ensembles using four-part harmony or by charismatic soloists such as "Sister Rosetta" Tharpe (also from Cotton Plant)—added to the folk music soundscape of the Arkansas Delta. Blues and gospel also contributed to the development of commercial rock and roll, many of whose pioneers, including Johnny Cash, Billy Lee Riley, and Sonny Burgess, were Arkansans who recorded just across the Mississippi River at the Sun Records studio in Memphis.

Folk Music in the Ozarks

Folklorist Vance Randolph was attracted to the Ozarks, where he had vacationed as a child, by the appeal of ballads, particularly the narrative folksongs from England and Scotland that Harvard University professor Francis James Child had anthologized in the late nineteenth century and many of which dealt with knights and ladies in pseudo-medieval settings. Randolph—along with his wife, Mary Celestia Parler, who was a professor of English and folklore at the University of Arkansas (UA) in Fayetteville (Washington County)—was fascinated that Ozark "peasants" living in the early twentieth century as subsistence farmers in an isolated pocket of the United States were singing songs

about British nobility and royalty that could be traced in a few cases to the late Middle Ages. These songs tell pithy, dramatic, often lurid stories of young women seduced by supernatural beings ("Lady Isabel and the Elf-Knight"), intra-family murder ("Edward"), cruel young women who drive rejected suitors to their graves ("Barbara Allen"), and a woman so mean that the devil cannot stand to have her in hell ("The Farmer's Curst Wife").

Ozark singers supplemented these old narrative folksongs from the British Isles (known as "Child ballads" for the Harvard professor who edited and numbered the collection) with more recent songs from Britain and Ireland; with indigenous ballads that told stories of Robin Hood–like outlaws, Civil War battles (including the Battle of Pea Ridge), railroad disasters, and other American themes; and with sacred and secular folk lyrics that did not tell stories but rather conveyed moods or emotions.

Randolph worked primarily in the western Ozarks and produced one of the most comprehensive collections of American folksongs from a single American region: the four-volume *Ozark Folksongs*, which the State Historical Society of Missouri published between 1946 and 1950. One of Randolph's most gifted performers of folksongs was Emma Dusenbury, born in 1862, of Mena (Polk County), a traditional singer whose work is represented by some 116 songs in the nation's leading folksong archive at the Library of Congress.

A generation later, John Quincy Wolf was collecting ballads and other folksongs in the eastern Ozarks. Wolf made contact with folk singer Almeda Riddle of Cleburne County, as well as the Morris family of Timbo (Stone County). James Morris—as Jimmy Driftwood—became a well-known songwriter and popularizer of Ozark folksongs in the 1950s and 1960s.

Folksongs were the primary lure that drew early collectors to the Ozarks. Both Randolph and Wolf gathered substantial bodies of material and identified important performers of this material. Black folk music and instrumental music did not receive as much attention, however, although several Ozark string bands, featuring skilled fiddlers such as Absie Morrison, made recordings in the late 1920s.

Folk Revival in the Modern Era

Folk music in Arkansas has carried on into

the modern era, with many Arkansas performers and songwriters continuing, preserving, and reviving the traditions, while adding their own contributions (often influenced by other styles such as blues, country, and rock) along the way.

While some consider the revival period of the mid-twentieth century to be a rediscovery of folk music, for some musicians, such as Almeda Riddle and others, the traditional music never went away in the first place. Discovered by ballad collector Wolf in the 1950s, Riddle (born in 1898) became a prominent figure in America's folk music revival. Her memory of ballads, hymns, and children's songs was one of the largest single repertories documented by folksong scholars. Violet Brumley Hensley, a fiddle maker and musician born near Mount Ida (Montgomery County) in 1916, was designated as the 2004 Arkansas Living Treasure by the Arkansas Arts Council, which recognized Hensley as an outstanding Arkansan who actively preserves and advances the art form of fiddle-making. Hugh Ashley, who was born in 1915 near Wiley's Cove (Searcy County), wrote and recorded some of the earliest known recordings of Ozark folk music, was one of radio's original "Beverly Hill Billies," and wrote songs for five members of the Country Music Hall of Fame.

As part of the protest music aspect of the American folk tradition, John L. Handcox, born in 1904 in Brinkley (Monroe County), became the voice of the common sharecropper through the poems and songs he wrote for the Southern Tenant Farmers' Union (STFU), a federation of tenant farmers formed in 1934 in Poinsett County. Handcox joined the STFU in 1935 and "found out singing was more inspiring than talking...to get the attention of the people." Through Handcox's recordings for the Library of Congress, folk greats Woody Guthrie and Pete Seeger had discovered his songs by the 1940s, performing and recording them in subsequent years as labor protest songs. Handcox wrote protest songs into the Reagan era of the 1980s.

Paris (Logan County) native Zilphia Mae Johnson Horton, born in 1910, was an influential educator, folklorist, musician, and social justice activist who collected, adapted, performed, and promoted the use of folksongs and hymns in the labor and civil rights movements, notably the protest anthems "We Shall Not Be Moved" and "We Shall Overcome." Fellow protest/political musician Lee Hays, born in Little Rock in 1914, was one of the original members of the Almanac Singers, perhaps the first folksong popularizers to adopt a progressive political agenda, in 1940, and is best known for singing bass with the folk revival group the Weavers. According to historian Studs Terkel, the Weavers were responsible for "entering folk music into the mainstream of American life." Among the songs Hays is most known for are "If I Had a Hammer," "Roll the Union On," "Raggedy, Raggedy, Are We," "The Rankin Tree," "On Top of Old Smoky," "Kisses Sweeter than Wine," and "Goodnight Irene." Members of the Weavers who had been in the Almanac Singers—Hays and Pete Seeger—had politics that ran afoul of the McCarthy-era political climate, and they were blacklisted, with the Weavers disbanding in 1952 (although the group later reunited a few times).

With the way paved for a modern-day folk singer offering up traditional songs and forms, Jimmy Driftwood of Stone County (whose father was also a folk singer) became a major figure in the folk revival scene of the 1950s and 1960s, writing more than 6,000 songs. He gained fame in 1959 when Johnny Horton recorded Driftwood's song, "The Battle of New Orleans." Even after Driftwood had risen to fame on the national scene by the late 1950s, he continued living in rural Stone County where he was born, spending most of his time promoting and preserving the music and heritage of the Ozark Mountains.

Popular/Contemporary Folk Music of the 1960s and Beyond

The influence and merging of other musical styles such as country, blues, jazz, and rock is especially seen in the popular/contemporary folk genre that emerged in the 1960s, with the singer/songwriter serving as a central figure. Dan Hicks, born in Little Rock in 1941, is a cross-genre singer/songwriter specializing in a type of music he calls "folk jazz." He has served as front man for his band, the Hot Licks, off and on since 1968. Iris DeMent, born in Paragould (Greene County) in 1961, is a singer/songwriter who has lent her distinctive voice to folk, country, bluegrass, and gospel music, singing songs about family, religion, people, places, and politics. Another singer/songwriter is Lucinda Williams, who was born in Lake Charles, Louisiana, in 1953 but spent much of her childhood in Arkansas. She won a Grammy for Best Contemporary Folk Album in 1998 for what is often regarded as her masterpiece, *Car Wheels on a Gravel Road*.

In the mid-to-late 1980s, highly visible Little Rock street musicians and eccentrics Elton and Betty White put their unique stamp on the continuing folk traditions of Arkansas with their sexually explicit ukulele songs. In addition, folk-pop/rock performance duo Trout Fishing in America, based in northwest Arkansas, has been nominated for four Grammys and has released more than twenty albums.

Folk Music Organizations, Festivals, and Sites

The Rackensack Folklore Society was organized in 1963 for the purpose of perpetuating the traditional folk music of the people of Arkansas, particularly in the mountainous area of the north-central part of the state. Stone County was unique in having music-making families throughout its boundaries who founded the base of the Rackensack organization. The society was begun by Lloyd and Martha Hollister, who came from the Little Rock area in 1962 and settled in Stone County. A Pulaski County chapter of the Rackensack Folklore Society was formed in 1963 as a sister to the original chapter.

To capitalize on the rich "mountain music" and craft traditions of the area, Mountain View (Stone County) hosted the first annual Arkansas Folk Festival in 1963 under the sponsorship of the Ozark Foothills Handicraft Guild (later known as the Arkansas Craft Guild) and the Rackensack Folklore Society. In the first year, the event brought more than 2,500 visitors to Mountain View, which had a population of less than 1,000 at that time. The festival was a revival of the original 1941 folk music festival, the Stone County Folkways Festival.

Born out of the success of the Arkansas Folk Festival, the Ozark Folk Center State Park in Mountain View is dedicated to the preservation and perpetuation of Southern mountain folkways and traditions. When it opened in 1973, the park was hailed as a permanent home for traditional crafts and music and has since become one of the important institutions preserving this particular way of life. Jimmy Driftwood, who was involved in the establishment of Rackensack, performed at the center's spring 1973 grand opening, although he ceased his involvement Rackensack soon after amid disagreements about policies. He went on to establish the Jimmy Driftwood Barn north of Mountain View, which hosts weekly musical programs portraying the folk music of the area.

For additional information:

Arkansas State Parks–Ozark Folk Center. http://www.ozarkfolkcenter.com (accessed February 22, 2013).

Cochran, Robert. *Our Own Sweet Sounds: A Celebration of Popular Music in Arkansas*. 2nd ed. Fayetteville: University of Arkansas Press, 2005.

McNeil, W. K. "Singing and Playing Music in Arkansas." In *An Arkansas Folklore Sourcebook*, edited by W. K. McNeil. Fayetteville: University of Arkansas Press, 1992.

Wade, Stephen. *The Beautiful Music All Around Us: Field Recordings and the American Experience*. Champaign: University of Illinois Press, 2012.

Weissman, Dick. *Which Side Are You On? An Inside History of the Folk Music Revival in America*. New York: Continuum, 2005.

Adapted in part from the EOA's Folklore and Folklife entry by William M. Clements and the Arkansas Traveler entry by William B. Worthen

Staff of the Encyclopedia of Arkansas

GOSPEL / CONTEMPORARY CHRISTIAN

Musicologists and journalists have often provided conflicting definitions of the term "gospel music." Early African-American gospel was a blend of nineteenth-century hymns, spirituals, field songs, ragtime, and blues, while the religious music performed by white artists—an obvious antecedent to what would be labeled Southern gospel—incorporated folk, traditional hymns, and singing convention standards. Today's Christian music is often categorized by genre, reflecting the social, racial, ideological, and generational diversity of the Christian community. This diversity is shown in a contrast of pervading traditions, varied approaches to lyric writing, and stylistic exchanges between the sacred and secular. Throughout the evolution of gospel and contemporary Christian music, Arkansas has remained at the forefront, producing noteworthy pioneers of yesterday and molding trendsetters of today.

Several key figures in gospel music were born or based in Arkansas. While the music of some of these pioneers often transcended race, socio-economic status, and denominational differences, commercial gospel music as a whole has seemingly taken divergent paths depending on the race of its performers and their respective audiences. Black gospel has influenced secular popular music and rock and roll, while Southern gospel is regarded as a cousin to mainstream country music. Rhythm and blues (R&B) artists often incorporate black gospel's "call and response" technique, and Southern gospel and country performers frequently garner support from the same fan base. Regardless of the direction it has taken, however, gospel music remains rooted in evangelical Protestantism.

In the development of early gospel music, the role of the Hartford Music Company and its roster of important songwriters, namely E. M. Bartlett and Albert Edward Brumley, cannot be underestimated. Bartlett penned such timeless standards as "Everybody Will Be Happy over There" and "Victory in Jesus," while Brumley, Bartlett's protégé, arguably became the most recognized name in Southern gospel. His compositions—including "I'll Fly Away," "Turn Your Radio On," "I'll Meet You in the Morning," and "Jesus, Hold My Hand"—appear as well regarded in traditional gospel circles today as they were before sound recordings replaced singing convention songbooks, the primary medium in which early gospel music was mass marketed. Early black gospel recordings of Bartlett and Brumley songs show their widespread appeal.

Roberta Martin influenced black gospel music in much the same way as Bartlett and Brumley popularized gospel music among a predominantly white constituency. The Helena (Phillips County) native made her mark in Chicago, Illinois, where so many successful black gospel careers were launched. Martin's publishing house was a dominant force, and her groundbreaking group, the Roberta Martin Singers, helped pave the way during black gospel's golden age of the 1940s and 1950s for younger gospel artists who performed in the turbulent decades to follow.

Regarded as a rock and roll pioneer, "Sister Rosetta" Tharpe of Cotton Plant (Woodruff County) indelibly transformed gospel music, rising to prominence with "Rock Me," a version of Thomas A. Dorsey's "Hide Me in Thy Bosom." As part of John Hammond's *From Spirituals to Swing* concert in 1938, Tharpe influenced a wide range of secular and gospel artists, all the while stirring controversy over her decision to straddle the line between gospel and blues/jazz. Her music also bridged racial divides, particularly within music industry circles. Having already performed on the Grand Ole Opry stage in 1949, Tharpe made history once again in 1952 by recording Cleavant Derricks's "Have a Little Talk with Jesus" with country singer Red Foley. In addition to appearing with such white gospel artists as the Jordanaires and Sons of Song, Tharpe performed gospel music for some of the first integrated audiences in the American South.

Since the days of Bartlett, Brumley, Martin,

Timeline

• 1885 – Old Folks' Singing started as a dedication of a new Methodist church in Tull (Grant County). It is thought to be the oldest annual singing day west of the Mississippi River, and it continues today.

• 1918 – The Hartford Music Company, a gospel music publisher, was founded in Hartford (Sebastian County).

• 1926 – The Stamps Baxter Quartet, who would later be known as the Melody Boys, was formed. They went on to become the first gospel music group from Arkansas to have a television program and published the famed gospel song "Give the World a Smile." The group's rotating members performed together until 2012.

• 1932 – Albert E. Brumley, working for the Hartford Music Company, published "I'll Fly Away," which has been recorded more than 500 times by various artists.

• 1938 – "Sister Rosetta" Tharpe was signed to Decca Records. Tharpe's unique sound of edgy guitar mixed with bluesy gospel lyrics was influential to the gospel, R&B, and rock and roll genres.

• 1939 – Roberta Martin of Helena (Phillips County) established the Roberta Martin Studio of Music in Chicago, which distributed the works of several famous black gospel singers. Martin's group the Roberta Martin Singers influenced the golden age of black gospel in the 1940s and '50s.

• 1980 – Already famous R&B artist Al Green decided to begin recording only gospel music and received eight Grammy Awards in the gospel genre throughout his career; he later reentered the pop music world.

• 1991 – Point of Grace was formed, going on to record more than fifteen contemporary Christian albums and receive eight Gospel Music Association Dove Awards.

• 2011 – Country artist Collin Raye released the album *His Love Remains*, featuring inspirational gospel and contemporary Christian songs.

and Tharpe, artists with Arkansas connections have represented the state well in a variety of gospel music genres. Songs by Twila Paris, who took Christian music by storm in the 1990s, have become an integral part of Sunday morning worship across the country. The all-female contemporary Christian group Point of Grace, which was founded by four Ouachita Baptist University students in 1991 and went on to sell millions of records and score multiple number-one hits, continues to uplift and motivate younger worshipers. The rousing soul gospel of Smokie Norful resonates from urban megachurches to small-town storefront congregations. Joanne Cash, sister to country music legend Johnny Cash, performs a rich repertoire of country gospel. The award-winning trio the Martins offers tight family harmony and progressive Southern gospel fare.

Catholic recording artist John Michael Talbot, who got his start in music as part of the rock and roll band Mason Proffit, is the founder and leader of the Brothers and Sisters of Charity at the Little Portion Hermitage near Eureka Springs (Carroll County). In 2001, EMI Records gave Talbot, who has more than fifty albums to his name, an award to recognize his twenty-five years of Christian music ministry. In 2005, Talbot was inducted into the Arkansas Entertainers Hall of Fame.

Also worth noting is the number of largely secular Arkansas recording artists who have enjoyed critical and commercial success in gospel music. The most significant of these are soul singer Al Green and country music icon Johnny Cash. Green, best known for such R&B hits as "Let's Stay Together," returned to his gospel roots in the 1980s, netting eight Grammy Awards and performing with Patti LaBelle in the 1982 Broadway revival of the gospel musical *Your Arms Too Short to Box with God: A Soaring Celebration in Song and Dance*. In 1979, Cash independently released the double gospel album *A Believer Sings the Truth*, eventually garnering support from Columbia Records after the album hit number forty-three on the Country Music Top 50. There were several Rosetta Tharpe standards on the album, including "Strange Things Happening Every Day," for which Cash seemingly ad-libbed ("Everywhere it seems so strange / People down here stealin' airplanes" and "Well, we say that we want peace / But we're killin' each other like beasts") in apparent response to

recent hijackings and the Vietnam War. Other mainstream artists from Arkansas who have attained noteworthy record sales, chart success, or major industry awards in Christian music include country stars Glen Campbell, Barbara Fairchild, Tracy Lawrence, and Collin Raye, whose thought-provoking single "What If Jesus Comes Back Like That" preceded his gospel/inspirational album by more than a decade.

In spite of the successes enjoyed by today's soloists, gospel music is widely associated with group performance, whether in the form of a mass choir, mixed group, or all-male quartet. While the popularity of old-fashioned singing conventions has waned, various forms of gospel music remain integral to the modern communal worship experience.

Today, gospel and contemporary Christian music is thriving in Arkansas. Though the hugely popular Sundown to Sunup Gospel Sing was relocated from Springdale (Washington and Benton counties) to Missouri, where it is known as the Albert E. Brumley Memorial Gospel Sing, other popular events, such as Old Folks' Singing in Tull (Grant County), remain. Furthermore, long-held traditions are being preserved due to the persistence of institutions like the Brockwell Gospel Music School and Jeffress/Phillips Music Company, the state's only remaining seven-shape gospel publisher. Meanwhile, new generations of singers, songwriters, and musicians continue Arkansas's long, distinguished record of excellence in the field of Christian music.

For additional information:

Boyer, Horace Clarence. *How Sweet the Sound: The Golden Age of Gospel*. Urbana: University of Illinois Press, 1995.

Deller, David. "The Songbook Gospel Movement in Arkansas: E. M. Bartlett and the Hartford Music Company." *Arkansas Historical Quarterly* 60 (Autumn 2001): 284–300.

Goff, James R., Jr. *Close Harmony: A History of Southern Gospel*. Chapel Hill: University of North Carolina Press, 2002.

Heilbut, Tony. *The Gospel Sound: Good News and Bad Times*. New York: Simon & Schuster, 1971.

McNeil, W. K., ed. *Encyclopedia of American Gospel Music*. New York: Routledge, 2005.

Wald, Gayle F. *Shout, Sister, Shout!: The Untold Story of Rock-and-Roll Trailblazer Sister Rosetta Tharpe*. Boston: Beacon Press, 2007.

Wilson, Charles Reagan, and William Ferris, eds. *Encyclopedia of Southern Culture*. Chapel Hill: University of North Carolina Press, 1989.

Greg Freeman

JAZZ

With New Orleans, Louisiana, and Kansas City, Missouri, emerging as the booming urban epicenters of jazz music and inevitably spilling this music and culture across interstate lines, Arkansas began to see a number of touring "territory bands" sprout up around the state in the late 1910s and early 1920s. Some of the first included Sterling Todd's Rose City Orchestra; the Quinn Band out of Fort Smith (Sebastian County); and the Syncho Six out of Helena (Phillips County), led by banjo player Eugene Crooke.

All three bands were at some point joined by Arkansas's first major jazz musician, pianist Alphonso E. "Phonnie" Trent. Trent played with the Rose City Orchestra and the Quinn Band during his teenage years before eventually taking over Crooke's Syncho Six in 1923 and changing the band's name to the Alphonso Trent Orchestra.

By 1925, the band had found a residency at the Adolphus Hotel in Dallas, Texas, becoming the first black musicians to be broadcast on the radio (on Dallas's 50,000-watt WFAA AM). It was, according to jazz historian Gunther Schuller, "the most idolized and advanced band of the Southwest." The band also featured two of Arkansas's most talented early jazz artists: Lawrence Leo "Snub" Mosley of Little Rock (Pulaski County) and Hayes Pillars of North Little Rock (Pulaski County). Snub Mosley was a jazz trombonist, composer, and band leader whose career spanned more than fifty years, which included stints in the 1930s with Claude Hopkins, Fats Waller, and Louis Armstrong. Mosley is probably best remembered today as creator of his own unique instrument—the slide saxophone. Saxophonist Hayes Pillars would, in 1934, alongside James Jeter, take control of the Alphonso Trent Orchestra and later form the Jeter-Pillars Orchestra.

Around this time, Arkansan Eugene Staples (born in 1893) began the notorious hot jazz band Blue Steele and His Orchestra in Atlanta, Georgia, enlisting tenor saxophonist Pat Davis of Little Rock. In 1925, future icon Louis Jordan began making a name for himself playing alto saxophone in Brady Bryant's Salt and Pepper Shakers out of Brinkley (Monroe County). The mid-to-late 1920s also saw an emergence

of jazz in El Dorado (Union County), driven by the number of dance halls popping up in the wake of the city's oil boom. There, Jordan played briefly in Jimmy Pryor's Imperial Serenaders, one of a number of El Dorado bands whose short tenures were a result of the city police's crackdown on Prohibition-era nightclubs.

The 1930s saw several music venues emerge around central Arkansas, hosting some of the biggest national names in jazz. The Cinderella Gardens and Dance Palace, the Dreamland Ballroom, and the Mosaic Temple, all in Little Rock, became frequent stops for the leading bands in the Southwest as well as national artists such as Ella Fitzgerald, Nat King Cole, and Duke Ellington.

While Little Rock was becoming a major regional hub for popular acts, a student at the Arkansas School for the Blind, Al Hibbler, began

Timeline

• 1893 – Eugene Staples, founder of Blue Steele and His Orchestra, was born.

• 1923 – Bob Dorough, best known as the composer and musical director for *Schoolhouse Rock!*, was born.

• 1925 – Louis Jordan began his jazz career by playing alto saxophone in Brady Bryant's Salt and Pepper Shakers.

• 1925 – The Alphonso Trent Orchestra was hired to play in the Adolphus Hotel ballroom in Dallas, Texas, becoming the first black musicians broadcast on American radio (Dallas's 50,000-watt WFAA AM).

• 1942 – Al Hibbler began singing with Duke Ellington's band.

• 1943 – Louis Thomas Hardin, adopting the name Moondog, moved to New York City and began playing his own experimental fusion of jazz and classical minimalism.

• 1966 – Pharoah Sanders released *Tauhid*, which had a major impact on the free-jazz movement.

• 1971 – Art Porter Sr. began hosting *The Minor Key*, a musical variety program on the Arkansas Educational Television Network.

• 1984 – The Eureka Springs Jazz Festival Jazz Eureka was founded.

• 1992 – The Hot Springs Jazz Fest was founded.

• 1994 – The Arkansas Jazz Heritage Foundation started the Arkansas Jazz Hall of Fame.

singing in local bands, eventually joining Jay McShann's orchestra in Kansas City for a year and a half in 1942–43 before moving on to front Duke Ellington's band for the next eight years, where he found national success and critical acclaim as a voice that bridged the styles of jazz and rhythm and blues (R&B).

Two of the most idiosyncratic, forward-thinking figures in 1950s jazz have Arkansas connections, as well. The first is Bob Dorough, born in Cherry Hill (Polk County), who is best known as the composer and voice of *Schoolhouse Rock!*. However, in 1954, Dorough was hired by boxer Sugar Ray Robinson. Robinson, who was taking a break from the ring to star in a song-and-dance revue, brought in Dorough as the show's music director. Over the following years in Paris, France, Dorough performed nightly gigs at a famous Parisian jazz mainstay, the Mars Club; performed with Louis Armstrong and Count Basie; recorded with fellow "hip vocalese" singer Blossom Dearie; and released *Devil May Care*, his first of several albums.

Art Porter Sr. at the piano; circa 1980s.

Courtesy: Butler Center for Arkansas Studies, Central Arkansas Library System

The second key 1950s figure is Louis Thomas Hardin, who spent his late teens and early twenties in Batesville (Independence County), enrolling at Arkansas College (now Lyon College) for one year, before moving to New York City in 1943 at the age of twenty-seven. There, the young eccentric pianist took the name Moondog and began dressing like the Norse god Odin, earning him the nickname "the Viking of Sixth Avenue." An experimentalist to the core, Moondog fused third-stream jazz and classical minimalism, earning the praises of, notably, Charlie Parker, Charles Mingus, and Philip Glass.

Another Arkansan to fuse jazz and classical styles, Walter Norris, has been hailed by some jazz historians as one of the greatest jazz pianists of all time. A key member of the West Coast jazz scene of the late 1950s, Norris played piano on the ground-breaking album *Something Else!: The Music of Ornette Coleman* (1958), joined the Charles Mingus Quintet in 1976, and, in between, served as the director of entertainment for the New York City Playboy Club from 1963 to 1970.

One of the biggest names in Arkansas's jazz history is pianist Arthur Lee (Art) Porter Sr., who performed mostly within the state. A vocal teacher by day and jazz pianist by night, he founded the popular Art Porter Jazz Trio. He hosted a musical variety program, *The Minor Key*, on the Arkansas Educational Television Network, which began in 1971 and lasted for a decade. Another program, *Porterhouse Cuts*, was a series of ten shows that aired in thirteen states. His son Art Porter Jr. of Little Rock was a creative composer whose work ranged across jazz, R&B, funk, and ballads.

While the melding of classical and jazz forms has been a major trend throughout Arkansas's jazz history, Pharoah Sanders, born Ferrell Sanders in Little Rock, is one of the major founding figures of the decidedly anti-classical/formalist free-jazz movement. While still enrolled at Scipio Jones High School in North Little Rock in the late 1950s, Sanders was a regular at Little Rock's downtown jazz clubs. After a brief stint in San Francisco, California (where he was known as "Little Rock"), Sanders relocated to New York in 1961, where he played with a number of jazz luminaries, including Sun Ra and Don Cherry. By 1965, Sanders was collaborating extensively with John Coltrane, influencing Coltrane with his deconstructive, free-jazz dissonance. Between 1966 and 1971, Sanders released five albums that are considered defining points of the free-jazz movement: *Tauhid* (1966), *Karma* (1969), *Deaf Dumb Blind (Summum Bukmun Umyun)* (1970), *Thembi* (1971), and *Black Unity* (1971).

Arkansas's continuing interest in jazz can be seen through the number of local jazz festivals that began popping up around with state, with the Eureka Springs Jazz Festival being founded in 1984 and the Hot Springs Jazz Fest following in 1992.

The Arkansas Jazz Heritage Foundation was established in the early 1990s to "educate the general public about the historical significance of Arkansas's musical heritage" through organizing weekly jazz sessions and, since 1994, maintaining the Arkansas Jazz Hall of Fame, which regularly honors Arkansans of note in the field of jazz. Members of the Arkansas Jazz Hall of Fame include Phonnie Trent, Al Hibbler, Bob Dorough, and Art Porter Jr. The following artists are members of both the Arkansas Jazz Hall of Fame and the Arkansas Entertainers Hall of Fame: Art Porter Sr., Louis Jordan, Pharoah Sanders, and Walter Norris.

For additional information:
Arkansas Jazz Heritage Foundation. http://www.arjazz. org/ (accessed March 26, 2013).

Cochran, Robert. *Our Own Sweet Sounds: A Celebration of Popular Music in Arkansas*. 2nd ed. Fayetteville: University of Arkansas Press, 2005.
Kernfield, Barry. *The New Grove Dictionary of Jazz*. New York: Grove's Dictionaries, 2002.
Rice, Marc. "Frompin' in the Great Plains: Listening and Dancing to the Jazz Orchestras of Alphonso Trent, 1925–44." *Great Plains Quarterly* 16 (Spring 1996): 107–115.
Rinne, Henry. "A Short History of the Alphonso Trent Orchestra." *Arkansas Historical Quarterly* 45 (Autumn 1986): 228–249.

John Tarpley

ROCK

Although the roots of rock and roll music can be traced back much farther, the genre made its musical debut in the early 1950s with artists such as Little Richard, Elvis Presley, and Jerry Lee Lewis, all of whom helped shape what rock music has become. The music of the 1950s gave way to the 1960s and the popularity of surf music, as well as the very significant "British Invasion." Arkansas musicians played an important part in this burgeoning genre.

In the mid-1960s, Little Rock (Pulaski County), along with many other mid-sized American cities, saw an explosion in the formation of garage bands, all of which began competing for performance spots at school, fraternity, and country club engagements. This excitement quickly spread to other Arkansas cities and towns. Musicians from around the state flocked to Little Rock to take part in the action. Bands began performing at Moses Melody Shop in Little Rock for Saturday KALO radio broadcasts and cut their demos at Jaggars Recording Studio. Others taped sessions for commercial release through the My Records label and E&M Recording Company.

Along with local success came national recognition, and many musicians from Arkansas achieved national and international success. Kingsland (Cleveland County) native Johnny Cash, though predominantly known for his success as a country artist, influenced the careers of many rock artists of the era. Newport (Jackson County) native Sonny Burgess is best known as one of the original rock and roll recording artists

One of Arkansas's many garage bands, My Records recording artists the Checkmates; circa mid-1960s.
Courtesy: Harold Ott/Psych of the South

for Sun Records in Memphis, Tennessee. Glen Campbell, a Pike County native, is an acclaimed pop/country singer and songwriter whose succession of hits includes "By the Time I Get to Phoenix," "Wichita Lineman," and "Rhinestone Cowboy"; in the mid-1960s, he played guitar and sang harmonies as a temporary replacement for Brian Wilson in the Beach Boys.

Huntsville (Madison County) native Ronnie Hawkins and Levon Helm, a Marvell (Phillips County) native, were both known for their work with the Canadian group the Band as well as for their solo careers. Dale Hawkins Jr., cousin to Ronnie Hawkins, is known for his rockabilly roots, and the sound he created came to be known as "Swamp Rock." This unique type of music of the late 1960s is characterized by genre influences such as zydeco, Cajun, blues, and pop. Black Oak Arkansas, a southern hard rock band fronted by Black Oak (Craighead County) native "Jim Dandy" Mangrum, reached great musical success in the 1970s. Randy Goodrum, born in Hot Springs (Garland County), is a Grammy Award–winning adult contemporary music songwriter and producer who penned such 1980s rock hits as "Foolish Heart" and "Oh Sherrie."

As in other places, rock music in Arkansas was spawned from a variety of genres ranging from country to blues to rockabilly. During the 1970s and 1980s, rock music began taking on other forms such as punk and what became known as metal, and the Arkansas scene continued to evolve and expand during the 1980s to include a unique punk and metal scene. In the late 1980s, an underground music scene emerged in Arkansas that grew rapidly in popularity and notability. During this time, teens began booking their own shows, selling their own records, and even starting small independent record labels. This led many young bands to success opening for national acts while giving them the opportunity to write, record, and market their own music. This process helped them build a tight-knit underground community that existed

Little Rock band Mulehead reproducing the famous Who photograph for album art; 2001.   Photo: Matthew Martin

and flourished for several years, as documented in the 2007 film *Towncraft,* which features Little Rock bands Ho-Hum (whose lead singer Kevin Kerby later formed Mulehead), American Princes, and others.

More recent times have seen other musicians and bands succeed in the rock genre, including the Arkansas-based band Evanescence, whose 2003 major-label debut *Fallen* catapulted them onto the charts. Little Rock native Ben Nichols is the frontman for the Memphis, Tennessee–based Lucero, an alt-country-rock band that formed in 1999. Beth Ditto of Judsonia (White County) formed her punk-rock group Gossip in Olympia, Washington, the same year. Pop musician Kris Allen of Conway (Faulkner County) was the winner of *American Idol* in 2009 and has gone on to release two albums as of 2012; he was inducted into the Arkansas Entertainers Hall of Fame in 2010.

Arkansas's emerging underground metal scene is most prevalent in the Little Rock metropolitan area. Bands such as Rwake, Deadbird, and Vore, as well as Christian death metal band Living Sacrifice, are making their mark. Venues in Little Rock such as Downtown Music and Vino's, as well as the Soundstage in Conway, frequently host metal shows promoting local talent.

Arkansas is also home to several notable venues that have hosted a number of major concerts over the years. These include Barton Coliseum, Verizon Arena (formerly known as Alltel Arena), and Robinson Center Music Hall. Several of the larger universities such as the University of Arkansas (UA) in Fayetteville (Washington County), University of Central Arkansas (UCA) in Conway, and Arkansas State University (ASU) in Jonesboro (Craighead County) also host a va-

Timeline

• 1965 – Originally called the Knowbody Else, the band that would become Black Oak Arkansas was formed.

• 1969 – The Band (with Levon Helm singing and drumming) released its eponymous album, *The Band*, including "The Night They Drove Old Dixie Down," "Up on Cripple Creek," "Across the Great Divide," "Look Out Cleveland," and "King Harvest (Has Surely Come)."

• 1975 –Rolling Stones guitarists Ron Wood and Keith Richards were pulled over for reckless driving and arrested in the Arkansas town of Fordyce. They were on their way to Dallas, Texas, after playing a show in Memphis, Tennessee.

• 1995 – Rock critic Robert Palmer of Little Rock published *Rock & Roll: An Unruly History*.

• 2002 – The city of Toronto, Canada, proclaimed October 4, 2002, "Ronnie Hawkins Day." A singer and bandleader from Huntsville (Madison County), Hawkins is best known for starting the group the Hawks, which later became the Band.

• 2007 – The film *Towncraft*, documenting the unique punk and metal scene in Arkansas during the 1970s and '80s, was released.

• 2009 – The Arkansas General Assembly designated a segment of U.S. Highway 67 the "Rock 'n' Roll Highway" to pay homage to the rockabilly and early rock and roll artists who performed at venues along the highway.

riety of national acts. Smaller venues such as Juanita's and the Revolution Room host up-and-coming national acts as well as local artists and bands.

Many recording studios can be found across the state, some of which are noted for recording and producing songs by national acts. The careers of many local artists were launched from demos and full-length albums recorded at studios such as Crystal Recording Studios in Bryant (Saline County), Hawk's Nest Studio in North Little Rock (Pulaski County), and Winterwood Recording Studios in Eureka Springs (Carroll County).

Over the years, Arkansas musicians and fans have kept up with the local music scene through *Night Flying*, a free, monthly music publication launched on December 8, 1980, by Peter Read. It quickly gained notoriety and still remains a prominent musical resource throughout the state, the only publication of its kind in Arkansas focusing on local music and musicians.

For additional information:

Cochran, Robert. *Our Own Sweet Sounds: A Celebration of Popular Music in Arkansas*. 2nd ed. Fayetteville: University of Arkansas Press, 2005.

Horne, Margaret Suzanne Huckett. "Power and Performance: Punk and Metal Music in a Small Southern Town." PhD diss., University of Arkansas, 2008.

The Little Rock Sound, 1965-69. Liner notes by Bill Jones. Little Rock: Butler Center for Arkansas Studies, 1999.

Matson, Richard, director. *Towncraft*. DVD. Matson Films, 2007.

Nightflying: The Entertainment Guide. http://www.nightflying.com (accessed February 13, 2013).

Sweet Sounds Exhibition. Old State House Museum Online Collections. Sweet Sounds Collection.

Elizabeth Whitaker

ROCKABILLY

Rockabilly, a musical genre that appeared in the mid-1950s, is an early form of rock and roll initially performed by white musicians from the mid-South. Several Arkansans became leading rockabilly songwriters and performers.

A distinctly American phenomenon, rockabilly was strongly influenced by developments of the post–World War II period. These include the introduction of the single-play 45 rpm record, the early phases of the civil rights movement, and the increasing mobility and purchasing power of teenagers. Characterized by a blues structure and a moderately fast tempo, rockabilly music celebrated a world of cars, parties, fast living, and sexual relationships. Its use of slang, much of it from African-American origins, and its themes of rebellious youth and self-indulgence, caused disfavor in many conservative groups.

Arkansas musicians had formative influence on the development of rockabilly. They include the jump blues of Louis Jordan, the rhythmic gospel style of "Sister Rosetta" Tharpe, and the hillbilly boogie sound of Wayne Raney. Early references to rockabilly as "hillbilly bop" suggest its origins in country music and western swing, with additional traces of bluegrass and honky-tonk. Arkansas rockabilly artists were influenced by the increasing popularity of radio barn dance shows in the early 1950s. Foremost among these were at the Grand Ole Opry from Nashville, Tennessee, and the *Louisiana Hayride* from Shreveport, Louisiana. These broadcasts were emulated in Little Rock (Pulaski County) with *Barnyard Frolics*, a live performance venue for local talent and regional performers.

Rockabilly was also strongly influenced by rhythm and blues and the evolution of acoustic country blues into the new, up-tempo electrified style of Howlin' Wolf, Sonny Boy Williamson, Robert Lockwood Jr., and other early stars of the *King Biscuit Time* radio show from Helena (Phillips County).

These varied influences reflect the major demographic and economic changes of the postwar period, a time when large populations of rural black southerners relocated to northern cities. The typical rockabilly artist reflected those significant changes. He was born in early 1930s, came from a middle or lower economic class, and by the mid-1950s was working in a trade or blue-collar job. Arkansans with rural backgrounds who had known the harsh realities of tenant farming and picking cotton were common in this group. They were keenly aware of the popularity and success of Elvis Presley, whose touring schedule included more than three dozen Arkansas shows in 1954 and 1955.

Many Arkansas musicians who transitioned to other styles began their careers in the rockabilly mode, including Johnny Cash, Conway Twitty, Levon Helm, Narvel Felts, and Sleepy LaBeef. Other Arkansans, such as Sonny Burgess, Billy Lee Riley, and Ronnie Hawkins, stayed closer to their original rockabilly sound over the decades. Numerous other Arkansas musicians performed and recorded rockabilly with limited recognition outside their musical communities.

Rockabilly music was played at bars, clubs, honky-tonks, college fraternity parties, and dance halls—places where people could dance and drink with some abandon. Some establishments were small, rough country venues where farmers in bib overalls arrived on tractors, seeking evenings of excessive drinking, fighting, and flirtation. Other clubs, such as Beverly Gardens in Little Rock, could accommodate 200 to 300 people. The largest club in Arkansas at this time was the Silver Moon in Newport (Jackson County), which could seat more than 800 people.

While rockabilly music owes much of its sound and character to the blues, Arkansas law and custom in the 1950s prohibited integrated social encounters, particularly where dancing occurred. Black musicians performed at clubs where rockabilly was played, and integrated bands were not uncommon, but black Arkansans seldom attended these clubs as patrons.

At the height of the rockabilly era in the late 1950s, many Arkansas rockabilly groups, such as Sonny Burgess and the Pacers and Billy Lee Riley and the Little Green Men, had recorded for Sun Records and were rising to national attention. Dale Hawkins, a member of the Rockabilly Hall of Fame, specialized in creating a sound (called "Swamp Rock" by some) that went on to help shape rock and roll music. In May 13, 1957, the Little Rock television affiliate of CBS began broadcasting *Steve's Show*, hosted by Steve Stephens and featuring local teenagers who danced to hit records as rockabilly artists and other performers lip-synched the words.

The rockabilly era ended with the decade, with several of its national stars in new engagements. Sonny Burgess's "Sadie's Back in Town," released by Sun Records on December 31, 1959, could be considered the last rockabilly hit of the era. The popular music industry was shifting to a softer format and more banal subject matter than rockabilly's fast cars, rowdy women, and rebellious partying. Arkansas rockabilly artists either modified their styles or retired from the music business. A rockabilly revival in the 1970s brought renewed attention to the genre, while European audiences have maintained a nearly cult-like devotion to the original sound. Younger Arkansans, such as Jason D. Williams of El Dorado (Union County), continue to perform in a traditional rockabilly mode.

Timeline

• 1943 – Billy Lee Riley's father bought Riley his first guitar.

• Early 1950s – Arkansas rockabilly artists were influenced by the increasing popularity of radio barn dance shows. These were emulated in Little Rock with *Barnyard Frolics*.

• Mid-1950s – Rockabilly, or "hillbilly bop," emerged as a genre.

• 1956 – Narvel Felts joined the Rockets and became the band's front man.

• 1957 – The Little Rock television affiliate of CBS began broadcasting *Steve's Show,* featuring local teenagers dancing to hit records by rockabilly and early rock and roll artists.

• 1957–1959 – Dale Hawkins charted four times in these years. A member of the Rockabilly Hall of Fame, he specialized in "Swamp Rock," which helped shape rock and roll music.

• 1959 – Sonny Burgess released "Sadie's Back in Town" on Sun Records, which many consider the last rockabilly hit of the era.

• 2009 – Rock 'n' Roll Highway 67 was designated to recognize the importance of the rockabilly/early rock and roll bands that traveled and played along the route in the 1950s; many thought it should be called the "Rockabilly Highway."

For additional information:

Altschuler, Glenn. *"All Shook Up": How Rock 'n' Roll Changed America*. Oxford: Oxford University Press, 2003.

Burke, Ken, and Dan Griffin. *The Blue Moon Boys: The Story of Elvis Presley's Band*. Chicago: Chicago Review Press, 2006.

Cochran, Robert. *Our Own Sweet Sounds: A Celebration of Popular Music in Arkansas*. 2nd ed. Fayetteville: University of Arkansas Press, 2005.

Dregni, Michael. *Rockabilly: The Twang Heard 'Round the World—An Illustrated History*. Minneapolis, MN: Voyageur Press, 2011.

Marcus, Greil. *Mystery Train: Images of America in Rock 'n' Roll Music*. New York: Plume, 1997.

McNutt, Randy. *We Wanna Boogie: An Illustrated History of the American Rockabilly Movement*. Fairfield, OH: HHP Books, 1988.

Morrison, Craig. *Go Cat Go: Rockabilly Music and Its Makers*. Urbana: University of Illinois Press, 1996.

Toches, Nick. *Country: The Twisted Roots of Rock 'n' Roll*. Cambridge, MA: Da Capo Press, 1996.

Marvin Schwartz

BLUES / R&B — LUTHER ALLISON (1939–1997)

Blues guitarist and singer Luther Allison was born in Arkansas, but like many of his contemporaries in the rural South, he rose to fame in cities far from his original home. His style exemplified the soulful blues of the west side of Chicago, Illinois, where he moved with his family as a child. Later, in 1977, when the popularity of the blues faded in the United States, he began touring Europe extensively and became an international star.

Born in Widener (St. Francis County) on August 17, 1939, Luther Allison was the fourteenth of fifteen children, all of whom were musically inclined, born to parents who were cotton farmers. He was exposed to gospel music as a young child, although he quickly became enthralled with the flourishing blues scene in Chicago upon his family's arrival there in 1951. At age sixteen, he was leading the first of his many bands, one of which was presciently named the Rolling Stones. His first major breakthrough as a popular solo artist was his acclaimed performance at the Ann Arbor Blues Festival in Michigan in 1969. In 1972, he was one of the few blues performers who ever signed a recording contract with Detroit's Motown Records.

Allison started touring in Europe almost exclusively in the late 1970s and settled in Paris, France, in 1984. He was adored in Europe, receiving what one critic described as "an overdose of respect," and cut one album, *Serious*, while in France—this was released by the Blind Pig label in the United States in 1987. Fifteen years after moving to Europe, Allison returned to America in triumph, and in 1994, he began recording for

Luther Allison in concert.
Courtesy: Ruf Records

Chicago's Alligator Records, an association that led in 1996 and 1997 to his winning five W. C. Handy Awards and fifteen Living Blues Awards. He released *Soul Fixin' Man* in 1994, *Blue Streak* in 1995, and *Reckless*, which was nominated for a Grammy, in 1998.

In 1997, at the height of one of the most astonishing comebacks in blues history, he was diagnosed with inoperable lung cancer. He died on August 12, 1997, at University Hospital in Madison, Wisconsin. The Ruf label released *Hand Me Down My Moonshine*, an all-acoustic album with Allison and his son Bernard, in 1998, and the following year, Alligator Records released Allison's two-CD set, *Live in Chicago*. Ruf has since released other Allison albums, including 2009's *Songs from the Road*.

For additional information:
Herzhaft, Gerard. *Encyclopedia of the Blues*. Fayetteville: University of Arkansas Press, 1997.
Luther Allison. http://www.luther-allison.com/ (accessed February 8, 2013).
Stambler, Irwin, and Lyndon Stambler. *Folk and Blues: The Encyclopedia*. New York: St. Martin's Press, 2001.

Jim Kelton

BLUES / R&B — JOSHUA ALTHEIMER (1911–1940)

Joshua Altheimer was one of the Delta's most prolific blues pianists. Altheimer mastered the emerging boogie-woogie style of the 1930s as he accompanied some of the legendary blues musicians of his era.

Joshua Altheimer was born on May 17, 1911, in Pine Bluff (Jefferson County) to Silas Altheimer and Verdis Pruitt Barnes Altheimer. He played his first years in Arkansas, perform-

ing during the late 1920s. It is not clear whether during this period Altheimer knew blues legend "Big Bill" Broonzy, who was from his home county and who was raised just a few miles from where he was born.

By the 1930s, Altheimer had moved to Chicago, Illinois, and was playing with the likes of John Lee Sonny Boy Williamson, Washboard Sam, Jazz Gillum, and Lonnie Johnson. From

1937 to 1940, he played on more than fifty tunes for Broonzy, who described him as "the best blues piano player I ever heard." The 1956 *Guide to Jazz* also called Altheimer "the greatest blues pianist on records." Altheimer was an accompanist in the 1939 recording session in which Lonnie Johnson recorded with an electric guitar for the first time.

Altheimer died in Chicago on November 18, 1940, from complications due to pneumonia. Though he never recorded solo material, he was part of a cadre of talented blues pianists such as Roosevelt Sykes, Tampa Red, Leroy Carr, and others who helped define pre–World War II blues.

For additional information:
"Joshua Altheimer." AllMusic.com. http://www.allmusic.com/artist/joshua-altheimer-mn0000282497 (accessed March 21, 2013).

Komara, Edward, ed. *Encyclopedia of the Blues*. Vol. 1. New York: Routledge, 2006.

Panassié, Hugues, and Madeline Gautier. *Guide to Jazz*. Boston: Houghton Mifflin, 1956.

Jimmy Cunningham Jr.

MISCELLANEA | ARKANSAS ENTERTAINERS HALL OF FAME

The Arkansas Entertainers Hall of Fame in Pine Bluff (Jefferson County) was created to honor Arkansans who have made outstanding contributions to the entertainment industry. Honorees include performers, non-performing contributors (such as writers, directors, and producers), and pioneers in the entertainment industry.

In 1985, the Arkansas General Assembly authorized the establishment of a museum honoring Arkansans who have made a considerable contribution to the entertainment industry. The first inductees were honored in 1996. The following year, the state legislature transferred the Arkansas Entertainers Hall of Fame to the Department of Parks and Tourism, along with $300,000. Several cities competed to host the museum. Pine Bluff was eventually chosen, with the Pine Bluff Convention and Visitors Bureau receiving $250,000 to establish the Hall of Fame. On October 2, 1998, the Hall of Fame opened with a permanent home in the Pine Bluff Convention Center.

The board of the Arkansas Entertainers Hall of Fame selects honorees for induction, with nominations coming from the artists themselves or from other individuals. After a review of applications to determine if the nominee meets the basic criteria of Arkansas connection and national significance, among other factors, the nominations are held until the board's annual meeting, at which time they are voted upon. Board members are appointed by the governor, and the board now holds an induction ceremony every two years.

A life-size animatronic statue of Johnny Cash greets visitors with some of the most popular songs of his career. Many other well-known Arkansas entertainers, both performing and non-performing, who have been inducted into the Hall of Fame have contributed artifacts to the exhibits that represent their achievements. For example, the museum houses Bob Burns's "bazooka" as well as the musical instruments and clothing of other performers.

Among the inductees into the Arkansas Entertainers Hall of Fame are radio personalities Chet Lauck and Norris Goff ("Lum and Abner"); musical talents Al Green, the Browns, Patsy Montana, Levon Helm, "Lefty" Frizzell, and Jimmy Driftwood; singer/songwriter and television and motion picture actor Ed Bruce; composer William Grant Still; orchestra conductor Sarah Caldwell; jazz pianist Walter Norris; opera singer Barbara Hendricks; Broadway and motion picture performer William Warfield; gospel songwriter Albert E. Brumley; movie actors "Broncho Billy" Anderson, Julie Adams, Mary Steenburgen, Billy Bob Thornton, Dick Powell, and Alan Ladd; entertainment promoter Jim Porter; author John Grisham; screenwriter James Bridges; motion picture sound and camera lens inventor Freeman Owens; television producer and director Harry Z. Thomason; Broadway producer Elizabeth Williams; and Broadway musical performer Lawrence Hamilton.

Arkansas Entertainers Hall of Fame Inductees

1996
Glen Campbell	Billstown/Delight
Johnny Cash	Kingsland
Jimmy Driftwood	Timbo
Randy Goodrum	Hot Springs
Al Green	Forrest City
Wayland Holyfield	Mallet Town

Alan Ladd ... ...Hot Springs
Tracy Lawrence ... ... Foreman
Lum and Abner (Chet Lauck and Norris Goff)... ... .. Mena
Art Porter Sr.. ... ...Little Rock
Patsy Montana ... ... Beaudry
Dick Powell ... ...Mountain View
Charlie Rich ... ... Colt
Mary Steenburgen.. ... ... Newport
Harry Thomason ... ... Hampton
Billy Bob Thornton.. ... ...Hot Springs

1998
Bob Burns ... ... .Greenwood
The Browns ... ... .Sparkman
Melvin Endsley ... ... .Drasco
Jim Ed Brown ... ... Sparkman/Pine Bluff
Levon Helm ... ...Turkey Scratch
Bonnie Brown.. ... ... Sparkman/Pine Bluff
Floyd Cramer ... ...Huttig
Maxine Brown. ... ...Sampti, LA/Pine Bluff
Louis Jordan . ... Brinkley
Mark Wright . ... Fayetteville
Jerry Van Dyke ... ... Benton
Conway Twitty. ... ... .Helena

2000
Julie Adams ... ...Little Rock
K. T. Oslin. ... ...Crossett
James (Jim) Bridges ... ... Paris
Sarah Caldwell ... ... Fayetteville
Skeets McDonald . ...Rector
Art Porter Jr... ... ...Little Rock
Broncho Billy Anderson.. ... ...Pine Bluff
Pharoah Sanders ... ...Little Rock
William Warfield ... ...Helena
Twila Paris ... ... Springdale

2002/2003
Ronnie Dunn ... ... .El Dorado
Barbara Hendricks ... ... Stephens
John Grisham ... ... Jonesboro
William Grant Still ... ...Little Rock
Steve Stephens ... ... Newport
Freeman H. Owens.. ... ...Pine Bluff
Walter Norris ... ...Little Rock

2005
Collin Raye. ... ...De Queen
John Michael Talbot ... .. Little Rock/Eureka Springs
Ed Bruce ... ... Keiser
Elizabeth Williams ... ... Arkadelphia
Jim Porter ... ...Little Rock
Lefty Frizzell.. ... ... El Dorado

Lawrence Hamilton. ... ... Foreman
John Weston ... ... .Brinkley/Smale
Albert Brumley ... ... Hartford Music Institute

2007
Beth Brickell.. ... ... .Camden
Gil Gerard ... ...Little Rock
Laurence Luckinbill. ... ... Fort Smith
Gail Davis ... ...McGehee
BJ Sams. ... ...Little Rock
Jack Mitchell. ... ...Bella Vista
Sonny Burgess ... ... Newport
Sarah Tackett ... ...Conway

2008
Tess Harper ... ... Mammoth Springs
Ronnie Hawkins. ... ... Huntsville/Fayetteville
Wayne Jackson ... ... .West Memphis
Joe Nichols ... ... .Rogers
Wilburn Brothers.. ... ... Hardy
Sonny Boy Williamson. ... ...Helena
Ed Wilson ... ...Rison

2010
Kris Allen . ...Conway
Lisa Blount . ... Fayetteville
Jim "Moose" Brown ... ... Jonesboro
Barbara Fairchild ... ...Knobel
Albert King ... ...Forrest City
George Newbern.. ... ...Little Rock
Mark Stallings . ... .McCrory
Jerry McKinnis. ... ... Flippin
Charles B. Pierce ... ...Hampton

2013
Gary Weir ... ... North Little Rock
Bill Carter ... ...Rector
Louie Shelton .. .. North Little Rock
Rosetta Nubin Tharpe.. ... ... Cotton Plant
Mike Utley.. ... ...Blytheville

For additional information:
Arkansas Entertainers Hall of Fame. http://www.arkansasentertainershalloffame.com/ (accessed February 8, 2013).
Cofer, Brian. "Hall of Fame for Entertainers Opens Friday." *Arkansas Democrat-Gazette*, September 27, 1998, pp. 1B, 8B.
Pine Bluff Convention and Visitors Bureau. http://www.pinebluffcvb.org/ (accessed February 8, 2013).
Slivka, Judd. "Pine Bluff Panel's Pick to House Hall of State Stars." *Arkansas Democrat-Gazette*, February 18, 1997, pp. 1B, 8B.

Bob Purvis

The annual Arkansas Folk Festival takes place on the third weekend in April in Mountain View (Stone County). Held since 1963, the event attracts thousands of people to the small mountain community, where the livelihood of many residents is based on tourism. The town has become nationally renowned for its folk music, and the downtown area is a popular place for impromptu "pickins" as musicians gather informally to perform.

The Arkansas Folk Festival has its roots in the Stone County Folkways Festival, which was held on August 20, 1941, in the Ozark National Forest near Blanchard Springs (Stone County). The festival was sponsored by the Stone County Extension Homemakers clubs and included musical performances and a jig dance contest. About 2,500 people attended, and hopes were high to make the festival an annual event, but the beginning of World War II later that year prevented a second annual festival the following summer.

The festival was revived in 1963 during the birth of a regional tourism effort. Glen Hinkle, the chairman of the Stone County Development Council, and Lloyd Westbrook, the county extension agent, were among the planners of the festival. They drew in the Ozark Foothills Handicraft Guild, which had held its first show the year before in Batesville (Independence County). Also, the local Tourist and Recreation Committee (a subcommittee of the Rural Development Agency) had sponsored a regional Dogwood Drive for the previous few years. The planners decided to combine the different events into one big spring festival. Westbrook then approached Jimmy Driftwood, who had performed at the 1941 festival and had since become a national figure in the folk music arena. Westbrook and his fellow organizers expected Driftwood to bring other famous musicians to the area for the festival, but Driftwood instead suggested that they feature local amateur talent. At that time, he began to organize the Rackensack Folklore Society, who became featured performers at the festival. The festival opened on April 19, drawing 2,500 people to the initial performances. An estimated 3,800 people attended the two concerts held the following night, though the city of Mountain View had, at the time, a population of about 1,000 people.

Attendance at the festival peaked in the 1970s with the height in popularity of folk music and the free-spirited audience that followed it. The festival was extended over two weekends in its most popular phase; as of 2013, the event features three official days of activities sponsored by the Mountain View Area Chamber of Commerce. A parade of local dignitaries, floats depicting area heritage, antique cars, and other entries is a main attraction. Musicians gather throughout the downtown area, and merchandise vendors display and sell their wares. Special programs such as living history forums and talent shows vary from year to year. Unofficial observers have estimated that between 20,000 and 30,000 people attend per year.

The Arkansas Craft Guild, which maintains its headquarters and gallery in Mountain View, worked in 2008 to re-establish handmade crafts as an important aspect of the festival. That year, the festival premiered the Artisans Market on the Square, a juried arts and crafts show and sale organized by the newly formed Mountain View Area Artisans Council.

For additional information:
"History of the Arkansas Folk Festival." *Heritage of Stone* 22, no. 2 (1998): 1–23.

Lori Freeze

Participants and attendees at the Arkansas Folk Festival situated in front of the courthouse on the square in downtown Mountain View.
Courtesy: Arkansas Department of Parks and Tourism

ARKANSAS SYMPHONY ORCHESTRA

The Arkansas Symphony Orchestra, based in Little Rock (Pulaski County), provides opportunities for the residents of the state to hear and to perform quality instrumental music. The current orchestra, which incorporated in 1966, is the successor to several previous and shorter-lived attempts to create a sustainable performing group.

Most reports of musical performances in early Arkansas history are of vocal performances, brass ensembles, concerts by amateur groups, recitals by pupils of individual teachers, or church-sponsored events. No regularly performing instrumental groups available for public enjoyment appear in reports until after the turn of the twentieth century. During the early years of 1900s, music clubs over the state, as well as individual music lovers, became vocal about the desirability of musical education for the young and their wish for quality musical performances for the enjoyment of the citizenry.

In 1933, the Little Rock Civic Symphony was organized and directed by Laurence Powell of the music department at Little Rock Junior College as part of the college's music program. Members of this all-student and all-volunteer group performed regularly scheduled concerts for six years. The business community, having become aware of the economic value of offering cultural opportunities, began to give some support; however, despite a fundraising drive spearheaded by the Business and Professional Women's Club, continuing financial difficulties caused the group to disband.

From the beginning, efforts to establish a viable symphony organization were plagued by financial and organizational problems. Between 1939 and the early 1960s, orchestra activity was characterized by frequent changes of name and of directors. Groups known as University Civic Orchestra, Arkansas Pop Orchestra, University Concert Society, and the Arkansas Orchestra Society kept activity alive, but none had secure backing, and none survived for long. Conductors who were knowledgeable and interested either left the state or took other positions. Two organizations from this period had somewhat better success than the majority. The State Symphony Orchestra, sponsored by the Arkansas Philharmonic Society and by music clubs across the state, emerged in 1941 and attracted bigger audiences than previous groups. In addition to performing its regularly scheduled concerts, it accompanied ballet and opera productions. It survived—under the direction of successive conductors William Hacker, Joseph Blatt, and Sidney Palmer—until 1952. In 1956, the Little Rock Philharmonic, organized under the direction of Robert Rudolf, who was aggressive in programming and taking the orchestra to various parts of the state, performed many concerts until Rudolf's departure in 1959.

Dedicated musicians, remaining from previous groups, persisted in efforts to maintain a symphony orchestra, performing occasional concerts under the direction of guest conductors but lacking regular rehearsal and performance space, a dependable source of financial support, and a financial or organizational structure. Once again, in 1960, the musicians reorganized as the Arkansas Symphony Orchestra and gave concerts irregularly under the direction of Vasilios Priakos, who was an experienced and talented director but whose impractical ideas led the organization into debt. Although Priakos's tenure was brief, he is considered the first of the continuing Arkansas Symphony Orchestra's directors. Stability began to emerge in the early 1960s with the organization of two supportive groups—the Arkansas Orchestra Society, which serves as a sponsoring and governing body and is made up of interested supporters, business people, and music lovers, and the Arkansas Symphony Orchestra Guild, a highly effective fundraising auxiliary organized as a nonprofit organization. Glen Owens of the music faculty of Little Rock University—now University of Arkansas at Little Rock (UALR)—was pressed into service as manager and conductor in conjunction with his work at the university. Owens, with help from Orchestra Society leadership and the Guild, instituted firmer organizational structure and secured financial assistance from individual members of the orchestra and the Guild, a grant from the National Endowment for the Arts and the Arkansas Arts and Humanities Council, and assurance of matching money guaranteed by a group of individual backers. With these assets, debts were paid off, and the Orchestra Society was cleared for incorporation as a functioning business organization in January 1966.

The orchestra was able to move into suitable

quarters: first, into an 1890s house in the Quapaw Quarter of downtown Little Rock, then to the fourth floor of a building at St. John's Center, the headquarters of the Catholic Diocese of Little Rock, in the Pulaski Heights section of the city. In 1996, it secured a long-term lease on a separate building, Byrne Hall, at St. John's. Concerts which, in earlier days, had been held in the auditoriums at UALR and Hall High School were moved to Robinson Center Music Hall, and a full-time, musically trained and business-oriented executive director was hired. In January 2013, the orchestra signed a lease for space in the M. M. Cohn Building in downtown Little Rock.

David Itkin, director of the Arkansas Symphony Orchestra 1993–2009.
Photo: Dixie Knight

From 1969 to 1971, the musicians were directed by a number of guest conductors. Dr. Francis McBeth of the music faculty at Ouachita Baptist University (OBU) in Arkadelphia (Clark County) had directed the orchestra several times as a guest conductor and, in 1971, took the responsibility on a regular basis. He filled the position until 1973, before returning to full-time work in composing and teaching at OBU. Three other conductors—Kurt Klippstatter, William Harwood, and Robert Henderson—served from 1973 until 1993. When David Itkin was chosen as director in 1993, he was selected from a field of 231 applicants. In 2010, Philip Mann was selected after a search of over a year.

The Masterworks Series by the full orchestra and the Art of Chamber Music concerts by smaller ensembles, including several quartet groups, are aimed primarily at adults and emphasize classical symphonic and chamber music. Masterworks concerts in several seasons have featured concert performances of stage works such as Prokofiev's ballet *Romeo and Juliet* and Puccini operas *Tosca* and *Turandot*. Three world premiere performances of orchestral works have been presented. The orchestra continues the practice, introduced early in its history, of programming selections that include massed choral groups from colleges around the state. A number of national and international figures have performed with the orchestra at special concerts, among them Yo-Yo Ma, Van Cliburn, Marilyn Horne, and Itzhak Perlman.

The Pops Live Series attracts various audiences interested in more contemporary music, jazz, show tunes, and standard popular compositions and performers. It often features acclaimed national and international personalities, including, among many others, Doc Severinsen, James Earl Jones, Olivia Newton-John, Shirley Jones, and Liza Minnelli. A Christmas Gala program has long been a popular feature of the Pops Series.

A strong Youth Orchestra program is designed primarily to offer opportunities for student musicians to experience group performances. It gives concerts annually at Horace Mann Junior High School in Little Rock and at Hot Springs Village (Garland and Saline counties) and is available for appearances elsewhere. An Arts Partners program takes music into schools and introduces young people to quality music performed by professionals. The Crayon Concert Family Series is aimed at families with younger children.

One aim of the orchestra is to make orchestral music accessible to as many people as possible. Innovative programming, designed to attract a wide variety of tastes and to increase listeners' acquaintance with musical repertoire, has attracted many people to orchestra performances. The orchestra does "run out" concerts in various Arkansas cities, such as Harrison (Boone County), Monticello (Drew County), Hot Springs (Garland County), Hot Springs Village, Arkadelphia, Helena-West Helena (Phillips County), Mount Ida (Montgomery County), and more than fifty other communities. The musicians play for an estimated 250,000 people annually at the symphony's various concerts.

For additional information:
Arkansas Symphony Orchestra. http://www.arkansassymphony.org/ (accessed December 13, 2012).
The Arkansas Symphony Orchestra: On the Edge of the Future. Little Rock: Arkansas Symphony Orchestra, 1998.
The Stella Boyle Smith 35th Anniversary Historical Recording. Two CDs with booklet compiled by Eric Harrison. Little Rock: Arkansas Symphony Orchestra, 2000.

Katherine Stanick

HUGH ASHLEY (1915–2008)

Hubert Carl (Hugh) Ashley lived a life revolving around country and western music and public service. He wrote and recorded some of the earliest known recordings of Ozark folk music, was one of radio's original "Beverly Hill Billies," and wrote songs for five members of the Country Music Hall of Fame.

Hugh Ashley was born on September 27, 1915, near Wiley's Cove (Searcy County). He was the first of four boys born to Hobart Ashley and Lillie Holstead Ashley. At seven, he rode a mule five miles from Sulphur Springs (Searcy County) to Leslie (Searcy County) for his first piano lesson, and at thirteen, he joined his father's musical group, the Ashley Melody Men, playing guitar, singing, and yodeling. The Ashley Melody Men played on early radio stations in the Ozarks and made some of the first known recordings of Ozark folk music, with RCA Victor. Ashley wrote most of the music, traveling with the Ashley Melody Men as far as Dallas, Texas, and Memphis, Tennessee, for recording sessions.

Around 1929, talent scouts from *The Beverly Hill Billies* radio program on KNBC in Los Angeles, California, at the advice of Ashley's father, discovered the fourteen-year-old Ashley. After a short audition, Ashley left for Los Angeles and arrived at the airport, where a large crowd, assembled as a result of the promotional activities of KNBC, greeted him. He played the role of Little Hubert Walton for two summer seasons, returning for school in Searcy County. Country Music Hall of Famer Jimmie Rodgers would later thank Ashley for helping to popularize what would become known as country music. When Ashley chose not to return to California for a third summer, he was replaced by a Searcy County classmate, Elton Britt.

Ashley graduated from Marshall High School and attended the University of Arkansas (UA) in Fayetteville (Washington County), studying vocal techniques and piano. In the early 1930s, Ashley again left for the West Coast to play, write, and record music in Los Angeles and Las Vegas, Nevada, for the next decade. During World War II, Ashley was drafted in 1943 and served as a sergeant of entertainment in the Army Special Services. He was stationed at Letterman's Army Hospital in San Francisco, California, and provided musical entertainment for wounded Pacific-theater soldiers. It was here that Ashley met Helen Restvedt, a Red Cross volunteer, whom he married in Clinton (Van Buren County) after his discharge from the army in 1946.

Ashley and his wife settled in Harrison (Boone County), opening Ashley's Music Store in 1946. Beginning in the 1950s, Ashley found success in song writing for the growing number of country music recording artists in Nashville, Tennessee. Among those who recorded Ashley's songs were five members of the Country Music Hall of Fame: Red Foley, Brenda Lee, Bill Monroe, Jim Reeves, and Porter Wagoner. Brenda Lee recorded Ashley's song "One Step at a Time," her first hit. Ashley also helped Nashville talent scouts discover the music of Jimmy Driftwood. In 1964, Jim Reeves was scheduled to record a whole album of Ashley's songs but was killed in a plane crash.

In the late 1960s, Ashley began a long career in public service. He was the mayor of Harrison from 1970 to 1974; served on the Harrison City Council (1968–1970, 1975–1976); and served two terms as state representative (1977–1980). Ashley was awarded the Heritage Award by the Democratic Party of Arkansas for a life of public service in Arkansas.

In his later years, Ashley turned to conservation efforts on his family farm in Searcy County and continued to run his music store. He is the only person ever named Arkansas Tree Farmer of the Year by the Arkansas Forestry Association for two separate tree farms. In addition, he was named Outstanding Tree Farmer for the Southern Region (covering thirteen states) by the American Forestry Association. Ashley was also appointed by Governor Bill Clinton to serve on the Arkansas Forestry Commission.

Ashley died at his home in Harrison on October 31, 2008. He was survived by three daughters.

For additional information:

Dewoody, Celia. "Ashley Lives Music." *Harrison Daily Times*, February 17, 2008. Online at http://harrisondaily.com/ashley-lives-music/article_4720bc0b-1079-5bfb-825c-f9770c20e380.html (accessed February 26, 2013).

McCorkindale, Colter. "In Memoriam: Hugh Ashley, 1915–2008" *Arkansas Times*, November 20, 2008. Online at http://www.arktimes.com/arkansas/in-memoriam-hugh-ashley-1915-2008/Content?oid=934054 (accessed February 26, 2013).

Chad Causey

GOSPEL / CONTEMPORARY CHRISTIAN E. M. BARTLETT (1885–1941)

With the exception of his protégé, Albert E. Brumley, no other Arkansas figure contributed more to the development of the Southern gospel music genre than singer, songwriter, and publisher Eugene Monroe Bartlett Sr.

E. M. Bartlett was born on December 24, 1885, in the small community of Waynesville, Missouri, but he and his parents eventually relocated to Sebastian County, Arkansas. Educated at the Hall-Moody Institute in Martin, Tennessee, and William Jewell College in Liberty, Missouri, Bartlett received training as a music teacher.

In 1917, Bartlett married Joan Tatum; they had two children.

As an aspiring songwriter, Bartlett became an employee of the Central Music Company, a publisher of shape-note singing convention books based in Hartford (Sebastian County), which was owned by shape-note singing school instructor David Moore and songwriter Will M. Ramsey. Following Ramsey's move to Little Rock (Pulaski County), Bartlett persuaded Moore and John A. McClung to partner with him in 1918 to establish the Hartford Music Company, one of Southern gospel's first significant publishing companies. The company published some of Bartlett's first compositions as well as other early Southern gospel songs, including McClung's popular "Just a Rose Will Do." From Hartford Music's inception to 1935, Bartlett served as the company's president, facilitating its expansion to include branch offices in other cities and states.

In addition to the Hartford Music Company's music publishing interests, Bartlett established the Hartford Music Institute, a shape-note school, in 1921, and began publishing *The Herald of Song*, a monthly magazine covering the quartets Hartford sponsored to promote its products. Albert E. Brumley, the best-known Southern gospel songwriter of all time, attended the Hartford school in 1926 courtesy of Bartlett's financial generosity. Bartlett mentored Brumley, published his first songs, and eventually employed him at Hartford Music.

A diverse songwriter, Bartlett penned singing convention favorites such as "Everybody Will Be Happy Over There" and "Just a Little While," songs that were popularized by the leading gospel music quartets of the day, including Hovie Lister & the Statesmen, the Stamps Quartet, the Blackwood Brothers, and the Blue Ridge Quartet. In an era in which the exchange of music between white and black recording artists and writers generally benefitted white artists and black writers the most, Bartlett's song "He Will Remember Me" was recorded by at least two important African-American gospel groups, the Sensational Nightingales and the Staple Singers, as well as black gospel legend Albertina Walker. Revealing his sense of humor, Bartlett also produced light-hearted fare such as "You Can't Keep a Good Man Down" and "Take an Old Cold Tater and Wait," a country music hit for Grand Ole Opry star Little Jimmy Dickens.

In 1939, a stroke rendered Bartlett partially paralyzed and unable to perform or travel. Amid such bleak circumstances, he wrote his final and most beloved song, "Victory in Jesus," an optimistic number that has been sung by millions in worship services and recorded by gospel's biggest names.

Bartlett died on January 25, 1941. He is buried at the Oak Hill Cemetery in Siloam Springs (Benton County). Posthumously, Bartlett was inducted into the Gospel Music Association's Gospel Music Hall of Fame in Nashville, Tennessee, in 1973.

For additional information:

Collins, Ace. *Turn Your Radio On: The Stories Behind Gospel Music's All-time Greatest Songs*. Grand Rapids, MI: Zondervan, 1999.

Deller, David. "The Songbook Gospel Movement in Arkansas: E. M. Bartlett and the Hartford Music Company." *Arkansas Historical Quarterly* 60 (Autumn 2001): 284–300.

Goff, James R., Jr. *Close Harmony: A History of Southern Gospel*. Chapel Hill: University of North Carolina Press, 2002.

Greg Freeman

BAZOOKA

Although today it is more commonly applied to the anti-tank weapon widely used during World War II, or to a product of Topps Chewing Gum, the name "bazooka" was originally given to a novelty wind instrument created by native Arkansan radio and film personality Bob Burns. Spanning the musical gap between a trombone and a slide whistle, the bazooka produces a narrow range of notes with a tone that is more comical than dulcet.

Burns developed the bazooka one evening, as early as 1905, during band practice at Hayman's Plumbing Shop in Van Buren (Crawford County). Burns blew into a gas pipe that made a noise described as sounding like a "wounded moose." Inspired by this, he developed a new instrument from two interconnecting pipes, a slide handle, a whiskey funnel, an inset trombone-like mouthpiece, and possibly other obscure internal parts. He called it a "bazooka," a word he later copyrighted in 1920. The name was most likely formed from "bazoo," a slang term meaning "a windy fellow."

Like the trombone, the bazooka is played with variably tense buzzing lips blowing air into a mouthpiece and a slide moving to change the overall tube length. The slide is manipulated to produce vibrato and harmonic shifts.

Burns practiced his new instrument constantly, becoming good enough to play it in the Silver Cornet Band. During World War I, Burns became a sergeant in the U.S. Marine Corps, going overseas with the Eleventh Regiment, U.S. Marines, American Expeditionary Force. Later, he became the leader of the U.S. Marine Corps jazz band in Europe and introduced the bazooka to the troops there, making it part of the band's performances by 1918. As Bob "Bazooka" Burns, he began a long career in radio in 1931, playing his bazooka in between jokes and tales about fictitious hillbilly relatives back home in Arkansas.

During World War II, U.S. soldiers dubbed a commonly used portable rocket launcher a "bazooka" due to physical similarities the launcher had with the instrument. After World War II, Topps Chewing Gum, Inc., produced a popular patriotic bubblegum called "Bazooka" that the company claimed was named directly after Burns's instrument—not the weapon.

Bob Burns and his bazooka. Courtesy: UALR Center for Arkansas History and Culture

Although the instrument has been taken up by few musicians, Burns has not been the only bazooka performer to date. Sanford Kendrick, a member of the western swing band Bob Skyles and His Skyrockets, was known for playing the instrument, as well as mid-twentieth-century New Orleans, Louisiana, jazz musician Noon Johnson, who played a bazooka he constructed from parts of an old brass bed.

Few of the original Burns bazookas remain today. This is mostly due to Burns's comedic habit of destroying them on stage at the end of his performances as part of the entertainment. One remains on display at the Arkansas Entertainers Hall of Fame in Pine Bluff (Jefferson County).

For additional information:
"Bob 'Bazooka' Burns, the Arkansas Traveler, 1890–1956." Van Buren, Arkansas. http://www.vanburen.org/bob_burns.php (accessed February 14, 2013).

Chapman, Robert. "Clarity and Uncertainty about Bazooka." *American Speech* 69 (Autumn 1994): 328–331.

Aaron Miller

BEATLES—STOPOVER

In 1964, the world's most popular music group, the Beatles, visited the Lawrence County town of Walnut Ridge. Though brief, their visit left a lasting impact on the community and has recently been the subject of a documentary movie.

That year, the popularity of the Beatles was without rival. George Harrison, John Lennon, Paul McCartney, and Ringo Starr were mobbed by teenage fans at each public appearance. The Fab Four, as they were dubbed, had five singles in the top five slots on the *Billboard* charts. Their first film, *A Hard Day's Night*, appeared in 500 U.S. theaters. The group's first appearance on

Sculpture commemorating the 1964 Beatles stopover at Walnut Ridge.

Photo: Mike Polston

The Ed Sullivan Show drew an estimated seventy-three million viewers. In their legendary 1964 concert tour, they performed thirty-two shows in thirty-four days.

On September 18, 1964, the group finished a concert at Memorial Coliseum in Dallas, Texas, and immediately boarded a plane owned and operated by Reed Pigman. (Pigman owned American Flyers Airlines out of Dallas; the Beatles chartered one of Pigman's planes during the 1964 tour.) Pigman owned a ranch in Alton, Missouri, that would serve as a getaway before the group's final U.S. concert of the year, which would be in New York. Before traveling to Alton, the Beatles made a brief stop in Walnut Ridge. The Walnut Ridge airport provided the ideal spot for the group to change planes before heading to Missouri. The runway was built as a training facility during World War II and could handle large aircraft. Also, the Beatles could avoid the crush of screaming fans by landing at a secluded airport at the edge of a small town.

Just after midnight, the plane began circling the Walnut Ridge airport and approached the runway. Nighttime aircraft landings were rare in Walnut Ridge in 1964. As the plane circled, three boys left the local teen hangout and raced to the airport to identify the unexpected visitors. To the boys' surprise, the Beatles departed the plane and quickly boarded a small aircraft headed for Missouri. Details about the secret landing quickly spread throughout Walnut Ridge. Disbelief turned to excitement as teenagers spent the weekend sharing information and spreading rumors about the Beatles' probable return to the airport on Sunday, September 20.

While most people attended Sunday morning church services, 200 to 300 people descended on the Walnut Ridge airport in anticipation of the Beatles' return. The plane that had carried the group across the United States sat on the runway waiting for their return from Missouri. Parents snapped photographs of their children next to the plane. Home movie cameras captured the crowd's excitement. The sounds of teenagers singing Beatles songs could be heard across the runway.

There were many false alarms that morning. Teenagers mobbed a local crop-duster mistaken for the Beatles' plane. Little did they know that McCartney and Harrison had arrived at the airport an hour early and watched the spectacle from an old truck parked across the runway.

Suddenly, a small commuter aircraft with Lennon and Starr landed and taxied up the runway. The two left the plane, walking through a gauntlet of polite but excited spectators. At the same time Lennon and Starr ascended the steps to the larger plane, the old truck that held Harrison and McCartney pulled up next to it. All four Beatles quickly boarded and left for their last U.S. concert of the year. For many of the Walnut Ridge teenagers, it was their only chance to see the Beatles in person.

Though the encounter lasted only moments, the memory of seeing the Fab Four at the height of Beatlemania has endured. The event has become the subject of a documentary featuring some of the people at the airport. On September 18, 2011, Walnut Ridge unveiled a monument, designed to look like the cover of the album *Abbey Road*, to commemorate the event. Walnut Ridge also renamed a downtown street Abbey Road. In 2011, the first Beatles at the Ridge festival was held, and in 2012, the town built a guitar-shaped plaza downtown modeled after Epiphone guitars played by John Lennon and George Harrison.

For additional information:

Bustillo, Miguel. "Beatles Said a Fast Hello, Goodbye but a Tiny Town Won't Let It Be." *Wall Street Journal*, September 19, 2011. http://online.wsj.com/article/SB10001424053111904106704576578662518738784.html (accessed February 8, 2013).

Hammer, David. "Walnut Ridge Residents Recall Unexpected Beatles' Encounter." *Jonesboro Sun*, September 18, 2004.

Koch, Stephen. "Fab Four Touchdown." *Arkansas Times*, September 15, 2005, p. 30. Online at http://www.arktimes.com/arkansas/fab-four-touchdown/Content?oid=862652 (accessed February 14, 2013).

Michael Bowman

AL BELL (1940–)

Al Bell is considered the driving force behind Stax Records as a producer, songwriter, and executive during the company's most productive period, from 1965 to 1975. He was responsible for promoting the careers of such talent as the Staple Singers, Isaac Hayes, and Otis Redding, among many others.

Al Bell was born Alvertis Isbell on March 15, 1940, in Brinkley (Monroe County). One of his earliest musical memories was that of listening to his father's Louis Jordan's records. In an interview published in 2001, Bell claimed Jordan, also a Brinkley native, as a distant relative. Bell's family moved to North Little Rock (Pulaski County) when he was five years old. After attending Catholic and Seventh-Day Adventist private schools, Bell attended Scipio A. Jones High School in North Little Rock, the public high school for African-American students during the period of segregation. During his junior and senior years there, he presided over the state honor society, the student council, and the audio visual society. The latter post put him in charge of the record player during school dances. Borrowing records from his fellow students to play at these "sock-hops," Bell began to develop an ear for popular music. He organized a talent contest between Scipio A. Jones High School in North Little Rock and Dunbar High School in Little Rock (Pulaski County) held at the Dunbar Community Center, an event he named "Radio Station T-O-U-G-H, Tough." The general manager of KOKY, a judge in the competition, asked Bell to come by the station the following week. Bell did so and hosted a gospel music program the following Sunday morning, as well as filling in for another disc jockey on a jazz program that evening. He shortened his name from Alvertis Isbell to Al Bell while working as a disc jockey.

Shortly after graduating from Scipio A. Jones High School, Bell attended Philander Smith College in Little Rock. While there, he was encouraged to go to Georgia to join Martin Luther King Jr. and the Southern Christian Leadership Council, where he would eventually become a student/teacher. Bell and King did not see eye to eye on how to respond to attacks on protestors. A particular incident in which Bell was spat upon and responded by lunging with a knife at his assailant made their philosophical disagreement

untenable. Bell left the organization and reenrolled at Philander Smith.

Bell then had an opportunity to be a disc jockey at WLOK in Memphis, Tennessee. Bell started his own label, Devore, and used the studio facilities at Stax Records. Stax had had some moderate success outside of the Mississippi Delta region with Booker T. & the MG's and their hit "Green Onions" in the early 1960s.

Bell married Linda Mae Purifoy on December 25, 1963, and they had two sons.

Bell took another disc jockey job in the Washington DC area but remained in touch with Stax owner Jim Stewart. Bell gained notoriety for being one of the only disc jockeys playing Stax music in the Washington DC area. Stewart began seeking Bell's advice, as he was creating a new market in the region for Stax music. In the fall of 1965, Bell officially joined Stax as head of promotion; problems with a distribution agreement with Atlantic Records had inspired the move by Stewart. However, Bell had again started a record label, this time called Safice, while working on the East Coast, and he also had a distribution agreement through Atlantic. Jerry Wexler at Atlantic told him that they were contributing money to pay Bell to improve the demand for Stax music, but the amount was a severe cut in pay for the multi-tasking Bell, who had a variety of income sources stemming from his connections in the music industry in Washington DC (for example, he had been involved in producing and engineering Grover Mitchell's "Midnight Tears," which was released on the Decca label). The eventual agreement was for Bell to try and turn the struggling record company around, and, if he succeeded, he would be given part ownership in Stax.

Moving from the business side to production, Bell engineered Isaac Hayes's debut album, *Presenting Isaac Hayes* (1967). However, Bell made his biggest contribution as a producer with the Staple Singers. He had been introduced to the group while working at KOKY in Little Rock, and Bell wrote their biggest hit, "I'll Take You There," while visiting North Little Rock for his brother Louis's funeral.

Stax began to have financial troubles after losing the rights to its back catalogs—including the biggest hits from Sam & Dave and Otis

Redding—to Atlantic, followed by the death of Redding in a December 1967 plane crash. The company regrouped by separating itself from Atlantic and creating multiple subsidiary labels to produce music for various genres, including country and jazz, in addition to the traditional Stax fare of soul, funk, and rhythm and blues. In July 1969, Stax reported sales of ten million singles within one year of its becoming independent, but a 1972 distribution deal with CBS turned bad for Stax and led to an unsuccessful $67 million antitrust lawsuit.

By 1974, Bell had acquired Stax from Jim Stewart, and it became the fifth-largest black-owned company in America, according to *Black Enterprise Magazine*, even as the company was facing total financial collapse. Bell was given an offer to sell from CBS but turned it down. He then attempted to move the label to Arkansas through talks with former governor Winthrop Rockefeller, who died before a deal could be concluded. Stax went bankrupt in December 1975, but Bell made another attempt to revive the label in 1978 through talks with Governor Bill Clinton. Clinton was interested in the economic benefits the label could bring to the state, but his first term as governor held unexpected challenges, and he was unable to win reelection, halting the plans for Stax's rebirth.

Bell moved to California and set up a management firm that represented artists such as Mavis Staples and Prince. Bell used the time to re-establish contacts in the music industry. He met with Berry Gordy at Motown, who was having distribution problems similar to those Bell had experienced at Stax. Bell took over as head of Motown Records Group for a time and began advising Gordy to sell the company. Bell started Bellmark Records and Alvert Music, which produced some significant hits, including Tag Team's "Whoomp! There It Is" (1993). He was involved in several of the first lawsuits over music "sampling" while in California.

By 2001, Bell was again living in North Little Rock. One of his sons was involved in the music business by that time and started Alpine Records with a studio in Bryant (Saline County).

Among his many honors, Bell was inducted into the Arkansas Black Hall of Fame in 2002, named the chairman of the Memphis Music Foundation in 2009, and received a Grammy Trustees Award in 2011. The Grammy Trustees award is given by the board of trustees of the Recording Academy and is considered a top music industry award.

For additional information:
"Al Bell." Memphis Music Foundation. http://www. memphismeansmusic.com/al-bell/ (accessed February 5, 2013).
Bell, Al. "Interview with Al Bell." October 1, 2008. Audio and video online at Butler Center AV/AR Audio Video Collection.
Hill, Jack W. "Alvertis Isbell." *Arkansas Democrat-Gazette*, November 16, 2008, pp. 1D, 6D.
Koch, Stephen. "Al Bell Takes Us There: An Interview by Stephen Koch." *Arkansas Review: A Journal of Delta Studies* 32 (April 2001): 49–59.
———. "Stax Up." *Arkansas Democrat-Gazette*, August 12, 2001, pp. 1E–2E.
"Trustees Award: Al Bell." http://www.grammy.com/news/ trustees-award-al-bell (accessed February 5, 2013).

Michael Hodge

MISCELLANEA | # Al Bennett (1926–1989)

Alvin Silas (Al) Bennett was a recording industry executive best known for his tenure as president and director of Liberty Records from 1958 to 1968. Known as a "music business wizard," Bennett is largely credited with the transformation of Liberty Records from a struggling start-up operation to a dominant force in the recording trade. "Alvin" of Alvin and the Chipmunks was named after Bennett.

Al Bennett was born in Joiner (Mississippi County) on September 21, 1926, to the farming family of Silas S. Bennett and Jessie Starling Bennett. The oldest of four children, he spent his early years working on the farm while attending Shawnee School, graduating in 1943. Bennett enlisted in the U.S. Army on November 5, 1945, for a one-year stint. After serving his commitment, he returned to Arkansas to farm. On February 15, 1946, he married Cathleen Whitlock of Sheridan (Grant County). The couple had three children: Wayne, Keith, and Adalah; Adalah later became a music industry executive in her own right.

By 1948, a series of farming and financial setbacks convinced Bennett to pursue a new career. Although he had little knowledge of phonograph records, he ultimately secured a job working as a salesman for Decca Records in Memphis, Tennessee. As his career progressed, he moved to Gallatin, Tennessee, to become national sales manager for Dot Records. In 1956, he relocated to Los Angeles, California, for Dot Records, later joining Hart Distribution before moving to Liberty Records, also in Los Angeles, in 1958 as vice president.

Liberty Records, founded by Simon Waronker in 1955, was struggling under massive debt and lacked the capital to exploit its catalogue of recordings. Under Bennett's leadership, Liberty Records soon became one of the fastest-growing companies in America. From its backlog of unreleased discs, Bennett selected "The Witch Doctor," and within twelve months, the company's debts were paid. His acquisition of artists such as Julie London, Spike Jones, Bobby Vee, and the Fleetwoods served to stabilize the company and expand its success. One of its most notable hits came with a series of novelty records begun in 1958 by Ross Bagdasarian under the pseudonym "David Seville." The three chipmunks in "The Chipmunk Song"—Alvin, Simon, and Theodore—were named after company executives Alvin Bennett, Simon Waronker, and Ted Keep.

In 1962, Liberty Records was sold to Avnet for $12 million. However, after two years of losses, Avnet sold Liberty back to Bennett for $8 million. In 1968, Liberty Records was sold again to TransAmerica Corp. for $38 million. Six months later, Bennett left Liberty and founded Cream Records. In 1977, Cream Records purchased Hi and Stax Records, two Memphis-based rhythm and blues powerhouses. In 1979, Bennett sold the Hi and Stax publishing companies and the Stax master recordings, but he retained the Hi masters.

Throughout his career, Bennett maintained a residence in Sherman Oaks, California, as well as in Joiner, owning and operating Benshaw Farms. He was also actively involved in numerous recording industry groups, including service as vice president of the American Record Manufacturing and Distribution Association, chairman of the Hollywood Museum, and chairman of the Entertainment Industry for Radio Free Europe. His accomplishments were honored by his home state in 1964 with his selection as Arkansas's "Man of the Year."

Bennett died on March 15, 1989, in Sherman Oaks. He is buried at Bassett Cemetery in Mississippi County.

For additional information:

Gray, Jerry. "Al Bennett: An Arkansas Native Gives Boost to 'Memphis Sound.'" *Arkansas Gazette*, August 21, 1977, p. 2E.

Kelly, Michael Bryan. *Liberty Records: A History of the Recording Company and Its Stars, 1955–1971*. Jefferson, NC: McFarland and Co., 1993.

Toney Butler Schlesinger

ROCK — BLACK OAK ARKANSAS

Black Oak Arkansas, a popular rock and roll band of the 1970s from rural Arkansas near Black Oak (Craighead County), was the first Arkansas rock band to have significant commercial success.

Originally called the Knowbody Else, the band was formed in 1965 by singer James "Jim Dandy" Mangrum from Black Oak and guitarist Ricky Reynolds from Manila (Mississippi County). The band was signed to Stax Records and released an album, *The Knowbody Else*, on Enterprise, a Stax subsidiary, as well as *Early Times*, which was released on Stax. Despite the failure of these albums, the band continued touring the nation and was "discovered" in California by Ahmet Ertegun of Atlantic Records, who signed the band in 1970. They changed their

Black Oak Arkansas early in their career; 1972.
Courtesy: Bob Ketchum, Cedar Crest Studios

name to Black Oak Arkansas and released the eponymous album *Black Oak Arkansas* in 1971 on Atco, a subsidiary of Atlantic.

The Atco debut, which mixed hard rock, down-home Dixie boogie, and quasi-mystical country music, featured Mangrum on vocals and washboard, Reynolds on guitar, Harvey "Burley" Jett of Marion (Crittenden County) and Stanley "Goober" Knight from Little Rock (Pulaski County) on guitars, Pat "Dirty" Daugherty from Jonesboro (Craighead County) on bass guitar, and Wayne "Squeezebox" Evans on drums. Besides the three-guitar harmony, the band's sound was characterized by Jim Dandy's gravelly voice.

The album benefited from the airplay of "underground" radio programs such as the late-night program *Beaker Street* on KAAY (AM 1090 out of Little Rock), which introduced the band to a national audience by making such songs as "Lord Have Mercy on My Soul," "When Electricity Came to Arkansas," "Hot and Nasty," and "Uncle Lijah" staples of its program.

Following the success of *Black Oak Arkansas*, the band toured extensively from 1972 to 1977 and became known for its high-energy shows and Mangrum's overt sexuality. In those years, the band was one of the highest grossing live acts in the United States. The blond, long-haired Mangrum performed bare-chested and wore tight, white spandex pants, influencing such performers as David Lee Roth, Jesse James DuPree, and Axl Rose in later years.

After the Atco debut album, Tommy Aldridge replaced Wayne Evans on drums, as the band became a more professional touring unit. In 1972, the band released two well-received albums, *Keep the Faith* and *If An Angel Came to See You, Would You Make Her Feel At Home?* In 1973, the album *Raunch 'N' Roll Live* documented the fire of their live performances. Jimmy Henderson replaced Harvey Jett on guitar in June 1974.

The follow-up album, 1973's *High on the Hog*, featured the band's only Top 40 hit, a fiery ver-

Black Oak Arkansas vocalist Ruby Starr at her home in Oakland (Marion County); 1976. Photo: Mike Keckhaver

sion of LaVern Baker's rhythm and blues classic "Jim Dandy," which featured a duet between Mangrum and female singer Ruby Starr, who began touring regularly with the band. *High on the Hog* peaked at No. 52 on the *Billboard* album charts.

In 1974, the band released the album *Street Party*. Their 1975 album *Ain't Life Grand*, which featured a version of the Beatles' "Taxman," was the last for the classic lineup of the band.

Black Oak Arkansas then signed with MCA and released *X-Rated* (1975), *Balls of Fire* (1976), and *10-Year Overnight Success* (1976). By 1977, Mangrum was the only original member remaining in the band, which had not only left a legacy of high-energy Arkansas rock but had also raised hundreds of thousands of dollars for state benefits, including Arkansas Children's Hospital.

The band released two albums on Capricorn, *Race with the Devil* (1977) and *I'd Rather Be Sailing* (1978). After Mangrum recovered from a heart attack in 1984, he reunited with Reynolds to release *Ready as Hell* on HM USA. Mangrum then released *The Black Attack is Back* in 1986. The band's later work, however, was relatively lackluster compared with the early Atco records.

A well-received greatest-hits package, *Hot and Nasty*, was released on Rhino in 1992, and a "King Biscuit Flower Hour" live set was released in 1998.

Despite a heart attack in the 1980s and a bad car accident in 1991, Mangrum continued to put together various incarnations of the band throughout the 1990s. He reunited again with Reynolds and Daugherty to release *The Wild Bunch* on the Cleopatra label in 1999.

In 2002, Rhino released a retrospective DVD, *Black Oak Arkansas: The First 30 Years.*

For additional information:
Black Oak Arkansas. http://www.blackoakarkansas.net/ (accessed February 6, 2013).

George-Warren, Holly, and Patricia Romanowski, eds. *The Rolling Stone Encyclopedia of Rock & Roll.* New York: Rolling Stone Press, 2001.

Hutson, Cecil. *Analysis of the Southern Rock and Roll Band Black Oak Arkansas.* New York: Edwin Mellen Press, 1996.

Hutson, Kirk. "Hot 'N' Nasty: Black Oak Arkansas and Its Effect on Rural Southern Culture." *Arkansas Historical Quarterly* 54 (Summer 1995): 185–211.

Bryan Rogers

CLASSICAL / OPERA GRETHA BOSTON (1959–)

Gretha Denise Boston is a celebrated mezzo-soprano and Tony Award–winning actress. She made her Carnegie Hall debut in 1991 in Mozart's *Coronation Mass* and won the 1995 Tony for Best Featured Actress in a Musical for her role as Queenie in the Broadway revival of *Showboat*; she was the first Arkansan to be so honored. The same role earned Boston the Theatre World Award as Outstanding Debut Artist. She was also nominated for the Helen Hayes Award for Outstanding Lead Actress in a Non-Resident Production for the 2000–01 season at the Kennedy Center in Washington DC for her performance in *It Ain't Nothin' But the Blues*.

Gretha Boston was born in Crossett (Ashley County) on April 18, 1959, the eldest of seven children of Delores Tucker Boston and Curtis Joe Boston Sr. Her early musical training was in the Gates Chapel African Methodist Episcopal Church and in her high school choir, where she was encouraged by Bill Stroud, then head of the school's music department, and by C. T. Foster, her band director. She graduated from Crossett High School in 1977.

Boston attended North Texas State University (now the University of North Texas) in Denton, Texas, earning her bachelor's degree in music and performance. As a member of the NTSU A Capella Choir, she recorded Mendelssohn's *Walpurgisnacht* with the Royal Philharmonic Orchestra in London, England. After graduation, she attended the University of Illinois at Urbana-Champaign, where she was a two-time winner in the D'Angelo International Young Artists Competition. She studied with Johnson Wustman at the University of Illinois, with Margaret Hoswell in New York City, and with Maestro Franco Iglesias, also of New York. Boston has performed in concert in St. Louis, Missouri; Champaign, Illinois; and Santa Barbara, California.

Boston made her debut at Carnegie Hall in May 1991 in Mozart's *Coronation Mass* and returned later in Beethoven's *Ninth Symphony*. Her operatic roles include Amneris in *Aida* (at the University of Illinois, the Intiman Theater in Seattle, Washington, and the Denver Center), Maddelena in *Rigoletto* (New York Grand Opera), and Maria in *Porgy and Bess* (Buffalo Philharmonic and Opera Delaware). Her choral works include *Messiah*, *Elijah*, and Verdi's *Requiem* (New York Grand Opera).

Boston has appeared on television in PBS's *An Enchanted Evening: A Salute to Oscar Hammerstein* and has also appeared on the *David Letterman Show* and the *Today Show*, as well as the television dramas *Hope and Faith* (2004), *Law and Order* (2001), and *Law and Order: Criminal Intent* (2004).

Crossett native Gretha Boston was inducted into the Arkansas Black Hall of Fame in 1997.
Courtesy: Harwood Management

In 2002, Boston played Bloody Mary in the national tour of *South Pacific*, starring Robert Goulet. In December 2002, she performed as the character Ethel in the musical *Let Me Sing* at the Charlotte Repertory Theater in North Carolina. Later that year, she acted the role of Lola in the play *Jar the Floor*, also in Charlotte. In the field of musical comedy, Boston has performed the role of Velma Crowns in *Portraits of Black Women in Church Hats* in Buffalo, New York (Studio Arena), Rochester, New York (GEVA Theater), and Washington DC (Arena Stage.)

Boston lives in New York City. She was elected to the Arkansas Black Hall of Fame in 1997.

For additional information:

"Gretha Boston." Internet Movie Database. Online at http://www.imdb.com/name/nm0098253/ (accessed February 8, 2013).

Gretha Boston. Arkansas Black Hall of Fame. http://www.arblackhalloffame.org/honorees/page.aspx?id=180 (accessed February 25, 2013).

Bill Norman

COUNTRY — ELTON BRITT (1913–1972)

Elton Britt was a popular country singer of the 1940s, with a yodeling style most often compared to Jimmie Rodgers. His most popular song, "There's a Star Spangled Banner Waving Somewhere," was the first country performance awarded a gold record for selling more than a million copies. Britt also was a heavy influence on most subsequent yodelers in country music.

James Elton Baker was born on June 27, 1913, to James M. Baker and Martella Baker in Zack (Searcy County), a small community in the Ozarks. He was the youngest of five children and was plagued with heart trouble most of his life. Because he was not expected to live, his parents did not name him until he was a year old. He was named after his father and Elton Wilson, a local doctor who was able to keep him alive during his first year of life. Because his health was so delicate, he was pampered by his family, who called him "Cute," a nickname used throughout his early years.

Baker acquired a love of music from his family. At the age of ten, he purchased his first guitar, a $4.95 instrument ordered through the mail from Montgomery Ward. A short time later, he heard the records of Jimmie Rodgers and was so impressed that he learned to yodel. He reportedly learned breath control while swimming underwater for several minutes at a time, which enabled him to sustain his yodel for an unusually long time.

In 1930, Baker was asked to replace his friend Hugh Ashley, another young yodeler from Searcy County who worked under the name of Hobart Walton in the Beverly Hill Billies, a popular group broadcasting almost daily over KMPC in Los Angeles, California. Although he was only scheduled to stay in Los Angeles, California, for six weeks, this step eventually took Baker from Hollywood to New York City and other places during his long musical career. Glen Rice, an employee with the McMillan Oil Company that owned KMPC, decided that James Elton Baker did not sound hillbilly enough, so he gave him the name Elton Britt.

During his stay with the Hill Billies, Britt entered into the first of his four marriages. In February 1934, he wed Margaret Scott, a fifteen-year-old relative of his brother Vernon's wife. Seven months later, in September 1934, Margaret was killed in an automobile accident in Cleveland, Oklahoma. In 1935, Britt married Jeannie Russell, a Canadian citizen who died two days after the birth of their second child on June 9, 1937. In 1942, he wed his third wife, Penny, a long-time Britt fan; this marriage lasted until 1958, when the couple divorced. Finally, he married Janet Counts, a woman twenty-five years his junior, staying with her until 1970. Britt had children by each wife except the first, but none followed him into the world of music.

Britt's first recordings were probably made with the Beverly Hill Billies, but it is impossible to determine on which of their several discs he appeared. His first documented recordings came in August 1933 for the Conqueror label as part of a group called the Wenatchee Mountaineers. About a year later, in June 1934, Britt made his first significant recording, "Chime Bells" (which later became a signature song), with his brother Vernon, with whom he recorded off and on for several years during the 1930s. The piece showcased his trademark yodeling. Later versions were recorded in 1939 and 1948, the latter making its way onto the *Billboard* charts.

Britt recorded with RCA Victor from 1937 to 1956, during which time he had several hit singles. These include "Someday" (1944), "Detour" (1946), "Candy Kisses" (1949), and "Quicksilver" (1950). His biggest hit by far was the patriotic wartime number, "There's a Star Spangled Banner Waving Somewhere" (1942), with estimates of its sales ranging from one to four million.

Britt appeared in at least two movies. His performances in *The Last Dogie* (1933) and in the Charles Starrett western *Laramie* (1949) did nothing to advance his career. He may also have appeared in Universal's *The Prodigal Son* (1949), but there is no evidence it was ever released.

During the 1950s, Britt made a habit of retiring and coming out of retirement. When he retired in 1960, it was to wage an unsuccessful campaign for president of the United States on the Democratic ticket. This was generally viewed as a publicity stunt dreamed up by Aubrey Mayhew, his sometime manager. Shortly afterward, he returned to entertaining, and he had his last major hit with a seven-minute yodeling song, "The Jimmie Rodgers Blues," in 1968.

On June 22, 1972, Britt suffered a heart attack and died in a McConnellsburg, Pennsylvania, hospital the next day. He is buried in the Odd Fellows Cemetery in Broad Top, Pennsylvania. Later, a monument listing many of his hit songs was erected over his grave.

For additional information:

Cochran, Robert. *Our Own Sweet Sounds: A Celebration of Popular Music in Arkansas.* 2nd ed. Fayetteville: University of Arkansas Press, 2005.

"Elton Britt." AllMusic.com. http://www.allmusic.com/artist/elton-britt-mn0000176830 (accessed February 12, 2013).

McNeil, W. K., and Louis Hatchett. "There's a Star Spangled Banner Waving Somewhere: The Story Behind Its Success." In *Country Music Goes to War*, edited by Charles K. Wolfe and James E. Akenson. Lexington: University Press of Kentucky, 2005.

William K. McNeil

This entry, originally published in *Arkansas Biography: A Collection of Notable Lives*, appears in the *Encyclopedia of Arkansas Music* in an altered form. *Arkansas Biography* is available from the University of Arkansas Press in Fayetteville.

GOSPEL / CONTEMPORARY CHRISTIAN   BROCKWELL GOSPEL MUSIC SCHOOL

The Brockwell Gospel Music School offers instruction in choral and instrumental musical techniques for those who desire the improvement of church music. It operates every summer on a small campus in Brockwell (Izard County) at the intersection of State Highways 9 and 56. It was founded in 1947 as the Brockwell Music School, assumed its present name in 1962, and operates at its original site.

The singing-school tradition goes back to the time of the Second Great Awakening on the American frontier in the first years of the nineteenth century. This tradition contributed significantly to the growth and power of the great revivals that especially captivated gospel-hungry settlers in the frontier South in the first third of the century. Itinerant singing "masters" gave musical instruction to far-flung, often musically illiterate students. The students learned rudiments of music and the basics of Christian teaching for the purpose of their spiritual improvement.

In Arkansas, such instruction was offered both by itinerant teachers and more formal schools operating in stable locations, including the Hartford Music Institute, which opened in Hartford (Sebastian County) in 1921. People in Izard County have long kept the singing-school tradition alive, with the Izard County Singing

Brockwell Gospel Music School in Brockwell.

Photo: Mike Keckhaver

Convention, which was founded in 1910, and a rich history of hosting singing masters who conducted musical instruction in local churches for many years before and after the founding of the singing convention. Building on this tradition, Orgel Mason, L. L. Floyd, Steve Jones, Jeff Cooper, and Thomas and Ethel Brockwell founded the Brockwell Music School.

Mason was a musician and piano tuner who began singing gospel music as a teenager and worked as a young man for the legendary Stamps-Baxter Music Company in Dallas, Texas. Stamps-Baxter ran a hugely popular marketing and promotional network throughout the South, as well as a successful network of gospel music schools under the name of the Stamps-Baxter Normal Music School. Mason became convinced the school could be replicated in north-central Arkansas to train amateur musicians without the commercialization so often present in the gospel music industry. The Izard County Singing Convention's leader Lindsey Floyd, Mason, and friends and relatives of Mason and Floyd did the initial work in establishing the school, drawing support and students from the singing convention, which existed apart from the Brockwell School.

To teach the first classes, Mason and his co-workers recruited the Home State Quartet of Little Rock (Pulaski County), one of the numerous gospel singing groups of the day that traveled the South performing, selling copies of their original gospel tunes, and promoting the publishing company that kept their songs in print. The school's leaders used teachers from throughout Arkansas and occasionally other southern states and prided themselves on always staffing the school with highly trained, skilled musicians. Teachers usually gave up parts of their summer vacations to teach without pay to keep costs low enough so most interested students could attend.

The school began operation with a tabernacle as the centerpiece of the original campus but had to borrow classroom space in local homes and businesses. Classes occasionally met outside under shade trees. In conjunction with the Izard County Singing Convention, Brockwell School leaders developed a campus of several buildings. They moved frame structures to the school through the 1970s, constructed a cement-block classroom building in 1991, and added a large auditorium in 2005.

After Orgel Mason's death, longtime Brockwell teacher and manager Anna Floyd became the school's manager, assisted by Loye Mason, a graduate of the school.

Unlike their traveling predecessors, the instructors at the Brockwell School maintain a set two-week curriculum at the same site every summer. Students range from young children to senior citizens who come from around Arkansas and from other states to improve their musicianship. The school also offers instruction in sight reading, conducting, and composition, as well as in singing by ear and shape-note singing. It uses the same curriculum it always has, concentrating on four-part, Southern gospel harmony based on the shape-note system developed in the nineteenth-century songbooks *Southern Harmony* and *Christian Harmony*. The school has a loyal following among its graduates, many of whom have sent their own children to attend the school, including members of the family of famed gospel composer Luther Presley. The school has had an average annual attendance of about 120 since it began keeping records.

For additional information:
Floyd, Anna. "History of the Brockwell Gospel Music School." Unpublished manuscript. Brockwell Gospel Music School, Brockwell, Arkansas.
Massey, Tom. Interviews with Orgel Mason. Regional Studies Collection. Lyon College, Batesville, Arkansas.
Special issue on Brockwell. *Izard County Historian* 37 (July 2012).

David Stricklin

BLUES / R&B | "Big Bill" Broonzy (1893–1958)

Although William Lee Conley "Big Bill" Broonzy achieved fame and success in the Chicago blues scene and the folk revival in the United States and abroad, some of his earliest encounters with the blues and his earliest experiences as a performer and song writer were in Arkansas.

Sources differ as to the date and place of Big Bill Broonzy's birth. Broonzy himself claimed to have been born in Scott, Mississippi, on June 26, 1893 (though some sources say 1898). However, more recent research has him born near Lake Dick, Arkansas, on June 29, 1903, with the name Lee Conley Bradley. His parents were Frank Broonzy (Bradley) and Mittie Belcher, and he was one of seventeen children. Broonzy spent most of his childhood years in the Pine Bluff (Jefferson County) area. He began performing music at an early age, playing for social and church events on the fiddle, which he learned from his uncle Jerry Belcher. In addition to odd jobs as a musician, Broonzy also served briefly as a pastor in the Pine Bluff area before 1918.

Between the years 1917 and 1919, Broonzy served in the U.S. Army and was stationed in Europe. After his discharge in 1919, Broonzy returned to Arkansas for a brief time, playing in clubs around the Little Rock (Pulaski County) and Pine Bluff areas. In the early 1920s, Broonzy moved to Chicago, Illinois, where he switched instruments to the guitar, taught to him by Papa Charlie Jackson, and began a prolific recording career under the Paramount, Columbia, Bluebird, OKeh, and Chess record labels. Examples of his recording career can be found on numerous compilations. The most comprehensive collection is the twelve-volume anthology of the complete works of Big Bill Broonzy, which was produced by Document Records beginning in 1994.

Influenced by musicians such as Jimmie Rodgers, Blind Blake, Son House, and Blind Lemon Jefferson, Broonzy developed an amalgamated form of the blues. By combining ragtime and hokum blues with country blues, he created a style that foreshadowed the post–World War II Chicago sound, which was later defined by such artists as Muddy Waters and Willie Dixon.

In 1938, Broonzy filled in for Robert Johnson, who had died unexpectedly, at the Spirituals to Swing Concert produced by John Hammond at Carnegie Hall. The fame achieved from this event and a follow-up concert in 1939 established Broonzy as a key figure in the Chicago blues scene. While in Chicago, Broonzy recorded more than 300 songs and remained a popular and well-respected artist throughout the 1940s. His prolific musical output is evident from his fruitful solo career and his collaborations with other artists, such as singer/guitarist Brownie McGhee.

With the rise of electric blues in the early 1950s, Broonzy became an active supporter of the folk blues genre. In 1951, Broonzy took his first tour of Europe, where he was met with enthusiasm and appreciation. His appearances in Europe introduced the blues to European audiences and were especially influential in London's emerging skiffle and rock blues scene. Broonzy's success also set the stage for later blues artists such as Sonny Boy Williamson and Muddy Waters to play European venues. Broonzy toured Europe again in 1955 and 1957.

"Big Bill" Broonzy helped define the Chicago blues style.

Artists: Patterson and Barnes / From the Old State House Museum Collection

Broonzy's autobiography, *Big Bill Blues*, was published with the aid of Danish writer Yannick Bruynoghe in 1955. Shortly after his final tour in 1957, Broonzy was diagnosed with throat and lung cancer. He continued to perform until his death on August 14, 1958, in Chicago. He is buried in the Lincoln Cemetery in Blue Island, Illinois. Broonzy was inducted into the Blues Foundation Hall of Fame in 1980.

For additional information:
Broonzy, Bill, and Yannick Bruynoghe. *Big Bill Blues*. London: Cassell &Co., 1955.
Broonzy, Bill. *The Bill Broonzy Story*. CD box set. Polygram Records, 1999.
His Story: Big Bill Broonzy Interviewed by Studs Terkel. CD. Smithsonian Folkways, 2012.
House, Roger Randolph. "'Key to the Highway': William 'Big Bill' Broonzy and the Chicago Blues in the Era of the Great Migration." PhD diss., Boston University, 1999.
Palmer, Robert. *Deep Blues*. New York: Viking Press, 1981.
Riesman, Bob. *I Feel So Good: The Life and Times of Big Bill Broonzy*. Chicago: University of Chicago Press, 2011.

Robbie Fry

COUNTRY JIM ED BROWN (1934–)

Country and western music star Jim Ed Brown's career has spanned more than half a century since the early 1950s. He has been a solo vocalist and a member of two singing groups: the Browns and a duo consisting of himself and singer Helen Cornelius. He has performed on numerous radio and television programs, hosting some and starring on others, and has become a member of the Grand Ole Opry.

James Edward Brown was born in Sparkman (Dallas County) on April 1, 1934, to Floyd and Birdie Brown; he has two sisters. He grew up in the timber country near Pine Bluff (Jefferson County), and his father hauled logs for a living and was also a farmer. Brown formed a musical duo with his sister Maxine after they graduated from high school. They soon signed with California's Fabor Records and issued their first release, "Looking Back to See," in 1954. The song was a hit, but their contract with Fabor Robinson, proprietor of the company bearing his name, produced no royalties from its sales.

Nevertheless, the song—which the pair wrote during a period when they were performing on

Barnyard Frolics, a radio program originating on Little Rock (Pulaski County) station KLRA—carried them to modest national prominence. They joined the *Louisiana Hayride* radio lineup and began making regular appearances on the *Ozark Jubilee*, hosted by Red Foley, in 1955. The pair's younger sister Bonnie joined the group that same year, and the Browns, as they were known, started a steady climb to stardom. They first released the hit "Here Today and Gone Tomorrow." They then signed with RCA Records (at the behest of guitarist and executive Chet Atkins) in 1956 and quickly produced two number-one hits: "I Take the Chance" and "I Heard the Bluebird Sing."

After a two-year tour of duty as a draftee in the armed services, Brown reunited with his sisters, and together they struck gold in 1959 with "The Three Bells." It sold more than a million copies and was the first number-one country smash to cross over to number one on the pop and rhythm and blues charts. That was followed by two more hits: "The Old Lamplighter" and "Scarlet Ribbons." In 1963, the Browns joined the Grand Ole Opry.

The next few years brought more success to the group as Nashville, Tennessee, slowly changed its sound from the rustic hoedowns of the past to a contemporary orchestral style that was greatly influenced by the Browns. However,

by the mid-1960s, Maxine and Bonnie wearied of the struggle to sustain both family lives and show-business careers, causing them to retire from the trio.

Jim Ed Brown continued as a solo act, and, in 1966, he hit a solo peak with his classic "Pop-A-Top," which he followed with "Southern Loving," "Sometime Sunshine," and "Morning." He had a six-season occasional spot as co-host of the weekly syndicated TV series *Nashville on the Road*, starting in 1976. He then teamed with Helen Cornelius for a country duo act that resulted in the hits "Don't Bother to Knock," "Saying Hello, Saying I Love You, Saying Goodbye," and "Lying in Love with You."

Brown began working with The Nashville Network (TNN) in 1983. He was a prominent figure there for six years on the *You Can Be a Star* program. He went on, beginning in 2003, to host the *Country Greats Music Radio Show*. He remains a member of the Grand Ole Opry, on which he makes about thirty appearances a year.

For additional information:
Brown, Maxine. *Looking Back to See: A Country Music Memoir*. Fayetteville: University of Arkansas Press, 2005.
Jim Ed Brown. http://www.jimedbrown.com/ (accessed February 26, 2013).

Jim Kelton

COUNTRY   ## THE BROWNS

A vocal trio from southern Arkansas, the Browns had several country hits. They were also instrumental in the development of the elegant, often orchestral "Nashville sound," which replaced the string bands of earlier eras.

The Browns began as a duo featuring Jim Ed Brown, born in 1934 in Sparkman (Dallas County), and his sister Maxine, born in Campti, Louisiana, in 1931. Their sister Bonnie, born in Sparkman in 1938, joined the group in 1955.

The Browns grew up in the piney woods near Pine Bluff (Jefferson County), where their father, Floyd Brown, worked as a log hauler and farmer. The group began its recording career for Fabor Records in southern California shortly after Jim Ed and Maxine graduated from high school. Their first release, "Looking Back to See" (1954), was a hit, but their contract with Fabor Robinson, proprietor of Fabor Records, precluded them from collecting royalties for its sales.

In the early days, the Browns made regular appearances on the *Louisiana Hayride* radio show (where they met and befriended a young Elvis Presley) on KWKH in Shreveport, Louisiana, and the *Ozark Jubilee* TV program, broadcast from Springfield, Missouri, though the Browns really started their professional career on *Barnyard Frolics* on KLRA in Little Rock (Pulaski County). They met and toured with many country stars, including balladeer Jim Reeves, Eddy "The Tennessee Plowboy" Arnold, and Johnny Cash.

After years of second-rate tours and low pay, the Browns met master guitarist and record producer Chet Atkins and signed a lucrative contract through him with RCA Records in Nashville, Tennessee. Though the group had a few hits shortly after teaming with Atkins (including "I Take the Chance" by Ira Louvin and "Money"), 1959 proved to be their most successful year in the music business. Their single "The Three Bells" went to number one on the country and pop charts and sold more than a million copies. Their follow-ups, "Scarlet Ribbons" and "The Old Lamplighter," did almost as well. Their smooth harmonies not only put the Browns at the forefront of Nashville's emerging sophistication but fit in with the burgeoning folk music movement, allowing them to capitalize on the popularity of both.

When Jim Ed was drafted into the military, his sister Norma filled in for him until his discharge. Although making somewhat haphazard public appearances after Maxine and Bonnie married and had children, the Browns stayed together until 1967 and kept recording. They cultivated a strong following in Europe, and their albums still sell well there. Jim Ed had begun a solo career in 1965 and continued performing after the group broke up, most notably with singer Helen Cornelius. His biggest solo hit was the jukebox classic "Pop-A-Top," and he has been the recipient of numerous awards throughout the years for his solo work.

The Browns received many awards. In 1959, they were nominated for Grammy Awards as Best Country Vocal Group and Most Promising Pop Group but did not win. They joined the Grand Ole Opry in 1963 and were inducted into the Arkansas Entertainers Hall of Fame in 1998. In 1997, Germany's Bear Family label released a four-disc retrospective of the Browns under the title *The Three Bells*.

For additional information:

Brown, Maxine. *Looking Back to See: A Country Music Memoir*. Fayetteville: University of Arkansas Press, 2005.

"The Browns." AllMusic.com. http://www.allmusic.com/artist/the-browns-mn0000630603 (accessed February 13, 2013).

Jensen, Joli. *The Nashville Sound: Authenticity, Commercialization and Country Music*. Nashville, TN: Vanderbilt University Press, 1998.

Jim Kelton

GOSPEL / CONTEMPORARY CHRISTIAN — ALBERT E. BRUMLEY (1905–1977)

Albert Edward Brumley Sr. was one of the most successful American gospel song composers of the twentieth century, penning such standards as "I'll Fly Away," "I'll Meet You in the Morning," "If We Never Meet Again," "Turn Your Radio On," and many others. Between 1926 and 1931, he studied, lived, and worked at the Hartford Music Company in Hartford (Sebastian County) under the tutelage of its founder, Eugene Monroe (E. M.) Bartlett. Although Bartlett died in 1941, Brumley forever credited him as the chief mentor and inspiration behind his music and eventually purchased the Hartford Music Company in 1948.

Albert E. Brumley was born on October 29, 1905, in Indian Territory near present-day Spiro, Oklahoma. His parents, William Sherman Brumley and Sarah Isabelle Williams Brumley, were recent newcomers to the region, sharecropping cotton until they finally had enough money to buy their own farm outside nearby Rock Island, Oklahoma. The middle child of three boys, Brumley was five years old when his older brother, Bill, died of typhoid fever.

Music, both sacred and secular, formed an important part of Brumley's childhood. His parents were firmly committed Campbellite Protestants, but his father was also a noted fiddler, and his mother enjoyed singing parlor songs. Music was integral to the family's weekly church gatherings and house parties. Brumley completed public school in Rock Island through the tenth grade, and participation in his first shape-note singing school there, at age sixteen, ignited his lifelong passion for gospel music.

At age twenty, Brumley arrived virtually penniless on the doorstep of E. M. Bartlett, hoping to enroll at the renowned publisher's Hartford Music Institute. Bartlett graciously took the young

Portrait of Albert E. Brumley.
Courtesy: The Restoration Movement

man under his wing, even providing board at his own home. Bartlett's kindness paid off; Brumley published his first song for Hartford in 1927 ("I Can Hear Them Singing Over There") and eventually became one of Bartlett's finest staff songwriters. He also sang bass with the 1929 Hartford Quartet and became increasingly active as a singing-school teacher in the Oklahoma-Missouri-Arkansas tri-state area.

In 1931, Brumley married Goldie Schell and moved to Powell, Missouri, where he lived for the rest of his life and raised his six children. He continued working for Bartlett on part-time and freelance bases, and a string of successful songs published in the 1930s—mostly by Hartford and including "I'll Fly Away" (1932)—emboldened Brumley to try composing full time. By the early 1940s, he was earning $200 a month as a staff songwriter for the famous Stamps-Baxter Music Company in Dallas, Texas. In 1943, Brumley started his own publishing company, Albert E. Brumley and Sons, and he purchased the Hartford Music Company in 1948, acquiring the copyright to several of his most successful songs. Today, Albert E. Brumley and Sons/Hartford Music Company continues to operate in Powell under the direction of Brumley's son Robert.

In 1969, Brumley began the Sundown to Sunup Gospel Sing, which was held annually in Springdale (Washington and Benton counties) until 2001 and then in Fayetteville (Washington County) until 2005. It has continued in Lebanon, Missouri, every summer since 2006 as a four-day festival called the Albert E. Brumley Memorial Gospel Music Sing.

Thanks to their widespread use among early radio and recording artists, several of Brumley's songs became extremely popular among the general public. "I'll Fly Away" alone has been recorded well over 500 times and continues to be successful. Recent recordings include artists as diverse as Aretha Franklin, Alan Jackson, and Kanye West, as well as an appearance on the platinum-selling soundtrack for the film *O Brother, Where Art Thou?* (2000).

Albert E. Brumley died on November 15, 1977, and is buried in the Fox Cemetery just outside of Powell. Estimates of his total output range from 600 to 800 songs.

For additional information:

Deller, David Charles. "Sing Me Home to Gloryland: Arkansas Songbook Gospel Music in the Twentieth Century." PhD diss., University of Arkansas, 1999.

Goff, James R., Jr. *Close Harmony: A History of Southern Gospel.* Chapel Hill: University of North Carolina Press, 2002.

Hively, Kay, and Albert E. Brumley Jr. *I'll Fly Away: The Life Story of Albert E. Brumley.* Branson, MO: Mountaineer Books, 1990.

Malone, Bill C. "Albert E. Brumley: Folk Composer." *Bluegrass Unlimited* 21 (July 1986): 69–77.

Stubblefield, Paul. "Brumley is Ozark's Country/Gospel Songmaster." *Music City News* 14, no. 10 (1977): 25, 40.

Wolfe, Charles K. "'I'd Rather Be An Old-Time Christian': The Music of Albert E. Brumley." *Precious Memories* (May–June 1991): 15–18.

Kevin D. Kehrberg

BLUES / R&B — ROY BUCHANAN (1939–1988)

Leroy (Roy) Buchanan was a guitar innovator whose skill inspired an aptly titled documentary, *The Best Unknown Guitarist in the World.* For more than thirty years, the guitarist melded blues, country, jazz, and rock music into a unique sound.

Roy Buchanan was born on September 23, 1939, in Ozark (Franklin County), the third of four children born to Bill Buchanan and Minnie Bell Reed Buchanan. When he was two, the family moved to Pixley, California, a tiny San Joaquin Valley farming town, where his father was a farm laborer.

At age five, Buchanan learned a few guitar chords. When he was nine, his father bought him a red Rickenbacker lap steel guitar, and, by age twelve, he was playing lap steel with the Wawkeen Valley Boys. He also picked up the standard guitar and learned to play along with songs on the radio.

Buchanan formed a band called the Dusty Valley Boys and began to get professional work in the area's honkytonks. At sixteen, he left home to pursue a musical career in Los Angeles, California. A Los Angeles–area agent, Bill Orwig, enlisted Buchanan to play in a band called the Heartbeats. The band can be seen in the 1956 period film *Rock, Pretty Baby.* The band fell apart when Orwig left the members stranded in Oklahoma City, Oklahoma.

Buchanan was playing as staff guitarist on *Oklahoma Bandstand*, a television show in Tulsa, Oklahoma, when rocker Dale Hawkins hired him. They toured together for three years, and Buchanan's first appearance on a commercial recording was on Hawkins's hit "My Babe" in 1958. In 1961, Hawkins's cousin, Ronnie Hawkins, persuaded Buchanan to join his band.

In the summer of 1961, Buchanan married Judy Owens. They settled in the suburbs of

Washington DC and had seven children. Buchanan spent the 1960s playing in the DC area in such bands as the Snakestretchers. In 1969, he reportedly turned down a job with the Rolling Stones, preferring to play in local venues.

In 1970, John Adams, a producer for WNET television in Washington DC, made the documentary *The Best Unknown Guitarist in the World* about Buchanan. Airing in November 1971, it led to Buchanan's signing with the Polydor label. In 1972, Buchanan recorded two albums for Polydor: *Roy Buchanan* and *Second Album*. Both were critical, if not financial, successes. Through the 1970s, he recorded three more albums for Polydor, then three for Atlantic Records. From 1978 to 1985, he recorded no albums, but then he signed with Alligator Records, a Chicago, Illinois–based blues label, and in 1985 released *When a Guitar Plays the Blues*, his biggest success. It stayed on the *Billboard* charts for fifteen weeks and earned him a Grammy nomination for Blues Album of the Year. He recorded two more albums with Alligator, *Dancing on the Edge* (1986), which won the College Media Journal Award for Best Blues Album of the year, and *Hot Wires* (1988).

Buchanan's alcohol and substance abuse became persistent problems. On August 14, 1988, his wife called the police to their Reston, Virginia, home about a domestic disturbance, and he was arrested. He died that night in his jail cell, the cause officially recorded as suicide by hanging. But some still dispute this finding.

The guitar innovator never achieved major commercial success, but he had a great influence on many guitarists, including Jeff Beck, Danny Gatton, and Robbie Robertson. His work has

Roy Buchanan performing at the Electric Ballroom in Dallas, Texas; December 1976.
Photo: Michael Clay Smith

been featured on several posthumous releases, including *American Axe: Live in 1974* (Powerhouse Records), *20th Century Masters: The Millennium Collection* (Polydor), *Deluxe Edition* (Alligator), and *Guitar on Fire: The Atlantic Sessions* (Atlantic).

For additional information:

Carson, Phil. "The Life and Times of Roy Buchanan." *Vintage Guitar Magazine* (August 1999). Online at http://www.yee.ch/winter/rbuch_lifetimes.html (accessed February 19, 2013).

———. *Roy Buchanan: American Axe.* San Francisco, CA: Backbeat Books, 2001.

Roy Buchanan. http://www.roybuchanan.org/home.html (accessed February 8, 2013).

Bryan Rogers

ROCK   # SONNY BURGESS (1929–)

Albert Austin "Sonny" Burgess is best known as one of the original rock and roll recording artists for Sun Records in Memphis, Tennessee, and as one of the pioneers of rock and roll. He and his band, the Pacers, made a hit of his first recording, "Red Headed Woman," and the flip side, "We Wanna Boogie," both of which Burgess wrote. The record sold approximately 100,000 copies, a phenomenal number for that era. Burgess and the Pacers are still performing at various events in the United States and Europe.

Sonny Burgess was born on May 31, 1929, in Newport (Jackson County). His parents, Albert and Esta Burgess, raised him, his two brothers, and his three sisters on their farm near Newport. Burgess graduated from Newport High School in 1948. In 1950, he and three friends formed a boogie-woogie band they called the Rocky Road Ramblers. Those three friends were Kern Kennedy, Johnny Ray Hubbard, and Gerald Jackson. Both Hubbard and Kennedy became members of the original Pacers. In 2005, Kennedy was still with the Pacers, Jackson was the mayor of Tuckerman (Jackson County), and Hubbard was retired and living in Newport.

In 1954, following a stint in the U.S. Army (1951–1953), Burgess re-formed the band, calling them the Moonlighters after the Silver Moon Club in Newport, where they performed regularly. The Silver Moon was part of a circuit—including the B&I Club, Mike's 67 Club, and Porky's Roof Top Club—in the Newport area made by many up-and-coming performers. Stars such as Elvis Presley, Carl Perkins, Charlie Rich, Jerry Lee Lewis, and Conway Twitty got their start on the Newport club circuit.

At that time, Elvis Presley was performing in clubs and school gyms to promote his releases, and the Moonlighters opened for him four times. Elvis liked what he heard and told Burgess the band should go to Memphis and talk to Sam Phillips of Sun Records. They followed his advice, and Phillips told them to get a larger band together and come back. Thus, the Pacers were born, consisting of Kennedy on piano, Hubbard on upright "slap" bass, Russ Smith on drums, Joe Lewis on guitar, and Jack Nance on trumpet. Burgess provided the vocals and played guitar. Lewis came up with the new name for the band, inspired by the Pacer airplane. They played rhythm and blues and boogie-woogie music. Sonny and the Pacers returned to Memphis and recorded "Red Headed Woman" in 1955. The record, personally recorded by Sam Phillips, was released in 1956, and they were on their way to fame.

As popular as their recordings were, these did not compare with the band's energetic live show, unparalleled by the performers of that era. Their show included gyrating, stage sliding, and acrobatics. They even formed a human pyramid in the center of the dance floor without missing a beat in their music. They also had an act they called "Bug Dance," in which they jumped into the audience while performing. Burgess was known, too, for his red hair, dyed to match his candy-apple-red Fender guitar and his red suit.

Burgess married Joann Adams in 1956, and they raised two sons, Peyton and John.

Sonny Burgess and the Pacers continued recording with Sun Records until 1959. In those four years, they recorded five singles. In addition to their first record, they recorded "Thunderbird," "Ain't Got a Thing," "My Bucket's Got a Hole in It," and "Sadie's Back in Town."

Burgess left the band in 1960 and began working with Conway Twitty, who was raised in Phillips County. He left Twitty in 1965 and formed his own band, the King's Four. In 1972, he got what he called "a real job" as a salesman, and the King's Four broke up in 1974. Burgess continued working as a salesman and playing music on the side until 1986, when he was invited to a show in Washington DC that included rockabilly music, where he made a big hit. After that, Burgess traveled all over the world and became a sensation in Europe.

In 1999, Burgess was inducted into the Rock and Roll Hall of Fame of Europe. In 1998, the Smithsonian Institution made a video called *Rockin' on the River* that brought Burgess and the Legendary Pacers together again. In addition to Kennedy, the group now included Bobby Crafford, Jim Aldridge, Fred Douglas, J. C. Caughron, and Charles Watson II. They made two album-length recordings in the late 1990s: *They Came from the South* and *Still Rockin' and Rollin'.* In 2002, they were inducted into the Rockabilly Hall of Fame in Jackson, Tennessee. In 2005, they performed at numerous events in Arkansas, Texas, and Tennessee and toured Europe.

Between performances, Burgess and his wife live in Newport, where he has spent most of his life. He hosts a radio show, *We Wanna Boogie,* for KASU in Jonesboro (Craighead County). Burgess was awarded an Honorary Doctor of Music degree from Arkansas State University in Jonesboro on May 7, 2011.

Sonny Burgess and the Pacers Hits
"Red Headed Woman" (1956)
"We Wanna Boogie" (1956)
"Ain't Got a Thing" (1957)
"My Bucket's Got a Hole in It" (1957)
"Thunderbird" (1958)
"Sadie's Back in Town" (1960)

Sonny Burgess performing at the 2012 Arkansas Sounds music festival in Little Rock.
Photo: Mike Keckhaver

For additional information:
Escott, Colin. *Roadkill on the Three-chord Highway:*

Art and Trash in American Popular Music. New York: Routledge, 2002.

"Sonny Burgess." Delta Boogie. http://www.deltaboogie.com/deltamusicians/burgess (accessed February 8, 2013).

Sonny Burgess and the Legendary Pacers. http://www.legendarypacers.com (accessed February 8, 2013).

Paula Harmon Barnett

C

CLASSICAL / OPERA SARAH CALDWELL (1924–2006)

A member of the Arkansas Entertainers Hall of Fame, Sarah Caldwell was an internationally recognized American opera director, conductor, producer, and impresario. She was known for emphasizing the dramatic elements of opera in her productions with innovative stagings that often included spectacular visual effects. She also was known for performing and staging obscure operas that were performed only rarely because of their difficulty.

Sarah Caldwell was born on March 6, 1924, in Maryville, Missouri, but grew up in Fayetteville (Washington County). Her parents divorced when she was young, and her mother—piano teacher Margaret Carrie Caldwell Baker—later married Henry Alexander, who taught political science at the University of Arkansas (UA) in Fayetteville.

Recognized as a child prodigy, she was performing in public on violin by the age of ten and graduated from Fayetteville High School at fourteen. Caldwell went on to study psychology at UA but left after a year and a half. She studied violin at Hendrix College in Conway (Faulkner County) and won a scholarship to the New England Conservatory of Music. In 1946, she won a scholarship in viola at the Berkshire Music Center in Tanglewood, Massachusetts. In 1947, she staged Ralph Vaughan Williams's *Riders to the Sea* at Tanglewood. She served for eleven years as opera teacher Boris Goldovsky's chief assistant.

Caldwell moved to Boston to head the Boston University opera workshop in 1952. In 1957, she started the Opera Company of Boston with $5,000. There, she staged a variety of operas, establishing a reputation for producing difficult works under pressure. In 1975, Caldwell was featured on the cover of *Time* magazine. Caldwell became the first female conductor of the Metropolitan Opera the following year. She appeared with the New York Philharmonic Orchestra, the Pittsburgh Symphony Orchestra, and the Boston Symphony Orchestra. In 1978, she was the first recipient of the Kennedy Center Award for Excellence. She became artistic director of the New Opera Company of Israel in 1983. In 1996, she traveled to the White House, where President Bill Clinton and First Lady Hillary Clinton presented her with the National Medal of Arts.

Known for taking on interesting and difficult works, Caldwell said that she wanted "to perform music which is wonderful that for some odd reason we have not yet explored." Caldwell staged more than seventy-five operas, including such American premieres as Hector Berlioz's *Les Troyens* (1972), Sergei Prokofiev's *War and Peace* (1974), Roger Sessions's *Montezuma* (1972), Mikhail Glinka's *Ruslan and Lyudmila* (1977), Bernd Alois Zimmermann's *Die Soldaten* (1982), Peter Maxwell Davies's *Taverner* (1986), and Robert DiDomenica's *The Balcony* (1990).

Her opera company closed in 1991, over $5 million in debt. She took many guest teaching and guest conducting jobs after this, including a brief stint as distinguished professor of music at UA starting in 1999, but seldom worked in the United States.

Caldwell died on March 23, 2006, in Portland, Maine, at the age of eighty-two.

For additional information:

Duffie, Bruce. "Conversation Piece: Conductor Sarah Caldwell." http://www.bruceduffie.com/caldwell.html (accessed February 8, 2013).

Kessler, Daniel. *Sarah Caldwell: The First Woman of Opera.* Lanham, MD: Scarecrow Press, 2008.

"Music's Wonder Woman." *Time*, November 10, 1975, pp. 52–54, 59, 65. Online at http://www.time.com/time/magazine/article/0,9171,913688,00.html (accessed February 8, 2013).

Schudel, Matt. "Opera Conductor and Impresario Sarah Caldwell, 82." *Washington Post*, March 25, 2006, p. 6B. Online at http://www.washingtonpost.com/wp-dyn/content/article/2006/03/24/AR2006032401987.html (accessed February 8, 2013).

C. L. Bledsoe

GLEN CAMPBELL (1936–)

Glen Travis Campbell is a commercially successful and critically acclaimed entertainer whose career has lasted more than fifty years. As a guitarist, Campbell has appeared on recordings by a diverse range of artists, including Elvis Presley and Frank Sinatra. As a singer and solo artist, Campbell has sold millions of recordings and earned many awards. He has also starred in films and hosted his own television programs.

Glen Campbell was born on April 22, 1936, in the Billstown community, near Delight (Pike County). He was one of twelve children born to the farming family of Carrie Dell Stone Campbell and John Wesley Campbell. Many of his relatives were musicians, and young Campbell soon developed an interest in singing and playing. He received his first guitar at age four, performed in public by age six, and made occasional appearances on the local radio station.

Glen Campbell has played with or for:
- Elvis Presley
- Dean Martin
- The Mamas and the Papas
- Ricky Nelson
- Bobby Darrin
- Frank Sinatra
- The Monkees
- The Beach Boys

The Campbell family moved first to Houston, Texas, and then to Albuquerque, New Mexico, where teenaged Campbell began performing in nightclubs. Campbell dropped out of school in the tenth grade to spend more time on music. In 1956, he joined the Sandia Mountain Boys, a local band led by his uncle Dick Bills. Campbell stayed with the group until 1958.

In 1958, Campbell formed his own band, Glen Campbell and the Western Wranglers. In 1960, Campbell disbanded the group and moved to Los Angeles, California. He hoped to establish himself as a solo performer but found himself instead to be a sought-after studio musician and guitarist. He worked for a year with the instrumental rock group the Champs (of "Tequila" fame) before recording his first solo record in 1961. "Turn Around, Look at Me," recorded for Crest, was a minor hit and led to a Capitol Records contract for Campbell in 1962. Campbell's first single for Capitol, "Too Late to Worry—Too Blue to Cry," was more successful. Nonetheless, Campbell's solo career floundered for several years.

As a session musician, however, Campbell established himself as one of the premier guitarists of the era. He became associated with the "Wrecking Crew," as the group of leading Los Angeles studio musicians was known. The group included drummer Hal Blaine and keyboardist Leon Russell. With or without the Wrecking Crew, Campbell played guitar for sessions by producer Phil Spector, as well as on recordings by leading performers including Elvis Presley, Dean Martin, the Mamas and the Papas, Ricky Nelson, and Bobby Darrin. His guitar playing is featured on Frank Sinatra's "Strangers in the Night," the Monkees' "I'm a Believer," and many other hits. Campbell took a position with the Beach Boys from 1964 through 1965, playing guitar and singing harmonies as a temporary replacement for Brian Wilson.

After years backing other artists, Campbell finally realized the individual success he sought. His 1967 recording of John Hartford's "Gentle on My Mind" entered the *Billboard* Top 40 and earned Campbell two 1968 Grammy Awards for both Best Country Vocalist and Best Contemporary Vocalist.

Campbell's popularity soared after "Gentle on My Mind," and he produced a string of hit songs over the next ten years. He won three more Grammys for his 1968 hit "By the Time I Get to Phoenix." Hits continued through the 1960s and 1970s with "Wichita Lineman," "Galveston," "Rhinestone Cowboy," and "Southern Nights."

Campbell's entertainment success was not confined to music. His early groups had made occasional television appearances, but Campbell's guest spots on *The Smothers Brothers Comedy Hour* opened the door to television and film stardom. Campbell filled in as a summer replacement for the canceled Smothers Brothers' show in 1968 and was signed to his own CBS television program in 1969. A variety program, *The Glen Campbell Goodtime Hour*, ran from 1969 through 1971.

Although Campbell had only a few film roles, some were memorable. His appearance in the 1969 John Wayne film *True Grit* garnered Campbell a Golden Globe nomination for Best Newcomer. In 1970, Campbell played the title role in the feature film *Norwood*. Both films were based on novels by Arkansas author Charles Portis.

Campbell continued to enjoy chart success through the late 1970s. Among his more than seventy albums are several gospel albums recorded in the 1990s, one of which—*A Glen Campbell Christmas*—earned a Dove Award in 2000.

Campbell has been married four times. He and his first wife, Diane Kirk, were married in 1954; they had one child before divorcing in 1959. On September 20, 1959, Campbell married Billie Jean Nunley; they had three children before divorcing in 1976. Campbell then married Sarah Davis, the ex-wife of country singer Mac Davis, on September 3, 1976; they had one child and divorced in December 1980. During the early 1980s, a public affair with singer Tanya Tucker made Campbell the subject of tabloid headlines. In 1982, Campbell married his fourth wife, Kimberly Woollen; they had three children.

In 1994, Campbell published his autobiography, *Rhinestone Cowboy*. Campbell was a first-year inductee into the Arkansas Entertainers Hall of Fame in 1996, and was inducted into the Coun-

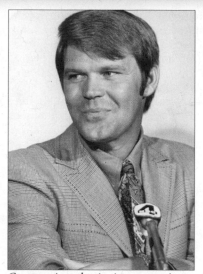

Grammy Award–winning country/pop music artist Glen Campbell; circa 1970s.

Courtesy: UALR Center for Arkansas History and Culture

try Music Hall of Fame in 2005. In August 2008, Campbell released a new album, *Meet Glen Campbell*. On June 22, 2011, Campbell made public that he had been diagnosed with Alzheimer's disease; he began a farewell tour in 2012. Campbell is slated to receive a lifetime achievement award from the Arkansas Entertainers Hall of Fame at its 2013 induction ceremony.

For additional information:
Campbell, Glen, with Tom Carter. *Rhinestone Cowboy: An Autobiography*. New York: Villard, 1994.
Glen Campbell. http://glencampbellshow.com/main.html (accessed February 6, 2013).
George-Warren, Holly, and Patricia Romanowski, eds. *The Rolling Stone Encyclopedia of Rock & Roll*. New York: Rolling Stone Press, 2001.

Terry Buckalew

JOHNNY CASH (1932–2003)

Johnny Cash was a world-renowned singer/songwriter of country music. With his deep, rich voice and often dark, often uplifting lyrics, he created a body of work that will be heard and remembered for generations to come.

J. R. Cash was born on February 26, 1932, in Kingsland (Cleveland County) to Ray and Carrie Cash. He had six siblings: Roy, Louise, Jack, Reba, Joanne, and Tommy. In 1935, the family moved to Dyess (Mississippi County), where they lived modestly and worked the land. The tragic death of Jack Cash in a 1944 sawmill accident haunted young J. R. for the remainder of his life. His mother introduced him to the guitar, and the local Church of God introduced him to music. He acquired a fascination for the guitar and a love for singing. Cash first sang on the radio at station KLCN in Blytheville (Mississippi County) while attending Dyess High School. Upon graduation in 1950, he enlisted in the U.S. Air Force after a brief search for work in Michigan.

Cash was stationed in Germany, where he bought his first guitar for five dollars and formed

his first band, the Landsberg Barbarians. After receiving an honorable discharge from the air force in 1954, Cash returned to San Antonio, Texas, where he married Vivian Liberto, whom he had met while in basic training four years

Kingsland native Johnny Cash.
Artists: Patterson and Barnes / From the Old State House Museum Collection

67

earlier. The couple settled in Memphis, Tennessee, where Cash took radio broadcasting classes at Keegan's School of Broadcasting and worked as an appliance salesman for the Home Equipment Company.

In Memphis, Cash met bass player Marshall Grant and guitarist Luther Perkins. They formed a band and soon were hired to perform once a week on Memphis radio station KWEM, which had recently moved from West Memphis (Crittenden County). In 1954, Cash and his band auditioned for Sam Phillips at Sun Records in Memphis. After several sessions, the trio recorded their first record, 78 rpm and 45 rpm, "Hey Porter" and "Cry, Cry, Cry" in 1955. It was Sam Phillips who gave Cash the name Johnny and labeled his band "Johnny Cash and the Tennessee Two." The release was successful and sold more than 100,000 copies. Cash toured feverishly, primarily through the tri-state area of Arkansas, Mississippi, and Tennessee—often with other Sun artists, such as Elvis Presley and Carl Perkins. When Sun Records released his second 78 rpm and 45 rpm record, "Folsom Prison Blues" and "So Doggone Lonesome" (1955), Cash was already a performing member on Shreveport's weekly radio program, *Louisiana Hayride*. Around this time, Cash quit his job as a part-time appliance salesman and pursued his music full time. In mid-1956, Cash left *Louisiana Hayride* to perform on the Grand Ole Opry, but his stint on the *Opry* was short because Cash preferred not to appear in Nashville every Saturday night.

Johnny Cash and wife June Carter Cash at Kingsland; March 20, 1976.
Courtesy: Arkansas History Commission

With his third release, "I Walk the Line" and "Get Rhythm" (1956), Cash established himself as a rising star. The recording peaked at No. 2 on the country charts and No. 19 on the pop charts. In 1957, Cash signed a lucrative recording contract with Columbia Records, taking effect the following year. At the end of 1957, Cash was the third-best-selling country artist in America and began appearing on national television programs such as *The Jackie Gleason Show*.

Sun Records continued to release Cash singles and albums until 1964, including his first No. 1 country single "Ballad of a Teenage Queen" (1958), just a few months before his Columbia record "Don't Take Your Guns to Town" (1958) reached the No. 1 spot. During the next decade, Columbia Records sold more than twenty million Cash albums worldwide.

Cash moved his family to California in 1961, which allowed him to pursue a limited acting career. He appeared on the television program *Wagon Train* (1959) and the movie *Five Minutes to Live* (1961). He continued acting throughout his career, appearing in a total of four theatrical movies, including *A Gunfight* (1971), as well as seven television movies.

The long tours and endless one-night gigs took a toll on many a performer, and in 1957, on a long road trip to Jacksonville, Florida, Cash began taking amphetamines to help stay awake. Members of his touring party were using them and were happy to share these "bennies" with Cash and his band. This was the start of an addiction that would plague Cash for the next decade. A bottle of 100 or so pills would cost less than ten dollars, and on the road, they were as important to Cash as his guitar.

During the 1960s, Cash maintained a hectic international touring schedule. His drug abuse increased, and his persona of the Man in Black took shape. In 1963 and 1964, Cash scored No. 1 country hits with "Ring of Fire" and "Understand Your Man," respectively. Cash was releasing theme albums such as his acclaimed album titled *Bitter Tears* (1964), which recounted the plight of the American Indian. Cash was branching out of country music and finding a whole new "folk" audience. He performed at the Newport Folk Festival in 1964, and it was around this time that Cash wrote a scathing letter to *Billboard* magazine blasting the country music establishment for ignoring his "new" music.

Cash's drug abuse continued. While on stage at the Grand Ole Opry, he used a microphone stand to smash footlights along the front of the stage. Months later, he was arrested in El Paso, Texas, for illegally purchasing hundreds of pills in Juarez, Mexico. Two years later, when Cash was again arrested in Lafayette, Georgia, he realized he needed help. However, that same year, Cash attempted to kill himself by driving alone to Chattanooga, Tennessee, and getting himself lost in a series of dark caves. He felt so despondent over his drug addiction and broken promises that he wanted to disappear. However, once deep inside the caves, he became religiously inspired and realized he had much more to live for. He found his way out of the caves and, at that point, decided to seek help for his drug addiction and renew himself religiously. June Carter, who had toured with Cash since the early 1960s, was instrumental in breaking his addiction by constantly reassuring him and never giving up on him. In early 1968, Vivian Cash was granted a divorce from her husband, and Cash promptly married June Carter.

On February 4, 1968, Cash triumphantly returned to Arkansas for a special "Johnny Cash Homecoming Show" at the Dyess High School gymnasium. Later that year, long-time friend and guitarist Luther Perkins died. Arkansan Bob Wootton, born in the small town of Paris (Logan County), joined Cash's band as a permanent replacement after literally coming out of the audience to play guitar during a concert in Fayetteville (Washington County) on September 17, 1968.

The year 1969 was a remarkable one for Cash. He was clean and sober, and he sold six and a half million albums. Cash toured the Far East; his album *Johnny Cash at San Quentin* went to No. 1 on the country and pop charts; he had two No. 1 country singles, "A Boy Named Sue" and "Daddy Sang Bass"; he recorded with Bob Dylan on Dylan's *Nashville Skyline* album; and ABC launched *The Johnny Cash Show*, which was filmed at the Grand Ole Opry and aired in prime time through 1971. On April 10, 1969, Cash returned to Arkansas for a much-anticipated concert at Cummins Prison in Lincoln County.

Cash began the 1970s with another No. 1 country song, "Sunday Morning Coming Down" (1970). He would not have another country No. 1 hit until 1976, when Columbia Records released "One Piece at a Time." Cash began spending time with his friend, evangelist Billy Graham, and in 1971 and 1972, he produced and filmed a movie in Israel about the life of Jesus Christ, titled *Gospel Road* (1973). Cash and Graham's friendship grew over the next thirty years, and Cash often appeared at Billy Graham Crusades held around the world. One such appearance was in Little Rock (Pulaski County) at War Memorial Stadium in September 1989. In 1975, Cash published his autobiography, *Man in Black*, which sold more than one million copies. He briefly re-

turned to television with *The Johnny Cash Show* as a 1976 summer replacement series and continued to tour the world throughout the 1970s and 1980s.

In 1980, Cash became the youngest person ever elected to the Country Music Hall of Fame. A year later, Cash found himself in Stuttgart, Germany, at the same time as old friends Carl Perkins and Jerry Lee Lewis. They went on stage together and recorded a live album titled *The Survivors* (1982).

In the early 1980s, Cash had eye surgery, broke several ribs, and damaged a kneecap, all on separate occasions, and again became addicted to pills. He was hospitalized in 1983 with internal bleeding that almost killed him. Upon regaining strength, he checked into the Betty Ford Clinic and remained clean until his death.

In 1985, Cash joined several of his friends for a couple of albums. *The Highwaymen* reached No.

1 on the country charts and featured Cash with Willie Nelson, Waylon Jennings, and Kris Kristofferson. Later that year, Cash returned to Sun Records in Memphis to record the album *Class of '55* with Carl Perkins, Roy Orbison, and Jerry Lee Lewis.

Cash published his second book, *Man in White*, in 1986. It chronicled the life of Paul the Apostle. That same year, Cash was dropped from Columbia Records, and he signed with Mercury/Polygram Records, with which he recorded four albums: *Johnny Cash is Coming to Town* (1987), *Water from the Wells of Home* (1988), *Boom Chicka Boom* (1989), and *The Mystery of Life* (1991). In 1989, Cash was elected to the Songwriters Hall of Fame.

The second Highwaymen collection, titled *Highwaymen II*, was released in 1990. It peaked in the top five on the country charts. During the 1990s, Cash received recognition from many organizations: the Rock and Roll Hall of Fame (1992), the Kennedy Center Honors for Lifetime Contribution to American Culture (1996), the

Arkansas Entertainers Hall of Fame (1996), and the Grammy Award for Lifetime Achievement (2000)—one of numerous Grammy Awards he received.

In 1994, Cash signed an unlikely contract with rap producer Rick Rubin and American Recordings and released a successful album, *American Recordings*. Cash's popularity soared. This release began a new series of acclaimed compact discs: *Unchained* (1996), *American III: Solitary Man* (2000), and *American IV: The Man Comes Around* (2002). These albums featured Cash recording songs written by such alternative rock performers as Soundgarden, Beck, and Nine Inch Nails. In March 2003, Country Music Television proclaimed Cash the "Greatest Man in Country Music."

In 1997, Cash published a new version of his autobiography, titled *Cash: The Autobiography*. That same year, he announced he had been diagnosed with a rare form of Parkinson's disease and was forced to give up touring. In 2001, the diagnosis was corrected when he learned he had autonomic neuropathy, a group of symptoms affecting the central nervous system. Throughout the final years of his life, Cash was frequently admitted to the hospital, suffering primarily from various stages of pneumonia.

On May 15, 2003, June Carter Cash died of complications from heart surgery. Almost four months later, on September 12, 2003, Johnny Cash died at Baptist Hospital in Nashville, Tennessee, from respiratory failure brought on by complications from diabetes—one of the many physical ailments Cash had been facing over the years. Cash is buried near his wife at Hendersonville Memory Gardens in Hendersonville, Tennessee.

The legend of Johnny Cash continues to inspire people around the world. In 2005, a major motion picture documenting the first half of his life, *Walk the Line*, was released and garnered both critical and commercial success.

Tourists continue to visit Dyess to see the place that was home to Cash during his youth. In 2011, Arkansas State University in Jonesboro (Craighead County) purchased Cash's boyhood home for a reported $100,000 and is working to restore the house to serve as a museum. In 2013, the United States Postal Service announced the release of a memorial stamp in honor of Cash.

For additional information:

Cash, Johnny. *Cash: The Autobiography*. San Francisco: Harper, 1997.

———. *Man in Black*. Grand Rapids, MI: Zondervan, 1975.

"Dyess Gets Ready to Greet Singing Star Johnny Cash at His Homecoming Show." *Arkansas Gazette*, February 2, 1968, p. 1.

Edwards, Leigh H. *Johnny Cash and the Paradox of American Identity*. Bloomington: Indiana University Press, 2009.

Hawkins, Martin. *Johnny Cash, The Sun Years*. London: Charly Holdings, Inc., 1995.

Johnny Cash Official Site. http://www.johnnycash.com (accessed February 6, 2013).

Moriarty, Frank. *Johnny Cash*. New York: MetroBooks, 1997.

Streissguth, Michael. *Johnny Cash: The Biography*. New York: Da Capo Press, 2006.

———. *Ring of Fire: The Johnny Cash Reader*. Cambridge, MA: Da Capo Press, 2003.

Tahmahkera, Dustin. "An Indian in a White Man's Camp: Johnny Cash's Indian Country Music." *American Quarterly* 63 (September 2011): 591–617.

Tost, Tony. *Johnny Cash's American Recordings*. New York: Continuum, 2011.

Eric Lensing

ROCK   CATE BROTHERS BAND

The Cate Brothers, identical twins Earl and Ernie (born Ernest), once exemplified the country-style rock and roll that flourished in the Ozark Mountains area of northwestern Arkansas, before adding rhythm and blues (R&B), soul, and funk to their approach in a distinctly unpretentious way.

The Cates were born in Fayetteville (Washington County) in 1942 and grew up in Springdale (Washington and Benton counties). Although not born to a musical family, the Cates taught themselves how to play their instruments and were heavily influenced during their teenage years by Ronnie Hawkins, whose ever-changing band, the Hawks, was at that time composed of the personnel who eventually became famous as Bob Dylan's backup ensemble, the Band: pianist Richard Manuel, keyboardist Garth Hudson, drummer Levon Helm, and guitarist Robbie Robertson. The northwestern Arkansas musical enclave was a diverse one, however, and the Cates heard not only renowned touring rock musicians

Ernie (left) and Earl Cate; 2012.   Photo: Mike Keckhaver

(1977), and *Fire on the Tracks* (1979). The group, which toured around the world, earned critical acclaim for its distinctive sound and a solid reputation for expert musicianship. *Cate Bros.* and *In One Eye and Out the Other* were produced by legendary Memphis, Tennessee, guitarist Steve Cropper, a member of Booker T. & the MG's and a mainstay of the celebrated Stax label throughout the company's 1960s heyday. *Fire on the Tracks* was produced by Tom Dowd, a renowned longtime producer and engineer for Atlantic Records.

During the 1970s and 1980s, the Cates toured nationally and internationally with the likes of Heart, Fleetwood Mac, and Queen. The Cates have earned a devoted following of their own and have continued to release albums, including *Radioland* (1995), *Struck a Vein* (1997), *Cate Brothers Band Live* (1999), and *Play by the Rules* (2004). These later albums have been described as hybrids of blues, rock, soul, and country.

Though they have never achieved the kind of far-flung success that was eventually accorded the Band (the Cates' most famous recording is probably "Union Man" from the 1975 *Cate Bros.* album), the Cates remain a well-respected band among their peers in the music world and have carried their style of classic rock into the twenty-first century.

but also worked with such local stars as vocalist Ken Owens while competing with Hawkins and Tolleson for a tough, knowledgeable regional audience. The Cates' band was originally called the Del-Reys, and they sang Everly Brothers–style harmonies when they were young, before they developed their own vocal personae. Earl Cate plays the guitar, while Ernie Cate plays the keyboard.

The Cates have remained close to the northwestern Arkansas clubs and festival activities, which revolve around the University of Arkansas (UA) in Fayetteville and have expanded to accommodate the booming regional commercial developments related to the growth of Walmart, Tyson Foods, and J. B. Hunt. But the Cates are also true to their musical roots in that theirs is a "country soul" unit, and they are masters of a kind of rhythmic eclecticism that is native to the cultural territory from which it emerged, bounded generationally by Bob Wills's western swing style and the Band's blend of hillbilly simplicity and blues depth.

In the 1970s, the Cates released four major-label albums (three on the Asylum label—a powerful force in rock music at the time—and one on Atlantic): *Cate Bros.* (1975), *In One Eye and Out the Other* (1976), *Cate Bros. Band*

For additional information:

Hawkins, Ronnie, and Peter Goddard. Ronnie Hawkins: Last of the Good Ol' Boys. Toronto: Stoddart, 1989.

Helm, Levon, and Stephen Davis. This Wheel's on Fire: Levon Helm and the Story of the Band. Chicago: Chicago Review Press, 2000.

Wallis, Ian. The Hawk: The Story of Ronnie Hawkins and the Hawks. Toronto: Quarry Press, 1996.

Wyeth, Wyndham. "Band of Brothers." Arkansas Life (May 2013): 78–83.

Jim Kelton

COUNTRY   CAROLINA COTTON (1925–1997)

Helen Hagstrom is best known for her country and western swing music and yodeling, as well as her appearances in numerous television specials, radio programs, and films under the name of Carolina Cotton. Nicknamed "The Yodeling Blonde Bombshell," Hagstrom was an entertainer and teacher throughout her life.

Helen Hagstrom was born on October 20, 1925, in Cash (Craighead County), where her parents, Fred and Helen Hagstrom, and maternal grandparents had a farm, growing many crops, including cotton and peanuts. During the Great Depression, Hagstrom's father moved his wife and two daughters to San Francisco, California. Hagstrom began performing in traveling stage shows with the O'Neille Sisters Kiddie Revue. Then, after regularly visiting KYA Radio to watch Dude Martin's Roundup Gang perform, she volunteered to replace the yodeler who left the band. It was then that she got her nickname "Carolina." The surname "Cotton" came later thanks to fans and a radio disc jockey named Cottonseed Clark.

In 1944, Hagstrom traveled to Hollywood to pick up costumes, and, though she had been told to wait in her hotel, she instead explored the city. During this outing, she bumped into songwriter Johnny Martin, who invited her to attend a Hollywood party. Soon after, he offered her a part in a film called *Sing Neighbor Sing*, and Hagstrom realized she had to choose between an entertainment career in the Bay Area or in Hollywood. She chose to move to Hollywood, where she joined the Spade Cooley Orchestra.

Carolina Cotton photo from Yodeling Blonde Bombshell Vol. 1.
Courtesy: CarolinaCotton.org

In 1945, Hagstrom married Deuce Spriggins, a member of the orchestra; the couple divorced in 1946. Hagstrom kept recording and performing. One of her most famous songs, "3 Miles South of Cash (in Arkansas)," was inspired by her upbringing in Arkansas. Throughout the 1940s and into the early 1950s, Hagstrom appeared in many films, including a low-budget film called

I'm from Arkansas (1944), which takes place in the fictional town of Pitchfork, Arkansas. In 1952, she appeared in two films with Gene Autry, *Blue Canadian Rockies* and *Apache Country*, which featured one of her most famous songs, "I Love to Yodel." These two films would be her last.

In the early and mid-1950s, Hagstrom began focusing much of her attention on performing for the military troops around Europe, Africa, and Asia. She also created short radio programs to entertain the troops. In 1956, Hagstrom married musician Bill Ates. The couple had a son and daughter but divorced a few years later.

Inspired by meeting many children around the world during her travels, Hagstrom decided to become a teacher. Though she was busy with her family, teaching, and even working part time at a department store, she still performed, especially at western film festivals, even in Little Rock (Pulaski County). Her song "3 Miles South of Cash (in Arkansas)" was a standard during these appearances.

Hagstrom retired from Mount Vernon Elementary School in Bakersfield, California, in 1997, and died on June 10, 1997, after battling ovarian cancer for three years.

For additional information:

Blevins, Brooks. *Arkansas/Arkansaw: How Bear Hunters, Hillbillies, and Good Ol' Boys Defined a State*. Fayetteville: University of Arkansas Press, 2009.

"Carolina Cotton." Western Music Association Hall of Fame. http://www.westernmusic.com/performers/hof-cotton.html (accessed February 26, 2013).

Carolina Cotton: The Official Site. http://www.carolinacotton.org/ (accessed February 26, 2013).

Lamsen, Chris, dir. *Soundies: A Musical History*. DVD. Liberation Entertainment, 2007.

Amber Hood

FLOYD CRAMER (1933–1997)

Pianist Floyd Cramer was one of the creators of what became known as the "Nashville sound," a style often seen as a forerunner of the slick, upscale pop/rock that emerged in Nashville, Tennessee, in the 1990s. Cramer released fifty solo albums, had a classic hit in the song "Last Date" in 1960, and accompanied Elvis Presley on such rock and roll hits as "Heartbreak Hotel." He was a longtime friend of producer and guitar virtuoso Chet Atkins and performed with other music luminaries, including Patsy Cline, Eddy Arnold, the Everly Brothers, Perry Como, and Roy Or-

bison. In the 1980s, he recorded a hit version of the theme from the *Dallas* TV series.

Born on October 27, 1933, in Campti, Louisiana, near Shreveport, Cramer spent most of his childhood in Huttig (Union County). He learned to play the piano by ear and developed a smooth, "slip-note" style that influenced countless other pianists. After graduating from high school, Cramer joined the *Louisiana Hayride* radio troupe and there met young Presley and many other country stars, among them Hank Williams Sr. and the Browns.

Cramer moved to Nashville in 1955 and quickly became associated with Atkins, saxophonist Boots Randolph, and producer/studio proprietor Owen Bradley. A versatile studio musician (his light touch suited a broad spectrum of pop styles), Cramer was amazingly prolific. His hits included a version of Bob Wills's "San Antonio Rose" and another instrumental milestone, "On the Rebound" (both released in 1961), which accentuated his slightly discordant (and blues-influenced) playing.

Between 1958 and 1962, eleven of Cramer's singles charted on *Billboard*'s Hot 100, a remarkable accomplishment for an instrumentalist in that era. He even topped himself with his No. 2 hit "Last Date." The No. 1 song at the time was Presley's "Are You Lonesome Tonight?" a ballad featuring Cramer on piano. Another hit on which Cramer played was Hank Locklin's "Please Help Me, I'm Falling," but it is estimated that he played on at least a fourth of the hits that constituted the archive of late 1950s and early 1960s "countrypolitan" orchestral Nashville bestsellers. Many consider him the most important pianist in country music history.

Cramer died of cancer on December 31, 1997. In 2003, he was elected to the Country Music Hall of Fame.

For additional information:

Cochran, Robert. *Our Own Sweet Sounds: A Celebration of Popular Music in Arkansas.* 2nd ed. Fayetteville: University of Arkansas Press, 2005.

"Floyd Cramer." Country Music Hall of Fame and Museum. http://countrymusichalloffame.org/full-list-of-inductees/view/floyd-cramer1 (accessed February 26, 2013).

Malone, Bill C. *Country Music U.S.A.* Austin: University of Texas Press, 1985.

Jim Kelton

D

BLUES / R&B   CeDell Davis (1926–)

Ellis CeDell Davis is a blues musician and recording artist who helped bring blues from its rural southern roots into the twenty-first century. He employs a unique slide guitar style and performs the traditional Delta blues he learned growing up in and around Helena (Phillips County). Although he was a longtime professional musician, recordings of his music were not available until 1983. Since then, he has recorded several albums and become a favorite with a new generation of blues fans.

CeDell Davis was born on June 9, 1926, in Helena, where his mother worked as a cook but was also known as a faith healer. At age four, Davis went to live with relatives on the E. M. Hood Plantation near Tunica, Mississippi. There, he befriended Isaiah Ross, who went on to blues fame as "Doctor Ross." The youngsters learned music together, and by age seven, Davis had learned harmonica and rudimentary guitar skills he honed on an improvised one-string instrument called a diddley bow.

Davis returned to Helena in the mid-1930s. He contracted polio at age nine and was left partially paralyzed. After nearly two years in a Little Rock (Pulaski County) hospital, Davis could walk only with crutches and had limited use of his arms and hands. He had to relearn guitar, and this greatly shaped his unusual style and sound. Although right handed, Davis plays with his left hand dominant, in nonstandard tunings, fretting the strings with a table knife used as a slide. The resulting sound has become Davis's trademark, though it can seem out of tune to some listeners.

At fourteen, Davis began making a living performing at juke joints and on street corners in Helena. The older bluesmen in the area influenced him. In the 1940s, Helena was home to Robert Lockwood Jr., Sonny Boy Williamson, Roosevelt Sykes, and a host of blues greats. Davis worked with many of the local artists, most notably slide guitar great Robert Nighthawk.

After a brief stay in St. Louis, Missouri, in 1945, Davis returned to Helena and the Delta. He continued to play locally and was an occasional guest on *King Biscuit Time* and other programs on Helena's KFFA radio. In 1953, Davis began a ten-year stint with Nighthawk.

Davis followed Nighthawk to St. Louis in 1957, joining a network of Arkansas natives working there, including Williamson, Sykes, and Frank Frost. Soon after moving to St. Louis, Davis was involved in a serious accident. While he performed at a nightclub with Nighthawk and drummer Sam Carr, a fight broke out. Panicked

Bluesman CeDell Davis demonstrating his unique playing style.
Photo: Paul Barrows

1993 solo debut, *Feel Like Doin' Something Wrong*. Davis then became active in recording studios, releasing the albums *The Horror of it All*, *CeDell Davis*, and a greatest-hits collection over the next few years, all on Fat Possum, a record company based in Oxford, Mississippi.

His belated recording debut and subsequent follow-ups made Davis a regular on the blues festival circuit. He has toured the United States and has performed or recorded with an eclectic array of musicians, including jazz great Ornette Coleman, Bruce Hampton, and Palmer. He is still active in music; members of rock bands R.E.M. and Screaming Trees appeared on his most recent release, 2002's *Lightning Struck the Pine*.

In 2001, Davis's "She Got the Devil in Her" was covered by Buddy Guy on his *Sweet Tea* album. In 2004, he received a Lifetime Achievement Award for Blues from the Delta Cultural Center, which also features Davis memorabilia.

Davis performed in Little Rock in October 2012 with several noted musicians, including Barrett Martin (formerly of Screaming Trees) and Peter Buck (formerly of R.E.M.). While he did not play the guitar, as a stroke has left him without the use of his right arm, he sang from his wheelchair.

patrons trampled Davis, who suffered severe injuries. He stayed in a hospital for months and has been wheelchair bound since. Davis stayed in St. Louis four more years, continuing to work with Nighthawk, Carr, and Frost.

He returned to Arkansas in 1961, settling in Pine Bluff (Jefferson County), where he lives today. In a 2000 interview, Davis said he has been married several times and has three children and several stepchildren.

Despite a lengthy and accomplished career, Davis did not record until the late 1970s, when folklorists included his music on the compilation album *Keep It to Yourself: Arkansas Blues, Volume I*, released by Rooster Records in 1983 (and rereleased in 2006 by Stackhouse Records with the help of Helena-West Helena's Delta Cultural Center). His reputation was enhanced by prominent mention in musician and critic Robert Palmer's widely read *Deep Blues*, originally published in 1981. Davis and Palmer became friends and playing partners. Palmer produced Davis's

For additional information:

Bogdanov, Vladimir, Chris Woodstra, and Stephen Thomas Erlewine, eds. *All Music Guide to the Blues: The Definitive Guide to the Blues*. San Francisco: Backbeat Books, 2003.

Cochran, Robert. *Our Own Sweet Sounds: A Celebration of Popular Music in Arkansas*. 2nd ed. Fayetteville: University of Arkansas Press, 2005.

Palmer, Robert. *Deep Blues*. New York: Viking Press, 1981.

Pearson, Barry Lee. "CeDell Davis' Story and the Arkansas Delta Blues." *Arkansas Review: A Journal of Delta Studies* 33 (April 2002): 3–14.

Terry Buckalew

FOLK | IRIS DEMENT (1961–)

Arkansas native Iris DeMent has used her distinctive voice to sing folk, country, bluegrass, and gospel music. She has written songs about family, religion, people, places, and political ideas in a time when few were doing so.

Iris DeMent was born on January 5, 1961, in Paragould (Greene County), the youngest of fourteen children. Her parents, Patrick Shaw and Flora Mae DeMent, were farmers on an is-

land in the St. Francis River outside Paragould. When Iris was three, her father lost his factory job after a failed attempt to unionize, and the family hit hard times, sold the farm, and moved to Buena Park, California. They lived there until she was seventeen and then moved to Sacramento, California. Eventually, her parents and some of her siblings moved back to Arkansas.

The family had a love of music, and not just

the kind they heard at Pentecostal services in Arkansas and California. DeMent's father played fiddle at dances during his early years in Arkansas and later at Pentecostal church services. Her brothers, sisters, and mother played piano and sang. Her older sisters—Zelda, Reba, Regina, and Faye—had a gospel group, the DeMent Sisters, who recorded one album. DeMent quit high school and moved to the Midwest, where she supported herself by cleaning houses and working as a waitress.

It was not until she was in her late twenties, living first in Kansas and then briefly in Nashville, Tennessee, that DeMent began to consider a career as a singer/songwriter. During her years working a series of day jobs, she gradually built up her confidence by playing at open-mike nights in clubs and coffeehouses. She came to the attention of folk label Rounder/Philo Records after she enlisted the help of producer Jim Rooney, who helped her get a recording contract, leading to her debut album, *Infamous Angel*, in 1992. It was produced by Rooney and endorsed on the liner notes by singer/songwriter John Prine.

Warner Bros. Records rereleased the album in 1993 after noticing the strong word-of-mouth praise it earned, along with sales of approximately 80,000 copies. The album included "After You're Gone" and "Mama's Opry," two songs about her parents, the latter of which featured Emmylou Harris on harmony vocals. The song "Our Town" was used as the credits rolled in the final episode of the TV series *Northern Exposure*. Another song, "Let the Mystery Be," was used in the opening sequence of a movie, *Little Buddha*, starring Keanu Reeves. Her version of "Whispering Pines" was used on the soundtrack of a Robert Redford movie, *The Horse Whisperer*.

DeMent's songs—some inspired by, and some in reaction to, her fundamentalist upbringing—have earned her more critical than commercial success. Many of her songs express her openness and reluctance to embrace rigid doctrines.

She released a second album, *My Life*, in 1994; its liner notes featured her memorial to her father, who died in 1992. Her third album, *The Way I Should*, came out in 1996 and marked a move into political topics (including the songs "There's a Wall in Washington," "Quality Time," and "Wasteland of the Free"). Her political topics have earned her comparisons with Bruce Springsteen, Jackson Browne, Bonnie Raitt, and other musicians who have criticized American government and its politicians. She co-wrote "This Kind of Happy" with Merle Haggard (who had praised her version of his song, "Big City," on *Tulare Dust*, a Haggard tribute CD) and sang a duet with Delbert McClinton on "Trouble," the final cut of *The Way I Should*.

DeMent's fourth album, *Lifeline* (2004), marked her departure from Warner Bros. to record for her own label, Flariella Records, named for her mother. The album's thirteen songs are old hymns, save for DeMent's "He Reached Down." Her singing is also heard in several movie soundtracks, including the 2010 version of *True Grit*.

On November 21, 2002, DeMent married fellow singer/songwriter Greg Brown, a troubadour from Iowa. They divide their time between her house in Kansas City, Missouri, and the house he built in recent years in southern Iowa.

In October 2012, DeMent's *Sing the Delta*, consisting of twelve original songs, was released on the Flariella label.

For additional information:
Brockmeier, Kevin. "Iris Dement." *Oxford American* 58 (2007): 129–134.

Iris DeMent. http://irisdement.com/ (accessed February 8, 2013).

Jack W. Hill

Singer/songwriter Iris DeMent, from Paragould..
Courtesy: Warner Bros. Records, Inc.

DIAMOND STATE CHORUS

The Diamond State Chorus is the performance group of the Greater Little Rock Chapter of the Society for the Preservation and Encouragement of Barber Shop Quartet Singing in America, Inc. (SPEBSQSA). The international men's singing group, also known as the Barbershop Harmony Society, has more than 34,000 members. It was founded on April 11, 1938, in Tulsa, Oklahoma.

The local chapter is a grandchild of the Memphis, Tennessee, chapter. In 1952, seven barbershoppers from Memphis went to Stuttgart (Arkansas County) to start a chapter. The subsequent Grand Prairie Chorus attracted the attention of a quartet from Little Rock (Pulaski County)—The Four Specs—which made the 120-mile round trip to Stuttgart for a couple of years before deciding to form a chapter in Little Rock. The original four were Fred Holder Jr., Dr. Joe Norton, William Bard, and Richard H. Hawn. Two dozen other men attended the first meeting in Little Rock. The Greater Little Rock Chapter was chartered on March 5, 1955.

That group chose as its name the Capitol City Chorus. In the early 1970s, the chapter changed its name to the Diamond State Chorus. It was part of the Dixie District when it was formed but was switched to the Southwest District in 1978. Arkansas has four other Barbershop Harmony Society chapters: Greater Ozarks, based in Bentonville (Benton County); Northwest Arkansas, based in Springdale (Washington and Benton counties); Greater Fort Smith in Sebastian County; and Hot Springs in Garland County.

The Diamond State Chorus at any one time has forty to fifty singers who perform as a single group and in several four-man quartets, singing tenor, lead, baritone, and bass. Members, who range in age from the twenties to the eighties, are from throughout central Arkansas, from Clarksville (Johnson County) and Hot Springs to Pine Bluff (Jefferson County) and Jacksonville (Pulaski County). Members include students, doctors, accountants, lawyers, mechanics, social workers, corporate executives, and retirees. They specialize in the close-knit, a cappella harmony that is the signature of barbershop singing.

The chorus has won many competitions as part of the Northeast Region of the Southwestern District of the Barbershop Harmony Society. District winners—both chorus and quartet—

earn the right to compete at the annual national convention.

The chorus performs primarily in the greater Little Rock area, singing for church groups, civic functions, and business events. In a typical year, the chorus appears before more than 3,000 people in more than twenty performances. It has opened events, such as ribbon cuttings and grand openings, sung at the opening and half-time at sporting events, and provided entertainment for conventions and other meetings.

The group meets most Monday evenings, practicing its singing and showmanship. All males are welcome to attend, from teenagers to retirees. The chorus earns income through paid performances, annual dues, an annual show, singing Valentines, and corporate sponsors. The money is used to provide scholarships for young musicians and for such expenses as music and a director. The annual show features the chorus, each of its quartets, and often an award-winning guest quartet from out of state.

Each February, quartets from the chorus offer singing Valentines, which cost $40 to $100; they include "a romantic song, a sentimental card and an instant photograph." The chorus cooperates with the Top of the Rock Chorus, its female counterpart, to give buyers a choice of a male or a female quartet.

For additional information:
Barbershop Harmony Society. http://www.barbershop.org (accessed February 23, 2013).
Diamond State Chorus. http://www.diamondstatechorus.com/ (accessed February 23, 2013).

C. Dennis Schick

Diamond State Chorus with director Donald Q. Snow; February 2004.
Courtesy: Lou Anderson

BOB DOROUGH (1923–)

Robert Lrod Dorough is a composer, lyricist, and musician best known for his jazz compositions and 1970s *Schoolhouse Rock!* shorts on ABC Saturday morning television.

Bob Dorough was born on December 12, 1923, in Cherry Hill (Polk County), the oldest of four children of Robert Lee Dorough, an automobile and insurance salesman, and Alma Audrey Lewis, a housewife and Singer sewing machine instructor. Dorough's unusual middle name was suggested by his aunt. He attended elementary schools in De Queen (Sevier County), Mena (Polk County), and Texarkana (Miller County) and graduated from Plainview High School in Plainview, Texas, where the family moved in 1934. The Plainview High School bandmaster inspired Dorough musically and gave him free lessons in harmony and the clarinet to complement his previous training in violin, piano, and singing.

Dorough attended three semesters at Texas Tech University before being drafted into the U.S. Army in February 1943. Because of a punctured eardrum, present since childhood, he was placed in limited service and was never sent overseas. He received a medical discharge in December 1945. While in a military Special Services band, Dorough wrote many arrangements and played in various musical groups. Dorough returned to school after his discharge and earned a Bachelor of Music degree from North Texas State Teachers College (now University of North Texas) in 1949. He moved to New York City after graduation to pursue a master's degree from Columbia University but dropped out before completion after his GI Bill funds were depleted.

Dorough married Jacqueline Wright in 1945. They divorced in 1953. He married Ruth Corine Meinert in 1960; they had one daughter. Meinert died of cancer in 1986. Dorough married Sally Shanley in 1994.

After leaving Columbia University, Dorough supported himself as a piano player. In 1952, he met boxing champion Sugar Ray Robinson, who was learning a tap routine at the Henry LeTang Dance School. The retired boxer hired Dorough to be his music director in his new career in show business, and they toured Canada and the United States, with Dorough either at the piano or conducting big bands for Robinson's act. They went to Paris, France, where Dorough remained after Robinson decided to return to the boxing ring, playing nightly at the Mars Club, a famous Right Bank boîte, for six months (1954–1955).

Dorough's first song to be recorded was "Devil May Care," written with Terrell Kirk. It was recorded in 1953 by the Les Elgart Band. His first full-length album, also titled *Devil May Care*, was a jazz album issued by Bethlehem Records in 1956. He has recorded and released more than fifteen solo

Composer, lyricist, and musician Bob Dorough.   Photo: Richard Newhouse

albums and has been featured on more than twenty albums by different artists, including Miles Davis and Blossom Dearie. Dorough also has dabbled in acting, appearing in one episode of the television series *Have Gun, Will Travel* (1959), in the movie *Chasers* (1994), as well as voicing (uncredited) a character for the animated television series *Drawn Together* (2005).

In 1971, Dorough was commissioned by David B. McCall, president of a New York advertising company, to set the multiplication tables to music to make learning numbers easier. He wrote and recorded eleven songs for McCall, including "Three Is a Magic Number." McCall approved the release of the songs for a commercial album, titled *Multiplication Rock*, which was issued by Capitol Records in 1973.

The advertising executives considered ideas for tie-ins with the album, settling finally on an animated adaptation, drawn by Tom Yohe. The idea was pitched to television network ABC, which at the time was looking for more kid-friendly materials for the Saturday morning schedule. The network's head of children's programming approved the

---

Bob Dorough:
Film & Television

Have Gun, Will Travel (1959)
Chasers (1994)
Drawn Together, voice acting (2005)
Schoolhouse Rock! (wrote 22 of 52 songs)

Schoolhouse Rock! Episodes
"Three Is a Magic Number" (1973)
"My Hero Zero" (1973)
"Elementary, My Dear" (1973)
"The Four-Legged Zoo" (1973)
"Lolly, Lolly, Lolly, Get Your Adverbs Here" (1974)

three-minute skits, which the General Mills company sponsored. The first four segments of *Schoolhouse Rock!* premiered on ABC on January 6, 1973, with "My Hero Zero," "Elementary, My Dear," "Three Is a Magic Number," and "The Four-Legged Zoo." Following "Multiplication Rock" came "Grammar Rock," which featured songs such as "Lolly, Lolly, Lolly, Get Your Adverbs Here"; "History Rock" (originally known as "America Rock"), featuring "Mother Necessity"; and "Science Rock." Dorough wrote twenty-two of the fifty-two songs for the series, including the series theme song "Schoolhouse Rocky." He served as musical director for the series, which ran on ABC's Saturday morning lineup from 1973 to 1985. The network began re-running the series in 1993.

Dorough continues to produce jazz albums and perform around the world. He and his wife live in Pennsylvania.

For additional information:
Bob Dorough. http://www.bobdorough.com (accessed February 8, 2013).
Giddins, Gary. "Bob Dorough Endures." *The Village Voice*, May 16, 2000, p. 130.
Vann Hall, W. "Bob Dorough: Academic Hipster Mixes Math and Music." *Music Educators Journal* 72 (November 1985): 28–30.
"The Voice of Schoolhouse Rock on the Series at 40." NPR Music, January 6, 2013. http://www.npr.org/2013/01/06/168699556/the-voice-of-schoolhouse-rock-on-the-series-at-40 (accessed January 7, 2013).

Timothy G. Nutt

COUNTRY — DR. SMITH'S CHAMPION HOSS HAIR PULLERS

During the height of the great string band era of the 1920s, one of the largest and most popular string bands in Arkansas was Dr. Smith's Champion Hoss Hair Pullers. Originally founded to promote tourism in the area of Izard County, the band went on to achieve a modicum of regional success before succumbing to the Depression.

Dr. Smith's Champion Hoss Hair Pullers was founded by Dr. Henry Harlin Smith, a surgeon for the Missouri Pacific Railroad who lived in the Calico Rock (Izard County) area. On his travels with the railway, he found that he was often working to dispel the backward image that many people outside of Arkansas had of the region. Smith thought that if more people were to visit Calico Rock and enjoy the area's natural beauty, it could change the negative misconception that was so prevalent.

Courtesy: Kenny Rorrer

As a way to promote the area and tourism, he organized a fiddle contest in Calico Rock. Smith was not a musician himself, but he knew that a rich crop of talented musicians lived in and around Izard County. The contest was held in January 1926. From the winners of the contest, Dr. Smith formed a band with the whimsical name of "Dr. Smith's Champion Hoss Hair Pullers"—a unique but fitting name derived from the fact that fiddle bows are strung with horse hair.

Smith also assembled a group of vocalists from the winners of the contest and called them the "Hill-Billy Quartet."

Smith took the Champion Hoss Hair Pullers and the Hill-Billy Quartet to Hot Springs (Garland County) as ambassadors of the Calico Rock area. As part of his introduction before each show, he proudly extolled the natural beauty of Izard County and promoted the virtues of the area as a vacation destination.

Dr. Smith's Champion Hoss Hair Pullers enjoyed a couple years of popularity, which earned them several radio performances on KTHS in Hot Springs and a recording session in Memphis, Tennessee, for Victor during September 1928. Three 78 rpm records, a total of six songs, were recorded at this session. Members of the band for these recordings included James Clark Duncan and Bryan Lackey on fiddles, Leeman Bone on guitar, and Ray Marshall on mandolin.

Over the years, the band's roster changed several times. Members of the various incarnations of Dr. Smith's Champion Hoss Hair Pullers and the Hill-Billy Quartet included Leeman Bone on guitar and vocals, Graydon Bone on vocals, George Dillard on fiddle, James Clark Duncan on fiddle, Roosevelt Garner on vocals,

Homer T. Goatcher on vocals, J. Odie Goatcher on vocals, Owen Hunt on fiddle, Bryan Lackey on fiddle, Ray Marshall on mandolin, W. P. McLeary on fiddle and guitar, Hubert Simmons on vocals, and Luther Walker on fiddle.

By late 1929, the Depression began to take a toll on the music industry as well as tourism. Dr. Smith's Champion Hoss Hair Pullers and the Hill-Billy Quartet continued to play throughout Izard County until 1930, when Dr. Smith determined that the band no longer served its original purpose as ambassadors of tourism, and the group was disbanded.

For additional information:

Cochran, Robert. *Our Own Sweet Sounds: A Celebration of Popular Music in Arkansas.* 2nd ed. Fayetteville: University of Arkansas Press, 2005.

Echoes of the Ozarks. Vol. 2. CD. County Records, 1996.

Lindley, Helen C. "The Hoss Hair Pullers and Hill-Billy Quartet." *Izard County Historian* 5 (April 1974): 9–13.

Tosches, Nick. *Country: The Twisted Roots of Rock 'N' Roll.* New York: Da Capo Press, 1996.

Wolfe, Charles K. *Classic Country: Legends of Country Music.* New York: Routledge, 2001.

Ed Hopkinson

FOLK — JIMMY DRIFTWOOD (1907–1998)

Jimmy Driftwood was a prolific folk singer/ songwriter who wrote more than 6,000 songs. He gained national fame in 1959 when Johnny Horton recorded Driftwood's song "The Battle of New Orleans." Even after Driftwood had risen to fame, he continued living in rural Stone County, spending most of his time promoting and preserving the music and heritage of the Ozark Mountains.

Jimmy Driftwood was born James Corbett Morris in West Richwoods (Stone County) near Mountain View (Stone County) on June 20, 1907, to Neal and Allie Risner-Morris. He was given the name Driftwood as the result of a joke his grandfather had played on his grandmother. When the two went to visit their new grandson, Driftwood's grandfather arrived first and wrapped a bundle of old sticks in a blanket. When Driftwood's grandmother arrived, she was handed the bundle and remarked, "Why, it ain't nothing but driftwood."

Music played a large role in Driftwood's life from his earliest years. His father, a farmer by trade, was also an accomplished folk singer, and it was through him and other local musicians that Driftwood was first exposed to the songs of the Ozarks. While still a small child, Driftwood learned to play the guitar his grandfather had made from a piece of a rail fence and other salvaged materials. He would continue to play this unusual-looking instrument throughout his career; it became his trademark and is currently on display in the Arkansas Entertainers Hall of Fame in Pine Bluff (Jefferson County).

Driftwood was a good student during his eight short school terms in the one-room school at Richwoods (Stone County). Although he had

Jimmy Driftwood of Mountain View, a prolific folk singer/songwriter who achieved fame for his song, "The Battle of New Orleans"; circa 1955.

Courtesy: Arkansas History Commission

not attended high school, he passed the Arkansas Teachers Exam when he was sixteen. He spent the next few years teaching in one-room schoolhouses in Prim (Cleburne County), Roasting Ear Creek (Stone County), Timbo (Stone County), and Fifty-six (Stone County), while attending high school in Mountain View. After graduating in 1928, he attended Arkansas State Teachers College (now the University of Central Arkansas) in Conway (Faulkner County), before eventually attending John Brown College (now John Brown University) in Siloam Springs (Benton County). In addition to teaching, Driftwood played the fiddle at local dances and other venues to earn money for college.

Driftwood left college before receiving a degree and rambled for a while, eventually ending up in Arizona. While in Phoenix, he won a local talent show, which led to weekly performances on a local radio station. He left Phoenix in 1935 and returned to Stone County to teach in Timbo. Although he had been writing songs and poetry for years, it was at Timbo that Driftwood began teaching his students history through song. It was also there that he fell in love with a former student, Cleda Johnson. They were married on November 26, 1936. The couple had three sons.

After his marriage to Cleda, Driftwood continued to teach at area schools as well as write songs and play folk music. In 1947, the couple was able to purchase the 150-acre farm where they would live the rest of their lives. After years of taking summer and night classes, Driftwood finally received his BSE degree from Arkansas State Teachers College on May 29, 1949, and, with it, became principal of the school in Snowball (Searcy County).

In the early 1950s, Driftwood began testing the waters of commercial music. He submitted songs he had written to several record companies, including Blasco Music Company and Shelter Music, both in Kansas City, Missouri. Both Shelter and Blasco recorded some of Driftwood's material, but with little commercial success. In 1957, Driftwood went to Nashville, Tennessee, and auditioned for RCA record executive Don Warden, who signed him to a recording contract. Driftwood, under the guidance of RCA's Chet Atkins, recorded his first album, titled *Jimmy Driftwood Sings Newly Discovered American Folk Songs*, in less than three hours. It was released in 1958 and saw limited success. The album featured "The Battle of New Orleans," a song Driftwood had composed in 1936 to help his students differentiate between the War of 1812 and the Revolutionary War. The song was a hit among those who heard it, but the strict broadcast standards of the day virtually excluded it from the airways because of the words "hell" and "damn" in the lyrics. After the release of Driftwood's album, he quit his job as principal of Snowball School and began making regular appearances at such popular country music venues as the Grand Ole Opry in Nashville, Tennessee; the *Ozark Jubilee* in Springfield, Missouri; and the *Louisiana Hayride* in Shreveport, Louisiana, where he met Johnny Horton, who expressed an interest in recording "The Battle of New Orleans." Driftwood revamped the song's lyrics to make them acceptable for radio.

Horton's recording of "The Battle of New Orleans" stayed on top of the country singles chart for ten weeks in 1959 and also held the top spot on the pop charts for six weeks. Partially because of the popularity of this song, Driftwood was asked to perform his traditional American music for Soviet premier Nikita Khrushchev during his visit to the United Nations in 1959. Driftwood and Horton took Song of the Year honors at the second Grammy Awards ceremony in 1959. Driftwood's "Wilderness Road" also received a Grammy nomination for Best Folk Performance of the Year in 1959, and the same year, Eddie Arnold received a Grammy nomination in both country and folk categories for his version of Driftwood's most-recorded song, "Tennessee Stud."

Driftwood received another Grammy nomination for the 1961 song "Billy Yank and Johnny Reb." During the next few years, Driftwood, often joined on stage by Cleda, performed at Carnegie Hall, the Grand Ole Opry, and major folk festivals. On March 31, 1962, Driftwood was elevated from a regular guest to starring member of the Grand Ole Opry. He also returned to the educational profession in 1962, teaching folklore at the University of Southern California in Idyllwild. Driftwood also released his final album on the RCA label, *Driftwood at Sea*. However, the album sold poorly, and Driftwood longed to return to Stone County.

In 1963, Driftwood returned to Timbo. He helped to form the Rackensack Folklore

Singer/songwriter Jimmy Driftwood playing the fiddle at his home in Timbo; circa 1964.
Courtesy: Arkansas History Commission

Society, was one of the visionaries in creating the Arkansas Folk Festival in Mountain View, and was a leading force in the establishment of the Ozark Folk Center. Having more national notoriety than anyone else involved in Arkansas's folk scene, Driftwood was largely responsible for promoting and securing funding for folk celebrations and the folk center. He astounded city officials by obtaining $2.1 million toward the construction of the center from the Ways and Means Committee of the House of Representatives.

Driftwood also became involved in environmental issues. He helped secure the designation of the Buffalo River as the first national river and helped persuade the United States Forest Service to develop and promote the Blanchard Springs Caverns. He held several prominent positions, including chairman of the Arkansas Parks and Tourism Commission, member of the Advisory Committee of the John F. Kennedy Center for the Performing Arts and the National Advisory Board for the National Endowment for the Arts, and musicologist for the National Geographic Society, producing *Music of the Ozarks*, the society's first album of American folk music

In 1975, Driftwood was relieved of his position as musical director of the Ozark Folk Center. This controversial removal caused a backlash among Driftwood's friends and musical companions in the Rackensack Folklore Society. The majority of Rackensackers, who had been the heart of the folk center's programs, cut ties with the folk center and left in search of a new performance venue. Driftwood purchased a three-acre plot of land north of the folk center, and by 1976, he and the Rackensackers had built a simple wood-frame building for the performance of traditional Arkansas folk music.

Driftwood died on July 12, 1998, in Fayetteville (Washington County), where he had been hospitalized. His ashes were scattered on his farm near Timbo.

For additional information:

Jimmy Driftwood Legacy Project. http://www.jimmydriftwoodlegacyproject.com (accessed February 8, 2013).

Lucas, Ann Davenport. "The Music of Jimmy Driftwood." *Mid-America Folklore* 15 (Spring 1987): 27–41.

Streeter, Richard Kent. *The Jimmy Driftwood Primer.* Calhoun, GA: The Jimmy Driftwood Legacy Project, 2003.

Zac Cothren

COUNTRY   RONNIE DUNN (1953–)

With a slew of chart-topping singles to his credit as half of the duo Brooks & Dunn, Ronnie Dunn established himself as a member of the most award-winning duo in country music. Though Arkansas is not considered his home state, he has earned a spot in its musical history.

Ronnie Gene Dunn was born on June 1, 1953, in Coleman, Texas, to Jesse Eugene Dunn and Gladys Inez Thurmon Dunn. His father was a musician who also worked in the oil fields and drove trucks; his mother was a devout Baptist who, in the 1960s, lived in El Dorado (Union County) and worked as a bookkeeper at the First National Bank and then as a telephone operator at Warren Brown Hospital. Dunn played the saxophone in El Dorado's school band while also honing his musical ear by listening to Ace Cannon records purchased for him by his father. He moved around the country, attending thirteen schools in twelve years in El Dorado, western Texas, New Mexico, and Oklahoma. After graduating from high school, he enrolled at Abilene Christian College in Texas with plans to become a Baptist preacher, but he was asked to leave the school after he was seen performing music in bars. Dunn then continued performing in Tulsa, Oklahoma.

In 1990, Dunn moved from Tulsa to Nashville, Tennessee, where he was subsequently introduced to Kix Brooks. The two songwriters quickly formed a partnership. Brooks & Dunn's first album, *Brand New Man* (1991), spawned the hit single "Boot Scootin' Boogie." The duo has since produced more than twenty hits and won more awards than any other duo in the genre of country music.

Dunn has three children with his wife, Janine, whom he married on May 19, 1990.

Brooks & Dunn have been named "Entertainers of the Year" three times by the Academy of Country Music (ACM) and once by the Country Music Association (CMA). In 2008, the duo published their first novel *The Adventures of Slim and Howdy*, with collaborator Bill Fitzhugh. Dunn was inducted

Ronnie Dunn customized guitar pick.
Courtesy: Old State House Museum Collection

into the Arkansas Entertainers Hall of Fame in 2002/2003. In August 2009, the duo announced it would split up upon completion of its last tour in 2010.

In 2011, Dunn released his first solo album, titled *Ronnie Dunn*.

For additional information:
Brooks & Dunn. http://www.brooks-dunn.com (accessed February 26, 2013).

Hill, Jack. "Brooks, Dunn to Play Something Country." *Arkansas Democrat-Gazette*, August 24, 2007, pp. 6W–7W.

"Ronnie Dunn Story." Online at http://rons_hangout.tripod.com/bio.html (accessed February 26, 2013).

Sculley, Alan. "For Brooks & Dunn, the Work Never Ends." *The Herald & Review*, August 15, 2008.

Elizabeth Whitaker

FOLK — EMMA DUSENBURY (1862–1941)

Emma Hays Dusenbury was an outstanding traditional singer; her work is represented by some 116 songs in the nation's leading folksong archive at the Library of Congress.

Emma Hays was born on January 9, 1862, probably in Habersham County or Rabun County, Georgia, to William Jasper Hays and Mary Jane Pitts. She came to Arkansas with her parents and four siblings in 1872, staying first in Crittenden County but eventually settling in Baxter County, near Gassville. Some-

Emma Dusenbury (right), with daughter Ora; circa 1930.
Courtesy: Special Collections, University of Arkansas Libraries, Fayetteville

time after 1880, she married Ernest Dusenbury, who was from Illinois. Two years later, they had a daughter. In about 1894 or 1895, she suffered a serious illness that left her blind.

Before settling near Mena (Polk County) in about 1907, Dusenbury lived an itinerant life; her husband worked railroad and packing plant jobs, and the whole family picked cotton in the summers. Dusenbury's husband died in 1933, leaving the family to live in poverty.

During the late 1920s and early 1930s, guided by F. M. Goodhue, a teacher at a nearby radical labor school, Commonwealth College, Dusenbury was recorded by some of the best-known folksong collectors in the region and nation. John Lomax, Vance Randolph (whose *Ozark Folksongs* lists November 1928 as the date of his first collecting from her), and Sidney Robertson all visited, as did poet John Gould Fletcher and Little Rock (Pulaski County) composer and symphony director Laurence Powell. All were greatly impressed; Lomax wrote in his autobiography that she sang continuously for two days and recorded more traditional Anglo-American ballads than any other singer.

Dusenbury's one brush with celebrity came in 1936 when she sang in Little Rock as part of the celebration of Arkansas's statehood centennial. Her photograph appeared in the newspaper, along with two feature articles about her (one written by Powell) that are even today the primary sources of information about her. Powell later based the final movement of his *Second Symphony* on three of her traditional songs.

Dusenbury's repertoire was more than simply large—it was remarkably varied, including many rarely recorded songs in addition to the old Anglo-American ballads especially prized by the collectors of the period. "Abraham's Proclamation," for example, a scoffing number denouncing President Lincoln's Emancipation Proclamation and believed by scholars to originate in blackface minstrelsy, has been collected from no other singer.

Dusenbury died on May 6, 1941; she is buried, as Emmer Duesberry, in the small community of Rocky (Polk County), near Mena.

For additional information:
Cochran, Robert. "'All the Songs in the World': The Story of Emma Dusenbury." *Arkansas Historical Quarterly* 44 (Spring 1985): 3–15.

Emma Dusenbury Folksong Collection. Special Collections. University of Arkansas Libraries, Fayetteville, Arkansas.

Robert B. Cochran

This entry, originally published in *Arkansas Biography: A Collection of Notable Lives*, appears in the *Encyclopedia of Arkansas Music* in an altered form. *Arkansas Biography* is available from the University of Arkansas Press in Fayetteville.

ROCK — E&M RECORDING COMPANY AND MY RECORDS

In the 1960s, Little Rock (Pulaski County) was home to E&M Recording Company, a studio owned by Earl Fox. The initials in the company name stood for "Earl" and "Myrna," Fox's wife. Through his two independent record labels, E&M Recording Company and My Records, which he established later, Fox provided a creative outlet and commercial venue for local singers and musical groups. My Records, in particular, played an important role in nourishing the creative energy released in the late 1960s profusion of central Arkansas rock and roll groups.

In 1959, Fox built a sound studio behind his house at 1612 South Buchanan Street in Little Rock; this was an avocational enterprise, which he undertook for his love of music and his desire to promote local bands. He adapted an old radio board for recording purposes. After three years, Fox rented a building at 12th Street and University Avenue for his growing business. He began issuing singles and albums under the E&M label. The music Fox recorded included jazz, blues, gospel, country, and rock. A notable local rock hit was Bobby Garrett's "Vampire" (1962).

In the 1960s, Fox moved his studios to 2911 West Markham Street because he needed more space. With the post-Beatles boom in the number of area "garage bands," Fox began recording hopeful groups on his new label, My Records, a subsidiary of E&M that enjoyed regional success with such singles as "I'll Find a Way" by the Romans (1966), "Suzanne" by the Egyptians (1966), "Burnin' Up the Wires" by the Dutch Masters (1967), "Midnight to Six Man" by the Culls (1967), "Tears of Blue" by the Coachmen (1967), and "Ain't No Need" by Merging Traffic (1967), who signed with Decca in 1968 and achieved minor national success with the single "Bit by Bit."

By the end of the decade, however, most of the local groups had disbanded. Fox continued his recording business, producing commercial and political jingles as well as music, but in the 1970s, he finally sold E&M; My Records had died two years earlier when the first wave of garage bands began disbanding as their members graduated from high school and went their separate ways. In 1999, the Butler Center for Arkansas Studies released an archival compact disc, *The Little Rock Sound, 1965–69*, featuring a representative selection of the My Records catalogue.

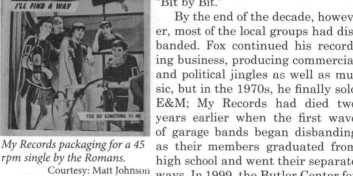

My Records packaging for a 45 rpm single by the Romans.
Courtesy: Matt Johnson

For additional information:
The Little Rock Sound, 1965–69. Liner notes by Bill Jones. Little Rock: Butler Center for Arkansas Studies, 1999.

William B. Jones Jr.

ROCK — EVANESCENCE

Evanescence, a popular alternative rock band from Little Rock (Pulaski County), is known for its dark themes and lyrical melodies.

Evanescence was established in 1999 when teenagers Amy Lee and Ben Moody (former lead guitarist) were at a summer camp in Arkansas. They started writing music together, playing together, and recording at their parents' houses. Eventually, the band gained worldwide recognition. Before deciding on the name Evanescence (which means dissipation or a disappearance, as with vapor), the group went through several names, including Childish Intentions and Stricken. The line-up included Lee as lead singer and pianist, guitarists John LeCompt and Terry Balsamo, bassist Will Boyd, and drummer Rocky Gray. Ben Moody left the band in October 2003.

Evanescence's music is a combination of classical-style music and hard rock. Amy Lee trained

Evanescence Albums/Media
Origin (2000)
Fallen (2003)
Daredevil movie soundtrack (2003)
Anywhere But Home, DVD (2004)
The Open Door (2006)
Evanescence (2011)

in classical piano for nine years, and the band uses a choir and string instruments. The rest of the band has the hard rock sound that gives the band the "alternative" label. This blend has led to several hits, such as "Bring Me to Life" and "My Immortal," both of which were in the top ten on the *Billboard* Hot 100. "Bring Me to Life" also reached No. 1 in the United Kingdom. These songs are found on *Fallen*, the band's first studio album released in 2003, and the *Daredevil* movie soundtrack. *Fallen* was ranked third on the *Billboard* 200 in June 2003 and was in the top ten for almost a year. In 2004, the band won Grammy Awards for Best Hard Rock Performance ("Bring Me to Life") and Best New Artist. *Origin*, an early full-length album (2000), contained several notable pieces, such as "Field of Innocence," "Anywhere," and "Lies."

The band's DVD, *Anywhere But Home* (2004), includes tour footage and a few new songs. In 2006, bassist Will Boyd left the band. Later that same year, Evanescence released its second studio album, *The Open Door*. On October 11, 2011, the band released its third studio album, the eponymous *Evanescence*.

Amy Lee in concert with Evanescence. Photo: Daigo Oliva

For additional information:
Evanescence. http://www.evanescence.com (accessed November 26, 2012).
Pareles, Jon. "In Every Note, the Pangs of the Heart." *New York Times*, November 2, 2011, http://www.nytimes.com/2011/11/03/arts/music/evanescence-at-terminal-5-review.html?_r=0 (accessed November 16, 2012).

Esther Jennings

DALE EVANS (1912–2001)

Dale Evans was an actress, author, and songwriter who was raised in Osceola (Mississippi County), where she attended school and met her first husband. She rose to fame as America's "Queen of the West" (sometimes called "Queen of the Cowgirls") alongside her fourth husband, Roy Rogers ("King of the Cowboys"). She starred in movies, television shows, and evangelical Christian programs. Evans wrote twenty-eight inspirational books and composed many songs, including the popular song of faith, "The Bible Tells Me So," as well as the iconic American standard, "Happy Trails."

Dale Evans was born in her grandparents' home at Uvalde, Texas, though her family lived in the nearby town of Italy. Her father, Walter Smith, was a middle-class farmer who also owned and operated a hardware store in the small town of Italy, which had about 1,000 residents. Her mother, Betty Sue Hillman Smith, was a homemaker. The evidence of her birth was an affidavit from her parents saying she was born Frances Octavia Smith on October 31, 1912, which she used for her driver's license and passport until it was misplaced in 1954. Requesting a birth certificate from the Texas Bureau of Vital Statistics, she was surprised to see it in the name of Lucille Wood Smith, born on October 30. Her mother insisted that she was born Frances Octavia and that the record keepers were wrong, though even her mother was unsure of the date, so October 31 was officially adopted.

At the age of three, she made her gospel singing solo debut at the Baptist church in Italy. When she was seven, the family—including her younger brother, Hillman—moved to Osceola, after her father's brother told stories of bountiful cotton fields in the Arkansas community. He failed to mention floods, boll weevils, and mosquitoes, and she later said the family's first year in Arkansas was "neither financially rewarding nor joyous." The next year was more successful.

After being taught the basics of reading, writing, and arithmetic by her mother, she entered school in Osceola for the first time at age seven. After spending a half year in the first grade, she was moved ahead to the third. She would also skip the seventh grade, arriving in the eighth grade at age eleven, at which point she suffered a nervous breakdown and was ordered to spend the summer in bed.

Even then, she took piano lessons, but her instructor quit, saying the child refused to practice her scales and instead improvised her own songs. She returned to school at age twelve as a freshman in high school. At a weekly public dance held at the courthouse, she met an older boy, Thomas Fox, and eloped with him at age fourteen. Lying about their ages, they were married at the home of a local minister in Blytheville (Mississippi County).

They moved to Memphis, Tennessee, where their son, Thomas Fox Jr., was born. She was seventeen when they were officially divorced in 1929, her husband believing that he was too young to be tied down to a wife and child.

In Memphis, she took courses in business school and worked as a secretary while aspiring to become a singer. After working at a bus company, she found a higher-paying job at an insurance agency, where her boss heard her singing at her desk. With his help, she found occasional work as a radio singer at WMC and WREC on programs sponsored by the insurance company. She became a local radio show regular under the names Frances Fox and Marian Lee.

(Some sources state that, in 1929 in Memphis, she married August Wayne Johns, divorcing in 1936. There were no children. In her au-tobiography, *Happy Trails*, she does not mention this union.)

Seeking a larger radio market, she moved with her son Tommy to Chicago, Illinois, in 1930, where she found few job prospects and was diagnosed with acute malnutrition. After recovering, she and Tommy moved to Louisville, Kentucky, where she found both a job at station WHAS and her final stage name. Station manager Joe Eaton renamed her Dale Evans because it was easy for radio announcers to pronounce. She gained popularity as a singer on the air and in clubs around Louisville.

However, her son became ill, and she decided to return to Texas so that he could stay with her parents, who had left Arkansas for their farm near the town of Italy. She found work as a singer at station WFAA in Dallas, joining her family in Italy on weekends. While in Texas, she heard from Robert Dale Butts, a pianist and orchestra leader she had known in Louisville. He moved to Dallas, also finding work at WFAA, and they were married in 1937.

With her son staying with her parents, the couple moved to Chicago, where Butts found work with the local NBC radio affiliate and she found singing jobs with big bands. One such engagement with the Anson Weeks Orchestra took her on a cross-country tour that lasted a year, including eight weeks in Los Angeles, California. There were no immediate job offers in California, but after the two returned to Chicago, she was invited by Hollywood agent Joe Rivkin to do a screen test for the movie *Holiday Inn* (released in 1942) with Bing Crosby and Fred Astaire. While she did not win the part, Rivkin became her agent, subtracting seven years from her age. He also encouraged her to remove her wedding ring and changed some details of her biography,

Actress, author, and songwriter Dale Evans of Osceola; circa 1950.

Courtesy: Roy Rogers–Dale Evans Museum, Branson, Missouri

most notably promoting the story that Tommy was her younger brother, not her son.

By 1942, Evans was signed to a one-year contract by 20th Century Fox and appeared in the films *Orchestra Wives* and *Girl Trouble* that same year. She became a regular on the *Edgar Bergen* radio show broadcast nationally from Hollywood, and she joined a USO troupe during World War II.

Moving from Fox to Republic Pictures, she worked in such western films as *In Old Oklahoma* (1943) opposite John Wayne. In 1944, *The Cowboy and the Senorita* paired her with cowboy star Roy Rogers (born Leonard Franklin Slye). They proved a popular pair and continued to co-star in such films as *Yellow Rose of Texas* (1944), *Lights of Old Santa Fe* (1944), and *Utah* (1945).

The acting team of Rogers and Evans was a success. Off screen, in 1945, Dale Evans was divorced from her husband, and the next year, Rogers's wife, Arlene Wilkins Rogers, died of an embolism one week after giving birth to their son, Roy Rogers Jr. (called Dusty). On December 31, 1947, Rogers and Evans were married at the Flying L Ranch near Davis, Oklahoma, where they had just completed filming *Home in Oklahoma*. After their wedding, they ended the falsehood about Tommy being Dale's brother and acknowledged him as her son.

In addition to Dale's son and Roy's children (Cheryl, Linda Lou, and Dusty from his marriage to Arlene), the couple had a daughter, Robin Elizabeth Rogers, on August 26, 1950. Robin died two years later of complications of Down's Syndrome, inspiring Dale to write a book in her honor, *Angel Unaware*. The couple became foster and adoptive parents to other special needs children: Dodie; Marion; Deborah Lee; who died in a bus accident at age twelve; and John David (Sandy), who died in an accident while in the peacetime army in Germany. To honor their lives, Evans wrote the books *Dearest Debbie* and *Salute to Sandy*.

In 1950, Dale Evans wrote the song, "Happy Trails," which Roy Rogers used as his theme song. Writing the lyrics on an envelope, she taught the melody to Rogers and the singing group, Sons of the Pioneers, only minutes before their radio show.

The couple made thirty-five films together and founded their own production company, Roy Rogers Productions. They created *The Roy Rogers Show* (1951–1957), *The Roy Rogers and Dale Evans Show* (1962), and *Happy Trails Theatre* (1986–1989). In 1973, they appeared in a television special called *Saga of Sonora*. In 1968, Roy Rogers licensed his name to a restaurant chain whose creators chose him as their namesake for his all-American wholesomeness; there were more than 600 restaurants at the chain's peak, many of which hosted personal appearances by Evans and Rogers.

Evans starred in her own weekly Christian TV program, *A Date with Dale*, from 1996 until her death in 2001. The couple owned a ranch in Apple Valley, California, and founded the Roy Rogers–Dale Evans Museum in nearby Victorville, where they often greeted fans. In 2003, the museum moved to Branson, Missouri, where the Roy Rogers Jr. family was involved in the daily operations of the 26,000-square-foot museum and the Happy Trails Theater, featuring live performances by Roy Rogers Jr. On October 6, 2009, the owners announced that the operation would close in December 2009 due to the economic downturn as well as declining attendance

Evans holds three stars on the Hollywood Walk of Fame, was inducted into the Texas Country Music Hall of Fame (2000) and the Cowgirl Hall of Fame (1995), and received the Cardinal Terrence Cook Humanities Award (1995).

After more than fifty years of marriage to Evans, Rogers died of heart failure in 1998. Evans died of heart failure on February 7, 2001. She was survived by six children, sixteen grandchildren, thirty-two great-grandchildren, and six great-great-grandchildren. She is buried beside Rogers at Sunset Hills Memorial Park in Apple Valley, California. Her work continues through the Roy Rogers–Dale Evans Happy Trails Foundation for abused children, which sponsors the annual Roy Rogers–Dale Evans Western Film Festival, which began in 1998, near their former ranch in California.

For additional information:

Enss, Chris, and Howard Kazanjian. *The Cowboy and the Senorita*. Guilford, CT: Falcon Press, 2004.

Rogers, Dale Evans. *Rainbow on a Hard Trail*. Tarrytown, NY: Revell Books, 1999.

Rogers, Dale Evans, and Roy Rogers, with Carlton Stowers. *Happy Trails: The Story of Roy Rogers and Dale Evans*. Waco, TX: Word Books, 1979.

White, Raymond. *King of the Cowboys, Queen of the West: Roy Rogers & Dale Evans*. Madison: University of Wisconsin Press, 2006.

Nancy Hendricks

COUNTRY BARBARA FAIRCHILD (1950–)

Throughout her career, Barbara Fairchild has been an influential singer and songwriter in both country and gospel music.

Barbara Fairchild was born in Lafe (Greene County) on November 12, 1950, to Opal and Ulys Fairchild. She was raised in Knobel (Clay County) until she and her family moved to St. Louis, Missouri, when she was thirteen. Fairchild's passion for performing began early; she first performed in front of an audience at age five in a school talent show.

Two years after moving to St. Louis, Fairchild released her first single, "Brand New Bed of Roses," for the Norman label, and it appeared on local television channels. After graduating from high school, Fairchild moved to Nashville, Tennessee, to pursue a career in country music. Within a few months, Fairchild met with Jerry Crutchfield of the MCA label, who was impressed with her songwriting talent. He soon hired her as a writer for MCA and sent her recording of "Love Is a Gentle Thing" to Columbia Records, landing Fairchild a record deal as well as a spot in the top seventy on the country charts. Fairchild then released several somewhat successful singles, as well as three albums: *Someone Special* (1970), *Love's Old Song* (1971), and *A Sweeter Love* (1972).

Fairchild's greatest country music achievement was "The Teddy Bear Song" from her third album. This number-one country single and top-forty pop single also garnered Fairchild a Grammy nomination. She later received another Grammy nomination in the Music for Children category with "Lullaby for Teddy." Between 1972 and 1978, Fairchild released several albums, such as *Love Is a Gentle Thing* (1974), and charted ten singles, such as "You've Lost that Lovin' Feelin'" and "Cheatin' Is."

After this period, her country career reached something of a plateau, and none of her recordings between 1978 and 1980 achieved top-forty status. She moved to San Antonio, Texas, in an effort to repair her failing marriage with Randy Reinhard and to spend time with her children. The two eventually divorced, and she later married evangelistic singer/songwriter Milton Car-

roll in 1982. They divorced in 2002, and she later married Roy Morris, a gospel singer/songwriter with whom Fairchild has recorded several albums.

In 1986, Fairchild returned to Nashville in an unsuccessful attempt at making a comeback in country music. It was not until 1989, when she was invited to join the gospel group Heirloom, that she began recording music again. From 1989 onward, Fairchild recorded only gospel music and has had a successful career through solo as well as collaborative albums. In 1990, Heirloom released the album *Apples of Gold*, which had two successful singles, "Prayin' up a Storm" and "Suffer the Little Children."

Barbara Fairchild in Branson, Missouri.
Photo: Lou Sander

In 1991, Fairchild released her first solo gospel album, *The Light*. In 1992, she moved to Branson, Missouri, to perform in *The Mel Tillis Show*, a stint that lasted two years. She was also a regular on *The Jim Stafford Show* in 1993. That same year, she started her own show in Branson. She also began a weekly Sunday morning worship service at Music City Centre theater with her husband, in addition to regularly touring the country performing with him.

In 2000, Fairchild embarked on a tour titled "Take America Back," in which she honored veterans as well as current U.S. troops. She is a spokesperson for Feed the Children, a sponsor for the Foster Grandparents Organization, and a member of Concerned Women of America.

Fairchild has appeared on several television shows, such as *The Gene Williams Country TV Show* in Branson, *Ralph Emery's Nashville Now* on CNN, and *Country Music Reunion*, hosted by Bill Anderson on RFD-TV. On September 21, 2003, Fairchild was inducted into the George

D. Hay Music Hall of Fame, and in September 2010, she was inducted into the Arkansas Entertainers Hall of Fame.

For additional information:

Barbara Fairchild. http://www.barbarafairchild.com (accessed March 1, 2013).

"Barbara Fairchild." Branson Tourism Center. http://www.bransontourismcenter.com/bransonarticle85.htm (accessed February 25, 2013).

Finzer, Beth. "Singer Fairchild Sets Out to Take America Back." *Arkansas Democrat-Gazette*, Northwest Edition, June 2, 2000, p. 2.

Darby Burdine

ROCK | TAV FALCO (1945–)

Tav Falco is an innovative rock musician who combines rockabilly, blues, and fractured noise in a genre known as psychobilly. He has created films and documentaries about musicians and the cultural scene in Memphis, Tennessee, in addition to touring across the globe. The *New York Times* describes Falco as a "singer, guitarist and researcher of musical arcane who hasn't let his increasingly technical expertise and idiomatic mastery compromise the clarity of his vision."

Tav Falco was born Gustavo Antonio Falco on May 25, 1945, to Rita Rose Falco on the East Coast. After his mother married Horace Homer Nelson, a sailor from Arkansas, they settled in the rural land between Gurdon (Clark County) and Whelen Springs (Clark County), where Falco was raised. Falco moved to Memphis in the late 1960s and started his career as a documentary filmmaker with an art-action group called TeleVista. He trained in photography and filmmaking under famous photographer William Eggleston during his early years in Memphis. Falco then began seeking out blues and rockabilly artists to film their performances, filming artists such as R. L. Burnside, Charlie Feathers, and Jessie Mae Hemphill. Inspired by the performances of these artists and becoming interested in the relationship between performer and observer, Falco began playing the guitar. His first performance was in 1978 at the Orpheum in

Tav Falco (right) with George Reinecke and Lorette Velvette of Panther Burns.
Photo: Mike Keckhaver

Memphis in the middle of a concert by Mud Boy & the Neutrons, in which he played a few songs and then proceeded to use a chainsaw to shred his guitar to pieces; he then promptly passed out. This outrageous performance was met with mixed reactions, but Falco certainly revealed his capacity to captivate an audience with his unique sound, style, and performance methods.

In 1979, Falco formed a group called Panther Burns, named after the legend of a plantation in Mississippi that supposedly was terrorized by a panther to the point that the people living on the plantation trapped the panther in a canebrake and set it on fire. The earliest members of the frequently changing group were Falco, Alex Chilton, and James Luther (Jim) Dickinson. The group has lived up to the intensity of their name; they quickly gained popularity in the Memphis area for their unusual harsh noise, and their shows became extremely popular, featuring guests such as rockabilly legend Charlie Feathers. Panther Burns released their first EP in 1981, titled *Behind the Magnolia Curtain*. The album was met with a great deal of success, and the group's members decided to move to New York City to further their musical careers. In 1982, they released their first and only major record label album, *Blow Your Top*. Although this album was not very successful on the charts and met with mixed reviews, it did garner the group a spread in Andy Warhol's *Interview* magazine, as well as attention from several *New York Times* critics. Throughout the 1980s and 1990s, Falco traveled back and forth between Europe and the United States, touring with Panther Burns throughout Europe and playing several small roles in films in America such as *Great Balls of Fire, Wayne County, Downtown 81*, and *Highway 61*. Falco also studied and observed Latin music and dancing, particularly the tango, and danced the tango in the film *Dans Le Rouge du Couchant* in Paris, France, in 2003.

Falco continued performing with Panther

Burns between 2005 and 2010 at several large venues such as the "It Came from Memphis" series in London, England, in 2005; the Arthur Nights Festival in Los Angeles, California, in 2006; the Fondatin Cartier in Paris in 2007; the Strade Blu Festival in Tredozio, Italy, in 2008 (headliner); the Alternatilla Festival in Mallorca, Spain, in 2009; and the Barreiro Rocks Festival in Lisbon, Portugal, in 2010. The band then became Tav Falco and the Unapproachable Panther Burns, releasing *Conjurations: Séance for Deranged Lovers* in May 2010.

In addition to performing music and acting, Falco has created several short films on varying subjects, but mostly regarding "underground" city life in Memphis. Five of the films were added to the official archive of the Cinémathèque Française in Paris in 2006. Falco also collabo-rated with rock writer Erik Morse in writing a two-volume encyclopedia titled *Mondo Memphis*, which is a musical history and psychogeographic study of Memphis, released in 2011 (vol. 1) and 2012 (vol. 2).

For additional information:
Morse, Erik. "Tav Falco." *Bomb Magazine* (Spring 2008). http://bombsite.com/issues/103/articles/3102 (accessed March 18, 2013).
"Tav Falco." AllMusic.com. http://www.allmusic.com/artist/tav-falco-mn0000016147 (accessed March 18, 2013).
"Tav Falco." http://www.limbos.org/tavfalco/ (accessed March 18, 2013).
"Tav Falco: Sexual, Abandoned, Political." *L.A. Record*, November 10, 2011. http://larecord.com/interviews/2011/11/10/tav-falco-sexual-abandoned-political (accessed April 17, 2013).

Darby Burdine

CLASSICAL / OPERA "FAYETTEVILLE POLKA"

"Fayetteville Polka" was written by Austrian immigrant Ferdinand Zellner in honor of his adopted hometown of Fayetteville (Washington County). It was accepted for publication in 1856, becoming what is said to be the first published piece of sheet music by an Arkansan.

Ferdinand Zellner came to the United States in 1850, when the showman P. T. Barnum brought Swedish soprano Jenny Lind from Europe to the United States on a concert tour that ran through 1852. Called the "Swedish Nightingale," she was one of the greatest coloratura sopranos of the nineteenth century, possessing a voice of outstanding range and quality. Zellner, a young Austrian violinist, accompanied her on her prestigious U.S. tour.

At the end of Lind's U.S. tour in 1852, she returned to Europe, but Zellner stayed in Arkansas. By 1854, he was professor of music at Sophia Sawyer's Fayetteville Female Seminary. In her journal, Marian Tebbetts of Fayetteville, a student at the time, noted that while he was so educated in music as to have been Lind's violinist, he could not sing. Therefore, he concentrated on teaching, performing on the violin, and writing music.

In 1856, Zellner traveled to St. Louis, Missouri, and visited the noted musical publishing house Balmer and Weber. That year, Balmer and Weber published his composition, "Fayetteville Polka," written in honor of his adopted town. The lively three-part polka was dedicated to Katy Smith, a student at Sawyer's school who came from a prominent local family. According to the Old State House Museum in Little Rock (Pulaski County), "Fayetteville Polka" was the first piece of sheet music by an Arkansan to be published.

Sheet music for "Fayetteville Polka."
Courtesy: Special Collections, University of Arkansas Libraries, Fayetteville

The song was well received at the time of its publication and is still performed by regional musicians at events sponsored by the Washington County Historical Society and other local organizations. It was the theme song for the play *Second to None*, which was presented at the Walton Arts Center in 1999.

For additional information:
Allison, Charlie. "Ferdinand Zellner: Fayetteville's First Composer." *Flashback* 62 (Spring 2012): 3–26.
Banes, Marian Tebbetts. *The Journal of Marian Tebbetts Banes.* Fayetteville, AR: Washington County Historical Society, 1977.
Campbell, William S. *One Hundred Years of Fayetteville 1828–1928.* Fayetteville, AR: Washington County Historical Society, 1977.

Nancy Hendricks

Narvel Felts (1938–)

Albert Narvel Felts is a singer and songwriter best known for a string of commercially successful country music recordings in the 1970s. Over the course of his career, Felts has been known for performing a wide range of music, including rockabilly, pop, R&B, soul, and gospel, but it is his traditional country and rockabilly recordings that gained him the most attention.

Sheet music to the Narvel Felts's recording of "Reconsider Me"; 1969.

Courtesy: Old State House Museum Collection

Narvel Felts was born on November 11, 1938, near Keiser (Mississippi County) to Albert and Lena Felts. In 1953, when he was fourteen, the family, including Felts and his older sister Ogareeda, relocated eighty miles north to the community of Powe, Missouri.

As a teenager, Felts taught himself to play a guitar that, he has said, "was held together with wire." He bought the guitar with $15 he had saved from working in the cotton fields. This was the same guitar he was playing when a deejay "discovered" Felts singing a cover of "Blue Suede Shoes" during a talent show at his high school in nearby Bernie, Missouri. The rockabilly performance led to a Saturday afternoon program on KDEX in Dexter, Missouri.

Felts recorded for Sun Records in the 1950s, where he has said he was mentored by Roy Orbison and Johnny Cash. In the early 1950s, he joined the Rockets and became the front man for the band in 1956. The group cut records for Mercury Records, five of which were released as singles in 1959. Throughout the 1960s, he continued to pursue his music career but also focused on his young family, including wife Loretta (Stanfield) and children Stacia and Narvel "Bub" Felts Jr. (who would grow up to tour as the drummer in his father's band until his death in 1995 at age thirty-one in a traffic accident).

Sometime in the mid-1970s, Felts's manager began to promote him as a solo act. Felts had his first success on the charts in 1973 with a country cover of the song "Drift Away," a big mainstream hit for Dobie Gray that same year. It was the first of a string of hit songs throughout the decade, first on the Cinnamon label and, after it folded, for the Dot label, which was owned by ABC at the time.

His 1975 single "Reconsider Me" peaked at number two on the country music charts in the United States; the song was a number-one country music hit in Canada. When ABC Records was absorbed by MCA, Felts lost his contract and has since released only sporadic albums on minor labels. He never again charted an album or single.

Felts is a member of the Rockabilly Hall of Fame. He lives in Malden, Missouri.

For additional information:
"Narvel Felts." Allmusic.com. http://www.allmusic.com/artist/narvel-felts-mn0000375287 (accessed March 13, 2013).
"Narvel Felts." My Kind of Country. http://www.mkoc.com/narvelfelts/bio.htm (accessed March 13, 2013).
Whitburn, Joel. *Joel Whitburn Presents Hot Country Songs 1944 to 2008*. Menomonee Falls, WI: Record Research 2009.

Keith Merckx

Fiddlin' Bob Larkan & His Music Makers

Fiddlin' Bob Larkan was a well-known country fiddle player whose Music Makers band played on the radio stations of charlatan medical messiahs Dr. John R. Brinkley and Norman Baker and made a number of recordings. The group's song "Higher Up the Monkey Climbs" became notorious for its suggestive, ribald lyrics. Although "Larkan" was the correct spelling of Bob Larkan's name, record companies and even his hometown newspaper in his obituary rendered the name "Larkin."

Robert William (Bob) Larkan was born on November 18, 1867, in New York City, his father having migrated from Ireland and his mother from England. A musical child, he learned the violin, banjo, and guitar. The family moved to Boone County, Missouri, by 1870. In 1888, he married a woman named Hattie (Harriett) and moved first to Tollville (Prairie County) and then settled in Hazen (Prairie County). His wife played the organ, and their nine daughters and five sons formed the base of a well-known local band. Larkan acquired the nicknames "Fiddlin' Bob" or "Uncle Bob" after winning a number of fiddling contests. On one occasion, his winning prize consisted of twelve dollars, a barrel of flour, and twenty-six chicks; the chicks he raised in a box by his bed. In 1927, he was proclaimed the champion fiddler of the state of Arkansas after being picked by listeners in a fiddle contest held by KUOA, at that time the radio station of the University of Arkansas (UA) in Fayetteville (Washington County). According to the news release, Larkan was also a composer, played on a Stradivarius violin, and held the title of the state's champion live-bird shooter. In 1928, he won the fiddling contest for a second time.

With the advent of radio, the group began playing on local stations. The notorious quack doctor John R. Brinkley created station KFKB in 1923 in Milford, Kansas, and used country music to attract a large audience and to lure patients to his hospital. By 1925, Fiddlin' Bob Larkan & His Music Makers were playing two morning shows and another in the afternoon, accounting for two and a half hours of air time. The family was still living in Milford in 1930. After Brinkley was forced off the air in Kansas and opened XER in Mexico, the group briefly followed. They also played for another infamous medical entrepreneur, Norman Baker, on his radio station, XENT. The group probably disbanded before 1940 as Larkan's asthma worsened.

Their enduring fame came from the twelve songs they recorded for the OKeh and Vocalion record companies in February and November of 1928. The Music Makers consisted only of family members, with Larkan's son Forrest playing the piano, and his daughter Alice and her husband, William Sherbs, on guitars. In addition to "Higher Up the Monkey Climbs" (also known as "The Seneca Square Dance"), in which Larkan also sang the lyrics, and the risqué "The Women Wear No Clothes At All," the group also played tributes to Arkansas with "Arkansas Waltz" and "Prairie County Waltz."

Bob Larkan died of asthma on January 23, 1942, at his home in Hazen. The local newspaper described him as a "retired farmer and sportsman," mentioning that he had run the state's trapshooting contest for the Peters Ammunition Company. He was survived by five sons and seven daughters and is buried at DeValls Bluff (Prairie County). The *Arkansas Gazette* seems not to have mentioned his death.

For additional information:

Juhnke, Eric S. *Quacks and Crusaders: The Fabulous Careers of John Brinkley, Norman Baker, and Harry Hoxsey*. Lawrence: University Press of Kansas, 2002.

Russell, Tony. *Country Music Originals: The Legends and the Lost*. New York: Oxford University Press, 2007.

———. *Country Music Records: A Discography*. New York: Oxford University Press, 2004.

Michael B. Dougan

COUNTRY   "LEFTY" FRIZZELL (1928–1975)

William Orville "Lefty" Frizzell was virtually the prototype of what became known as honky-tonk singers—plainspoken vocalists whose regional roots were immaterial because they sounded as friendly as a storytelling neighbor. Willie Nelson remarked that "without Lefty Frizzell, a lot of us singers wouldn't have a style."

Lefty Frizzell was born on March 31, 1928, in Corsicana, Texas, but he soon moved from one small town to another in Arkansas, Louisiana, and Texas as the son of an oilfield worker. Country singer David Frizzell is his younger brother. He debuted as a singer on radio station KELD in El Dorado (Union County) when he was twelve, and he acquired his nickname in a schoolyard brawl. He is widely regarded as one of the most influential singers in country music history.

At eighteen and already married, Frizzell began appearing on radio station KGFL in Roswell, New Mexico. These radio appearances, as well as his concerts, were immensely popular and landed him recording deals with the Columbia label. His first hit single was "If You've Got the Money, Honey, I've Got the Time" in 1950. His next, the same year, was the flip side, "I Love You a Thousand Ways," a song he composed while serving a six-month jail term for statutory rape. He was invited to appear at the Grand Ole Opry in 1950. His last No. 1 hit was "Saginaw, Michigan" in 1964.

Frizzell was not praised in his lifetime as a definitive country singer, but he influenced multitudes that came after him. He virtually crooned his lyrics in a conversational, vowel-rolling style that made hardcore honky-tonk music palatable to many who otherwise shunned it. Among his most famous recordings was his original 1959 version of "The Long Black Veil," an "instant" folk song written by Danny Dill and Marijohn Wilkin, which became an international standard in Frizzell's stark, no-frills reading of it.

Frizzell made recordings until his July 19, 1975, death, which was caused by a stroke (possibly a consequence of his almost lifelong addiction to alcohol). He is buried in Goodlettsville, Tennessee. In 1982, he was inducted into the Country Music Hall of Fame.

For additional information:
Hemphill, Paul. *The Nashville Sound: Bright Lights and Country Music.* New York: Simon and Schuster, 1970.
Horstman, Dorothy. *Sing Your Heart Out, Country Boy.* Nashville, TN: Country Music Foundation Press, 1996.
"Lefty Frizzell." Country Music Hall of Fame and Museum. http://countrymusichalloffame.org/full-list-of-inductees/view/lefty-frizzell (accessed February 26, 2013).

Jim Kelton

G

GARAGE BANDS

ROCK

With the arrival of the Beatles on American shores in 1964, the "British Invasion" became a national pop-culture phenomenon. Representing the second generation of rock and roll, wave after wave of English rock groups—such as the Rolling Stones, the Animals, and the Who—followed the Beatles during the next two years. Teenagers across the United States were inspired to form four- or five-member bands patterned after their British role models. Because they often practiced in garages, these amateur groups came to be known as "garage bands."

Like many mid-sized American cities, Little Rock (Pulaski County) witnessed a mid-1960s explosion in the number of neighborhood teenage groups, all competing for school, fraternity house, or country club engagements. Other cities and towns in Arkansas, such as Hot Springs (Garland County), Fayetteville (Washington County), Jonesboro (Craighead County), and Pine Bluff (Jefferson County), experienced the garage-band boom, but Little Rock offered several advantages to groups hoping for a shot at fame. Aspiring rock stars found their favorite

My Records recording artists Merging Traffic; circa mid-1960s.
Courtesy: Harold Ott/Psych of the South

records at Moses Melody Shop on Main Street and occasionally performed there for Saturday KALO radio broadcasts. Some cut demo discs at Jaggars Recording Studio on South Johnson Street, while others who wanted a shot at the Top 40 taped sessions for commercial release through E&M Recording Company and My Records at 2911 West Markham Street. (Although most of the bands cutting records were from Little Rock, out-of-town groups such as the Egyptians, from Hot Springs, also recorded for the My Records label.)

The Spyders were among the first of the Little Rock garage bands, forming in 1964. The band was made up of Ralph Payne, lead guitar; Wally Lehle, rhythm guitar; Dane Fulmer, vocals; Ron Hughes, vocals; Doug Fulmer, drums; and Jim Vaughter, bass. The group made one recording at Jaggars Studio, in one take with one microphone.

The Checkmates featured Mark Abernathy, lead vocals; Jim Pearsall, bass; Mike McCarroll, drums; Larry Storthz, rhythm guitar and vocals; and Chip Payne, lead guitar.

Another early group, the Coachmen, was one of the most popular and long-lasting, featuring vocalist Dave Mayo; drummer Steve Hockersmith; guitarists Tommy Roberts and Johnny Baumgardner; and bassist Buck McArthur. Their self-released 1966 single, "Jamie" / "Stand By Me," harkened back to pre-Beatles rhythm and blues influences, while their 1967 My Records release showcased two polished, original songs, the ballad-like "Tears of Blue" and the Stax-Volt-flavored "I've Had Enough."

Matching the Coachmen in professional perfectionism and popularity were the Romans, consisting of Gary Hall (lead vocals, rhythm guitar), Phil Miller (lead guitar), Rocky Hestes (keyboard, vocals), Charles Wycott (bass), and Greg Kempner (drums). The group had a local hit with a 1966 My Records single, the Byrds-influenced "I'll Find a Way." Reconstituted in 1967 as Merging Traffic, the group expanded with new members Richard Shook (bass, vocals), Bob Younts (sax, vocals), Bobby Lincoln (trumpet), and Jim Matthews (who replaced Kempner on drums). After scoring well locally with the 1968 My Records release "Ain't No Need," on which the band displayed a mastery of the Memphis horn sound, Merging Traffic was signed by Decca, a major label, and had a minor national hit with "Bit By Bit."

A band that blended what would come to be called "alternative" music with mainstream pop and soul was the Culls. Steve Baldwin (vocals), Dan Kenner (lead guitar), Mike Anders (rhythm guitar), Dub Elrod (bass), and Jim Orahood (drums) explored lesser-known material by the Yardbirds, Them, and the Kinks. Their 1967 My Records cover of the Pretty Things' "Midnight to Six Man," paired with the Burt Bacharach standard, "Walk on By," received a lot of radio airplay and became a kind of cult favorite, surfac-

Little Rock's Dutch Masters; circa mid-1960s.

Courtesy: Harold Ott/Psych of the South

ing some years later on a British album devoted to American garage bands.

Another notable Little Rock group of the era was the Dutch Masters, an experimentally daring group with a proto-punk attitude, headed by Blake Schaefer. The Light Brigade, a true house-party band led by brothers Lonnie and Ronnie Cole, lasted longer than any of the others, playing gigs across the southeast United States for several years. The garage bands of the 1960s set the stage for the growth of a vibrant rock-music scene in Little Rock with the garage-band revival of the 1980s and 1990s. The efforts of these various bands were archived on a compact disc, *The Little Rock Sound, 1965–69*, compiled by Bill Jones and issued by the Butler Center for Arkansas Studies in 1999.

For additional information:

Hall, Ron. *Playing for a Piece of the Door: A History of Garage and Frat Bands in Memphis*, 1960–1975. Memphis: Shangri-La, 2001.

Hicks, Michael. *Sixties Rock: Garage, Psychedelic, and Other Satisfactions*. Urbana: University of Illinois Press, 1999.

The Little Rock Sound, 1965–69. Liner notes by Bill Jones. Little Rock: Butler Center for Arkansas Studies, 1999.

William B. Jones Jr.

FOLK

OLLIE GILBERT (1892–1980)

Both a local and national celebrity, Ollie Eva Woody Gilbert, known popularly as Aunt Ollie, performed with Jimmy Driftwood, Woody Guthrie, and many other folk musicians who have come to define the voice of the Great Depression. Venues ranged from friends' and family members' front porches and living rooms in the Ozark Mountains to Cow Palace in San Francisco, California; the Grand Ole Opry in Nashville, Tennessee; and Madison Square Garden in New York City.

The eighth of thirteen children of James (Jim) Franklin Woody and Mary Minerva Balentine Woody, Ollie Eva Woody was born on October 17, 1892, in the Hickory Grove area of Stone County. She learned to play the banjo at the age of five. Her instrument was made from a garden gourd with a squirrel hide stretched over it, and

it had horsehair strings. The stories her mother told about the Civil War and the family's move from Tennessee to settle in Arkansas greatly influenced her life and her music.

On July 29, 1909, just a few months before her sixteenth birthday, she married twenty-four-year-old Ewell Oscar Gilbert. They had eight children. Her husband not only was a banjo picker himself but was known for his beautiful singing voice. Together, they played at parties, church gatherings, and other social occasions.

Ollie Gilbert was recorded by noted folklorist and musicologist Alan Lomax when he made his "Southern Journey" in 1959–1960, and appeared in his collection when it was released by Prestige Records in the early 1960s. She recorded more than 400 songs for Max Hunter. Folklorist John Quincy Wolf recorded her multiple times,

Ollie Gilbert playing banjo at her home; circa 1970.
Courtesy: Larry Gilbert

including her performances at the Arkansas Folk Festival in 1963 and 1964. She was an early member of the Rackensack Folklore Society and sang on volume one of *The Rackensack* (Rimrock, 1972) and later volumes released by the society.

She performed across the state and nation, including at three separate concerts given at the University of California at Los Angeles Folk Festival on May 14–16, 1965, as well as the Festival of American Folklife on July 1–5, 1970, at the National Mall in Washington DC. In 1972, she was recorded on the album *Music of the Ozarks: A Sounds of the World Recording* (National Geographic Society, 1972). In 1977, she appeared in *All You Need Is Love: The Story of Popular Music*, a seventeen-part television documentary series first broadcast in 1976, as well as on the Alan Lomax album *The Gospel Ship* (New World Records, 1977).

Gilbert continued performing, especially at the Arkansas Folk Festival, up until her death on September 17, 1980. She and her husband are buried at Timbo Cemetery.

For additional information:
Blevins, Brooks. *Hill Folks: A History of Arkansas Ozarkers and Their Image*. Chapel Hill: University of North Carolina Press, 2002.
Cochran, Robert. *Our Own Sweet Sounds: A Celebration of Popular Music in Arkansas*. 2nd ed. Fayetteville: University of Arkansas Press, 2005.
John Quincy Wolf Jr. Collection. Regional Studies Center. Lyon College, Batesville, Arkansas. Online at http://web.lyon.edu/wolfcollection/ (accessed April 29, 2013).
Max D. Hunter Collection of Ozark Folksongs, 1956–1976. Springfield-Greene County Library, Springfield, Missouri. Online at http://maxhunter.missouristate.edu/ (accessed April 29, 2013).
Shoudel, Pearl W. *Some Remarkable Women of Arkansas*. Little Rock: Arkansas IWY Co-ordinating Committee, 1977.

Freda Cruse Hardison

COUNTRY | LONNIE GLOSSON (1908–2001)

Lonnie Elonzo Glosson popularized the harmonica nationwide and had a hand in several hit songs during a time when radio stations employed harmonica orchestras. From a young age, Glosson's ability and versatility on the harmonica stood out.

Lonnie Marvin Glosson was born the seventh of eleven children on February 14, 1908, in Judsonia (White County) to Cora Busby Glosson and George H. Glosson. He later changed his middle name to Elonzo because he did not like the uncle after whom he was named. Glosson's mother taught him the harmonica after he earned money to buy the instrument by picking cotton: "She showed me how to play 'Home Sweet Home,' and I took it from there." His father owned a boat dock and bait shop and picked mussel shells for a button factory in Newport (Jackson County). George Glosson's parents had come to Prospect Bluff (later renamed Judsonia)

Lonnie Glosson; circa 1985.
Courtesy: Ozark Cultural Resource Center

from North Carolina in the 1850s.

Hoboing around the United States, Lonnie Glosson earned a living playing harmonica in barber shops, on street corners, and on radio stations. From KMOX in St. Louis, Missouri, Glosson went to WLS's *National Barn Dance* in Chicago, Illinois, where he was paired with Gene Autry. Glosson recorded for Paramount's Broadway label in the early 1930s and also recorded for the Decca and Mercury labels. Glosson's early records were of the hillbilly boogie variety, but to survive as a performer, Glosson had to be versatile; he could just as easily sing and play a blues, gospel, or pop song. He also played guitar. The Country Music Hall of Fame cites his 1936 song, "Arkansas Hard Luck Blues," as "an early example of the talking blues popularized by Woody Guthrie and Bob Dylan."

In 1930, Glosson married Ruth Moore of

Providence (White County); they soon divorced but remarried again in 1931 and eventually had six children. His partnership with harmonica player Wayne Raney of Wolf Bayou (Cleburne County) also lasted decades. By 1938, they had a program on KARK radio in Little Rock (Pulaski County), later hosting a national show on WCKY in Cincinnati, Ohio. Glosson and Raney also sold millions of mail-order harmonicas over the airwaves. In 1949, their "Why Don't You Haul Off and Love Me," with Raney on vocals and Hot Springs (Garland County) native Henry Glover producing, reached number one on the charts. They recorded several songs with the Delmore Brothers, including the Delmores' massive hit, "Blues Stay Away From Me," co-written and produced by Glover, the same year.

Glosson delved more into gospel as the years wore on, self-issuing songs such as "For Christmas Give Jesus Your Soul." Nicknamed "the Talking Harmonica Man," he toured mainly in schools. He continued performing into his nineties. Glosson died on March 2, 2001, in Searcy (White County) weeks after his ninety-third birthday and is buried in Kensett (White County).

He received the Ozark Pioneer Music Award in 1999 and was inducted into the George D. Hay Country Music Hall of Fame in 2000.

For additional information:

Kingsbury, Paul, ed. *The Encyclopedia of Country Music*. New York: Oxford University Press, 1998.

"Lonnie Glosson." AllMusic.com. http://www.allmusic. com/artist/lonnie-glosson-mn0000228017 (accessed February 26, 2013).

Stephen Koch

BLUES / R&B — AL GREEN (1946–)

Al Green is one of Arkansas's best-known singers, with a career that has ranged from rhythm and blues (R&B) to pop to gospel and a combination. Green's distinctive falsetto singing style continues to thrill fans old and young, and he remains an active soul singer from an era that also produced Sam Cooke, Otis Redding, and Marvin Gaye.

Al Greene (he later dropped the last "e") was born on April 13, 1946, in Forrest City (St. Francis County) and grew up in a large family that sang gospel music. When his sharecropper father moved the family to Grand Rapids, Michigan, Green was only nine but sang with his siblings in the Green Brothers. When he began listening to the non-gospel sounds of Jackie Wilson, Green's father dismissed him from the group. He was sixteen.

Green was later recruited by a local band, the Creations, later renamed Al Green and the Soul Mates, and in 1967, they recorded a single, "Back Up Train," which hit No. 5 on the R&B charts. After a couple of years of struggling, Green was in a Midland, Texas, club in 1969 when he met Willie Mitchell, a Memphis, Tennessee, bandleader and an executive with that city's soul record label, Hi Records. Mitchell persuaded Green to move to Memphis and let Mitchell shape his career and sound.

Green's first chart hit, "Tired of Being Alone," reached No. 11 in 1971. It was followed at the

R&B and gospel singer Al Green.
Artists: Patterson and Barnes / From the Old State House Museum Collection

end of that year by his only No. 1 hit, "Let's Stay Together." He had six other Top 10 hits, all released between 1972 and 1974.

Fame and fortune followed, but Green suffered a couple of infamous career-changing moments. A former girlfriend entered Green's home while he was bathing, poured a pot of boiling grits on him, then used his gun to kill herself. The 1974 incident resulted in second-degree burns on Green's stomach, arm, and back. Two years later, he bought a church, paying for the building using a blank piece of paper as a check. The church, the Full Gospel Tabernacle, is on Hale Road in Memphis, not far from Elvis Presley's famous residence, Graceland. Green was ordained the pastor of his church, but it was another three years before he gave up his pop music career; he fell off an Ohio stage in 1979 and viewed the incident as a message from God.

Green then began recording and performing gospel music exclusively and has earned eight Grammy Awards in the gospel genre. Although his 1980s albums were devoid of pop sounds, he did a 1982 stint on Broadway with Patti LaBelle in a gospel musical, *Your Arms Too Short to Box with God*, and he recorded a duet with Annie Lennox (then one-half of Eurythmics), "Put a Little Love in Your Heart," on the soundtrack of the 1988 Christmas movie *Scrooged*.

In 1984, documentary filmmaker Robert Mugge released a film, *Gospel According to Al Green*, which covered Green's early life and contained footage shot in his church. Lyle Lovett teamed with Green in 1994 on a Grammy-winning song, "Funny How Time Slips Away," which was part of a collection of duets, *Rhythm, Country and Blues*. Green toured a bit and appeared on network television shows. In 1997, he got the

Al Green: Paired Up

On Broadway with Patti LaBelle in gospel musical *Your Arms Too Short to Box with God* (1982)

Duet with Annie Lennox (Eurythmics) "Put a Little Love in Your Heart" on soundtrack for the Christmas movie *Scrooged* (1988)

"Funny How Time Slips Away" with Lyle Lovett, on collection of duets *Rhythm, Country and Blues* (1994)

box-set treatment for the first time with *Anthology*, a four-disc set. In 2004, another four-disc set, *The Immortal Soul of Al Green*, was released.

In 1995, Green was inducted into the Rock and Roll Hall of Fame and also released his first secular album in years, *Your Heart's in Good Hands*. In 2000, HarperEntertainment, an imprint of HarperCollins Publishers, published his 343-page autobiography, *Take Me to the River*. In 2004, he was inducted into the Gospel Music Hall of Fame.

As the twenty-first century began, Green returned fully to the world of pop music and touring by reuniting with Willie Mitchell, the producer who had guided Green's early career. The two, who had not collaborated since 1985, worked together on *I Can't Stop*, Green's 2002 debut on Blue Note Records, and the follow-up, *Everything's OK*, in 2005. In 2008, Green released *Lay It Down*. He lives in Memphis, where he continues to serve as a pastor to his church.

For additional information:
Al Green. http://www.algreenmusic.com/ (accessed February 8, 2013).
Green, Al. *Take Me to the River*. New York: HarperEntertainment, 2000.
Mugge, Robert, dir. *Gospel According to Al Green*. VHS, DVD. Winstar, 1999.

Jack W. Hill

H-I

GOSPEL / CONTEMPORARY CHRISTIAN

HARTFORD MUSIC COMPANY AND INSTITUTE

The Hartford Music Company, located in Hartford (Sebastian County), was founded in 1918 by Eugene Monroe (E. M.) Bartlett, a businessman from Waynesville, Missouri, who wanted to publish gospel music. Specifically, he was interested in teaching people how to sight read a song, using shape notes, which would enable them to read music and sing with or without an instrument. Hartford was the perfect location for a gospel music company; the railroad ran east and west through town, with connecting rails all over the United States, thus allowing the easy transport of paper and supplies as well as students.

Bartlett, president of the Hartford Music Company, printed from electrotype plates for his songbooks, published semiannually. The books were shipped all over the United States and were used at singing conventions and schools. Training schools, or "normals," were held twice a year at Hartford to teach the shape-note style, which uses an assigned shape for each tone on an eight-note scale. This made it easier for the average person to read music.

The forerunner of the Hartford Music Company was the Central Music Company, owned by songwriter Will M. Ramsey and David Moore. Moore was a lifetime resident of Hartford who also owned the David Moore Store, selling organs, pianos, phonographs, and other musical instruments, along with music books, especially gospel. When Ramsey moved to Little Rock (Pulaski County) in 1918, Bartlett persuaded Moore and John A. McClung to partner with him in establishing the Hartford Music Company, with Moore as business manager. By 1931, the company was printing and shipping more than 100,000 books a year to thirty-five states and two foreign countries. A branch plant was established in Nacogdoches, Texas, where 20,000 books were published each year. Other branches were in Fort Smith (Sebastian County); Powell, Missouri; Tulsa, Oklahoma; Cullman, Alabama; and Houston, Texas. The company used more than 80,000 pounds of paper in these books, making it one of the state's largest publishing companies.

Bartlett sold only 15,000 copies his first year. The usual price was twenty-five cents. He wrote most of the songs, though familiar hymns were added as fillers or by popular request. His most famous song that is still published today is "Victory in Jesus." Bartlett formed the Hartford Music Institute to coincide with the Hartford Music Company, hiring instructors to teach voice, piano, piano tuning, rudiments, harmony, and stringed instruments.

When Bartlett retired in 1931, John McClung became president and sole owner of the company. He had co-owned it in the 1920s and bought it outright on February 20, 1931. He authored a number of songs, including "Just a Rose Will Do," "Death Will Never Knock on Heaven's Door," and "Standing Outside." Bartlett and McClung taught singing schools all over Arkansas as well as in Illinois, Texas, Missouri, Oklahoma, Alabama, and Kansas.

After McClung died in 1942, the company was sold to Floyd Hunter, Waldo Pool, Otis Echols, and Oliver Cooper, who moved it to Hot Springs (Garland County). Albert E. Brumley

Hartford Music Company in Powell, Missouri.
Courtesy: The Restoration Movement

(who wrote "I'll Meet You in the Morning" and "I'll Fly Away") bought the company in 1948 and moved it to Powell, Missouri, where it is today as a part of the Brumley Music Company.

The Hartford Music Company was one of many such publishing companies in the first half of the twentieth century. The schools they held provided an outlet for their songs and easy access to "new" gospel music. Only a few remain, yet "convention style singing" is prevalent in many locations in Arkansas.

For additional information:
Crouch, Mary. *Music from the Hills and Valleys*. Hartford, AR: 2000.
Deller, David. "The Songbook Gospel Movement in Arkansas: E. M. Bartlett and the Hartford Music Company." *Arkansas Historical Quarterly* 60 (Autumn 2001): 284–300.

T. J. (McClung) Gibson and John R. Way

DALE HAWKINS (1938?–2010)

Delmar Allen (Dale) Hawkins Jr., a member of the Rockabilly Hall of Fame, specialized in creating a sound (called "Swamp Rock" by some) that helped shape rock and roll music. Hawkins was successful in many roles in the music industry: singer, songwriter, recording artist, producer, arranger, band leader, musician, TV host, disc jockey, and promoter. *Billboard* magazine lists Hawkins's *Suzie Q* album in its Top 100 most valuable albums in the development of rock and roll. His first cousin, Ronnie Hawkins, rose to fame with the musical group the Band.

Different sources have reported different birth dates for Hawkins (given the practice in the 1950s for promoters to alter birth dates to make their clients more appealing to a younger audience), but he was most likely born on August 22, 1938, on Goldmine Plantation in Louisiana. His father, Delmar (Skipper) Hawkins, was a road musician and, at one time, a member of the band Sons of the Pioneers, while his mother, Estelle Taylor Hawkins, was a teacher. He had one brother, Jerry, who went on to become a recording artist on Ebb records and head the Musicians Union in Shreveport, Louisiana. Hawkins's father left when Hawkins was three years old. Although Hawkins grew up not knowing his father, he spent much of his youth with his father's family on his aunt Annabel Hawkins's farm and attended a few years of school in

St. Paul (Madison County).

Hawkins often listened to Hank Williams and Hank Snow on the radio. He learned about gospel music at a church in St. Paul and from musicians he met in Louisiana. He learned blues music while picking cotton in Louisiana, with country blues singers, and by following his maternal grandfather, federal marshal Jessie Clinton Taylor, on his rounds to clubs and cafés. Hawkins bought his first guitar at the age of thirteen with money he earned selling *Grit* newspapers.

Hawkins joined the navy at the age of sixteen and served for a year and a half. He moved to Bossier City, Louisiana, and, while attending college, worked part time at Stan's Record Shop in Shreveport. There, he met Leonard Chess (Chess Records/Checker Records) and later recorded his first hit on Chess's Checker label, the self-penned "Suzie Q" (1957). Stan Lewis, owner of Stan's Record Shop, and E. Broadwater also received co-writing credits, though in a later interview, Hawkins stated that the writing credits were taken out of his control and should have been given to himself and James Burton.

Hawkins was one of the few white artists who recorded for Checker, a label that produced rhythm and blues records. Hawkins performed at the Apollo Theater in New York City two weeks before the reputed first white artists, Buddy Holly and the Crickets, arrived on the scene.

Hawkins's records charted four times between 1957 and 1959: "Suzie Q" (1957), "La-Do-Dada" (1958), "A House, a Car and a Wedding Ring" (1958), and "Class Cutter (Yeah, Yeah)" (1959).

Hawkins nurtured many great guitarists in his band, including Rock and Roll Hall of Fame member James Burton; Fred Carter Jr., who later went to work for Ronnie Hawkins; and Roy Buchanan. Hawkins gave Joe Osborn his first gig as a session guitarist on "La-Do-Dada." Other band members were future Newbeats Dean and Marc Mathis; Country Music Hall of Fame and Rock and Roll Hall of Fame member Floyd Cramer; Rock and Roll Hall of Fame member Scotty Moore; Rockabilly Hall of Fame member Dominic Joseph (D. J.) Fontana; Carl Adams; and Kenny Paulsen.

In 1960, Dick Clark helped Hawkins become the host of *The Dale Hawkins Show*, featuring rock and roll music and teenage dancers on WCAU-CBS TV in Philadelphia, Pennsylvania. The show lasted a year and a half.

Hawkins married Paulette Hale in 1962, and they had two sons.

In the mid-1960s, Hawkins moved into the production side of records. He went back to Shreveport and worked for Stan Lewis's Jewel and Paula record labels. He undertook all aspects of the record production process, including road work to promote the records. During this time, Hawkins worked with Joe Stampley and the Uniques on "Not Too Long Ago" (1965) and "All These Things" (1966). In 1966, he moved to Tyler, Texas, to become president of ABNAK Records. He produced a big hit for the Five Americans, "Western Union" (1967), as well as John Fred and the Playboys' "Judy in Disguise (With Glasses)" (1968), and Bruce Channel's "Mister Bus Driver" and "Keep On" (1968). While in Texas, Hawkins served as Southwest vice president of Columbia Records.

In 1968, he moved to Los Angeles, California, to become RCA's West Coast Head of A&R (Artist & Repertoire). For the next three years at RCA, he worked with artists such as Harry Nilsson and Michael Nesmith.

In the early 1970s, Hawkins got hooked on prescription drugs and moved his family back to Louisiana. He and Paulette divorced. In the late

Dale Hawkins performing in 2009.   Photo: Ken King

1970s, Hawkins battled chemical dependency at a Veterans Administration hospital. He moved to Arkansas in 1978.

Filmmaker Moe Emerson of El Dorado (Union County) produced a thirty-minute profile of Hawkins for the Arkansas Educational Television Network (AETN) in 1989. During the 1990s, Hawkins worked as a volunteer disc jockey for community radio station KABF and was a featured performer at White Water Tavern in Little Rock (Pulaski County). Hawkins was also featured on VH-1's *Where Are They Now?* in the mid-1990s.

Hawkins co-starred in a 120-minute documentary by filmmaker Robert Mugge, *Rhythm 'N' Bayous: A Roadmap to Louisiana Music*. He continued to compose, record, and produce his own music, releasing the album *Back Down in Louisiana* in 2007. He lived in North Little Rock (Pulaski County) for about twenty years and recorded at his Hawk's Nest Studio.

Hawkins died on February 13, 2010, in Little Rock. He is buried at Riverside Cemetery in St. Paul.

For additional information:

Dewitt, Howard A. "Dale Hawkins: Oh Suzie-Q and Beyond." *Blue Suede News* (Fall 1997): 16–22.

Laffoon, Janis. "An Interview of Dale Hawkins" *Nightflying* (October 1987): 11–13.

Martin, Douglas. "Dale Hawkins Dies at 73; Rockabilly Author of 'Susie Q.'" *New York Times*, February 18, 2010. Online at http://www.nytimes.com/2010/02/18/arts/music/18hawkins.html?_r=0 (accessed February 27, 2013).

Marymont, Mark "Hawkins Begins TV Enterprise with 'Risky Fifties' Collection." *Arkansas Democrat-Gazette*, February 26, 1989, p. 4G.

———. "'Suzie-Q' among 100 Most Valuable Albums." *Arkansas Gazette*, September 17, 1989, p. 5G.

Billie J. Abbott

RONNIE HAWKINS (1935–)

Ronald Cornett (Ronnie) Hawkins, a rock and roll singer and bandleader, is known primarily for starting the group the Hawks, which later became the Band.

Ronnie Hawkins was born on January 10, 1935, in Huntsville (Madison County). His father, Jasper Hawkins, was a barber, and his mother, Flora Cornett Hawkins, was a schoolteacher. In 1945, the family, which included Hawkins's older sister Winifred, moved to Fayetteville (Washington County). Hawkins was educated in the city's public schools, graduating from Fayetteville High School in 1952. During his high school and college years, Hawkins formed his first bands, which played such Fayetteville venues as the Tee Table, the Bubble Club, and the Shamrock Club. A physical education major at the University of Arkansas (UA) in Fayetteville, he developed an outrageous stage persona that earned him such nicknames as "Rompin' Ronnie" and "Mr. Dynamo." His camel walk predated Michael Jackson's moonwalk by three decades, and his back flips became an integral part of his live act.

Hawkins did not complete college. Instead, he joined the army and was stationed at Fort Chaffee in Fort Smith (Sebastian County) and Fort Sill, Oklahoma. After finishing his service, he moved to Helena (Phillips County), where he put together a touring band that included Levon Helm of Marvell (Phillips County) on drums. At the suggestion of Harold Jenkins (later known as country and western star Conway Twitty), the group headed for Canada in 1958.

Hawkins referred to Canada as "my promised land" upon being embraced there by an audience hungry for authentic American rock and roll. Always on the lookout for talented players to mold into Hawks, he assembled between 1958 and 1961 a roster that included Rick Danko, Garth Hudson, Richard Manuel, and Robbie Robertson, who, along with Helm, would back Hawkins until 1963, when they left to tour with Bob Dylan. Eventually, the quintet would name itself the Band and record such classics as "The Night They Drove Old Dixie Down," "Up on Cripple Creek," and "The Shape I'm In." *The Last Waltz*, Martin Scorsese's 1978 documentary, captures the group at its zenith, backing a diverse assemblage of artists, including Eric Clapton, Joni Mitchell, Neil Diamond, and their old mentor Hawkins, whose version of Bo Diddley's "Who Do You Love?" is one of the film's highlights.

During his long career, Hawkins has had only two hit records in America. In 1959, "Forty Days," his reworking of Chuck Berry's "Thirty Days," and his version of Young Jesse's "Mary Lou" reached No. 45 and No. 26, respectively, on

Rock and roll singer Ronnie Hawkins, a native of Huntsville, with daughter Leah performing in Toronto, Canada; October 2004.
Courtesy: Carole Bozzato Timm

Fame, Hawkins was, in March of 2004, inducted into the Canadian Music Industry Hall of Fame.

In addition to appearances as himself in *The Last Waltz* and *Renaldo and Clara* (1978), Hawkins had minor dramatic roles in several motion pictures, including Michael Cimino's *Heaven's Gate* (1980). He hosted his own variety series, *Honky Tonk*, on Canadian television during the 1981–82 season. In 2004, he made a guest appearance on the Billy Ray Cyrus series *Doc*.

Hawkins and his wife, Wanda, make their home in Peterborough, Ontario, Canada. They have three grown children: Ronnie Jr., Robin, and Leah. In 2002, Hawkins was diagnosed with pancreatic cancer and was not expected to survive. But he defied the odds against him and recovered fully. In 2002, he released a new album, *Still Cruisin'*, to favorable reviews. He was inducted into the Arkansas Entertainers Hall of Fame in 2008.

For additional information:

Cochran, Robert. "Long on Nerve: An Interview with Ronnie Hawkins." *Arkansas Historical Quarterly* 65 (Summer 2006): 99–116.

Wallis, Ian. *The Hawk: The Story of Ronnie Hawkins and the Hawks*. Kingston, Ontario: Quarry Music Books, 1997.

Thomas Cochran

the U.S. charts. He fared much better in Canada, where he earned the 1982 Juno Award, equivalent to an American Grammy, as Best Male Country Vocalist. In 1996, he was presented the Walt Grealis Special Lifetime Achievement Award, one of the most esteemed honors in the Canadian music industry. The city of Toronto proclaimed October 4, 2002, "Ronnie Hawkins Day." A 2002 addition to Canada's Walk of

---

FOLK

LEE HAYS (1914–1981)

Lee Elhardt Hays was a singer best known as the big man who sang bass with the folk-music group the Weavers. According to historian Studs Terkel, the Weavers were responsible for "entering folk music into the mainstream of American life." Among the songs he is most known for are "If I Had a Hammer," "Roll the Union On," "Raggedy, Raggedy, Are We," "The Rankin Tree," "On Top of Old Smoky," "Kisses Sweeter than Wine," and "Goodnight Irene."

Lee Hays was born on March 14, 1914, in Little Rock (Pulaski County) to a strict Methodist preacher, William Benjamin Hays, and Ellen Reinhardt Hays. Hays's father was serving as editor of the *Arkansas Methodist* at this time but later went back to the pulpit. By the time Hays was twelve, he had lived in five different Arkansas towns: Little Rock, Newport (Jackson County), Paragould (Greene County), Conway (Faulkner County), and Booneville (Logan County). He started school in Arkansas and finished high school in Georgia as his father traveled the Methodist circuit.

Hays spent much of his life rebelling against his father's fundamentalism; he took up smoking and drinking at an early age and never gave them up. However, his church background provided a deep-seated religious element to his singing and songwriting. Some said Hays's political principles had a fundamentalist quality of their own.

Hays became a student at Commonwealth College in the late 1930s as America was deep into the Great Depression. This rural college located near Mena (Polk County) had dedicated itself to helping working men by promoting the organization of labor unions. Hays was appalled at the hardships endured by southern sharecroppers and laborers and thought that union activism was essential to American workers.

At Commonwealth, Hays dressed in overalls, attended labor-oriented classes, and worked with other students in the fields. New York playwright Eli Jaffe, a fellow student, recalled that Hays was "deeply religious and extremely creative and imaginative and firmly believed in the Brotherhood of Man." Hays also preached in area churches and wrote songs, plays, and stories.

Hays transformed hymns and black spirituals into songs about unions, sometimes substituting the word "union" for "Jesus." His labor-related ballads pleased his contemporaries so much that they raised sixty-five dollars to send him to New York City to gain a larger audience. In New York, Hays met Pete Seeger, another young political singer who became Hays's lifelong friend and collaborator. They dreamed of using folk music, the traditional music of the poor, to achieve political goals.

Hays and Seeger began singing with small local groups that included famous musicians such as Woody Guthrie, Leadbelly, Burl Ives, and Josh White. In 1940, Seeger created the Almanac Singers, who lived in a commune and coined the word "hootenanny."

The group broke up during World War II because Seeger enlisted in the army. After the war, Seeger and Hays tried to revive the group but failed. In 1948, in Seeger's Greenwich Village basement, Ronnie Gilbert, Fred Hellerman, and Hays joined Seeger in creating the Weavers, who, in the 1950s, brought folk music to a mass audience for the first time. The group took its name from a nineteenth-century play of the same name written by German playwright Gerhard Hauptmann that dealt with a strike among textile workers. Recording for Decca Records (and later for Vanguard), the group was highly successful with "Goodnight Irene," "On Top of Old Smoky," "So Long, It's Been Good to Know Ya," and "Kisses Sweeter than Wine." Seeger and Hays composed "If I Had a Hammer" while nonchalantly passing a notepad between them at a political meeting. Both considered themselves "political performers."

Unfortunately, the Weavers' success came during the McCarthy era. The Weavers were blacklisted and put under surveillance because of some members' political beliefs. They were barred from television, engagements were can-celed, and radio stations refused to play their music. They disbanded in 1952 but reunited in 1955 after a staged Carnegie Hall reunion of the band sold out. In the audience of this December 24, 1955, show were people who later created the Limelighters; the Kingston Trio; Peter, Paul and Mary; and Mitch Miller. In fact, Mary Travers of Peter, Paul and Mary later credited the Weavers with the success and the very existence of her own folk group.

Among the albums the Weavers cut were *Wasn't That a Time*, *Union Songs*, *Talking Union*, *Sod Buster Ballads*, *Deep Sea Chanteys*, *Gospel*, *Best of the Weavers*, *Goodnight Irene*, *Kisses Sweeter Than Wine*, and *Together Again*.

Hays was plagued by ill health, and the Weavers' farewell concert came in December 1963 at the Orchestra Hall in Chicago, Illinois. Seeger continued with his music, and Hays helped him write "We Shall Overcome." Hays lost both legs, which were amputated due to his diabetes, and his health continued to deteriorate.

In November 1980, a final concert was held at Carnegie Hall. Although Hays was almost unrecognizable in his wheelchair, the Weavers' music filled the hall. Nine months later, on August 26, 1981, Hays died from diabetic cardiovascular disease at his home in Croton-on-Hudson, New York. His body was cremated, and his friends met to mix the ashes with his compost pile.

For additional information:

Coogan, Harold. "The Ballad of Lee Hays." *Arkansas Times* (July 1988): 40–44.

Koppelman, Robert. "Lee Hays: A Literary Reconsideration." *Southern Folklore* 55, no. 2 (1998): 75–100.

Stambler, Irwin, and Grelun Landon, eds. *The Encyclopedia of Folk, Country and Western Music*. New York: St. Martin's Press, 1983.

The Weavers: Wasn't That a Time! Warner Bros., 1982.

Willens, Doris. *The Lonesome Traveler: A Biography of Lee Hays*. New York: W. W. Norton & Company, Inc., 1988.

Harold Coogan

This entry, originally published in *Arkansas Biography: A Collection of Notable Lives*, appears in the *Encyclopedia of Arkansas Music* in an altered form. *Arkansas Biography* is available from the University of Arkansas Press in Fayetteville.

ROCK | LEVON HELM (1940–2012)

Mark Lavon (Levon) Helm was best known as the drummer and singer for the Canadian rock group the Band. Following the demise of the Band, he continued to have a successful career leading his own band, as well as acting in nu-merous motion pictures.

Levon Helm was born on May 26, 1940, outside Elaine (Phillips County) to Nell and Diamond Helm. He had two sisters and one brother. He spent his childhood in Marvell (Phillips

County) working on the family cotton farm but was always encouraged to play and sing music at home and in church. Helm knew that he wanted to become a musician at age six, after seeing bluegrass musician Bill Monroe perform. He began playing guitar at age eight but was inspired shortly afterward to become a drummer after seeing a performance by F. S. Walcott Rabbit's Foot Minstrels, who had a left-handed drummer. He was also inspired by James "Peck" Curtis, the drummer for blues legend Sonny Boy Williamson, who frequently played in the area. Helm began spending time at the KFFA radio studio in Helena (Phillips County) listening to blues performers, and he watched live musical performances in Marvell. When he was twelve, he played guitar on the local music circuit accompanied by his sister Linda on washtub bass, performing at 4-H clubs and other civic-club gatherings. While in high school, he formed his first band, the Jungle Bush Beaters.

When he was seventeen, Helm got his first big break when he met Ronnie Hawkins, the rockabilly star born in Huntsville (Madison County), at the West Helena Delta Supper Club, where Hawkins was working sans drummer. The piano player knew Helm and suggested to Hawkins that the young drummer sit in with the band. Helm was asked to join the band, and once he graduated from high school in Marvell, he joined Hawkins's band, the Hawks, on the road.

Levon went with Hawkins to Toronto, Canada, where the rockabilly sound was popular. In 1959, Hawkins signed to Roulette Records, and the Hawks recorded two hit albums in 1959, *Forty Days* and *Mary Lou*. Along with Helm, Hawkins gradually put together a stellar version of the Hawks that, by 1961, included future Band members—pianist Richard Manuel, bassist Rick Danko, guitarist Robbie Robertson, and keyboard and saxophone player Garth Hudson, all Canadians.

> **Levon Helm: Hit Songs with the Hawks and the Band**
>
> "Leave Me Alone" (1964)
>
> "The Stones I Throw" (1964)
>
> "Go Go Liza Jane" (1964)
>
> "I Shall Be Released" (1968)
>
> "The Night They Drove Old Dixie Down" (1969)
>
> "Up on Cripple Creek" (1969)
>
> "Across the Great Divide" (1969)
>
> "Look Out Cleveland" (1969)
>
> "King Harvest (Has Surely Come)" (1969)
>
> "The Weight" (1969)
>
> "Rag Mama Rag" (1969)

Wishing to expand their musical horizons, the band eventually broke away from Hawkins and began performing as Levon and the Hawks, playing rhythm and blues, blues, and rock and roll. Helm was given top billing, not only because of his seniority in the band but also because he was a member of the musicians' union, while the others were not. In 1964, they released their first single, "Leave Me Alone," on which they were listed as the Canadian Squires. They released two more singles that year as Levon and the Hawks: "The Stones I Throw" and "Go Go Liza Jane."

Their reputation grew to the point that Bob Dylan asked them to be his backup band after he decided to amplify and incorporate more rock into his traditional folk music sound. The band accompanied Dylan on his 1966 tour of the United Kingdom, where they encountered some hostility to his new "electrified" sound. The hostility bothered Helm, so he went back home to Arkansas.

After Dylan's near-fatal motorcycle wreck in July 1966, Dylan and the backup band moved to a pink split-level house, affectionately named Big Pink, in Woodstock, New York, in 1967. There they rehearsed and recorded music that would be released in 1975 as *The Basement Tapes*. Helm reunited with the group later that year to perform on some of the songs on *The Basement Tapes*.

In the spring of 1968, the Band—the name they and Dylan used to refer to the combo—recorded the music that would become *Music from Big Pink*, a widely acclaimed debut album. Released on Capitol Records in 1968, the album combined country and western, Appalachian, R&B, gospel, Cajun, and old-fashioned rock sounds—a synthesis of American music that greatly contrasted with the psychedelic rock more common to the period. In *The Rolling Stone Album Guide*, Paul Evans wrote that the album was "the group's tour de force debut: Robertson's 'The Weight' and the Dylan/Manuel 'I Shall Be Released' encapsulated the Band's strengths—the lean grace of Robertson's guitar, the understated drive of Levon Helm's drumming, and especially the solo and ensemble brilliance of the group's three singers." Helm is credited on the album with mandolin and guitar in addition to vocals and drums.

Music from Big Pink peaked at No. 30 on the *Billboard* album charts, but the album had a huge impact on such rock luminaries as Eric Clapton, George Harrison, Pete Townshend, and Mick Jagger.

In 1969, the Band released its eponymous album, *The Band*, which included songs such as "The Night They Drove Old Dixie Down," "Up on Cripple Creek," "Across the Great Divide," "Look Out Cleveland," and "King Harvest (Has Surely Come)." In *The Rolling Stone Album Guide*, Evans called it "one of the richest and deepest records in rock history."

The album *The Band* broke into the *Billboard* Top 10 on the album charts in late 1969, and the single "Up on Cripple Creek" broke into the Top 30 in late 1969. Meanwhile, in England, the Band's fame grew as "The Weight" from their debut album reached No. 21 on the British charts. "Rag Mama Rag," a single from the second album, was a Top 20 hit in the U.K. in April 1970.

Meanwhile, Helm was living with Libby Titus in Woodstock, and on December 3, 1970, their daughter, Amy, was born.

The Band's popularity continued to grow, and they continued to tour and record albums, including *Stage Fright* (1970), *Cahoots* (1971), a live double album called *Rock of Ages* (1972), and *Moondog Matinee* (1973). In 1974, they reunited with Dylan to record the studio album *Planet Waves*. They also toured with him, releasing a live album, *Before the Flood*, which featured both Dylan and Band songs. In 1975, the double album *The Basement Tapes*, recorded with Bob Dylan in 1967, was finally released on Columbia Records. Subsequently, the Band released the albums *Northern Lights/Southern Crosses* (1975) and *Islands* (1977).

In 1976, Robbie Robertson announced that he was tired of the road and wanted the band to go out with one last hurrah. On Thanksgiving 1976, the Band performed their farewell concert, titled "The Last Waltz." The concert, featuring such friends of the Band as Eric Clapton, Dr. John, Muddy Waters, Neil Young, Van Morrison, Ronnie Hawkins, and Joni Mitchell, was recorded for a triple album released in 1978. A documentary film of the event, directed by Martin Scorsese, was also produced and released that year as *The Last Waltz*.

Following the break-up of the Band, Helm signed to ABC records and released *Levon Helm and the RCO All-Stars* in 1977. The album featured Steve Cropper, Duck Dunn, Booker T. Jones, Dr. John, Paul Butterfield, and Fred Car-

Levon Helm in Central Park, New York; 2007.

Photo: Daniel Arnold

ter Jr. Helm followed up with the album *Levon Helm* in 1978. In 1980, Helm released the critically acclaimed album *American Son* on MCA. Then in 1982 he released an album called *Levon Helm* on Capitol Records.

Meanwhile, Helm had embarked on an acting career. He played Loretta Lynn's father, Ted Webb, in *Coal Miner's Daughter* in 1980, as well as Captain Jack Ridley in *The Right Stuff* (1983). He also appeared in *End of the Line* (1988), which was filmed primarily in Little Rock (Pulaski County), *Staying Together* (1989), and *The Adventures of Sebastian Cole* (1998). In 2005, he was in the Tommy Lee Jones–directed *Three Burials of Melquiades Estrada*. He also played the ghost of Confederate general John Bell Hood in the film *In the Electric Mist* starring Tommy Lee Jones and John Goodman.

In 1981, Levon married Sandra Dodd.

The Band, without Robbie Robertson, who chose not to join the re-formed Band, got together in 1983 and toured regularly. Richard Manuel committed suicide in 1986, but the Band carried on, recording three albums in the 1990s: *Jericho* (1993), *High on the Hog* (1996), and *Jubilation* (1998).

In 1993, Helm, with rock writer Stephen Davis, published a book about the Band's rise to fame, *This Wheel's on Fire*. In 1994, Helm was inducted along with the other members of the Band into the Rock and Roll Hall of Fame.

In the late 1990s, Helm suffered from throat

cancer, which forced him to quit singing. Nonetheless, he formed a band, Levon Helm and the Barn Burners, with a group of Woodstock-area musicians. He also released his greatest-hits album, titled *The Tie That Binds: The Best of Levon Helm, 1975–1996*. At his home studio in Woodstock, he recorded an album titled *Souvenir* in 1997 with a Woodstock band called Crowmatix. He regularly performed with the Barn Burners, often with his daughter Amy on vocals.

In 2005, Levon began singing again, and in 2007, he released a new album, *Dirt Farmer*, on Vanguard, which garnered a Grammy in the Traditional Folk Album category. A second solo album, *Electric Dirt*, was released June 30, 2009. In Woodstock, he performed monthly Midnight Ramble shows at his home. He also toured seasonally with the Levon Helm Band and occasional guest performers.

Helm died on April 19, 2012, from throat cancer. In April 2013, a documentary about Helm titled *Ain't in It for My Health* was released in Manhattan. Set in Helm's New York home and

directed by Jacob Hatley, it features him discussing his music career and his home state.

For additional information:
Helm, Levon. "The Music." *Razor Magazine*, February 2004.
Helm, Levon, and Stephen Davis. *This Wheel's on Fire: Levon Helm and the Story of the Band*. Chicago: Chicago Review Press, 2000.
Hill, Jack W. "Arkansan, Rocker, Rambler Helm Dies at 71." *Arkansas Democrat-Gazette*, April 20, 2012, p. 2A.
Hoskyns, Barney. *Across the Great Divide*. New York: Hyperion, 1993.
Levon Helm Studios. http://www.levonhelm.com/ (accessed February 8, 2013).
Pareles, Jon. "Levon Helm, Drummer in the Band, Dies at 71." *New York Times*, April 19, 2012. Online at http://www.nytimes.com/2012/04/20/arts/music/levon-helm-drummer-and-singer-dies-at-71.html?pagewanted=1 (accessed April 19, 2012).
Scott, A. O. "Playing Notes That Linger." *New York Times*, April 19, 2013, p. C10. Online at http://movies.nytimes.com/2013/04/19/movies/aint-in-it-for-my-health-directed-by-jacob-hatley.html?_r=0 (accessed April 24, 2013).

Bryan Rogers

CLASSICAL / OPERA — BARBARA HENDRICKS (1948–)

Barbara Hendricks is an internationally recognized leading lyric soprano. Whether performing light soprano roles in traditional operatic repertory, demanding premieres of twentieth-century vocal music, song recitals, or jazz, Hendricks has been recognized as a leading artist since the mid-1970s. In addition, she is recognized internationally for her work for human rights and world peace.

Soprano Barbara Hendricks.
Courtesy: Butler Center for Arkansas Studies, Central Arkansas Library System

Barbara Hendricks was born on November 20, 1948, in Stephens (Ouachita County). The child of a Methodist minister, she lived in various small towns in Arkansas and Tennessee. She graduated from Horace Mann High School in Little Rock (Pulaski County). She enrolled at Lane College in Jackson, Tennessee, and transferred to the

University of Nebraska as a chemistry major. She graduated in 1969 with a BS in mathematics and chemistry.

Her musical activities to that point were in church and civic choirs. She was encouraged to attend the Aspen Music Festival in the summer of 1969 and there met the celebrated vocalist and teacher Jennie Tourel, who invited her to study at the Juilliard School in New York City after college. She moved to New York, winning several vocal competitions in the early 1970s and completed a voice degree from Juilliard in 1973.

Hendricks found success with the Mini-Met production of *4 Saints in 3 Acts* (1973) and a recording of *Porgy and Bess* (1974). She followed it up with debuts in San Francisco, California (1974); Paris, France (1982); and London, England (1982), as well as with the Metropolitan Opera in New York City (1987). Vocal recitals have been particularly important to her.

Hendricks lived in France and then in Switzerland with her husband, Martin Engstrom, a Swedish citizen whom she married in 1978. They have three children. Her interest in humanitarian activities led to her being named a goodwill ambassador in 1987 by the United Nations High

Commissioner for Refugees. She performed at an inauguration gala for President Bill Clinton's 1993 inauguration. She received an Honorary Doctor of Music from Juilliard in 2000.

For additional information:
"Barbara Hendricks." *Ebony* 45 (May 1990): 158–160.
Barbara Hendricks. http://www.barbarahendricks.com (accessed February 8, 2013).

Forbes, Elizabeth. "Barbara Hendricks." *The New Grove Dictionary of Music and Musicians.* New York: Macmillan Publishers, 2002.
Karp, Judith. "Barbara Hendricks." *Fugue* 3 (January 1979): 37–38.
Scherer, Barrymore Laurence. "Mimi with a Method: On Becoming Barbara Hendricks." *Opera News* 53 (August 1988): 8–12.

Floyd W. Martin

FOLK

VIOLET BRUMLEY HENSLEY (1916–)

Known as the "Whittling Fiddler," the "Stradivarius of the Ozarks," or more simply, the "Fiddle Maker," Violet Brumley Hensley, a fiddle maker and musician most of her life, was designated as the 2004 Arkansas Living Treasure by the Arkansas Arts Council. According to the Arts Council, this designation recognizes Hensley as an outstanding Arkansan who has elevated her work as a fiddle maker to the status of art and who actively preserves and advances the art form.

Violet Brumley was born near Mount Ida (Montgomery County) on October 21, 1916, to George Washington Brumley and Nora Springer Brumley. The Brumleys had two other daughters. She followed in her father's footsteps as a musician, and at the age of fifteen, Brumley told her father, who crafted his first fiddle at age fourteen in 1888, that she wanted to make a fiddle of her own. By observing her father's fiddle-making technique, she cut the pattern and dried the wood by the fireplace. She learned how to split the wood with a hatchet and use hand planes, homemade curved knives of her father's design, and other hand tools to carve and create her first instrument.

She made four fiddles from 1932 to 1934, before marrying her husband, Adren Hensley, when she was eighteen. Although raising nine children took most of her time, she continued to play music, and after taking up fiddle-making again in 1961, she made sixty-nine more instruments.

Hensley makes her fiddles from native woods and has used approximately 100 different types of wood. She favors certain woods for particular pieces of the fiddle, such as wild cherry and maple for the back, sides, and neck; spruce, pine, and buckeye for the top; dogwood for the tail piece; and persimmon for the pegs. Hensley's workshop is located in her home in Yellville (Mari-

on County), where she and her husband moved their family in 1968. Her workbench not only provides a place to build the musical instruments she makes, which are coveted for their quality workmanship and clear musical tones, but is also a place to repair fiddles.

Violet Brumley Hensley; circa 1970.
Courtesy: Violet Brumley Hensley

Hensley has given solo demonstrations and exhibits at the War Eagle Craft Show (1965), the Silver Dollar City National Craft Festival (1967 to the present), the Silver Dollar City Music Festival (1980–2001), the Smithsonian Folklife Festival (July 1970), and Northwest Mississippi Junior College (April 1974), as well at Arkansas schools and in Illinois, Minnesota, and Missouri.

She has appeared on television on numerous occasions in such shows as *The Beverly Hillbillies* (1969), *The Art Linkletter Show* (1970), *Captain Kangaroo* (1977), and *Live with Regis and Kathy Lee* (1992). In addition, she has been featured in the magazines *National Geographic* (1970), *Mature Living* (1987), and *Country Woman* (1991), among others. During the 1980s, she appeared weekly on radio station KCTT in Yellville. Her most recent television appearance was on Ozarks Public Television (KOZK/KOZJ) at Missouri State University in Springfield, Missouri, in the summer of 2006, in the program "Handcrafted Musical Instruments."

Hensley and family members have made three albums: *Old Time Fiddle Tunes* (1974), *The Whittling Fiddler and Family* (1983), and *Family Treasures* (2004). Hensley and family also recorded *Old-Time Hoedowns* in the early 1970s. Family members who have played with Hensley are daughters Lewonna Nelson and Sandra Flagg, son Calvin Hensley, and husband Adren Hensley. Son-in-law and guitarist Tim Nelson replaced Adren Hensley after his death in 1997 and joined family members in making *Family Treasures*.

Hensley's dedication to her art has led to local and national acclaim, including the 2004 Arkansas Living Treasure designation. She received the 1997 Living Treasure Award from Silver Dollar City in Branson, Missouri, and was inducted into its Hall of Fame. Hensley made her forty-first consecutive appearance at Silver Dollar City during its 2007 National Crafts Festival. Hensley is no longer making complete fiddles due to failing eyesight, but she is able to make some of the less intricate parts. She continues teaching others to make and play fiddles.

For additional information:

"Arts Council Names 2004 Arkansas Living Treasure." *Art Lines* (April–June 2004): 1, 7.

Parks, Michelle. "Music Maker." *Arkansas Democrat-Gazette*, November 14, 2006, pp. 3E, 6E.

Worster, Ann. "The Whittling Fiddler." *The Baxter Bulletin*, January 13, 2004, pp. 8–9.

Ann Phillips Worster

JAZZ — AL HIBBLER (1915–2001)

Albert George Edward (Al) Hibbler, a pop/jazz singer, was the first African American to have a radio program in Little Rock (Pulaski County). He was also the first blind entertainer to gain national prominence. He sang with the Duke Ellington Band for eight and a half years before he left to make five recordings as a solo artist; these became *Billboard* pop hits. Hibbler also became a prominent figure in the civil rights movement.

Sheet music for song recorded by Al Hibbler.

Courtesy: Old State House Museum Collection

Al Hibbler was born on August 16, 1915, in Como, Mississippi, to Hubert Hibbler and Lucy Prokes Hibbler, a farm family; some sources have reported that Hibbler was born in Tyro, Mississippi, while still others report he was born in Little Rock, but he always claimed Como as his birthplace. He had three brothers and one sister. Some reports claim that he was blind at birth, but others claim that he became blind at a young age. Hibbler's brother Hubert Jr. was also blind. The family moved to Arkansas in 1925, settling in Dell (Mississippi County).

In 1929, Hibbler's parents sent him to be educated at the Arkansas School for the Blind in Little Rock. Hibbler was a soprano in the school choir and developed into a baritone with perfect pitch.

Hibbler was the first black singer to have a radio program in Little Rock (1935–1936). He broadcast on the KGHI 7:45 p.m. daily program, whistling and singing his theme song, "Star Dust," to the accompaniment of Vivian Sparks on piano. In the 1930s, Hibbler sang with a number of bands from the East Coast when they came to Little Rock and performed at the Dreamland Ballroom on 9th Street. Hibbler got his first singing job with a band called the Yellow Jackets in 1935; they frequently performed at the Chat & Chew on 9th and State streets. In about 1935, he first sang with the Duke Ellington Band. Ellington told Hibbler, "If you ever make it to New York, come see me."

Hibbler met Dub Jenkins & His Playmates of Memphis, Tennessee, when they played a tour date in Little Rock. He left Little Rock with them in 1936 and stayed with them a year and a half. He then spent two years with Boots and His Buddies out of San Antonio, Texas, but left in 1942.

Hibbler never used a cane, so a band took on extra responsibility when he worked with them. When he auditioned for Jay McShann's band out of Kansas City, Missouri, jazz great Charlie Parker told McShann that he would quit if McShann failed to hire Hibbler. McShann replied, "Ok, I'll hire him, but you'll have to look after him." In July 1942, Hibbler made his recording debut with McShann's band in New York City. Hibbler quit McShann's band after a year, recalling later that he "bummed around New York City for a while."

In 1943, eight years after he met Ellington in Little Rock, Hibbler went to visit him at the Hurricane Club in New York and worked for him for eight and a half years. Ellington described Hibbler's style as "tonal pantomime." Ellington asked Bob Russell to write words to a tune he had previously written and titled, "Concerto for Cootie." The new title, "Do Nothin' Till You Hear from Me" (1943), had special meaning for Hibbler and Ellington, and they recorded it several times over the years. In 1947, Hibbler recorded, with Ellington's band, the song, "Don't Be So Mean to Me, Baby," written by Peggy Lee and Dave Barbour. That same year, he was presented with the Esquire New Star Award for Male Singer. In all, Hibbler made eighty-two recordings with the Duke Ellington Band before he left over a salary dispute and started a solo career in 1951.

In 1955, Hibbler bought a house in Teaneck, New Jersey, with money he earned from his *Billboard* pop hit, "Unchained Melody." By 1956, he had earned enough money from his second solo *Billboard* pop hit, "He," to finish paying off the house. His other solo *Billboard* pop hits were "After the Lights Go Down Low" (1956), "11th Hour Melody" (1956), and "Never Turn Back (1956).

Hibbler's version of "Unchained Melody" was the featured song in the movie *Unchained* (1955). In 1957, he sang the title song in the movie *Nightfall*. He also appeared occasionally on television, such as on the *Steve Allen Show*, in the 1950s through the 1970s.

Hibbler played a noteworthy role in the civil rights movement, marching with Martin Luther King Jr. and being arrested for civil disobedience in New Jersey in 1959 and in Birmingham, Alabama, on April 10, 1963, where he was picketing in front of the Trailways Bus Station. The police did not put Hibbler in jail but rather took him back to his hotel.

Record companies were reportedly concerned about how Hibbler's involvement in the civil rights movement would affect record sales, and his singing career waned during this time. Frank Sinatra, however, signed Hibbler as one of his first solo artists on Sinatra's Reprise label. Sinatra called Hibbler and Ray Charles his "two ace pilots."

Hibbler was married three times. He had a son, Albert Jr., by his first wife and a daughter, Malaurie, by his second wife.

Hibbler played himself in the movie *Texas Tenor: The Illinois Jacquet Story* (1992). He lived his last few years in Chicago, Illinois, where his mother and siblings moved after leaving Arkansas. He died on April 24, 2001, in Holy Cross Hospital in Chicago. He is buried at Lincoln Cemetery in Worth, Illinois.

For additional information:

"Al Hibbler (1995 Lifetime Achievement Award)." Arkansas Jazz Hall of Fame. http://www.arjazz.org/artists/hof/1995/95_al_hibbler.html (accessed February 8, 2013).

Hill, Jack W. "Blind Singer Sets Benefit." *Arkansas Democrat*, May 9, 1986, p. 4W.

McCarthy, Albert. *Big Band Jazz*. New York: Bookthrift Co., 1984.

Ratliff, Ben. "Al Hibbler, a Singer with Ellington's Band, Dies at 85." *New York Times*, April 27, 2001. Online at http://www.nytimes.com/2001/04/27/arts/al-hibbler-a-singer-with-ellington-s-band-dies-at-85.html (accessed February 26, 2013).

Billie J. Abbott

FOLK   DAN HICKS (1941–)

Dan Hicks is a cross-genre singer/songwriter specializing in a type of music he refers to as "folk jazz." He has served as front man for his band, the Hot Licks, off and on since 1968.

Daniel Ivan Hicks was born on December 9, 1941, in Little Rock (Pulaski County), the only child of Ivan L. Hicks—a career military man—and Evelyn Kehl Hicks. The family moved to northern California when Hicks was five years old. The family settled in Santa Rosa, and Hicks has resided in the area north of San Francisco ever since.

Hicks started playing drums in grade school and played snare drum in his high school marching band. At age fourteen, he was accompanying high school bands at area dances. Hicks enrolled at San Francisco State College (now San Francisco State University) in 1959 to study broadcasting. It was at this point that he first took up the guitar. He joined the Bay Area folk scene, singing and playing in coffeehouses around San Francisco.

In the mid-1960s, Hicks became the drummer for a band known as the Charlatans. He also sang and played guitar for the band, which he has described as "kind of dysfunctional… [with] no real management, and it was just kind of some loose guys." In 1968, Hicks formed his own acoustic band to open shows for the Charlatans and called it Dan Hicks & His Hot Licks.

Musician Dan Hicks, a Little Rock native.
Courtesy: Dan Hicks

The first record from the new band, *Original Recordings*, was released the following year on Epic Records. It was a commercial failure, after which the band signed with Blue Thumb Records. Three albums followed in quick succession. *Where's the Money?* (1971), *Striking It Rich* (1972), and *Last Train to Hicksville* (1973) were all commercially successful and popular with critics. It was therefore surprising to many when Hicks broke up the band in 1973 at the height of their popularity. Of this move, Hicks has said, "I didn't want to be a bandleader anymore. It was a load and a load I didn't want. I'm basically a loner."

For the next fifteen years, Hicks chose a lower profile, playing solo acoustic shows; writing commercial jingles for products such as Levi's, Bic Lighters, and Ball Park Franks; and composing scores for films and television programs—most notably the score for the animated Ralph Bakshi film *Hey Good Lookin'* (1982). Hicks's songs were featured in the popular television shows *The Sopranos* and *The Osbournes*, and Hicks appeared in the Gene Hackman legal drama *Class Action* (1991), performing two songs in the film. During this period, Hicks was involved in only two musical projects that resulted in commercially released music; both were relatively obscure and remain somewhat rare.

In 1998, Hicks poised himself for a return to the mainstream when he signed a deal with Surfdog Records. This resulted in *Beatin' the Heat* (2000), which became his first release with the newly re-formed Hot Licks since 1973. Since then, he has released a number of studio albums and collaborated with artists such as Jim Keltner, Gibby Haynes, Van Dyke Parks, Willie Nelson, and Jimmy Buffett. Hicks's music is featured regularly on the Buffett-affiliated Sirius/XM satellite radio station Radio Margaritaville. In 2009, Hicks released *Tangled Tales*, his fifth album with Surfdog Records. Hicks and his band released a Christmas album in 2010.

Hicks maintains an active tour schedule and continues to experiment with a number of musical genres including rock, jazz, country, bluegrass, western swing, and Americana. Hicks and his wife, Clare, live in Mill Valley, California.

For additional information:

Dan Hicks. http://www.danhicks.net/ (accessed March 6, 2013).

"Dan Hicks." Allmusic.com. http://www.allmusic.com/artist/dan-hicks-p86519/biography (accessed March 6, 2013).

Hoskyns, Barney. *Beneath the Diamond Sky: Haight-Ashbury, 1965–1970*. New York: Simon & Schuster, 1997.

Libertore, Paul. "At Age 67, Musician Dan Hicks Keeps His Fingers on His Guitar." *Silicon Valley Mercury News*, May 7, 2009. Online at http://www.mercurynews.com/ci_12323390?IADID (accessed March 6, 2013).

McDonough, Jack. *San Francisco Rock—The Illustrated History of San Francisco Rock Music*. San Francisco: Chronicle Books, 1985.

Perry, Charles. "Enigmas on Thin Ice." *Rolling Stone* (August 30, 1973): 70–73.

Sculatti, Gene, and Davin Seay. *San Francisco Nights—The Psychedelic Music Trip, 1965–1968*. New York: St. Martin's Press, 1985.

Selvin, Joel. *Summer of Love*. New York: Dutton, 1994.

Keith Merckx

COUNTRY

WAYLAND HOLYFIELD (1942–)

Wayland Holyfield is a prolific country music writer and recording artist who wrote one of Arkansas's official state songs, "Arkansas (You Run Deep in Me)." He is a member of the Nashville Songwriters Hall of Fame and the Arkansas Entertainers Hall of Fame.

Wayland D. Holyfield was born in Mallet Town (Conway County) on March 15, 1942. He attended grade school in Springfield (Conway County) and Little Rock (Pulaski County) and graduated from Hall High School in Little Rock in 1960—after attending high school in Mabelvale (Pulaski County) during the Lost Year of 1958–59 when Little Rock's high schools were closed. He attended Hendrix College in Conway (Faulkner County) on a basketball scholarship and then the University of Arkansas (UA) in Fayetteville (Washington County), earning a BA in marketing from UA in 1965. After graduating, he worked in sales and advertising.

During and after college, Holyfield played guitar and sang in groups called the Rebels and the General Store. Holyfield married Nancy Selig of Conway; they have three children. The couple moved to Nashville, Tennessee, in 1972 so Holyfield could pursue a songwriting career.

Holyfield has written and co-written many songs that have been recorded by famous musicians, including Anne Murray, George Strait, Brooks & Dunn, Julio Iglesias, Conway Twitty, the Oak Ridge Boys, and the Statler Brothers. His first Top 5 hit (co-written with Bob McDill and Chuck Neese) was "Rednecks, White Socks and Blue Ribbon Beer," recorded by Johnny Russell. Two years later, in 1975, his song "You're My Best Friend," recorded by Don Williams, reached number one on the charts. Other notable songs that Holyfield either wrote or co-wrote include "'Til the Rivers All Run Dry" (1977), "Some Broken Hearts Never Mend" (1977), "Could I Have This Dance" (1980), "Only Here for a Little While" (1991), and "Meanwhile" (1999). The Grammy-nominated "Could I Have This Dance" is a popular wedding song.

Holyfield's song "Arkansas (You Run Deep in Me)" was commissioned by Arkansas Power and Light Company for Arkansas's sesquicentennial in 1986; the song was adopted by the state legislature as one of Arkansas's official state songs in 1987. Holyfield performed the song at President Bill Clinton's inauguration in 1993. It was also used as a nightly sign-off theme in the 1980s and 1990s for the Arkansas Educational Television Network.

Holyfield has served as chairman and vice chairman of the Nashville Songwriters Foundation. Holyfield is also active in promoting the rights of songwriters, and he serves on the board of directors of the American Society of Composers, Authors and Publishers (ASCAP).

Holyfield has received numerous honors and awards, including ASCAP Country Writer of the Year in 1983. He was inducted into the Nashville Songwriters Hall of Fame in 1992 and the Arkansas Entertainers Hall of Fame in 1996.

For additional information:
"Interview with Wayland Holyfield." July 24, 2010. Audio online at Butler Center AV/AR Audio Video collection.
"Wayland Holyfield." Arkansas Entertainers Hall of Fame. http://arkansasentertainershalloffame.com/home2/?p=124 (accessed March 6, 2013).
"Wayland Holyfield." Nashville Songwriters Foundation. http://www.nashvillesongwritersfoundation.com/h-k/wayland-holyfield.aspx (accessed March 6, 2013).

Ali Welky

FOLK | ZILPHIA HORTON (1910–1956)

Zilphia Horton was an influential educator, folklorist, musician, and social justice activist who collected, adapted, performed, and promoted the use of folksongs and hymns in the labor and civil rights movements, notably "We Shall Not Be Moved" and "We Shall Overcome." These two, respectively, became labor and civil rights movement anthems. She served as the first cultural director of the Highlander Folk School in Tennessee—the precursor of today's Highlander Research and Education Center, founded by her husband Myles Horton—until her untimely death in 1956.

Zilphia Mae Johnson was born in Paris (Logan County) on April 14, 1910, the second child of Robert Guy Johnson, a coal mine superintendent, and Ora Ermon Howard Johnson, a schoolteacher. She was the eldest of four daughters.

Paris was a prosperous and growing community with a population of approximately 1,500 in 1910. The city's prosperity was based on coal mining, which was concentrated in a narrow band of coal fields located along the Arkansas River Valley. Johnson's father worked for the Paris Purity Coal Company. His ample income provided the family with an affluent lifestyle, including private music lessons for Zilphia, who began studying piano at age five and became an accomplished classical musician.

Johnson attended the College of the Ozarks (later the University of the Ozarks) in Clarksville (Johnson County), where she studied drama and music. She graduated in 1931.

In 1930, the Reverend Claude Williams became pastor of Paris's Cumberland Presbyterian church, which Johnson attended. Williams's ministry stressed solidarity with victims of social injustice, which appealed to working-class parishioners and young people such as Johnson and future folk singer Lee Hays, who regarded both Williams and Johnson as mentors. Despite the church's significant growth during his tenure, Williams's political and social views provoked community elites and congregational elders who, in 1935, ousted him from the pulpit.

Like Hays, Johnson was greatly influenced by Williams in ways that would help to chart the course of her life. In 1934, she joined him in an effort to unionize her father's coal mine. Myles Horton summarizes a pivotal episode from this period: "[Zilphia] got mixed up with Claude Williams....Claude was trying to organize the workers in Guy Johnson's mine for the Progressive Miners' Union....Zilphia got involved in this attempt to organize her dad's mine. Her father told her she had to stop going to Claude Williams's church, and if she didn't, he was going to throw her out of the house. She just ignored him, he disowned her, and some friends of mine sent her to Highlander."

Soon after she arrived at Highlander Folk School in early 1935, she and Myles Horton were married. Not long afterward, Myles mediated a partial reconciliation between his wife and father-in-law. The couple lived modestly at Highlander for many years and worked for the causes to which they had committed themselves. They had two children.

As Highlander's cultural director, Zilphia Horton pioneered the mobilization of folk culture resources, especially music, in the service of social justice causes. Her multifaceted work spanned a wide range of expressive arts, all of which aimed at educating and empowering oppressed people. Pete Seeger recalled the talent and temperament she brought to this work, and Lee Hays credited her with motivating him to become a folk singer.

Best known of Horton's many accomplishments, and illustrative of her work with many other songs, is her role in making an old hymn into the iconic anthem of the 1950s and 1960s

civil rights movement, "We Shall Overcome." In October 1945, she learned the version sung on the picket line during a tobacco workers' strike in Charleston, South Carolina, by Lucille Simmons, who had changed the words "I'll overcome" to "We will overcome." It soon became Horton's favorite song. She added verses to the song, such as "We'll walk hand in hand," and changed the tempo. Later, she taught it to Pete Seeger, who changed "We will" to "We shall" to make it easier to sing. Over a period of years, in large measure through Horton's influence, the protest song spread throughout the labor and civil rights movements, and beyond, eventually becoming an international anthem of social justice movements. Civil rights leader Julian Bond observed, "People tell me that you can go anywhere in the world today and there's somebody singing this song."

Horton died in Nashville, Tennessee, on April 11, 1956, just before her forty-sixth birthday from acute kidney failure from uremic poisoning following accidental ingestion of a typewriter cleaning solution.

For additional information:

Adams, Frank. *Unearthing Seeds of Fire: The Idea of Highlander*. Winston-Salem, NC: John F. Blair, 1975.

Austin, Aleine. "Zilphia." *Social Policy* 21 (Winter 1991): 49–52.

Brown, Jim, director. *We Shall Overcome: A Stirring Tribute to This International Civil Rights Anthem*. VHS. Arlington, VA: PBS Home Video, 1990.

Horton, Myles. *The Long Haul: An Autobiography*. New York: Teachers College Press, 1989.

Schmidt-Pirro, Julia, and Karen M. McCurdy. "Employing Music in the Cause of Social Justice: Ruth Crawford Seeger and Zilphia Horton." *Voices: The Journal of New York Folklore* 31 (Summer–Spring 2005). Online at http://www.nyfolklore.org/pubs/voic31-1-2/socjust1.html (accessed February 26, 2013).

Zilphia Horton Folk Music Collection. Manuscript Section. Tennessee State Library and Archives, Nashville, Tennessee.

Greg A. Phelps

CLASSICAL / OPERA — HOT SPRINGS MUSIC FESTIVAL

The Hot Springs Music Festival is a non-profit organization whose dual mission is, first, to provide exceptionally talented young musicians with intensive mentoring to prepare them for the early stages of their professional careers, and, second, to have them share the music they make with people in central Arkansas. To fulfill its mission, the festival organization produces a two-week annual event by the same name every June in the historic downtown district of Hot Springs (Garland County).

The festival was founded in 1995 by Richard Rosenberg, an orchestra conductor and music educator, and Laura Rosenberg, an arts administrator. Prior to founding the festival, Richard Rosenberg had been acting director of orchestras at the University of Michigan, associate conductor of the London Classical Players, and music director of the Pennsylvania Ballet, as well as a guest conductor of orchestras across the United States and in Europe. Laura Rosenberg had served as director of production for the Chamber Music Society of Lincoln Center, as concert director at Northwestern University, and as director of the Old First Concerts series in San Francisco.

They had observed weaknesses as well as evolving opportunities in the classical music field during the course of their careers and designed an event-based organization to help musicians adapt to this changing environment. The Rosenbergs chose the city of Hot Springs after a nationwide search for a community that possessed a significant but underutilized historic district, natural beauty, an easily accessed location, an ability to accommodate visitors of all socioeconomic levels, and a strong history of volunteerism.

In preparation for each festival season, young musicians from all over the world apply to become "apprentices." Their applications are competitively evaluated by "mentors," fully established, mid-career musicians from major symphony orchestras and conservatory faculties. Once selected, the apprentices meet their mentors in Hot Springs to rehearse and perform side by side in a full-immersion schedule of symphony orchestra, chamber orchestra, chamber music, and opera repertoire. Every apprentice is provided full scholarship and housing at the festival, plus access to career-building seminars and master classes. On average, 100 to 125 apprentices participate in the program each year; their scholarships are funded by a variety of individual, family, foundation, business, and corporate sponsors.

One unique feature of the Hot Springs Music Festival is that the entire music-making process,

rehearsals as well as concerts, is open to the public. Another is that the venues are non-traditional, encompassing hotel ballrooms, churches, and a historic gymnasium. Every aspect of the concert-going experience has been reevaluated: the musicians perform in casual black street clothes, and audiences are encouraged to participate in the relaxed atmosphere.

Since the Hot Springs Music Festival's inaugural season in 1996, it has been part of the visual and performing arts community that has spurred a renaissance of Hot Springs' previously neglected historic downtown district. In collaboration with organizations such as the Hot Springs Documentary Film Institute, the Hot Springs Gallery Walk Association, ArtBlast, and the University of Arkansas Elderhostel, it has helped to make "cultural tourism" a major economic force in the city.

In addition to its impact within Arkansas, the Hot Springs Music Festival has gained an international reputation for resurrecting, performing, and recording the music of underappreciated American composers, particularly the "Creole Romantics" of nineteenth-century New Orleans, Louisiana: Louis Moreau Gottschalk, the Lambert family, and Edmond and Eugène Dédé. The festival's recordings have received repeated National Public Radio broadcasts and are distributed worldwide on Naxos Records.

More than 20,000 people attend the festival's on-site events each year. The festival's apprentice alumni, including many native Arkansans, are employed throughout North America, South America, Europe, Asia, Africa, and Australia in orchestras, concert halls, and music conservatories.

For additional information:
Hot Springs Music Festival. http://www.hotmusic.org (accessed February 26, 2013).
Villani, John. *The 100 Best Arts Towns in America*. 4th ed. Woodstock, VT: The Countryman Press, 2005.

Laura Rosenberg

BLUES / R&B

HOWLIN' WOLF (1910–1976)

Chester Arthur Burnett, known as Howlin' Wolf, was one of the most influential musicians of the post–World War II era. His electric blues guitar, backing his powerful, howling voice, helped shape rock and roll.

Chester Burnett was born on June 10, 1910, in White Station, Mississippi, four miles north-

east of West Point, Mississippi, to Leon "Dock" Burnett, a sharecropper, and Gertrude Jones. His parents separated when he was one year old; his father moved to the Mississippi Delta to farm, and he and his mother moved to Monroe County, Mississippi, where she became an eccentric religious singer who performed and sold self-

Electric bluesman Howlin' Wolf.
Artists: Patterson and Barnes / From the Old State House Museum
Collection

penned spirituals on the street.

Burnett got the nickname "Wolf" because his grandfather would scare the youngster by telling him that the wolf in the woods would get him if he misbehaved. The rest of the family would then call him "Wolf" and howl at him.

When he was still a child, Burnett's mother sent him away to live with his uncle, who was particularly hard on him, whipping him with a bullwhip and making him eat separately from the rest of the family. At age thirteen, he ran away from home and moved to the Mississippi Delta. He eventually found his father and his father's new family on a plantation near Ruleville, Mississippi, and he began working on the plantation.

While there, Charlie Patton, the most popular musician in the Delta, showed him a few chords on the guitar. In January 1928, Burnett's father bought him a guitar, and he began to play regularly, eventually teaming with Patton, who taught him many tricks of showmanship.

Preferring the life of a blues musician to the harsh life of sharecropping, Burnett began wandering the delta regions of Mississippi and Arkansas, playing music anywhere he could make money. He was a giant of a man, standing over six feet three inches and weighing some 275 pounds, and he became well known in the region as a blues performer, not only for his showmanship but also for his large size and loud, howling voice.

In 1933, the Burnett family left Mississippi and moved to a large Arkansas plantation in Wilson (Mississippi County). In early 1934, they moved to the Nat Phillips Plantation on the St. Francis River approximately fifteen miles north of Parkin (Cross County). Despite his commitment to his music, Burnett faithfully returned each spring to plow his father's land.

Burnett began traveling in Oklahoma and all over the south, but Arkansas remained his main stomping ground. He learned to play harmonica from blues legend Sonny Boy Williamson and added it to his performing arsenal. Along with Williamson, Burnett also performed in the 1930s alongside Robert Johnson, Son House, Johnny Shines, Willie Brown, and Robert Lockwood Jr.

Burnett enlisted in the army, for which he was not well suited. After serving in the army, Burnett returned home to farm on the Phillips Plantation. Then he went to Penton, Mississippi, for two years, farming by day and playing music by night. In Penton, he met Katie Mae Johnson, and they were married on May 3, 1947.

In 1948, Burnett moved to West Memphis (Crittenden County). He took a job in a factory there, but the area's blues clubs were the real draw for him. West Memphis, then a town bustling with blues clubs and gambling, was at the forefront of the newly amplified blues music, and Burnett adapted quickly. He assembled a blues band in the area called the House Rockers and made a commitment to make music his career. While Muddy Waters was giving birth to electric blues in Chicago, Illinois, Burnett was doing the same thing in West Memphis.

Beginning in 1948, Burnett was performing on local radio station KWEM in West Memphis (he both produced and sold advertising for his program), where he attracted the attention of record producer Sam Phillips in Memphis, Tennessee. Phillips's recordings of "Moanin' At Midnight" and "How Many More Years" were leased to Chess Records and became a double-sided hit, making *Billboard* magazine's R&B top ten.

In September 1951, Burnett signed with the Chess label, and the Chess brothers convinced him to move to Chicago in the winter of 1952. His wife refused to follow him, and their marriage, which had been rocky, ended. Upon arriving in

Chicago, Burnett broke into the scene quickly and assembled a band in the West Memphis style. Among his band members was a young guitarist from West Memphis, Hubert Sumlin, who would stay with Burnett for the remainder of Burnett's career.

In 1954, he recorded "Evil," his biggest hit to that point, which landed on the *Cash Box* magazine Hot Chart. It was also the first of many tunes that Willie Dixon wrote for Burnett. As his audience grew, he toured more widely, and in 1955, he played New York's Apollo Theater. That year he made *Cash Box* magazine's list of the top twenty-five male R&B vocalists. By that time, only Muddy Waters rivaled his popularity in the blues arena.

In 1956, Burnett recorded his masterpiece work, "Smokestack Lightnin'." The hit peaked at number eleven on both the *Cash Box* Hot Chart and *Billboard*'s R&B chart. Over the next five years, Burnett recorded many hits: "I Asked For Water," "Who's Been Talking," "Sitting on Top of the World," "Spoonful," "Wang Dang Doodle," "Back Door Man," "Goin' Down Slow," "I Ain't Superstitious," and "Red Rooster." In 1959, Burnett released his first album on Chess, *Moaning in the Moonlight*, which was followed in January 1962 by *Howlin' Wolf*, sometimes referred to as the "Rocking Chair" album. Greil Marcus of *Rolling Stone* magazine called it "the finest of all Chicago blues albums."

On March 14, 1964, Burnett married Lillie Handley Jones, who was from Alabama. She was a property owner and a smart money manager, and they settled in south Chicago. She would remain with him until his death.

Burnett's later hits included "Tail Dragger" (1962); "Built for Comfort," "300 Pounds of Heavenly Joy," "Hidden Charms" (all in 1963); and "Love Me Darlin'" and "Killing Floor" (both in 1964).

In September 1964, he traveled to Europe as part of the 1964 American Folk Blues Festival, touring with such blues artists as Sonny Boy Williamson, Lightnin' Hopkins, Willie Dixon, and Sleepy John Estes. "Smokestack Lightnin'" was a huge hit in Great Britain, and Burnett commanded headliner status on the tour.

Burnett garnered wider exposure through the folk movement and British Invasion remakes of his classic blues songs. In 1965, he appeared on the ABC-TV show *Shindig* with the Rolling Stones, who had a number-one hit in England with "Red Rooster." Over the next several years, he played the prestigious Newport Folk Festival, the Berkeley Folk Festival, and the Ann Arbor Blues Festival. In that period, he released the albums *Real Folk Blues* (1966) and *More Real Folk Blues* (1967). In 1968, he released *Howlin' Wolf*, often referred to as the "electric" Howlin' Wolf album.

Despite failing health, including a 1969 heart attack, high blood pressure, and kidney problems, Burnett continued to tour and record. In May 1970, he went to London, England, and recorded *The London Howlin' Wolf Sessions* with such British rock stars as Eric Clapton, Mick Jagger, Bill Wyman, Charlie Watts, Steve Winwood, Ringo Starr, and Ian Stewart. It became the only Howlin' Wolf album to appear on the *Billboard* 200, spending fifteen weeks on the chart and peaking at number nineteen.

In early 1971, Wolf released the album, *Message to the Young*, which was considered his "psychedelic" record, as well as the nadir of his recording career. In May 1971, Burnett had a second heart attack, and doctors discovered that his kidneys were failing. He began to get hemodialysis treatments and was ordered by doctors to stop performing. But he would not quit, and three months later, he was the opening night headliner at the Ann Arbor Blues Festival.

In early 1972, Burnett cut the live album *Live and Cookin' at Alice's Revisited*. In August 1972, he received an honorary doctorate from Chicago's Columbia College. In August 1973, he recorded his final studio album, *The Back Door Wolf*. In 1975, he was nominated twice for a Grammy Award for Best Traditional or Ethnic Album for *Back Door Wolf* and *London Revisited*, a repackaging of the *London* sessions recorded by both him and Muddy Waters.

On January 7, 1976, Burnett was diagnosed with a brain tumor. He underwent surgery from which he never recovered. He was removed from life support and died on January 10, 1976. He is buried at Oak Ridge Cemetery in Chicago.

Burnett was elected to the Blues Foundation Hall of Fame in 1980 and was inducted into the Rock and Roll Hall of Fame in 1991. In 1994, the great bluesman was honored on a U.S. postage stamp.

For additional information:

Cohodas, Nadine. *Spinning Blues into Gold: The Chess Brothers and the Legendary Chess Records*. New York: St. Martin's Press, 2000.

George-Warren, Holly, and Patricia Romanowski, eds. *The*

Rolling Stone Encyclopedia of Rock & Roll. New York: Rolling Stone Press, 2001.

Guralnick, Peter. "Howlin' Wolf: What Is the Soul of a Man?" *Oxford American* 75 (2011): 60–65.

"Howlin' Wolf." Rock and Roll Hall of Fame and Museum. http://rockhall.com/inductees/howlin-wolf/bio/ (accessed February 8, 2013).

Lott, Eric. "Back Door Man: Howlin' Wolf and the Sound of Jim Crow." *American Quarterly* 63 (September 2011): 697–710.

Marsh, Dave, and John Swenson, eds. *The Rolling Stone Record Guide.* New York: Random House/Rolling Stone Press, 1979.

Segrest, James, and Mark Hoffman. *Moaning at Midnight: The Life and Times of Howlin' Wolf.* New York: Pantheon Books, 2004.

Bryan Rogers

J

GOSPEL / CONTEMPORARY CHRISTIAN JEFFRESS/PHILLIPS MUSIC COMPANY

The Jeffress/Phillips Music Company, located in Crossett (Ashley County), is one of the five remaining seven-shape gospel publishing companies in the United States and is the sole seven-shape gospel music publisher in the state of Arkansas.

William Nolin Jeffress.
Courtesy: Jeffress/Phillips Music

While known best as a rural tradition, shape notes, sometimes referred to as character or patent notes, are visual cues that act as points of reference, creating a unique notational style composed of geometric figures. This teaching mechanism led to the development of a rich and varied canon of American folk hymnody notated and practiced in shape notes, of which seven-shape gospel music comprises one specific tradition.

Successor to the Jeffress Music Company, Jeffress/Phillips Music is a family-run operation. William Nolin Jeffress, founder of the original Jeffress Music Company, studied the rudiments of music theory and composition at the Hartford Music Institute and began his shape-note publishing career with the Hartford Music Company in Hartford (Sebastian County). After establishing the Jeffress Music Company in 1944, Jeffress published his first songbook, *Holy Light: A Book of Gospel Songs for Conventions, Churches, Schools, Etc.*, on January 19, 1945. Jeffress led the company with his wife, Essye DhuAn Estelle, until her death in 1974. In 1975, he married Audie Lindsey and continued to run the publishing company until his death in 1985.

Jeffress's widow led the company until her death in 1996, at which point Jeffress's nephew, Marty Phillips, reorganized the company as Jeffress/Phillips Music.

Jeffress/Phillips Music publishes an annual songbook of new seven-shape gospel compositions. Phillips learned the trade of shape-note composing and publishing from his uncle and began typesetting the annually published songbooks at age twelve. After receiving a degree in business from the University of Arkansas (UA) in Fayetteville (Washington County) in 1973, Phillips continued to work for the company; his wife, Ann, began to work in the business when they married in 1974.

In addition to publishing a yearly songbook that is sold throughout Arkansas and the southeastern region of the United States, the company has long contributed to the singing school community in Arkansas. The Jeffress School of Gospel Music is hosted each summer at Beech Street Baptist Church in Crossett. The singing school is primarily staffed by members of the Jeffress and Phillips families, including siblings of William Nolin Jeffress and their offspring. The school offers instruction to both beginning and advanced students, including courses in basic and intermediate rudiments, advanced harmony and songwriting, directing, and sight singing, as well as private instruction in voice, guitar, and piano. In 1999, Marty and Ann Phillips and Trisha Watts published *Rudiments of Music: A Complete Study of the Basics of Music from Definitions of Musical Terms to a Summation of Key Signatures* for use in the Jeffress School of Gospel Music and in other singing schools around the country. In 2004, the Phillipses collaborated on another teaching tool, *Understanding Four-Part Harmony: A Simplified Concept of the Art of Harmonizing Music: Done So Through the Use of*

Shape and Round Notation.

In 2000, Jeffress/Phillips Music began publishing a quarterly newsletter, *The Good News*, which was later renamed *What's Happening*. This newsletter has more than 130 subscribers across ten states. Marty and Ann Phillips travel widely each summer to teach at singing schools across the region. Their work at singing schools in Mississippi, Alabama, Tennessee, Texas, Louisiana, and North Carolina helps sustain the tradition of seven-shape gospel music within Arkansas and the greater southeastern region of the United States.

For additional information:

Deller, David. "The Songbook Gospel Movement in Arkansas: E. M. Bartlett and the Hartford Music Company." *Arkansas Historical Quarterly* 60 (Autumn 2001): 284–300.

Jeffress/Phillips Music Company. http://jeffressphillipsmusic.com/ (accessed March 21, 2012).

Meredith Doster

BLUES / R&B — "LITTLE WILLIE" JOHN (1937–1968)

William Edgar "Little Willie" John was a powerful rhythm and blues vocalist and songwriter who recorded several hit songs, including the original version of "Fever" at age eighteen.

Little Willie John was born on November 15, 1937, in Cullendale (Ouachita County). He was one of ten children. His father, Mertis, was a logger in northern Louisiana and southern Arkansas; his mother, Lillie, played guitar and sang gospel songs, teaching them to her children. His sister Mable, also raised in Ouachita County, recorded as a Raelette for Ray Charles and solo for Stax Records.

In 1942, the Johns moved to Detroit, Michigan, so Mertis could pursue factory work. The eldest children, including Willie, formed a gospel quintet in the 1940s. A powerful and emotive vocalist, the teenaged John also gained notice singing at solo amateur shows—including the attention of performer Johnnie Otis, who reportedly tried to get him a recording contract but was turned away because John was too young.

Producer, musician, and arranger Henry Glover of Hot Springs (Garland County) signed John to King Records in June 1955 after encountering him in New York City, when John was seventeen. Nicknamed "Little Willie" due to his short stature, John also had a short temper and considerable insecurity about his height—all made worse by his propensity to abuse alcohol. After a brief tenure with the Paul "Hucklebuck" Williams orchestra, John was dumped for misbehavior. Glover, who produced country, R&B, and rock hits and wrote such songs as "Drown in My Own Tears" and "California Sun," said he first heard John sing one day at 5:00 p.m.; he was so impressed, they were in the studio recording by 8:00 p.m.

John recorded a version of "All Around the World" the day the original Titus Turner version was released. His debut reached R&B's top five in 1955, and John's follow-ups charted at fifth and sixth—including one written by his brother Mertis Jr. When he was barely eighteen, John cut the first version of the evergreen "Fever" in Cincinnati, Ohio, on March 1, 1956, with Glover producing.

Through the late 1950s and early 1960s, John kept charting songs—1959's "Let Them Talk," 1960's "Sleep," 1961's "Take My Love." But increasing alcoholism and weakening sales caused King Records to drop him by the fall of 1963. He hit the club circuit without a recording contract, although King continued to issue his material from its vaults.

John was arrested in Miami, Florida (where he had moved probably in 1957 or 1958) for attacking a man with a broken bottle in August 1964. That same month, the Beatles cut several versions of their club favorites for the band's rushed *Beatles for Sale* sessions—including "Leave My Kitten Alone," a 1959 R&B and pop charter for John that charted again with its reissue in December 1960. But the song, co-written by John, was ultimately left off the Beatles album.

In October 1964, John killed a man at an after-hours party in Seattle, Washington. The man had apparently taken a chair from one of the women accompanying John. John confronted the man, who promptly punched him. In retaliation, John rose with a knife and stabbed the man.

Then twenty-six years old, he was charged with murder. He posted $10,000 bond and continued touring, returning for trial in 1965. Convicted of manslaughter, he began serving his eight- to twenty-year sentence at Walla Walla

State Penitentiary on July 6, 1966. He died nearly two years later, on May 26, 1968, in the maximum security facility. Rumors of prison beatings or other foul play have always surrounded his death.

After John's death, one-time opening act James Brown recorded a tribute album, *Thinking of Little Willie John and a Few Nice Things*. Brown had since signed with John's former label and become its biggest artist.

Johnnie Taylor of Crawfordsville (Crittenden County) was among the many R&B singers who later performed John's songs, including John's sister Mable.

In rock and roll, Phillips County native Levon Helm and Robbie Robertson of the Band are among those who have acknowledged John's influence. Robertson said John "opened up a door to something for me," and when he coordinated *The Color of Money* film soundtrack, he asked British rocker Robert Palmer to contribute to the project a version of John's overlooked 1963 rumba, "My Baby's in Love with Another Guy." Robertson also references John in his minor 1987 hit, "Somewhere Down the Crazy River." Retro-rockers the Blasters covered another obscure John single, 1960's "I'm Shakin'," and the Allman Brothers recorded a version of "Need Your Love So Bad." And from Peggy Lee to Madonna, the song "Fever" lives on through countless versions, but John's haunting, tortured vocals have yet to be replicated. He left a brief but profound musical legacy.

For additional information:
Bowman, Rob. *Soulsville, U.S.A.: The Story of Stax Records.* New York: Schirmer Books, 1997.
Hoffman, Steve. "Little Willie John." *Encyclopedia of the Blues.* New York: Routledge, 2005.
Koch, Stephen. "Big Voice, Big Hits, Big Trouble." *Arkansas Democrat-Gazette*, September 19, 1999, pp. 1E–2E.

Stephen Koch

GOSPEL / CONTEMPORARY CHRISTIAN — WILLA SAUNDERS JONES (1901–1979)

Willa Saunders Jones grew up in Little Rock (Pulaski County) during the first decades of the twentieth century before moving to Chicago, Illinois, where she became a prominent religious and cultural leader. Her crowning achievement was a passion play (a dramatization of Christ's life, death, and resurrection), which she wrote in the 1920s and produced for more than five decades in churches and eventually prestigious civic theaters. The play featured top musical talent, including Dinah Washington and Jones's close friend Mahalia Jackson, and drew support from such prominent figures as the Reverend Jesse Jackson Sr. and Chicago mayor Richard J. Daley. Her success in music as a soloist, accompanist, and choral director and in drama stemmed from early experiences in the African-American community of Little Rock and represented the dynamic cultural exchange between the urban South and North.

Willa Saunders was born in Little Rock to Ada Pulliam and George Washington Saunders on February 22, 1901; she had a twin sister who died in infancy and a half-brother. She grew up guided by a close-knit group of relatives in neighboring homes on the southwest side of the city. Her grandfather Joseph Davis was a charter member and prominent official of the Mosaic Templars of America, and her father served as pastor of First Baptist Church–Highland Park. Under his leadership, the church grew, and his position on the Home Missions Board of the National Baptist Convention, USA, offered his daughter early exposure to the denomination's organizational power. While socially situated in the black middle class, Saunders grew up poor. She learned to play piano on a piece of cardboard with charcoal-drawn keys, receiving instruction from a white neighbor girl.

Saunders attended Stephens Elementary School, graduating from the eighth grade with honors. She entered Arkansas Baptist College, where her father had previously taught, and took a wide range of liberal arts courses. Around the time she graduated with the equivalent of a high school diploma from Arkansas Baptist, she married her childhood sweetheart, George Washington Jones, who attended Philander Smith College. The couple put themselves through school by living with relatives and working menial jobs. Prior to the birth of their first child, George Jr., in January 1921, Jones worked at a laundry. Her husband earned enough at a lumberyard to afford regular payments on a house in North Little Rock (Pulaski County), into which the young family planned to move. The couple later had a second son, Charles, as well as a daughter, Betty Jane, who died soon after birth.

Jones lived in Little Rock when the city was a hub of black middle-class cultural activity. Influential composers William Grant Still and Florence Price were developing their craft, Carrie Still Shepperson (Still's mother) was producing various dramatic works, and Charlotte Andrews Stephens—the pioneering and widely respected black educator after whom Jones's primary school was named—was introducing local black citizens to community theater and the fundraising possibilities of music and drama. Mattie Albert Booker Pearry, the daughter of Arkansas Baptist College president Joseph A. Booker, probably had a more immediate influence on Jones than any other cultural leader. Through Sunday afternoon "community sings" at the school, Jones witnessed the power of spirituals and anthems to move both black and white audiences.

An unfortunate series of events foiled the Joneses' plan to move into their new home in North Little Rock. In March 1921, a white woman claimed that two black men had assaulted her, with one raping her. In Jones's presence, a vigilance committee entered her home and later strip-searched George Jones and his friend Emanuel West. When the alleged victim later identified West as the rapist, George Jones became the primary witness in a trial that garnered national media attention. Fearing those who attempted to lynch West, the Joneses fled Arkansas, although George Jones returned to defend his friend in court. (In spite of overwhelming evidence in favor of his innocence, and after a highly publicized initial trial that ended in a hung jury, a second jury sentenced West to life in prison, though Governor John E. Martineau later pardoned him.)

In Chicago, Willa Saunders Jones became a teacher and cultural leader similar to Pearry, Shepperson, and Stephens, signaling the significance of her Arkansas upbringing. By the 1930s, she sang with elite sacred choral groups and played organ for several Baptist churches. In 1933, Jones took the solo lead on Price's choral work "Banjo Song" before a large interracial audience at Chicago Orchestra Hall. In the 1940s and 1950s, she directed massive choruses across the country for the National Baptist Convention. Nothing brought greater acclaim and buttressed her religious authority more than the passion play. George Jones played the role of Christ for more than thirty years until his death in 1965, while she produced and directed the play until her death on January 15, 1979.

For additional information:

Hallstoos, Brian. "Pageant and Passion: Willa Saunders Jones and Early Black Sacred Drama in Chicago." *Journal of American Drama and Theatre* 19 (Spring 2007): 77–97.

———. "Willa Saunders Jones." In *African American National Biography*, Vol. 5, edited by Henry Louis Gates Jr. and Evelyn Brooks Higginbotham. New York: Oxford University Press, 2008.

———. "Windy City, Holy Land: Willa Saunders Jones and Black Sacred Music and Drama." PhD diss., University of Iowa, 2009. Online at http://ir.uiowa.edu/etd/371 (accessed February 26, 2013).

"Passion Play: Annual Chicago Presentation of All-Negro Religious Play Proves Big Box Office Draw." *Ebony,* (May 1950) 25–28.

Willa Saunders Jones Papers. Carter G. Woodson Regional Library. Chicago Public Library, Chicago, Illinois.

Brian Hallstoos

SCOTT JOPLIN (1868?–1917)

Known as the "King of Ragtime," Scott Joplin composed more than forty ragtime piano pieces, including "Maple Leaf Rag" (which sold more than a million copies) and "The Entertainer" (which was used in the 1973 film *The Sting*). He spent his formative years in Texarkana (Miller County), and his major opera, *Treemonisha*, is set in the plantation area of Rondo (Miller County) north of Texarkana.

Scott Joplin was born on November 24, 1867 or 1868, near Marshall, Texas. His father, Giles, was a former slave, and his mother, Florence, was a freed woman from Kentucky. The family moved to Texarkana early in Joplin's life so that his father could obtain work on the railroad. Joplin showed an early interest in the piano, and he practiced in the homes where his mother did domestic work. His teachers included Mag Washington, John C. Johnson, and Julius Weiss, a German immigrant who taught him piano technique and exposed him to the European opera music that influenced his later compositions.

Joplin left Texarkana at seventeen and traveled to Texas, Louisiana, Mississippi, and various places in Arkansas. In 1885, he joined the all-night ragtime piano competitions at Tom

Turpin's Silver Dollar Saloon in St. Louis, Missouri. His rail travels took him as far as Syracuse, New York.

Joplin arrived in Sedalia, Missouri, in 1894 and played in the Williams Brothers Maple Leaf Club; his famous "Maple Leaf Rag" (1899) took on the name of that club. His moniker, "The Entertainer," printed on the club business card, also became the name of one of his famous works. He took a music theory course at George R. Smith College in Sedalia around 1896 to learn how to notate the complicated rhythms of piano ragtime. This skill enabled his music to reach a wider audience through publication.

In 1899, John Stark, an agent for the Mason and Hamlin piano company, contracted with Joplin to publish "Maple Leaf Rag" for fifty dollars, plus royalties. Through nationwide sales at F. W. Woolworth stores, the song sold more than a million copies. This single publication freed Joplin from performing in honky-tonk saloons and enabled him to teach and compose.

Joplin married Belle Hayden in 1901, and the couple followed Stark to his new piano store in St. Louis. During this time, Alfred Ernst, conductor of the St. Louis Choral Symphonic Society, took an interest in Joplin. Encouragement from this European-trained conductor inspired Joplin to compose an opera and ballet. But his efforts resulted in little financial support from Ernst or from general audiences. A tour of his opera *The Guest of Honor* (1903) disbanded because of lack of interest.

Joplin divorced his first wife in 1904. He married his second wife, Freddie Alexander, in Little Rock (Pulaski County) on June 14, 1904, but she died of pneumonia ten weeks later. Finding solace in his work, Joplin went to New York City, where Stark had opened a new piano store and publishing company.

In 1909, Joplin married Lottie Stokes. By this time, he was known as the "King of Ragtime" because he had composed more than forty successful piano ragtime numbers and had published a sheet music booklet titled *School of Ragtime*. Stark continued to publish Joplin's piano works in New York, but he declined to publish Joplin's opera *Treemonisha*. The opera is set in the Red River region near Rondo and tells the story of a plantation girl who fights conjurors and voodoo magic to lead her people to freedom through education. Joplin mounted an unstaged version of the opera in 1915 at the Harlem Lincoln Theater, accompanying singers at the piano. But he died of tertiary syphilis two years later, on April 1, 1917, without having seen it produced with costumes and full orchestra. He is buried in St. Michael's Cemetery in Queen's County, New York.

Joplin's fame returned in the 1970s when "The Entertainer" was used in the film *The Sting*. *Treemonisha* was later performed at the Kennedy Center for the Performing Arts in Washington DC and at the Houston Grand Opera in Texas. In 1976, he was posthumously awarded the Pulitzer Prize for his contributions to American music.

Scott Joplin Notable Works

"Maple Leaf Rag," ragtime piano piece (1899)

"The Entertainer," ragtime piano piece (1902)

The Guest of Honor, opera (1903)

School of Ragtime, sheet music booklet (1908)

Treemonisha, opera (1911)

For additional information:

Albrecht, Theodore. "Julius Weiss: Scott Joplin's First Piano Teacher." *College Music Symposium* 19 (Fall 1979): 89–105.

Berlin, Edward A. *King of Ragtime: Scott Joplin and His Era*. New York: Oxford University Press, 1994.

Blesh, Rudi, and Harriet Janis. *They All Played Ragtime*. New York: Oak Publications, 1971.

Curtis, Susan. *Dancing to a Black Man's Tune: A Life of Scott Joplin*. Columbia: University of Missouri Press, 1994.

Ping-Robbins, Nancy R. *Scott Joplin: A Guide to Research*. New York: Garland Publishing, 1998.

Vanderlee, Ann, and John Vanderlee. "The Early Life of Scott Joplin." Unpublished manuscript. Texarkana Museum of History, Texarkana, Arkansas.

Stephen Husarik

BLUES / R&B ■ LOUIS JORDAN (1908–1975)

Louis Thomas Jordan—vocalist, bandleader, and saxophonist—ruled the charts, stage, screen, and airwaves of the 1940s and profoundly influenced the creators of rhythm and blues (R&B), rock and roll, and post–World War II blues.

Louis Jordan was born on July 8, 1908, in Brinkley (Monroe County). His father, Dardanelle (Yell County) native James Aaron Jordan, led the Brinkley Brass Band; his mother, Mississippi native Adell, died when Louis was young. Jordan studied music under his father and showed promise in horn playing, especially clarinet and saxophone. Due to World War I vacancies, young Jordan joined his father's band himself. Soon, he was good enough to join his father in a professional traveling show—touring Arkansas, Tennessee, and Missouri by train, instead of doing farm work when school closed. Show venues included churches, lodges, parades, picnics, or weddings; bands had to be ready to handle Charlestons, ballads, and any requests.

Jordan briefly attended Arkansas Baptist College in Little Rock (Pulaski County) in the late 1920s—he was later a benefactor to the school—and performed with Jimmy Pryor's Imperial Serenaders in Little Rock. He played saxophone and clarinet with the Imperial Serenaders and Bob Alexander's Harmony Kings in El Dorado (Union County) and Smackover (Union County) during their boom lumber and oil eras, getting twice the going five-dollars-per-gig rate in Little Rock. The Harmony Kings then took a job at Wilson's Tell-'Em-'Bout-Me Cafe in Hot Springs (Garland County); Jordan also performed at the Eastman Hotel and Woodmen of the Union Hall and with the band of Ruby "Junie Bug" Williams at the Green Gables Club on the Malvern Highway near town, as well as at the Club Belvedere on the Little Rock Highway. He rented a room at Pleasant and Garden streets in Hot Springs.

The lengths and legitimacy of his marriages are in some dispute. He first married Arkadelphia (Clark County) native Julia/Julie (surname unknown). He met Texas native singer and dancer Ida Fields at a Hot Springs cakewalk and married her in 1932, though he may have still been married to his first wife. He and Fields divorced in the early 1940s when he took up with childhood sweetheart Fleecie Moore of Brasfield (Prairie County), a dozen miles from Brinkley. They married in 1942. Moore is listed as co-composer on many hit Jordan songs, such as "Buzz Me," "Caldonia Boogie," and "Let the Good Times Roll." Jordan used her name to enable him to work with an additional music publisher; he had cause to regret it later, however, after she stabbed him during an argument, and though they reconciled for a time, he ended up divorcing her. Jordan married dancer Vicky Hayes in 1951 (and separated from her in 1960) and singer and dancer Martha Weaver in 1966.

In the 1930s, based in Philadelphia, Pennsylvania, Jordan found work in the Charlie Gaines band—playing clarinet and soprano and alto sax,

in addition to doing vocals—which recorded and toured with Louis Armstrong. The two Louises would later play duets when Jordan became a solo star. Jordan learned baritone sax during this period. In 1936, he joined nationally popular drummer Chick Webb's Savoy Ballroom Band. Ella Fitzgerald was the band's featured singer; Jordan played sax and got the occasional

Portrait of Louis Jordan.
Collage: Byron Werner

vocal, such as "Rusty Hinge," recorded in March 1937. In 1938, Jordan was fired by Webb for trying to convince Fitzgerald and others to join his new band.

Jordan's band, which changed American popular music, was always called the Tympany Five, regardless of the number of pieces. The small size of Jordan's Tympany Five made it innovative structurally and musically in the Big Band era. Among the first to join electric guitar and bass with horns, Jordan set the framework for decades of future R&B and rock combos. Endless rehearsals, matching suits, dance moves, and routines built around songs made the band; Jordan's singular brand of sophisticated yet down-home jump blues and vocals made it a success. His humorous, over-the-beat monologues and depictions of black life are a prototype of rap; his crossover appeal to whites calcified his popularity. Jordan charted dozens of hits from the early 1940s to the early 1950s—up-tempo songs like "Choo Choo Ch'Boogie" (number one for eighteen weeks) and "Ain't Nobody Here But Us Chickens" (number one for seventeen weeks), and ballads like "Is You Is Or Is You Ain't (My Baby)."

With Jordan's clowning for crowds, often overlooked was his musical talent. He could play a solo and delve into a rapid-fire vocal or routine without missing a beat. He demanded no less from his groups, among the most polished of their peers. Although Jordan's songs could depict drunken, raucous scenes—like "Saturday Night Fish Fry" (number one for twelve weeks) and "What's the Use of Gettin' Sober?"—he did not drink or smoke and could be quiet and aloof, in contrast to the jiving hipster he portrayed. Jordan was also a fine ballad singer—as songs such as "Don't Let the Sun Catch You Crying" and "I'll Never Be Free," sung with Ella Fitzgerald, show. He helped introduce calypso music to America and toured the Caribbean in the early 1950s, fooling natives with his faux West Indian singing accent.

Jordan said he chose to play "for the people"—no be-bop or self-indulgent solos, just Jordan's unique, fun urban blues. He also starred in early examples of music video—"Soundies," introduced in 1940—and longer films based around his songs, such as *Beware!* (1946), *Reet, Petite, and Gone* (1947), and *Look Out Sister* (1948). He cameoed in movies like *Follow the Boys* (1944) and *Swing Parade of 1946* (1946). Loved by World War II GIs, and selected to record wartime "V-discs," he remains known overseas today.

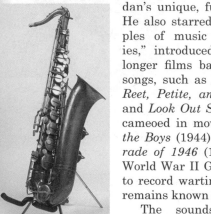

Louis Jordan's saxophone from 1939.

Courtesy: Old State House Museum Collection

The sounds Jordan pioneered conspired to slow his record sales as R&B and rock and roll emerged. His more than fifteen years on Decca—not counting his time there with Webb—ended in 1954; he sold millions of records for the company and performed duets with Armstrong, Bing Crosby, and Fitzgerald. During the late 1950s and early 1960s, Jordan released consistently engaging material, but for a variety of labels (Aladdin, Black Lion, RCA's X, Vik, and Ray Charles's Tangerine) and to decreasing results. Jordan continued to tour, including Europe and Asia in the late 1960s. He returned to Brinkley in 1957 for Louis Jordan Day. He spent much of the late 1960s and early 1970s without a recording contract. In 1973, Jordan issued a final LP, *I Believe in Music*, on the Black & Blue label.

Just over a year later, on February 4, 1975,

he died in Los Angeles, California. Jordan is buried in St. Louis, hometown of his widow, Martha.

A host of prominent musicians claim his influence, including Ray Charles, James Brown, Bo Diddley, and Chuck Berry. His songs have appeared in commercials, on TV, and in movies and have been recorded by dozens of popular artists. Tribute albums include Clarence "Gatemouth" Brown's *Sings Louis Jordan* (1973), Joe Jackson's *Jumpin' Jive* (1981), and B. B. King's *Let the Good Times Roll* (1999).

Jordan was inducted into the Rock and Roll Hall of Fame in 1987 and named an American Music Master by the Hall in 1999. A musical revue of Jordan's songs, *Five Guys Named Moe*, played on London's West End and Broadway in the 1990s. A nine-CD Decca retrospective was released by Germany's Bear Family in 1992. In Little Rock, the first Louis Jordan Tribute concert was held in 1997, with proceeds benefiting a Jordan bust in Brinkley by artist John Deering. Jordan was inducted into the Arkansas Entertainers Hall of Fame in 1998 and the Arkansas Black Hall of Fame in 2005. In 2008, the U. S. Postal Service released a stamp featuring Jordan as he appeared in the 1945 short film *Caldonia*.

For additional information:

Chilton, John. *Let the Good Times Roll: The Story of Louis Jordan and His Music.* Ann Arbor: University of Michigan Press, 1994.

Feather, Leonard. *The Encyclopedia of Jazz.* New York: Horizon Press, 1955.

Jancik, Wayne, and Tad Lathrop. *Cult Rockers.* New York: Simon & Schuster, 1995.

Sampson, Henry T. *Blacks in Black and White: A Source Book on Black Films.* Metuchen, NJ: Scarecrow Press, 1995.

Stephen Koch

This entry, originally published in *Arkansas Biography: A Collection of Notable Lives*, appears in the *Encyclopedia of Arkansas Music* in an altered form. *Arkansas Biography* is available from the University of Arkansas Press in Fayetteville.

K

MISCELLANEA | KAAY

KAAY (AM 1090) has been one of Arkansas's most influential radio stations since it came into being on September 3, 1962. The station incorporated a successful mixed format of music, religion, farm reports, and news that was

innovative for the time. Shortly after it had come on the air, KAAY was also utilized by the U.S. government to broadcast propaganda to Cuba during the Cuban Missile Crisis. In 1966, KAAY also successfully brought a new musical format to mid-America on the program *Beaker Street*. KAAY was born out of KTHS, the state's first 50,000-watt AM broadcast station. KTHS (which stood for "Kum To Hot Springs") officially came on the air in 1924 and was granted its new increased-power operating privileges in 1953 when it moved from Hot Springs (Garland County) to Little Rock (Pulaski County). Later, when LIN Broadcasting bought the station, Labor Day–weekend listeners were teased by a new, temporary format: that of radio announcers reading names and addresses out of the Little Rock phone book and welcoming them to "The Friendly Giant" over Henry Mancini's "Baby Elephant Walk."

Radio station KAAY's 7th Street studio in Little Rock; circa 1964.
Courtesy: Bud Stacey

Interestingly, the announcers' air names were taken from LIN Broadcasting's board of directors. The original line-up was Dub Murray ("Doc Holiday"), Jim Hankins ("Mike McCormick"), Wayne Moss (the first "Sonny Martin"), and Tom Bigby ("Buddy Karr")—the station's first music director, with the popular "Carpool Party." A religious block aired from 6:00 p.m. until 8:00 p.m., when Tom Campbell ("Rob Robbins") took the shift until midnight. From there, Howard Watson ("Ken Knight") took over until 6:00 a.m. Later, Dale Seidenschwarz was given LIN's comptroller's name, "Clyde Clifford," and went on to broadcast a very popular program called *Beaker Street*. As deejays left for other markets, their air names were dropped to the bottom of a list, and the next new announcer would pick up the air name at the top of the list. These names were patented by the station so that they could not be taken to competitors' markets. In some cases, a former announcer would be hired again by KAAY while his original air name was being utilized, so he used his real name; this happened with Wayne Moss in later years, as a "Sonny Martin" was on the air at the time.

KAAY was probably the first station in Arkansas to employ two full-time newsmen. The station would "scoop" the competition by having a news segment at a quarter to the hour and later at a quarter after the hour. KAAY also was successful in using original comedy in its programming. One highly successful program was *Ear on Arkansas*, a radio parody of *Eye on Arkansas* on television's Channel 11.

Top 40 music was the main format, but, in 1966, a new segment called *Beaker Street* was added. This program brought a totally different mixture of music during the late evening hours, including a selection of hard rock, blues, jazz, and more—music some termed "West Coast music." "Clyde Clifford," being both an announcer and licensed engineer, ran the "underground program" from the transmitter site in Wrightsville (Pulaski County), about twenty miles southeast of Little Rock. This not only allowed him to have the freedom to play the music (long album cuts) not heard anywhere else in the region but also gave a cost savings to LIN Broadcasting for having one person doing two jobs, as well as having the station on the air and productive over night. This was during a time when the Federal Communications Commission (FCC) had rules stating that an engineer had to be on duty at all times when a station was in operation. Because of the noise of the huge cooling fans on the RCA BTA-50F transmitter, Clifford played weird music in the background when his microphone was open for announcements.

Beaker Street settled into the 11:00 p.m. to 2:00 a.m. time slot and was followed by *Beaker Theater*, consisting of mystery programs from Great Britain. When the program was discontinued in 1972, Clifford left. However, the program was resurrected and aired again with different deejays.

KAAY radiated widely. The station's primary pattern blanketed nearly the whole state of Arkansas; its secondary pattern went well beyond the state's borders into the Gulf of Mexico, the Bahamas, Central and South America, and Canada. Rock musicians and other listeners in Cuba listened to KAAY nightly with Soviet-made transistor radios. There is an urban legend that U.S. troops heard the station in Vietnam, but there is no physical proof of this; however, a letter from a military installation in England verified KAAY's signal there. It is also documented that the station was heard in forty states and twenty-nine countries.

Because KAAY's signal pattern also covered Cuba, the station lent its services to the U.S. government to broadcast "Voice of America" programming to the Cuban people during the Cuban Missile Crisis of October 1962. The U.S. government had originally overlooked KAAY for this service, conflating it with KTHS, which was thought to be off the air. There were other stations already broadcasting to Cuba, but no one had the signal pattern KAAY had. Later, President John F. Kennedy honored station executives for this undertaking. This letter of commendation is displayed on the wall next to KAAY's original mixing board in the Museum of Discovery in Little Rock.

KAAY went through several owners, the original being LIN Broadcasting, followed by Multimedia and Sudbrink Broadcasting. In 1998, KAAY was sold to Citadel, the station's current owner. The last day KAAY broadcast Top 40 music was April 3, 1985. Clifford was given the honor of doing a one-hour *Beaker Street* on the last hour of the last day. *Beaker Street* was revived years later with Clifford as the host and was broadcast Sunday nights on Magic 105 FM, then KKPT 94.1 FM; it ceased broadcast at midnight on February 6, 2011. KAAY's current format is Christian talk radio and contemporary Christian music.

For additional information:

AM 1090 KAAY. http://www.1090kaay.com/ (accessed February 26, 2013).

"The Friendly Giant, KAAY, Little Rock, Arkansas." *Monitoring Times*. February 2010, p. 11.

Mighty 1090 KAAY. http://mighty1090kaay.blogspot.com/ (accessed February 26, 2013).

Robinson, Richard Cyril. "KAAY's 'Beaker Street' 1966–1977: Late Nights of Underground Radio Programming, from Little Rock to the Western Hemisphere, on the Airwaves of the Nighttime Voice of Arkansas." PhD diss., Southern Illinois University at Carbondale, 2009.

Melvin "Bud" Stacey

BLUES / R&B — ALBERT KING (1923–1992)

Albert King, one of the most influential blues guitarists of all time, was one of the three so-called "Kings of the Blues"—the triumvirate of B. B. King, Freddie King, and himself. His style of single-string-bending intensity—the essence of blues guitar—is evident in the approaches of thousands of acolytes, including Jimi Hendrix, Stevie Ray Vaughan, and Eric Clapton.

King was born Albert Nelson on April 25, 1923, on a cotton plantation in Indianola, Mississippi. He had twelve known siblings. His father, Will Nelson, an amateur guitarist, had a major impact on his music. Though he was mainly self-taught, he was inspired by Blind Lemon Jefferson. His singing in a family gospel group at a nearby church also influenced his music. He was one of the first major blues performers to cross over into "soul," commonly defined as a synthesis of blues and gospel.

Guitarist Albert King, one of the "Kings of the Blues."

Artists: Patterson and Barnes / From the Old State House Museum Collection

Not much is known about King's early years. He first played professionally in and around Osceola (Mississippi County), where he moved with his family in 1931 and where he heard such legendary Delta blues regulars as Elmore James and Robert Nighthawk while he played in a group named In the Groove Boys. In the early 1950s, he was in Gary, Indiana, where he briefly played drums behind Jimmy Reed, perhaps the most popular bluesman of the 1960s. He started recording in 1953 for the Parrot label, but he received little remuneration for that work, so he moved to St. Louis, Missouri. There, he recorded for the Bobbin and King labels. His most successful single was "Don't Throw Your Love on Me So Strong," which peaked at No. 14 on the rhythm and blues charts.

The most important event in King's career was his signing with Stax Records of Memphis, Tennessee, in 1966. He was accompanied by the "house" band, Booker T. & the MG's, one of the most skillful music ensembles of the rock era—made up of guitarist Steve Cropper, bassist Donald "Duck" Dunn, drummer Al Jackson Jr., and keyboard wizard Booker T. Jones. King honed his style in this homegrown (and independent) atmosphere, creating some of his most memorable recordings: "Born Under a Bad Sign," "Crosscut Saw," "I'll Play the Blues for You," and "As the Years Go Passing By."

He was so popular during this time that he was booked as the opening act for the premiere presentation at San Francisco's soon-to-be top rock and roll showcase, the Fillmore West, on February 1, 1968. Jimi Hendrix and John Mayall followed him onstage, but King stole the show and became a regular attraction at the Fillmore West. He also recorded one of his most powerful albums, *Live Wire/Blues Power*, there in 1968. In 1969, he recorded with the St. Louis Symphony Orchestra, becoming one of the first blues performers to unite blues and classical music.

For the rest of his life, he toured regularly (and often indiscriminately), always in the classic manner. He was a curiosity in that he was left-handed and played with his guitar upside-down and backward (simply flipping over the instrument). He was of the rough and rowdy "old school." He was reputed to carry a .45-caliber pistol in the waistband of his pants, and he was reported time and again as keeping a ready

submachine gun on his bus. But he was best known for his tireless entertainment value.

King died on December 21, 1992, in Memphis after a heart attack. There, he was honored with a jazz-style "blues funeral" procession down Beale Street with the Memphis Horns (Wayne Jackson and Andrew Love) playing "When the Saints Go Marching In." He was buried across the Mississippi River in Arkansas in Paradise Gardens Cemetery in Edmondson (Crittenden County), near his childhood home. He was inducted into the Arkansas Entertainers Hall of Fame in 2010 and the Rock and Roll Hall of Fame in 2013.

For additional information:

"Albert King." Rock and Roll Hall of Fame and Museum. http://rockhall.com/inductees/albert-king/ (accessed February 13, 2013).

Gordon, Robert. *It Came from Memphis*. New York: Atria, 2001.

Guralnick, Peter. *Sweet Soul Music: Rhythm and Blues and the Southern Dream of Freedom*. New York: Harper Collins, 1986.

Jim Kelton

BLUES / R&B KING BISCUIT BLUES FESTIVAL

The first weekend in October, the Mississippi River town of Helena-West Helena (Phillips County), about seventy miles southwest of Memphis, Tennessee, becomes a thriving community of blues musicians and their fans, gathered to enjoy the King Biscuit Blues Festival.

The festival grounds now lie along a levee, but during the early years, the festival was held on the back of a flatbed truck in front of an old train depot, which is now a museum and the site of the Delta Cultural Center on Cherry Street. Cherry Street, which parallels the Mississippi River, is a National Historic District and the historic commercial center of town. What began in 1986 as a one-day event with a crowd of 500 has become a three-day event with more than 100,000 people attending. The festival draws blues enthusiasts from around the nation and around the world. Despite Helena-West Helena's declining population, hotels and motels have few vacancies on festival weekend.

The festival now sprawls well beyond its initial 1986 boundaries. By 2013, there were six stages. Musicians are booked not only on the main stage but also on ones that include gospel

Performers on stage at the King Biscuit Blues Festival held in Helena-West Helena.

Courtesy: Arkansas Department of Parks and Tourism

choirs and other groups in addition to artists who perform more traditional Delta blues. One stage is called the Houston Stackhouse Stage in the morning and the Robert Junior Lockwood Stage in the afternoon, each named for a local blues legend. All along Cherry Street, vendors sell their blues-related crafts and food. The festival also hosts a barbecue competition.

The event frequently attracts blues musicians who play on street corners and can be heard throughout the grounds. Scattered among the vendors are artists who manage to plug their amps into a shop's outlet, allowing them to perform as small crowds gather and people toss coins into hats. Up and down the street, visitors can catch glimpses of well-known blues artists, and perhaps even a politician (Arkansas governor Mike Huckabee frequented the festival and even played bass guitar one year) or a mime troupe. Bicyclists compete in a morning race before the crowds become too large.

The festival's first day (Thursday) culminates with the announcement of local blues awards given to performers who competed prior to the festival. Longtime *King Biscuit Time* radio host "Sunshine" Sonny Payne often hands out the awards to young musicians as well as legendary artists, such as Pinetop Perkins, who was a regular, or Sam Carr, who appeared on the *King Biscuit Time* radio program in its early days. Others have included "T-Model" Ford, Frank Frost, Luther Allison, Big Jack Jackson, John Weston, Billy Lee Riley, Anson Funderburgh, Di Anne Price, and Vickie White. The festival's climax is on Saturday night, when a renowned guest artist performs.

The festival took its name from the *King Biscuit Time* radio program until 2005, when the festival's organizer, the Sonny Boy Blues Society, announced that the name would change to the Arkansas Blues and Heritage Festival because the New York firm that owned the rights to the King Biscuit name wanted too much money for its use. However, in 2010, the management of the festival succeeded in regaining the use of the name.

In the early twenty-first century, the festival began including panel discussions on the importance of the blues and the role radio has played in it. In 2001, the Delta Cultural Center hosted such a panel, which was scheduled just before Payne's program. At the cultural center, visitors may view a film loop that includes parts of past festivals while hearing Payne interviewing a guest or playing a song. His radio

booth is partitioned off from passersby, but the live show is easily accessible to guests.

In addition to storms and occasional equipment failure, each year brings a surprise or two. In 1998, Huckabee, a Baptist minister, married a couple on the main stage a year after they had met at the previous year's festival. During another festival, a strong wind knocked over a huge inflated Budweiser can next to the main stage, which organizers repaired as thousands watched. In 1996, Luther Allison continued playing as he left the main stage and meandered up and down the levee, wirelessly amplifying his guitar licks while photographers snapped pictures and the crowd went wild.

The festival attracts people from all walks of life. Despite changes in the music and the occasional non-traditional sound, as Payne once said, "Sooner or later they all come back to it."

For additional information:

King Biscuit Blues Festival. http://www.kingbiscuitfestival.com/ (accessed June 10, 2013).

Koon, David. "Fighting over a 'Biscuit.'" *Arkansas Times*, February 23, 2006.

Rotenstein, David S. "The Helena Blues: Cultural Tourism and African-American Folk Music." *Southern Folklore* 49 (Summer 1992): 133–146.

Webb, Robert Fry. "We Are the Blues: Individual and Communal Performances of the King Biscuit Tradition." PhD diss., Florida State University, 2010.

Richard Allen Burns

Street scene at the King Biscuit Blues Festival.
Courtesy: Arkansas Department of Parks and Tourism

KING BISCUIT TIME

In November 1941, KFFA, 1360 AM, the first local radio station in Helena (Phillips County), went on the air. Soon after its first broadcast, blues musicians Robert Lockwood Jr. and Sonny Boy Williamson approached owner Sam Anderson with a proposal to air a local blues radio show. Anderson liked the idea, but he knew the show would have to have a sponsor. He directed Lockwood and Williamson to Max Moore, the owner of Interstate Grocery Company, as a possible sponsor. Moore, who recognized the possibilities of marketing to African Americans, agreed to sponsor the show if the musicians would endorse his product. With a corporate sponsor, the *King Biscuit Time* radio program went on the air on November 21, 1941.

Soon, sales of King Biscuit flour greatly increased. With this success, Interstate Grocery began marketing Sonny Boy Cornmeal; the bags featured a drawing of Williamson sitting on an ear of corn and holding a piece of cornbread instead of his harmonica. The show, which aired daily at that time from noon to 12:15 p.m., featured Williamson and Lockwood. Soon afterward, drummer James "Peck Curtis" and pianist Dudlow Taylor joined the pair, rounding out the King Biscuit Entertainers. Later band members included Pinetop Perkins, Willie Love, Robert Nighthawk, and Houston Stackhouse. The show finalized its makeup in 1951 with the addition of host "Sunshine" Sonny Payne, who still hosts the show. The show could be heard within a fifty- to eighty-mile radius of Helena, including much of the Mississippi Delta and the outskirts of Memphis, Tennessee. *King Biscuit Time* was the first regular radio show to feature the blues and the first regular radio show to feature live blues performances. It was also one of the earliest examples of integrated radio in the South.

In addition to KFFA's groundbreaking accomplishments in broadcasting, the makeup of the King Biscuit Entertainers, Williamson's amplification of the harmonica, and Lockwood's jazz-influenced style are often cited as the prototype for the modern blues band. *King Biscuit Time*'s influence can be seen in the formation of radio stations throughout the mid-South, such as KWEM in West Memphis (Crittenden County); WDIA in Memphis; WROX in Clarksdale, Mississippi; and WLAC in Nashville, Tennessee. Guest artists on *King Biscuit Time* serve as a "who's who" of American music: Muddy Waters, Jimmy Rogers, Little Walter, James Cotton, and Levon Helm.

Broadcast on KFFA from the Delta Cultural Center five days a week from 12:15 to 12:45 p.m., *King Biscuit Time* is one of the longest-running radio shows in history. In 1992, KFFA was recognized for its importance in the history of radio and American music and was awarded a George Peabody Award for outstanding achievement in radio and broadcast journalism.

King Biscuit Time *at KFFA in Helena; 1942. Shown here are (left to right) Joe Willie Wilkins, Dudlow Taylor, Sonny Boy Williamson, announcer Herb Langston, James "Peck" Curtis, and Willie Love.*
Courtesy: Arkansas History Commission

For additional information:
Harvey, Hank. "How King Biscuit Blues Got Its Start in Helena." *Helena Daily World*, October 16, 1986, p. 18.
Palmer, Robert. Deep Blues. New York: Viking Press, 1981.

Robbie Fry

KING OF CLUBS

Part of an informal network of roadside nightclubs, often called roadhouses, the King of Clubs operated for more than fifty years under the ownership of Bob and Evelyn King until they sold the club in 2003. Located on U.S. Highway 67, just north of Swifton (Jackson County), the club was a familiar stop for some of the most famous pioneers in rock and roll music in the 1950s. These performers traveled constantly, making extra money and promoting their records by playing dances and shows in countless venues in cities, small towns, and in roadhouses such as the King of Clubs, which was especially favored by those who played the more southern form of rock

The King of Clubs on U.S. "Rock 'n' Roll" Highway 67, just north of Swifton; 2009. Photo: Mike Polston

and roll commonly termed rockabilly. Those who performed at the King of Clubs include Elvis Presley, Johnny Cash, Carl Perkins, Roy Orbison, Jerry Lee Lewis, Conway Twitty, Narvel Felts, Billy Lee Riley, and Sonny Burgess.

To passersby, the King of Clubs was an unremarkable white building on a gravel parking lot. Inside, the club consisted mostly of a large, dark, low-ceilinged room with pool tables in one corner and a small tiled dance floor framed by a horseshoe of chairs and small square tables. At the back of the room was a wooden stage rising about a foot above the dance floor. The club's modest appearance hid its success as a business and its formative influence on rock and roll, both of which grew from several factors, including its location. Many performers traveled in and out of nearby Memphis, Tennessee, to record their music for Sam Phillips's famed Sun Records and went up and down "Rock 'n' Roll" Highway 67 between Little Rock (Pulaski County) and St. Louis, Missouri, making one-night stands at the club easy to arrange. The fact that many of the performers who appeared at the King of Clubs early in their careers went on to become stars helped the club attract other artists. The club was also successful because it drew patrons from nearby Craighead, Independence, and Lawrence counties, where the sale of alcohol was illegal. Until it burned down on December 13, 2010, the club continued to operate and drew local bands, with Sonny Burgess and the Pacers appearing there occasionally.

For additional information:

Guralnick, Peter. *Last Train to Memphis: The Rise of Elvis Presley.* Boston: Little, Brown, 1994.

Jones, Pete. "The King of Clubs." *Arkansas Democrat-Gazette,* June 10, 2001, p. 1S.

Morrison, Craig. *Go, Cat, Go! Rockabilly Music and Its Makers.* Urbana: University of Illinois Press, 1998.

Stricklin, David, Malinda Huntley, and Caroline Bednar. Interview with Bob King. November 10, 2001. Regional Studies Center. Lyon College, Batesville, Arkansas.

David Stricklin

MISCELLANEA | KLIPSCH AUDIO TECHNOLOGIES

Klipsch Audio Technologies of Hope (Hempstead County) is one of the leading loudspeaker companies in the United States and a world leader in premium-quality audio products. The company's official motto, "A Legend in Sound," has also been applied to its founder, Paul Klipsch, who was eulogized as "a great inventor, engineer, scientist, pilot and legendary eccentric." Holding patents in acoustics, ballistics, and geophysics, Klipsch had a revolutionary vision for audio design and founded the company that bears his name in 1946.

Paul Wilbur Klipsch was born on March 9, 1904, in Elkhart, Indiana, to Oscar Klipsch and Minna Eddy Klipsch. As a boy, he enjoyed music and was fascinated with sound. At age fifteen, he built a radio receiver a year before the first scheduled commercial U.S. radio broadcast in 1920 at station KDKA in Pittsburgh, Pennsylvania. Klipsch attended college at New Mexico A&M (now New Mexico State University), graduating with a degree in electrical engineering in 1926.

He joined the radio division of General Electric, but in 1928, his passion for trains led him to Chile, where he was a locomotive supervisor for three years. Returning to the United States in 1931, he entered Stanford University and received a master's degree in electrical engineering. For the next ten years, he worked in oil exploration in Texas, researching the design of audio speakers in his spare time and submitting his first patent application for speaker horn design. With the coming of World War II in 1941, Klipsch was stationed at the Southwestern Proving Ground in Hope. After the war, he remained in Hope and devoted his career to designing and building superior loudspeakers. He rented a tin shack behind a dry cleaner in Hope, where he manufactured his first Klipschorn.

He registered the name Klipsch and Associates in 1946, though he did not hire his first employee until 1948, making his products by hand. From the company's beginnings in a virtual shed, Klipsch was granted twelve patents in acoustics (along with eight in geophysics and three in ballistics). The low-frequency section of the Klipschorn corner speaker was applied for in 1942 and granted in 1945. The high-frequency section was granted a patent in 1951. The Klipschorn as a complete system never received a patent for acoustical or electrical properties but was granted a patent for ornamental design in 1951. It is considered one of the finest loudspeakers ever made and is the world's only speaker to be in continuous production for over fifty years. The sound moves from the speaker using the walls of the corner of the room as part of the speaker to create a rich audio quality similar to an orchestral setting.

Klipsch's many awards and recognitions include being chosen 1985 Citizen of the Year in Hope, which named its municipal auditorium in his honor in 1995. In 2001, the Little Rock Arts and Humanities Promotion Commission recognized Klipsch with the Award of Distinction. His philanthropic activities in Arkansas include gifts to the Arkansas Ballet, Arkansas State University (ASU), Little Rock Symphony, and Wildwood Park for Performing Arts. His national honors include the Silver Medal from the Audio Engineering Society, induction into the Audio Hall of Fame in 1984, and his 1997 induction into the Engineering and Science Hall of Fame, where he was recognized along with fellow members Thomas Edison, Jonas Salk, and the Wright Brothers. Well into his nineties, he was active in his company, selling it to distant cousin Fred Klipsch in 1989. Though some of its speaker cabinet manufacturing and distribution operations remain in Hope, employing more than seventy people, Klipsch Audio Technologies is now based in Indianapolis, Indiana, using components from China. Specialty home speakers and commercial sound systems for movie theaters and the Hard Rock Cafe chain still garner Klipsch speakers high praise.

On May 5, 2002, Klipsch died at the age of ninety-eight.

Klipsch Audio Technologies continues to make some of the world's finest concert-quality loudspeakers, speaker systems, and electronic audio products, including theater-quality surround sound for the home, commercial audio products, and speakers for mp3 players. Along with the company-owned manufacturing and distribution facilities in Hope, the Klipsch Museum of Audio History is housed at 200 East Division Street. The museum is dedicated to the life and achievements of Klipsch, containing a replica of his office, model railroad trains he built, speakers, photographs, and other memorabilia. New Mexico State University also hosts a museum dedicated to the legacy of Paul Klipsch.

Paul W. Klipsch sitting atop a Klipsch Heresy speaker; 1989.
Courtesy: Butler Center for Arkansas Studies, Central Arkansas Library System

In 2011, the Audiovox company purchased Klipsch, though manufacturing still occurs under the Klipsch name.

For additional information:
Friedman, Mark. "Klipsch: Hope's Sweet Sound since 1946." *Arkansas Business*, July 31–August 6, 2006, pp. 1, 22–3.
Klipsch Audio Technologies. http://www.klipsch.com (accessed February 8, 2013).

Nancy Hendricks

L

ROCKABILLY

Sleepy LaBeef (1935–)

Sleepy LaBeef is a rockabilly musician who has been performing in the United States, Canada, and Europe for more than fifty years. He has shared the stage with a long list of greats, including Elvis Presley, Roy Orbison, Kenny Rogers, and Glen Campbell. Sometimes called the Human Jukebox, he is said to be able to play as many as 6,000 songs.

Sleepy LaBeef was born Thomas Paulsley LaBeff (the family name was originally LaBoeuf) in the oil-boom town of Smackover (Union County) on July 20, 1935, the youngest of ten children. His family owned a farm, raising livestock and growing cotton and watermelons, before selling the land to be drilled for oil. He got the nickname "Sleepy" in the first grade because of his heavy-lidded eyes that made him look only half awake. He later changed the spelling of his last name from LaBeff to LaBeef.

LaBeef has said that his musical influenc-

Sleepy LaBeef at the 2012 Arkansas Sounds music festival in Little Rock.
Photo: Mike Keckhaver

es include what he calls "root music: old-time rock-and-roll, Southern gospel and hand-clapping music, black blues, Hank Williams-style country" and, referring to his upbringing on a farm, "The original inspiration for real soul singin' is between the cotton rows, pullin' watermelons and puttin' 'em on the truck."

When he was fourteen, LaBeef traded a rifle to his brother-in-law for a guitar and taught himself how to play. At the age of eighteen, he moved to Houston, Texas, working for the highway department during the day and playing in clubs at night. After recording with a series of independent labels, he was signed by Columbia Records in 1964 and moved to Nashville, Tennessee. He then signed as the only artist with the reactivated Memphis, Tennessee, rockabilly label Sun Records in 1968, garnering a minor country hit with "Blackland Farmer" in 1971. In 1977, his tour bus (which had "Sun Recording Artist" painted on the side) caught fire on the Maine Turnpike, destroying most of his possessions but for some guitars he rescued. He settled in New England after the fire, leading the house band at Alan's Fifth Wheel Lounge in Amesbury, Massachusetts. Although he signed with Rounder Records in 1979 and remained based in New England, his tour bus in the 1990s had "Sun Sound" painted on the side, still paying homage to his

past with the legendary label of Elvis Presley.

Known primarily as a performer and an interpreter of songs, LaBeef has not had widespread success as a recording artist or song writer. While he has several notable albums, including *Nothin' But the Truth* (1987), *I'll Never Lay My Guitar Down* (1996), *Tomorrow Never Comes* (2000), and *Sleepy Rocks* (2008), he has always responded to the spontaneous nature of live shows with appreciative audiences. He has toured nearly nonstop all his professional life, aside from the months he spent filming the 1968 movie *The Exotic Ones* (also known as *The Monster and the Stripper*); at six-foot-six and more than 250 pounds, he was cast in the role of the swamp monster.

His first wife was a woman named Louise, with whom he performed gospel songs when he lived in Houston in the 1950s. He and his current wife Linda (who is also his manager) have five children.

Despite having to undergo heart surgery in 2003, LaBeef still maintains an active touring schedule into the twenty-first century. A concert/documentary film *Sleepy LaBeef Rides Again* was released in 2012. LaBeef was the twenty-fifth inductee into the Rockabilly Hall of Fame.

For additional information

Beuttler, Bill. "Sleepy LaBeef." *Downbeat* (October 1987): 14.

Guralnick, Peter. "Sleepy LaBeef: There's Still Good Rockin' Tonight." In *Rockabilly: The Twang Heard 'Round the World—An Illustrated History*, edited by Michael Dregni. Minneapolis, MN: Voyageur Press, 2011.

Schoemer, Karen. "Sleepy LaBeef's Living History Lesson." *New York Times*, March 8, 1991. http://www.nytimes.com/1991/03/08/arts/pop-jazz-sleepy-labeef-s-living-history-lesson.html (accessed March 9, 2013).

"Sleepy LaBeef." Rockabilly Hall of Fame. http://www.rockabillyhall.com/SleepyLB1.html (accessed March 9, 2013).

Vowell, Sarah. "The Lost Highway's Road Warrior." *GQ* (January 1998): 59–60.

Ali Welky

Marjorie Lawrence (1907–1979)

Marjorie Florence Lawrence, an Australian native and star soprano with the Metropolitan Opera Company of New York City, became an exemplar for endurance when she rebuilt her career after being stricken by poliomyelitis (commonly known as polio). Despite the profession-

al opinion that she would never sing again, she started over, first by singing from a wheelchair or platform, and then by managing to stand and sing. The subject of an Oscar-winning motion picture, *Interrupted Melody*, she later taught at Sophie Newcomb College at Tulane University and for an extended time at Southern Illinois University (SIU) at Carbondale. Beginning in 1941, Lawrence lived outside of Hot Springs (Garland County) and held summer opera coaching sessions at her ranch, Harmony Hills, which advanced the cause of classical music in Arkansas.

Marjorie Lawrence was born on February 17, 1907, at Dean's Marsh, Victoria, Australia, the fifth of six children of William and Elizabeth Lawrence. After graduating from the local school, she traveled to Melbourne without her father's permission to study voice with Ivor Boustead. After winning a vocal contest, she studied for three years under Cécile (Madame Dinh) Gilly in Paris, France. In 1932, she made her debut in Monte Carlo as a dramatic soprano, singing Elisabeth in Richard Wagner's *Tannhauser*. After more performances at Lille and Nantes, she arrived at the Paris Opera, making her debut there on February 25, 1933, as Ortrud, a mezzo role, in Richard Wagner's *Lohengrin*. She then moved back into dramatic soprano roles, singing Brunnhilde in *Die Walkure* and *Gotterdammerung*, as well other French and Italian soprano roles. She also recorded for Voix de son maitre (His Master's Voice). Particularly notable was her rendition of the final scene from Richard Strauss's *Salome*, which she sang in Oscar Wilde's original French text.

On December 18, 1935, she made her debut at the Metropolitan Opera House in New York, where she soon became a fixture, singing every season until 1940–41. On January 12, 1936, the astonished audience watched when, at the end of *Gotterdammerung*, she leaped upon her horse and rode into the fires of Siegfried's funeral pyre. Critics praised her performance of Rachel in Halévy's *La Juive*. Lawrence was also busy on the concert circuit; she returned to Australia for a concert tour and also performed at the Teatro Colón in Buenos Aires, Argentina.

On March 29, 1941, she married Dr. Thomas King, a young physician in New York City. Three months later, while rehearsing in Mexico City, she collapsed. Her husband rushed her to Hot Springs in hopes of alleviating her constant pain. First treated at St. Joseph's Hospital by Dr. George B. Fletcher, she improved to the point that she could go by ambulance daily to the Maurice Bathhouse. It was Fletcher who determined that she had been stricken by polio. Faced with the possibility of nearly total disability, the couple bought a home, which they later named Harmony Hills, from Mary Hedrick that was located on some 500 acres outside of Hot Springs. It remained Lawrence's home for most of her life, and there she wrote, "We have discovered the real joys of living."

In hopes of improving her condition, the couple consulted Sister Elizabeth Kenny, an international figure in polio-recovery practices. While Lawrence was being treated by her in Minneapolis, Minnesota, Dr. King learned how to care for Lawrence. One byproduct of these sessions was that Lawrence began to recover the use of her vocal cords. Her first public appearance came on December 21, 1941, at the First Christian Church in Miami, Florida, where the couple had gone for the winter.

Lawrence then worked at rebuilding her career, first on radio in 1942, where, of course, her wheelchair-bound condition was unimportant, and then at a Metropolitan Opera Guild luncheon and at a Town Hall recital. On December 27, 1942, she returned to the Metropolitan, singing from a couch the role of Venus in Wagner's *Tannhauser*. She performed in concerts extensively and, in 1943, sang the very demanding role of Isolde in Wagner's *Tristan und Isolde* in Montreal, with Sir Thomas Beecham conducting. A single Metropolitan performance followed in 1944, but General Manager Edward Johnson (who had partnered Arkansas's Mary Lewis in her operatic debut at the house in 1926), considered a wheelchair-bound Isolde to be "unsightly." Support, however, came from President Franklin Delano Roosevelt in 1943: "From an old veteran to a young recruit—my message to you is—'Carry on!'" She sang "The Star-Spangled Banner" at his 1945 inauguration and later met privately with him.

In 1944, she headed off to the Pacific Theater of World War II, performing for more than 50,000 GIs and "Diggers" (Australians), with special concerts for the critically wounded. The format consisted of her being seated behind a screen that would then be removed at the start of the concert. "Waltzing Matilda," which she recorded three times, was virtually her signature song. Even in a wheelchair, she still resembled "a big, blond bar maid."

In 1945, she toured Europe, singing the same mixture of songs and arias that she had featured in the Pacific. She thought she had done poorly during a command performance at Buckingham

Palace until she realized the audience members were wearing gloves. Subsequently, she sang with a number of English orchestras and added a new role, Amneris in Verdi's *Aida*, first at the Cincinnati Opera Company and then at the Opera in Paris. In occupied Germany, with Russians present, she sang with the Berlin Philharmonic in a program that included Tatania's "Letter Scene" from Tchaikovsky's *Eugene Onegin*, as well as her perennial concert favorite, the finale to *Gotterdammerung*. By 1947, her recovery had reached the point that she could stand and sing. This accomplishment was first displayed in a concert performance of Richard Strauss's *Elektra* with the Chicago Symphony conducted by Artur Rodzinski.

Meanwhile, she had been working on her autobiography. *Interrupted Melody: The Story of My Life* (1949) became a bestseller and, in 1955, was the basis for an Oscar-winning motion picture (for best writing, story, and screenplay). Eleanor Parker (who was nominated for an Oscar) played Lawrence, and soprano Eileen Farrell supplied the vocal numbers. Because Lawrence was best defined as a mezzo who had been induced to take on dramatic soprano roles and Farrell was a soprano, viewers got a slightly distorted notion of Lawrence's singing. The southern premiere of the film took place at the Malco Theatre in Hot Springs in 1955.

Lawrence moved into television, hosting from 1953 to 1954 a television show, *The Pause that Refreshes*, sponsored by the Coca-Cola Company. She sang publicly during a 1966 visit to Australia, and her last recording, appropriately of "Waltzing Matilda," was made there in 1976.

In 1957, Lawrence became artist-in-residence at Tulane University in New Orleans, Louisiana, where she taught voice at Sophie Newcomb College. In 1960, she moved to SIU in Carbondale, where she became professor of voice and director of opera workshops, remaining there until 1973. Summer workshops were held at Harmony Hills and included students from SIU and other schools. At the conclusion of the workshops, Lawrence presented her students in a public concert in the ballroom of the Arlington Hotel. She also sang with the Arkansas Symphony Orchestra.

Marjorie Lawrence as Brunnhilde at the Metropolitan Opera; 1938.
Courtesy: Dirk Koerschenhausen

In 1974, she began teaching at Garland County Community College (now National Park Community College) in Hot Springs and joined the faculty at the University of Arkansas at Little Rock (UALR) in 1975. Ohio University at Athens made her a doctor of humane letters in 1969, and in 1977, she became a dame Commander of the British Empire (CBE).

Lawrence died on January 13, 1979, in Little Rock (Pulaski County) and is buried in Greenwood Cemetery in Hot Springs.

Lawrence was one of the major operatic figures during her pre-polio days. Her career is documented by studio recordings ranging in date from 1928 to 1976 and by recorded radio broadcasts from the 1930s to 1950. Her courageous struggle with her disability highlighted the importance of a disease for which at that time there was no cure and no means of prevention. In her memoirs, and then as touched up by Hollywood, Lawrence gave this tragedy a voice and a face. When she attended the gala that marked the opening of the new home for the Metropolitan Opera at Lincoln Center, her students and admirers provided the funds that gave the hall wheelchair accessibility.

For additional information:

Hogarth, Will, and R. T. See. "Marjorie Lawrence: A Tribute in the Form of a Discography." *The Record Collector* 32 (January 1987): 3–18. Extensions, additions, and corrections to the discography appear in *The Record Collector* 33 (November 1988): 300–303; and *The Record Collector* 34 (May 1989): 98–100.

Jackson, Paul. *Saturday Afternoons at the Old Met: The Metropolitan Opera Broadcasts, 1931–1950*. Portland, OR: Amadeus Press, 1994.

Kolodin, Irving. *The Story of the Metropolitan Opera, 1883–1950*. New York: Alfred A. Knopf, 1953.

Lawrence, Marjorie. *Interrupted Melody: The Story of My Life*. New York: Appleton-Century-Crofts, Inc., 1949.

"Marjorie Florence Lawrence." *Australian Dictionary of Biography*. http://adb.anu.edu.au/biography/lawrence-marjorie-florence-7115 (accessed February 19, 2013).

Marjorie Lawrence Papers. Morris Library Special Collections. Southern Illinois University at Carbondale, Carbondale, Illinois.

Obituary of Marjorie Lawrence. *Arkansas Gazette*, January 14, 1979, p. 1A.

Mamie Ruth Abernathy and Michael B. Dougan

TRACY LAWRENCE (1968–)

With rural Arkansas beginnings, Tracy Lawrence took Nashville, Tennessee, by storm in the early 1990s to become one of the most popular country recording artists of that decade. Lawrence quickly gained a fan base with his physical appeal, vocal ability, good-guy image, and succession of hit songs.

Tracy Lee Lawrence was born on January 27, 1968, in Atlanta, Texas. Reared by his stay-at-home mother, JoAnn Dickens, and his step-father, Dwayne Dickens, a banker, Lawrence had two brothers and three sisters. In 1972, the Dickens family moved to Foreman (Little River County), where Lawrence sang in the choir of the local Methodist church and learned to play guitar. While his mother wanted him to become a Methodist minister, Lawrence aspired to be a singing star and first joined a band as a teenager.

In 1986, he entered Southern Arkansas University in Magnolia (Columbia County), where he studied mass communications, but he dropped out in 1988 to become lead singer for a Louisiana-based band. When the group disbanded in 1990, Lawrence set out for Nashville. Working a variety of jobs, he supplemented his income with prize winnings from various talent contests. Following one of the contests, he was offered a spot on the radio show *Live at Libby's* on WBVR in Daysville, Kentucky, where he commuted nightly to make his on-air appearance. On January 22, 1991, he performed in a showcase at the famed Bluebird Café in Nashville, and was offered a contract by manager Wayne Edwards. Subsequently, Edwards secured Lawrence a record deal with Atlantic Records.

Lawrence married rodeo barrel racer Frances Weatherford in 1993; they divorced in 1996. The following year, he married Dallas Cowboys cheerleader Stephenie (Stacie) Drew, but their marriage, too, ended in divorce. In 2000, Lawrence married his third wife, Becca; they have two daughters.

The release of Lawrence's debut album, *Sticks and Stones*, was delayed due to injuries he sustained on May 31, 1991, in a physical altercation with three robbers in the parking lot of a Nashville Music Row hotel. Lawrence was shot four times and required surgery. After a short hospital stay and rapid recovery, Lawrence resumed his career.

Released in late 1991, *Sticks and Stones* produced four singles on the *Billboard* country music chart. The title track spent one week at number one in January 1992. Having sold more than one million units, *Sticks and Stones* was certified platinum by the Recording Industry Association of America (RIAA). Subsequent Atlantic releases included *Alibis* (1993), *I See It Now* (1994), *Tracy Lawrence Live and Unplugged* (1995), *Time Marches On* (1996), *The Coast Is Clear* (1997), and *Lessons Learned* (2000), several of which were certified platinum or double platinum. From these albums came a string of major hits, including the chart toppers "Alibis," "Can't Break It to My Heart," "My Second Home," "If the Good Die Young," "Texas Tornado," and "Time Marches On." In 1994, Lawrence contributed "Renegades, Rebels and Rogues" to the soundtrack of the film *Maverick*.

After Atlantic's Nashville division closed in 2000, Lawrence released an album on the Warner Bros. label before joining the DreamWorks Records roster. *Strong*, his only DreamWorks project, came in 2003, and included the number-four single "Paint Me a Birmingham." In 2005, Mercury Nashville released a compilation of Lawrence's greatest hits. The following year, Lawrence partnered with his manager and brother, Laney Lawrence, to start Rocky Comfort Records. Lawrence released *For the Love* (2007), which contains "You Find Out Who Your Friends Are," his first number-one hit in more than a decade. In June 2009, Lawrence released *The Rock*, his first inspirational album. This was followed two years later by *The Singer*.

Atlantic Records publicity photo of Tracy Lawrence.
Courtesy: Old State House Museum Collection

In 1992, *Billboard* declared Lawrence the Best New Male Artist, and, in 1993, he garnered the prestigious Top New Male Vocalist award from the Academy of Country Music. In spite of the accolades, his image has been marred by controversy throughout the years. In 1994, Lawrence was charged with aggravated assault and carrying an unlicensed weapon after he claimed to have fired in self-defense at a group of teenagers on a freeway just outside of Nashville. Then, in mid-1998, Lawrence was accused of spousal abuse and was eventually convicted of misdemeanor battery and ordered to pay a $500 fine to a women's shelter.

Lawrence resides in suburban Nashville.

For additional information:

Cackett, Alan. *The Harmony Illustrated Encyclopedia of Country Music*. New York: Salamander Books, 1994.

Carlin, Richard. *Country Music: A Biographical Dictionary*. New York: Routledge, 2003.

Kingsbury, Paul, ed. *The Encyclopedia of Country Music: The Ultimate Guide to the Music*. New York: Oxford University Press, 1998.

McCloud, Barry. *Definitive Country: The Ultimate Encyclopedia of Country Music and Its Performers*. New York: Perigree, 1995.

Tracy Lawrence. http://www.tracylawrence.com (accessed February 8, 2013).

"Tracy Lawrence." Country Music Television. http://www.cmt.com/artists/az/lawrence_tracy/artist.jhtml (accessed February 8, 2013).

Greg Freeman

BLUES / R&B   CALVIN "SLIM" LEAVY (1940–2010)

Calvin James "Slim" Leavy, vocalist and guitarist, recorded "Cummins Prison Farm," a blues song that debuted on *Billboard*'s rhythm and blues chart on May 2, 1970, and stayed for five weeks, reaching No. 40. It was also the No. 1 song on the Memphis, Tennessee, station WDIA. Leavy was the first person charged under a 1989 Arkansas "drug kingpin law" targeting crime rings.

Calvin Leavy was born on April 20, 1940, in Scott (Pulaski and Lonoke counties), the youngest son of fifteen children born to the musical family of Johnny Leavy and Cora James Leavy. Both parents sang in the church choir at Mount Lake Baptist Church in Scott, and several family members played musical instruments. Leavy started out singing in the church choir and, as a teenager, sang with several gospel groups in the Little Rock (Pulaski County) area, including Sacred Fire, led by his oldest brother, Jake McKinley Leavy, and the Soul Savers. In 1954, he and his brother Hosea formed the Leavy Brothers Band. In addition to singing, Leavy played bass, drums, guitar, and piano. It was very popular in the Little Rock area, and, during the 1960s, they moved to Fresno, California, and toured the West Coast.

In December 1968, tired of big city life, they returned to Little Rock and played five nights a week at the 70 Club. Leavy's version of the "Tennessee Waltz," sung in the style of Sam Cooke, was very popular, and the club owner's wife offered to pay for recording time to do a demo tape at E&M Recording Company in Little Rock. After finishing the demo tape, the band still had time left and was approached by Bill Cole, who had written a song about Cummins Prison Farm.

Leavy improved the lyrics using information he had gained from a brother incarcerated at Cummins, and the band recorded it in one take. The song later became one of only twenty-seven blues songs to make the charts in 1970.

Leavy never recorded an album, but, during the 1970s, he recorded several 45 rpm records for Acquarian Records, Soul Beat Records, and Messenger Records: "Nothing But Your Love/I Won't Be the Last to Cry," "Cummins Prison Farm/Brought You to the City," "Cummins Prison Farm/That's Where I Am," "Give Me a Love (That I Can Feel)/Born Unlucky," "It Hurts Me Too/I've Got Troubles," and "Goin' to the Dogs Pt. 1/Goin' to the Dogs Pt 2."

In 1976, the Leavy Brothers Band did some recordings for the Arkansas Bicentennial Blues Project. Those recordings are archived at the University of Arkansas at Little Rock. In 1977, the band performed at the Beale Street Music Festival. Soon after, the band disbanded, but Leavy remained in Little Rock and formed Calvin Leavy and the Professionals, which was popular in the Little Rock area during the 1980s. They recorded "Is It Worth All (That I'm Going Through)/Funky Jam." Leavy also recorded "Big Four/It's a Miracle (What Love Can Do)" with Sonny Blake, Dan Craft, and Cyrus Hayes, as well as "What Kind of Love/Give Me Your Loving, Loving, Loving," "Free From Cummins Prison Farm/Enjoy Being Hurt By You," and "Thieves and Robbers/If Life Last Luck Is Bound to Change." His last performance before his incarceration was with the gospel group the Zion Five as a singer and bass player.

In 1991, Leavy was the first to be charged under the Arkansas "drug kingpin law" targeting organized crime rings. According to Pulaski County prosecutors, Leavy made three $1,000 payments to an undercover police officer to page him when police were about to make a raid. In July 1992, he was convicted of operating a continuing criminal enterprise, delivery of a controlled substance, public servant bribery, and use of a communication facility—a pager—in the commission of a felony. This was the first time that Leavy had been convicted of a felony. On July 10, 1992, he was sentenced by the Pulaski County Court to life plus twenty-five years. Interestingly, his incarceration began at Cummins Prison, and, while there, he sang "He Walks With Me—Part 1 (The Story of Moses)/He Walks With Me—Part 2 (The Story of Job)" with the Cummins Prison Farm Singers.

In 1995, Leavy petitioned for a writ of habeas corpus, but his petition was denied. In 2004, Governor Mike Huckabee commuted his sentence to seventy-five years. In 2007, Leavy applied for clemency, and the parole board recommended that it be granted. The following year, however, Governor Mike Beebe denied his request for clemency.

Leavy died on June 6, 2010, at Jefferson Regional Medical Center in Pine Bluff (Jefferson County). He had been due to be eligible for parole in November or December 2011. He was survived by sixteen children, two of his children having died before him.

For additional information:
Herzhaft, Gerard. *Encyclopedia of the Blues*. Fayetteville: University of Arkansas Press, 1997.
Kuhn, Jeff. "Calvin Leavy: The Story of Cummins Prison Farm." *Juke Blues* 52 (Winter 2002/3): 30–37.
Scott, Frank. *The Down Home Guide to the Blues*. Atlanta, GA: A Cappella Books: 1991.

Gwendolyn L. Shelton

CLASSICAL / OPERA — MARY LEWIS (1897–1941)

Mary Sybil Kidd Lewis was possibly the most publicized singer of the 1920s. Using her childhood training, she climbed her way to grand opera, gaining stage experience through vaudeville and operetta. Her career included radio performances and recordings with His Master's Voice, Victor, and RCA.

Mary Kidd was born on January 29, 1897, in Hot Springs (Garland County) to Charles and Hattie Kidd. Her father died about the time her brother was born two years later. Her impoverished mother moved with the children to Dallas, Texas. After the children lived in a series of foster homes, her brother was sent to Chicago, Illinois, to live with relatives. Her mother remarried but was unable to care for her children, and the child Mary Maynard (having taken her step-father's surname) was sickly and malnourished. In 1905, an elderly Methodist pastor, William Fitch, and his wife, Anna, took the young child into their home after having provided the girl with food and clothing for some time. Their own son, Frank, was a minister and had three children

Mary Lewis; circa 1925.
Courtesy: Special Collections, University of Arkansas Libraries, Fayetteville

about the same age as Maynard.

Anna Fitch tutored Maynard in schoolwork, and William Fitch trained her in music. In August 1906, the family moved to Eureka Springs (Carroll County), where Fitch was assigned to the First Methodist Episcopal Church. Maynard began to be noticed for her solos during the services.

In early 1908, William Fitch was named pastor of Trinity Methodist Episcopal Church in Judsonia (White County), where Maynard's vocal talents were noticed again. His health failing, Fitch was assigned to the Little Rock Mission in 1909. As a parsonage was not provided in this assignment, Anna Fitch returned to her home in Holmes County, Ohio, and asked her father for her anticipated inheritance; she soon returned to Little Rock (Pulaski County) carrying $4,000 in gold, which she used to build one of the first houses in the Pulaski Heights subdivision. This is the place Maynard called home.

In about 1912, chafing at the restrictions in the Fitch home, Maynard left to live with Henry Franklin Auten, a friend and influential

Arkansas politician, real estate agent, and entrepreneur. An orphan himself, Auten had taken in other disadvantaged children. He had heard Maynard sing and believed that she could establish a career singing. She enrolled in Little Rock High School, her first classroom experience, and received vocal lessons from Alice Henniger.

In 1915, Mary Maynard married J. Keene Lewis of Little Rock but left him to join a traveling vaudeville troupe. After she became famous, her ex-husband demanded his name not be used, so for publicity purposes she eliminated mention of the marriage and changed her birthday to January 9, 1900, making it appear that she left Little Rock as a teenager rather than a young married woman. She retained the surname of Lewis.

Vaudeville took Lewis to Hollywood, where she appeared in silent films before moving to New York City. She signed a contract with Florenz Ziegfeld as a prima donna in his *Follies of 1921*. Although all the Follies were spectacular, the *Follies of 1922* was climaxed by Charles LeMaire's "Lace Land," featuring elaborate costumes which achieved a theatrical glorification. Lewis herself wore a famous costume of peasant design with the lace treated with radium. The newly identified element provided a novel, eerie glowing quality in the dark. When the lights were turned off, the ghost of the dress and Lewis's face, luminous in the glow from the peasant cap of lace, were all that could be seen on stage while she sang "Weaving." About a month after the show opened, her health broke down. She spent three months in the hospital, probably from radiation poisoning, the first indication of her many health problems.

The salary of the *Follies* allowed her to undertake vocal studies with noted vocal coach William Thorner, who encouraged her to follow her dream of grand opera. After an audition with the Metropolitan Opera in New York, Lewis pursued further study and had her opera debut in Europe, as Marguerite in *Faust*, on October 19, 1923, in the Vienna Opera House. After achieving recognition, Lewis recorded in 1924–25 for His Master's Voice (HMV) in England. Returning home in the fall of 1925, Lewis received a contract with the Met for the next season. She debuted as Mimi in *La Bohème* on January 28, 1926.

On March 26, 1926, Lewis returned to Little Rock to receive the greatest demonstration of welcome accorded to any individual of the state up to that time. She arrived at Little Rock from Hot Springs, where she had given an operatic concert accompanied by Alice Henniger, her former teacher and friend. Lewis was welcomed by Governor Thomas Terral at the State Capitol, and she was presented a golden "Key of the City" by Mayor Charles E. Meyer.

Lewis recorded a second round in America in 1926–27 for HMV and Victor Talking Machine Co.

The first season at the Met ended with her sudden marriage to the Met's German bass/baritone, Michael Bohnen, on April 15, 1927. The ceremony was performed by New York's mayor, Jimmy Walker. The disastrous marriage to Bohnen and her own alcoholism began to take a toll on Lewis's career. The marriage ended in Hollywood in 1930, and Lewis sailed for Europe as the worldwide economic depression forced cuts in theatrical productions.

Lewis married Standard Oil Company vice president Robert L. Hague in Portland, Maine, on September 19, 1931. She spent the next few years traveling to Europe and back and was among the first to board the Hindenburg on its maiden flight to Germany in 1936. Although not performing professionally, she made many appearances for benefit causes. She appeared with John McCormack, the popular Irish tenor, at a fundraising concert for St. Benedict the Moor, a mission church, on December 17, 1933. She made radio appearances over New York's WYNC and WMCA stations in 1935. On January 30, 1936, Mary Lewis assisted with planning one of the celebrations in honor of President Franklin Roosevelt's fifty-fourth birthday. The nationwide benefits were a marathon effort to raise funds to help with the treatment of those afflicted with polio.

In 1937, Lewis made a substantial number of recordings for the Thesaurus series for radio broadcast. The discs were produced for NBC by RCA. A collection of her recordings from HMV, Victor Talking Machine Co., and the Thesaurus series has been re-mastered and reproduced on a set of CDs by Ward Marston, a music lover and sound engineer. The two-CD set by Marston Records of Swarthmore, Pennsylvania, *Mary Lewis, the Golden Haired Soprano*, was released in October 2005.

Lewis was separated from Hague, who later died on March 8, 1939, leaving her an estate that consisted of indebtedness. Lewis herself died on December 31, 1941, in New York, following a lengthy illness. After services in New York City, a second service was held on January 5, 1942, at the Second Baptist Church in Little Rock. She is buried in Pinecrest Memorial Park in Alexander (Pulaski and Saline counties).

For additional information:

Abernathy, Mamie Ruth Stranburg. "Mary Lewis, Lyric Soprano Hot Springs Native and Opera Singer." *The Record* 48 (2007): 165–167.

Dougan, Michael B. "A Touching Enigma: The Opera Career of Mary Lewis." *Arkansas Historical Quarterly* 36 (Autumn 1977): 258–279.

Marston, Ward. *Mary Lewis, the Golden Haired Soprano*. CD set and booklet. Swarthmore, PA: Marston Records, 2005.

Zeman, Alice Fitch. *Mary Lewis—The Golden Haired Beauty with the Golden Voice*. Little Rock: Rose Publishing Company, 2001.

Alice Zeman

LIVING SACRIFICE

Living Sacrifice is a Christian death metal band from Little Rock (Pulaski County) that has paved the way for Christian metal as a genre. The group gets its name from the Bible, Romans 12:1, which reads: "Therefore, I urge you, brothers and sisters, in view of God's mercy, to offer your bodies as a living sacrifice, holy and pleasing to God—this is your true and proper worship."

Living Sacrifice was formed in 1989 by bassist and vocalist Darren (D. J.) Johnson, drummer Lance Garvin, and guitarist Bruce Fitzhugh. Guitarist Jason Truby joined the band shortly after its founding. Fitzhugh and Garvin are the only members to have stayed in the band throughout its many changes in membership and sound, as well as its ebbs and flows in popularity. Living Sacrifice was inspired by local punk band Trusty to start creating original music, but the group had a difficult time starting out, as Christian metal was practically unheard of as a genre, particularly in Arkansas. However, when Vino's—a Little Rock pizzeria and brewery with a small space for concerts—opened in 1990, the band began playing there and gaining fans in its hometown.

The members of Living Sacrifice showed great skill instrumentally as well as in songwriting, and the band was soon signed to R.E.X. Records. The band released its first album, *Living Sacrifice*, in 1991. After touring and performing for both secular and Christian audiences nationwide, the band released its second album, *Nonexistent*, in 1992. The band quickly became popular

Early line-up of Living Sacrifice.
Courtesy: Dotty Oliver/*Little Rock Free Press*

with Christian teenagers, as its albums sounded instrumentally similar to secular metal bands such as Anthrax and Slayer but had Christian metal bands such as Believer and the Crucified as its main lyric influences.

In 1994, the band released its third album, *Inhabit*—its last with R.E.X., which was suffering financial problems. The band signed with the new Solid State Records, a division of the Christian label Tooth & Nail, which focuses on more extreme hard rock music. In 1995, founder Johnson left the band to pursue mission work outside of music, and Fitzhugh became the lead singer, though he continued playing guitar. Chris Truby joined as a bassist.

In 1997, the band released its fourth album, *Reborn*, recorded at Barry Poynter's studio in Little Rock, and began to gain more mainstream fans. As a result of this album, the band also received several offers to sign with larger mainstream recording companies but decided to re-sign with Tooth & Nail. Both of the Truby brothers left; Jason Truby went on to play in the rock band P.O.D. Arthur Green, from the band Eso-Charis, joined to play bass, and Rocky Gray joined and took over guitar. In 2000, the band released its fifth album, *The Hammering Process*, and toured the country with several metal bands, both secular and Christian.

By 2002, the band was beginning to fragment due to members committing to other projects outside of the band. Gray left the band to play drums for Evanescence, and Matt Putman replaced him as drummer for the remainder of the band's shows. Living Sacrifice released its sixth album, *Conceived in Fire*, that same year and began touring. The band ended the tour early, playing a farewell concert at Vino's on June 28, 2003. In 2005, the band released *In Memoriam*, a compilation album with three newly recorded songs.

On February 4, 2008, Living Sacrifice announced that it was re-forming. Band members Fitzhugh, Garvin, Green, and Gray all returned. The band immediately began a six-week tour and released a digital EP. In 2010, it released a new album, *The Infinite Order*, produced by Jeremiah Scott, which drew back many original fans while making its music accessible to a new generation. In 2010, the band headlined Tooth & Nail's "A Very Metal Christmas" tour and announced in December 2012 that it was beginning to write and record a new album at Fellowship Hall Sound recording studio in Little Rock.

For additional information:
"Living Sacrifice." Encyclopaedia Metallum. http://www.metal-archives.com/bands/Living_Sacrifice/3002 (accessed April 1, 2013).
"Living Sacrifice." Solid State Records. http://www.solidstaterecords.com/artists/51/Living_Sacrifice/ (accessed April 1, 2013).
"A Metal Band with a Message." *Arkansas Democrat-Gazette*, December 14, 2001, p. 4W.
Wilcox, Lauren. "Living Sacrifice Pioneered Music for Christians, Metal Heads Alike." *Arkansas Democrat-Gazette*, April 24, 2005, p. 6W.

Darby Burdine

BLUES / R&B ROBERT LOCKWOOD JR. (1915–2006)

Robert Lockwood Jr. was a blues guitarist celebrated for his progressive, jazz-like style, his longevity, and his role in many major events in the development of the blues. He was the only person who learned guitar directly from the legendary Robert Johnson, who often lived with Lockwood's mother during Lockwood's formative years. These factors have made a paradox of Lockwood's career. Although one of the most distinguished musicians of his time, Lockwood never prospered commensurately with his reputation. He was best known as an accompanist to more flamboyant stars, especially Sonny Boy Williamson and Little Walter Jacobs.

Lockwood was born on March 27, 1915, in Turkey Scratch, on the line between Phillips and Lee counties, twenty-five miles west of Helena (Phillips County). He was the son of Robert Lockwood and Esther Reese, of whom little or nothing is known. One source says that Lockwood moved briefly from Helena to St. Louis, Missouri, at age seven. He dropped out of school in the late 1920s.

Bluesman Robert Lockwood Jr.
Artists: Patterson and Barnes / From the Old State House Museum Collection

Lockwood first made music on his family's pump organ. He was in his late teens when he learned guitar from Johnson. Soon after, he acquired the nickname Robert Jr. because of his admiration for and emulation of Johnson.

At about age seventeen, Lockwood started playing professionally. He performed with Johnson, with Johnson's partner Johnny Shines, and with the freewheeling Williamson. He toured with some with them and performed all over the Delta, often playing on street corners for change. For decades, Lockwood performed professionally as Robert Jr. Lockwood until he wearied of the attention he received because of the name, as it connoted his being Johnson's stepson, a fact that he thought overshadowed his own achievements.

Johnson died in 1938, and Lockwood was more or less on his own. He made his first recordings in Aurora, Illinois, in 1941, performing as a guitarist on Doc Clayton's sessions for the RCA Bluebird label. That year, he teamed with Williamson once more, and they started hosting a noonday radio program, sponsored by the Interstate Grocery Company on Helena's KFFA. *King Biscuit Time* was the first regularly scheduled live broadcast of country blues. The show's band, in addition to star Williamson and his sideman Lockwood, consisted of rhythm makers James "Peck" Curtis and Dudlow Taylor.

Lockwood moved to Chicago, Illinois, in 1950 and performed with the historic group that provided backup for Chess Records stars Muddy

Waters and, in particular, Little Walter. Lockwood became a member of the band, the Aces, and played an important role in the development of the Chicago Shuffle, a blues innovation played on electrically amplified instruments that served as a prototype for classic rock and roll. In that period, he toured with Eddie Boyd and others.

In 1961, Lockwood moved to Cleveland, Ohio, where some reports indicate he was stranded in the midst of a shabby tour by Williamson. He eventually began to record under his own name. The recordings included "Steady Rolling Man" on the Delmark label and "Does Twelve" on Trix. Some earlier recordings for the Decca, Mercury, and Candid labels are difficult to find. Some of his earliest recordings, many in a style derived from Johnson, are collected on Yazoo's albums *Lonesome Road Blues* and *Windy City Blues*.

Lockwood sustained a career that went neither unheralded nor unrewarded, albeit underrated and under-compensated. He was inducted into the Blues Hall of Fame in 1989, received the National Heritage Fellowship Award (presented by Hillary Clinton) in 1995, and was inducted into the Delta Blues Hall of Fame in Cleveland, Mississippi, in 1998. In 2002, he received an honorary doctorate of music degree from Ohio's Cleveland State University. He had a street named for him in Cleveland—Robert Lockwood Jr. Way.

Lockwood continued to tour nationally and record one album a year until his death on November 21, 2006.

For additional information:

Buckalew, Terry. "'Steady Rolling Man': Arkansas Bluesman Robert 'Junior' Lockwood." *Arkansas Historical Quarterly* 53 (Spring 1994): 75–89.

Cobb, James C. *The Most Southern Place on Earth: The Mississippi Delta and the Roots of Regional Identity*. New York City: Oxford University Press, 1994.

Guralnick, Peter. *Feel Like Going Home: Portraits in Blues and Rock 'n' Roll*. Boston: Back Bay Books, 1999.

Hoffman, Larry. "Robert Lockwood, Jr." *Living Blues* 121 (May–June 1995): 13–29.

Inada, Mitsutoshi. "Robert Lockwood, Jr. (1915–2006): A Bridge between the Delta and Japan." *Arkansas Review: A Journal of Delta Studies* 43 (December 2012): 147–163.

Lee, Peter. "Robert Lockwood, Jr.: Unlocking Some Secrets." *Living Blues* 90 (March–April 1990): 32–35.

Palmer, Robert. *Deep Blues*. New York: Viking Press, 1981.

Robert Lockwood Jr. http://www.robertlockwood.com/ (accessed February 8, 2013).

Jim Kelton

M

ROCK — "JIM DANDY" MANGRUM (1948–)

James Leslie "Jim Dandy" Mangrum is the flamboyant frontman for the southern rock group Black Oak Arkansas, which reached its height of fame in the 1970s, charting ten albums and a hit single. According to author Ron Hall, "Jim Mangrum claims to be the first long-haired rock 'n' roller in Arkansas, and he may well have been." His often raunchy onstage antics and froggy, raspy voice have been cited as an influence on rock stars such as David Lee Roth and Axl Rose. After health problems and many incarnations of the band, Mangrum continues to record and perform with a group called Jim Dandy's Black Oak Arkansas.

James Leslie Mangrum was born in Benton Harbor, Michigan, on March 30, 1948, to J. C. and Elsie Mangrum, who were cotton farmers. He has two younger sisters. Mangrum attended high school in Monette (Craighead County), where Black Oak (Craighead County) children went to school before Monette's consolidation with Leachville (Mississippi County). Beginning around 1963—with boyhood friends Rickie Lee Reynolds, J. R. Brewer, and Keith McCann—Mangrum formed a rock and roll band, which, in his words, was "self-taught, loud and raw." After acquiring their sound equipment from Monette High School, where Mangrum was a sophomore in 1964, they were charged with eight area burglaries and sentenced in absentia to eight eight-year terms at Tucker Prison Farm, with the sentence later suspended. Mangrum left school, and he and the group headed for Craighead County's back woods.

According to Mangrum, the first place they rehearsed was in a bean elevator at a cotton gin near Black Oak. They called themselves the Knowbody Else at that time, winning a devoted local following by performing at nearby venues such as Reynolds Park in Paragould (Greene County). They moved to Memphis, Tennessee, where they recorded an album for Stax called *The*

Black Oak Arkansas singer Jim Dandy Mangrum, with his trademark washboard, performing at Barton Coliseum in Little Rock; 1977.

Photo: Ken King

Knowbody Else, but the recording did not sell well. They then moved to New Orleans, Louisiana, and finally California. In Los Angeles in 1968, they changed their name to Black Oak Arkansas, heralding the rise of southern rock bands such as Lynyrd Skynyrd and the Allman Brothers. At Atco Records in Los Angeles, they were one of the last acts signed personally by legendary music producer Ahmet Ertegun.

Ertegun saw potential in Mangrum's waist-length blond hair, raucous onstage antics, and white spandex pants (dubbed by rock critic Jay Sosnicki as "The Tightest Pants in Dixie"). Their first album for Atco, titled *Black Oak Arkansas*, was released in 1971. The year 1973 was the band's peak commercial year with the release of an album in March (*Raunch 'N' Roll Live*) and another in November (*High on the Hog*); both charted in the Top 100. That same year, their remake of the 1957 hit "Jim Dandy (to the Rescue)" featuring Mangrum with female vocalist Ruby Starr reached Number 25 on the *Billboard* Hot 100 as a single. That song established Mangrum's niche and enhanced the flamboyant persona of "Jim Dandy."

During the 1970s, Mangrum and the band toured constantly, with musicians coming and going. Their extensive touring schedule included opening for the hit group Iron Butterfly. Soon, however, Black Oak became the main attraction. The band, with Mangrum as one of its few consistent performers, recorded fifteen albums from 1971 through 1978, plus one collection and a re-release of their early album on Stax. The album *Ready as Hell* was released in 1984, though there is no evidence of a tour. But by the 1980s, the band's success had faded, most of the musicians had gone their separate ways, and no albums were released other than *The Black Attack is Back* in 1986. *Live on the King Biscuit Flower Hour 1976* was released in 1998, followed the next year by *The Wild Bunch*, on Capricorn and Cleopatra records respectively.

Mangrum has been married three times and has several children. He currently resides outside Memphis. Despite reported health problems, including heart attacks, Mangrum still performs whenever possible.

For additional information:

Black Oak Arkansas. http://www.blackoakarkansas.net (accessed February 25, 2013).

Hall, Ron. *Playing for a Piece of the Door: A History of Garage & Frat Bands in Memphis*, 1960–75. Memphis, TN: Shangri-La, 2001.

Hutson, Cecil. *An Analysis of the Southern Rock and Roll Band Black Oak Arkansas*. New York: Edwin Mellen Press, 1996.

Shiras, Ginger. "Black Oak Arkansas: Catching up on Family Doings of Multimillion Dollar Rock Band." *Arkansas Gazette*, January 23, 1977.

Nancy Hendricks

JAZZ ▌FRED MARSHALL (1938–2001)

Fred Calvin Marshall was a jazz musician, inventor, sculptor, and educator best known as the bassist in the Vince Guaraldi Trio, which recorded the soundtrack for the *Charlie Brown Christmas* television special. He began his musical career in Little Rock (Pulaski County) in the 1950s, later moving to Kansas City, Missouri, and California, where he became active in the thriving San Francisco musical scene in the 1960s.

Fred Marshall was born in Memphis, Tennessee, on October 4, 1938, to Calvin Abel Marshall and Helen Howard Marshall, although he was raised in Little Rock. His mother was an artist and an art teacher at Arkansas Polytechnic College (now Arkansas Tech University) in Russellville (Pope County). His mother's artistic creativity was an inspiration for Fred Marshall and his only sibling, Terry Marshall Williams.

Marshall began playing piano at age five and started playing bass and drums while attending Little Rock High School (now Central High School). He joined the musician's union at age fourteen, and, by age fifteen, he was playing in clubs on Little Rock's 9th Street, home to a thriving African-American club scene. "When I played down there I would have to duck down behind the bass when the police came," Marshall related. "Not only was I underage, I was also a white man playing in a black club."

Marshall attended college in Arkansas, Louisiana, and Oklahoma, eventually enrolling in the Kansas City Art Institute. He immersed himself in the Kansas City jazz scene, joining alto saxophonist Eddie "Cleanhead" Vinton's band and playing with musicians such as Etta James and Dinah Washington.

He moved to San Francisco in the early 1960s, where he became house bassist at San Francisco's famous jazz club, Bop City. He played with some of jazz's most important musicians, including saxophonists Ben Webster, Joe Henderson, and Dexter Gordon; trumpeter Maynard Ferguson; and singer Jimmy Rushing. He also played with fellow Little Rock native, saxophonist Pharoah Sanders.

Marshall, along with drummer Jerry Granelli, joined pianist Vince Guaraldi's trio in 1962, recording several Latin jazz albums together. The Vince Guaraldi Trio was invited to compose and perform music for the 1965 *Charlie Brown Christmas* television special, with Marshall playing an important role in creating the trio's sound. The soundtrack to *A Charlie Brown Christmas* has become a classic holiday jazz recording.

Marshall married Beverly Ann Bivens on February 13, 1965; they had one son and one daughter. The couple divorced in 1978.

Marshall and drummer Granelli joined Bill Ham to form Light Sound Dimension (LSD), which gave its first public performance in San Francisco in 1967 and played concerts worldwide over the course of several decades. Ham had created the light shows that accompanied many San Francisco concerts by such bands as the Grateful Dead, and Light Sound Dimension's performances incorporated Ham's visual displays with experimental jazz music. Marshall also played bass and guitar in several other bands, including the critically acclaimed band Delta Nine.

Marshall was a sculptor and welder and taught both skills at various schools. His sculptures were featured in a number of art shows, including several joint exhibits with his mother in Little Rock in 1961 that paired his sculptures with her abstract paintings.

He invented the megatar, which combined an Indian sitar and a guitar. He also collaborated with the Zeta musical instrument company to invent a small, portable bass that would fit in an airliner's overhead bin, which was marketed as the Zeta Upright. He held several patents associated with guitar neck construction and musical amplifier design. He taught music and bass and published *A Visual Approach to Music*, an instruction book for bass and music theory, in 1975.

In the early 1990s, Marshall formed the Marshall Arts Trio, with his son Joshi on saxophone and Steve Rossi on drums. The trio played together for nearly a decade.

Marshall died on November 14, 2001, of hepatic cirrhosis, and his ashes were scattered in Emeryville, California.

For additional information:

Hyde, Gene. "Renaissance Jazz Man." *Arkansas Democrat-Gazette*, July 16, 2000, pp. 1E, 2E. Online at http://www.runet.edu/~wehyde/fredmarshall.html (accessed February 23, 2013).

Obituary of Fred Calvin Marshall. *Arkansas Democrat-Gazette*, November 22, 2001, p. 6B.

Gene Hyde

GOSPEL / CONTEMPORARY CHRISTIAN ROBERTA MARTIN (1907–1969)

Roberta Evelyn Winston Martin Austin was one of the most significant figures during gospel music's golden age (1945–1960). A performer and publisher, she reached iconic status in Chicago, Illinois, where she influenced numerous artists (such as Alex Bradford, James Cleveland, and Albertina Walker) and had an impact on an entire industry with her innovation and business acumen.

Roberta Evelyn Winston was born in Helena (Phillips County) on February 12, 1907, one of six children of William and Anna Winston, proprietors of a general store. She began studying piano at age six. Her family relocated to Cairo, Illinois, before she was ten, and after arriving in Chicago in 1917, Winston played for various church functions, working with Thomas A. Dorsey, the "Father of Gospel Music," at Chicago's Pilgrim Baptist Church and eventually becoming choir director at the Windy City's Mount

Pisgah Baptist Church. Mildred Bryant Jones, choral director at Wendell Phillips High School where Winston attended, taught her in piano and choral directing, inspiring Winston later to attend Northwestern University, where she studied piano in anticipation of a career as a classical concert pianist.

While the date of her marriage to William (Bill) Martin and details of their subsequent divorce are uncertain, she was known as Roberta Martin at the onset of her career in the early 1930s.

In 1932, Martin joined Thomas Dorsey and Theodore Frye's Chicago-based Young People's Choir, and was eventually employed as the choir's pianist. A 1933 concert featuring the Bertha Wise Quartet led Martin to develop a new style of her own. That same year, Martin and Frye founded the Martin-Frye Quartet. Later renamed the Roberta Martin Singers, the group's early members included Robert Anderson, James Lawrence, Norsalus McKissick, Eugene Smith, Romance Watson, and Willie Webb. Martin accompanied the group as pianist but also sang the occasional solo. In 1947, she married James Austin; they had one son. In spite of a change in surnames, her stage name remained the same throughout her career.

The Roberta Martin Singers were a hit in the 1940s and 1950s, recording for the Apollo and Savoy record labels and earning several gold records. In the early 1940s, female voices—namely those of Bessie Folk and Delois Barrett—were added.

In 1939, Martin established her Roberta Martin Studio of Music, a Chicago-based gospel music publishing house, which distributed her compositions as well as those of James Cleveland, Dorothy Norwood, and Alex Bradford. Among the notable songs Martin published were "He Knows How Much We Can Bear" (1941), "Try Jesus, He Satisfies" (1943), "Only a Look" (1948), "I'm Just Waiting on the Lord" (1953), and "God Is Still on the Throne" (1959).

Though stricken with cancer, Martin reportedly refused painkilling drugs during the time leading up to her death on January 18, 1969, in Chicago, believing that God could perform a miracle. At her funeral, 50,000 black Chicagoans passed through Mount Pisgah Baptist Church to pay their last respects. Martin is buried at Chicago's Burr Oak Cemetery, where fellow Arkansan and gospel star "Sister Rosetta" Tharpe is buried. Martin was honored posthumously by the Smithsonian Institution in 1981 with a colloquium and by the U.S. Postal Service on July 15, 1998, with a commemorative postage stamp.

For additional information:

Boyer, Horace Clarence. How Sweet the Sound: The Golden Age of Gospel. Urbana: University of Illinois Press, 1995.

Heilbut, Tony. The Gospel Sound: Good News and Bad Times. New York: Simon & Schuster, 1971.

McNeil, W. K., ed. Encyclopedia of American Gospel Music. New York: Routledge, 2005.

Greg Freeman

CLASSICAL / OPERA   FRANCIS MCBETH (1933–2012)

William Francis McBeth was a world-renowned composer and conductor. He was the Trustees' Distinguished University Professor and resident composer at Ouachita Baptist University (OBU) in Arkadelphia (Clark County), where he served as chairman of the Department of Music Theory and Composition. The governor appointed him composer laureate of Arkansas in 1975. McBeth's compositions include works for all media, but he was influential in the development of the literature for wind symphony.

Francis McBeth was born on March 9, 1933, in Ropesville, Texas, to Joseph Phinis McBeth, a Baptist minister, and Lillie May Carpenter McBeth. He spent his youth in western Texas, where he began his musical training at an early age, studying piano with his mother and taking up the trumpet in second grade. McBeth had one brother and one sister.

McBeth attended Hardin-Simmons University (HSU) in Abilene, Texas, where he received his bachelor's of music in 1954. He received his master's of music in 1957 from the University of Texas at Austin and was awarded an honorary doctorate of music from HSU in 1971. He also studied at the Eastman School of Music in Rochester, New York.

While an undergraduate at HSU, McBeth played in the university band. From December 1952 to January 1953, the band traveled with U.S. Camp Shows to Europe. He served in the military from 1954 to 1956 with the 101st Airborne Band at Fort Jackson, South Carolina, and the 98th Army Band at Fort Rucker, Alabama. McBeth married Mary Sue White in 1953. They had two children.

McBeth was appointed band director at Ouachita Baptist College (now Ouachita Baptist University) in 1957. He remained at OBU, retiring in 1996 as chairman of the theory and composition department, resident composer, and the Lena Shepperson Professor of Music. In 1975, he was named composer laureate of Arkansas, the first composer laureate in the United States.

McBeth conducted the Arkansas Symphony Orchestra in Little Rock (Pulaski County) for many years before his retirement from the orchestra in 1973, at which time he was named Conductor Emeritus. During his tenure as conductor, McBeth transformed the ensemble into a professional orchestra with a permanent home, financial stability, and full-time professional players. In addition, McBeth conducted in forty-eight of the fifty states as well as Japan, Europe, and Australia.

Most of McBeth's music and books have been published by Southern Music Company of San Antonio, Texas. His publications include works for all media: piano, choral, chamber, orchestra, and band. Among his most frequently performed compositions are *Symphony No. 3* (which was awarded the Howard Hanson Prize in 1963); *Kaddish, Op. 57; Beowulf, Op. 71; Of Sailors and Whales, Op. 78; Through Countless Halls of Air, Op. 84;* and *Missa Brevis, Op. 82.* His passion for wind symphony music influenced its literature, and compositions of younger composers show his influence. McBeth was widely recognized as a clinician and lecturer and wrote a great deal about his own music and that of his contemporaries. Many of his articles were published in leading music journals, and he published three books on music theory and orchestration: *Effective Performance of Band Music* (1972), *New Theories of Theory* (1979), and *Twentieth Century Techniques of Composition for the Beginning Student* (1994). All of his major compositions have been recorded and are commercially available.

Francis McBeth, Arkansas Symphony Orchestra conductor, Little Rock; circa 1970.

Courtesy: University of Central Arkansas Archives, Arkansas Symphony Orchestra Collection

McBeth died on January 6, 2012, from complications of a stroke.

For additional information:

The ASCAP Biographical Dictionary of Composers, Authors and Publishers. 4th ed. New York: American Society of Composers, Authors, and Publishers, 1980.

Hanson, Aprille. "Composer's Life Was Music, More." *Arkansas Democrat-Gazette*, January 9, 2012, p. 2B.

Hitchcock, H. Wiley, and Stanley Sadie, eds. *The New Grove Dictionary of American Music*. New York: Grove's Dictionaries of Music, 1986.

Preston, Keith Y. "William Francis McBeth (b. 1933): Composer, Conductor, and Music Educator." DMA diss., Arizona State University, 2006.

Rehrig, William H. *The Heritage Encyclopedia of Band Music: Composers and Their Music*. Edited by Paul E. Bierley. Westerville, OH: Integrity Press, 1991.

"W. Francis McBeth." Sigma Alpha Iota Philanthropies, Inc. http://www.sai-national.org/phil/composers/wfmcbeth.html (accessed February 26, 2013).

George Keck

CLASSICAL / OPERA · ROBERT McFERRIN SR. (1921–2006)

Robert McFerrin Sr. was an African-American baritone opera and concert singer who became the first black male to appear in an opera at the Metropolitan Opera house in New York City, his debut following by less than three weeks the well-publicized breaking of the color barrier by contralto Marian Anderson. However, McFerrin's career at the Met was brief, being limited to ten performances in three seasons over three years. Although he sang in European opera houses and performed concerts extensively, he failed to attain major prominence. He is best remembered as the father of singer and conductor Bobby McFerrin, with whom he sometimes performed.

Robert McFerrin was born on March 19, 1921, in Marianna (Lee County) to Melvin McFerrin, a minister, and Mary McKinney McFerrin. He had seven siblings. McFerrin showed musical talent at an early age. The family moved to Memphis, Tennessee, when he was two, and he completed eight grades there. A talented siffleur (whistler), he joined a family gospel-singing trio at age thirteen. His father arranged for him to attend Sumner High School in St. Louis, Missouri. McFerrin intended to become an English teacher but changed his career plans after he joined the high school choir and received his first formal music instruction under chorus director Wirt Walton.

After graduation from high school in 1940, McFerrin was accepted at Fisk University in Nashville, Tennessee, but stayed only one year. In 1941, after winning a singing contest, he entered Chicago Musical College, where he studied under George Graham. In 1942, he won first prize in the Chicagoland Music Festival. After being drafted and serving in the army, he returned to college. In 1948, he moved to New York, where he became a student of Hall Johnson, a prominent figure in Afro-American music. He married Sara Copper in 1949; she was a Howard University graduate and singer who gave up her career to further his. She was also a polio victim and was in an iron lung while pregnant with their son, Robert Jr. (Bobby), one of their two children.

McFerrin's New York career began in 1949 with a small part in Kurt Weill's *Lost in the Stars*. His performance attracted the attention of Boris Goldovsky, who gave him a scholarship to study at the Tanglewood Opera Theatre outside of Boston, Massachusetts. There, in 1949, he made his operatic debut in Giuseppe Verdi's *Rigoletto*. He then joined Goldovsky's touring company, where he added roles in Charles Gounod's *Faust* and Christoph Willibald Gluck's *Iphigenie en Tauride*. In addition, he sang with the National Negro Opera company in Verdi's *Aida* and at the New York City Center Opera Company in the world premiere of William Grant Still's *Troubled Island*. Finally, he returned to Broadway for a revival of *Green Pastures* in 1951 and the following year for some performances in *My Darlin' Aida*, an updated version of the Verdi opera set in Memphis in 1861.

In 1953, urged on by his manager, he entered the Metropolitan Opera's "Auditions of the Air," which he won. Usually, the winner received a contract and six months of training. In McFerrin's case, he received no contract, and his training lasted for thirteen months. McFerrin did not object and later lauded the program for teaching him fencing, ballet, and other aspects of stage deportment.

The second African American and first black male to sing at the Metropolitan Opera, McFerrin debuted on January 27, 1955, when he was cast as Amonasro in *Aida*. Racial politics rather than sound musical values dictated his being cast as Amonasro. The black Ethiopian king (and father of Aida) has no love duets to sing with white women. At five foot seven inches tall and 140 pounds, the young McFerrin was hardly prepossessing on stage as an evil father-figure. His even but not large voice was not displayed to its best advantage. In addition, prior to the performance, he had never met the evening's female leads, Aida (Herva Nelli) or Amneris (Blanche Thebom).

A Town Hall recital found him in more congenial circumstances. McFerrin eventually sang only ten performances at the Metropolitan Opera. He did, however, record excerpts from *Rigoletto* in 1956 for the Metropolitan Opera Club. In addition, there exists a 1956 recording taken from a live broadcast of *Aida* from Naples, Italy. In 1958, he went to Hollywood to supply the vocals for Sidney Poitier's Porgy in the motion picture version of George Gershwin's *Porgy and Bess*. McFerrin and his wife decided to stay in California, where they became music teachers. In 1973, following their divorce, McFerrin moved back to St. Louis, where he lived until his death. In 1989, he suffered a stroke that affected his speaking but not his singing. He occasionally performed with his son, Bobby, and his daughter, Brenda. In 1994, he and William Warfield appeared in a Schiller Institute concert.

"I am not attempting to carry the load for all Negro singers," McFerrin had told the *New York Post* prior to his debut, but in reality the load he had to carry transcended vocal concerns. One major reason for his truncated career was management's fear of the reaction of audiences to seeing black males on stage as husbands or lovers of white females.

McFerrin died on November 24, 2006, in St. Louis. He is buried in Jefferson Barracks National Cemetery.

For additional information:

Jones, Randye. "Robert McFerrin." *Afrocentric Voices*. http://www.afrovoices.com/mcferrin.html (accessed February 8, 2013).

Obituary of Robert McFerrin Sr. *Arkansas Democrat-Gazette*, November 29, 2006, p. 8B.

"Robert McFerrin." *Opera News* 71 (February 2007): 71.

"Robert McFerrin Sr., 85, Operatic Baritone at Met, Dies."

New York Times, November 28, 2006. Online at http://www.nytimes.com/2006/11/28/obituaries/28mcferrin.html?_r=0 (accessed February 26, 2013).

Thomas, Naymond E. "Robert McFerrin: The First Black Man to Sing at the Metropolitan Opera Company." DMA diss., University of Oklahoma, 1988.

Michael B. Dougan

GOSPEL / CONTEMPORARY CHRISTIAN — MELODY BOYS QUARTET

The Melody Boys Quartet was a Southern gospel music group based in Little Rock (Pulaski County). The Melody Boys Quartet officially disbanded on December 31, 2012, at the end of the group's "Exit 63" tour, celebrating sixty-three years together.

The group had its origins in the late 1930s when Herschel Foshee, aided by Joe Roper, created the Stamps-Baxter Quartet. The group was named after the music publishing company founded by V. O. Stamps and J. R. Baxter in 1926; the publisher was established in Texas but later opened an office in Pangburn (White County). The quartet's original purpose was to sing and record the company's publications exactly as printed and thus aid in selling Stamps-Baxter songbooks to interested musical groups and churches.

In 1949, Foshee died from a heart attack and was replaced by the sixteen-year-old Gerald Williams, who was also the bass singer for the quartet. The group also ceased to be associated with Stamps-Baxter at this time. Joe Roper took over the group, and they renamed themselves Smilin' Joe Roper and the Melody Boys.

The quartet began to gain popularity throughout the 1950s. In addition to performing every weeknight as well as at different churches and music conventions every weekend, they began doing a radio broadcast program on the Little Rock station KARK-AM (now KARN) three times a day. The program consistently opened with the group's most popular song, "Give the World a Smile." The Melody Boys later became the first Southern gospel music group from Arkansas to have a television program; they began performing live on KARK TV in 1954. The Melody Boys also performed at the first National Quartet Convention in 1957 in Memphis, Tennessee.

In 1959, Roper left the Melody Boys to join the Prophets Quartet, and the group disbanded due to legal and financial problems. Gerald Williams spent the next several years trying to reunite the quartet under his direction. In 1966, Williams was legally able to give the reformed group its current name, the Melody Boys Quartet. However, several singers joined and left quickly throughout the next twenty years, and it was not until 1987 that the Melody Boys once again became firmly established. Williams maintained the name and led the group in many successful tours, as well as recording several albums and performing on television programs.

The Melody Boys recorded a number of albums over the years, and Williams was inducted into the Southern Gospel Music Hall of Fame at Dollywood in Pigeon Forge, Tennessee, on October 12, 2006. The band continued its touring and recording until its final performance at Geyer Springs Baptist Church in Little Rock on December 31, 2012. Williams currently resides in Little Rock.

For additional information:

Caillouet, Linda S. "Melodious Memories." *Arkansas Democrat-Gazette*, January 13, 2013, pp. 1E, 6E.

Melody Boys Quartet. http://www.themelodyboysquartet.com (accessed January 16, 2013).

"Melody Boys Quartet." *Southern Gospel History: Preserving the Legacy of Southern Gospel Music*. http://bradyswww.sghistory.com/index.php?n=M.Melody_Boys_Quartet (accessed January 16, 2013).

Darby Burdine

COUNTRY — PATSY MONTANA (1908–1996)

Patsy Montana was a pioneering female country music singer whose signature song, "I Want to Be a Cowboy's Sweetheart," was the first record by a female country artist to sell a million copies.

Patsy Montana was born Ruby Blevins on October 30, 1908, near Hot Springs (Garland County). She was the eleventh child and only daughter of farmer Augustus Blevins and his wife, Victoria. By the 1920 census, the family was living in Hempstead County. Raised on church songs, fiddle music, and the music of country star Jimmie Rodgers, Blevins headed to Los Angeles with her brother and sister-in-law in 1930; hoping to catch the public's eye, she changed the spelling of her first name to Rubye. She studied violin at the

Patsy Montana in western garb.
Courtesy: UALR Center for Arkansas History and Culture

University of the West (now known as the University of California at Los Angeles—UCLA) until a victory in a talent contest in 1931—she yodeled and sang Jimmie Rodgers songs—led to her own show on KMIC radio. Initially billed as "The Yodeling Cowgirl From San Antone," Blevins soon became Patsy Montana, a name given to her by singer/songwriter Stuart Hamblen while she was performing with the Montana Cowgirls on a KMIC show Hamblen hosted with cowboy star Monte Montana.

In 1932, after two years spent breaking into the music business in Los Angeles, Montana returned to Arkansas, where country singer Jimmie Davis heard her on KWKH in Shreveport, Louisiana, and invited her to sing back-up for him at his next recording session. She recorded four debut songs on that trip. A bigger break came in 1933 when she accompanied two of her brothers carrying a watermelon to the Chicago World's Fair and landed a job as vocalist for the Prairie Ramblers, a hugely successful Kentucky string band that appeared on radio station WLS. She then appeared regularly on the enormously popular *National Barn Dance*, a pioneering country-themed broadcast that started before the Grand Ole Opry, and recorded for the American Record Corporation. Montana also toured steadily, even after her marriage on July 4, 1934, to Paul Rose, who worked with WLS's touring shows. Her biggest hit, "I Want to Be a Cowboy's Sweetheart," composed by Montana herself, was recorded in 1935.

By this time, Montana was an established star with a clearly defined image as a "cowboy

Patsy Montana's boots.
Courtesy: Old State House Museum Collection

pal" who yodeled and dressed in the full western regalia favored by 1930s country stars, complete with gun and holster. Other songs followed in the same vein—"Sweetheart of the Saddle" (1936) and "I Wanna Be a Western Cowgirl" (1939), among others. Even more spirited were numbers such as "The She-Buckaroo" (1936) and "A Rip-Snortin' Two-Gun Gal" (1939)—in the former she portrays herself as a "man-hatin' lassie." In the 1940s, Montana contributed "Goodnight, Soldier" to the war effort and also recorded with such well-known groups as the Sons of the Pioneers and the Light Crust Doughboys.

Montana also appeared in several films, the best known being *Colorado Sunset* (1939) with Gene Autry. From 1946 to 1947, she had her own network radio show, *Wake Up and Smile*, on ABC, which featured her trademark greeting, "Hi, pardner! It's Patsy Montana," accompanied by the thunder of horses' hooves.

Montana returned to Arkansas in 1947, raising her two daughters, Beverly and Judy, doing radio shows on KTHS in Hot Springs, and appearing on Shreveport's *Louisiana Hayride*. Her husband's work eventually took the family to San Jacinto, California, but Montana continued to tour and make records into the 1990s, adding to her reputation as a hard-working professional entertainer. Between 1934 and 1992, she made more than 7,000 personal appearances in the United States, Canada, and Europe. In the fall of 1995, just before her eighty-seventh birthday, Montana played concerts in Hope (Hempstead County) and Little Rock (Pulaski County). She was frail and tiny in her boots and cowboy hat, but she sang and yodeled vigorously, closing as always with "I Want to Be a Cowboy's Sweetheart."

Patsy Montana died in San Jacinto, on May 3, 1996. Later that same year, she was inducted into the Country Music Hall of Fame. As long as women sing country songs in cowgirl outfits, Montana's niche in the pantheon of groundbreaking female country music stars is secure.

For additional information:

Bufwack, Mary A., and Robert K. Oermann. *Finding Her Voice: The Saga of Women in Country Music*. New York: Crown Publishers, 1993.

Kingsbury, Paul, ed. *The Encyclopedia of Country Music*. New York: Oxford University Press, 1998.

McCloud, Barry, and Ivan M. Tribe. *Definitive Country: The Ultimate Encyclopedia of Country Music and Its Performers*. New York: Berkley Pub. Group, 1995.

Robert Cochran

This entry, originally published in *Arkansas Biography: A Collection of Notable Lives*, appears in the *Encyclopedia of Arkansas Music* in an altered form. *Arkansas Biography* is available from the University of Arkansas Press in Fayetteville.

CLASSICAL / OPERA MOONDOG (1916–1999)

Louis Thomas "Moondog" Hardin Jr. grew up and learned to play the piano in Independence County. He later became a musician and composer admired in jazz, classical, and rock circles. He was also known for living on Manhattan streets dressed as a Viking and banging a drum.

Louis Hardin was born on May 26, 1916, in Marysville, Kansas, the son of an Episcopal minister, Louis Thomas Hardin Sr., and Norma Alves, a homemaker and teacher. He had one sister and one brother. The family moved around the Midwest when he was young. Playing tomtom at a Wyoming Arapaho dance at a young age fostered a life-long affection for Native American rhythms. As an adult, Hardin performed with the Blackfoot tribe.

While in Hurley, Missouri, in his early teens, he lost his sight while playing with a dynamite cap that exploded. Hardin went on to play drums in the Hurley school band, and he finished high school at the Iowa School for the Blind. In the early 1930s, the Hardins lived in St. Louis, Missouri, and Hardin attended the state blind school. In May 1936, Hardin's father became rector of St. Paul's in Batesville (Independence County). The family lived just east of Batesville in Moorefield (Independence County).

Hardin, who became known for wearing capes and having long hair, took piano lessons from area teacher Bess Maxfield. He attended Arkansas College (now Lyon College) for a year in 1936 and was in the college literary society. Hardin's mother left soon after the move to Arkansas, and the Hardins divorced. Louis Hardin Sr. remarried, and because of this, had to leave the church. The family remained in the state for some years after.

In 1942, Hardin obtained a scholarship to study music in Memphis, Tennessee, with the head of the Memphis Conservatory of Music. The next year, he moved to New York City and managed to meet Arturo Toscanini and Leonard Bernstein, all while busking and selling broadsides and sheet music of his songs in the street. In 1947, following the dissolution of his marriage to Virginia Sledge, Hardin adopted the stage name Moondog after a moon-fixated canine he remembered from Missouri. His marriage to Mary Whiteing Hardin produced a daughter, June; Hardin later fathered another daughter, Lisa Colins, out of wedlock.

When pioneering 1950s Cleveland, Ohio, rock and roll disc jockey Alan Freed called his radio program *The Moondog Rock and Roll Party*, using Hardin's song "Moondog Symphony" as background music, Hardin successfully sued Freed, with composer Igor Stravinsky testifying for Hardin.

Hardin had released a few 78 rpm singles, and in 1953, his debut album, *Moondog and Friends*, was issued; six more albums were released through the late 1950s. Hardin's music, which often consisted of poems spoken over jazzy rhythms and street noise, connected with Beat poets and others but not the mainstream. Hardin did not record again for a dozen years and then cut two albums for Columbia, shifting emphasis to his orchestral compositions and classical canons and rounds. He also did the arrangements for a Julie Andrews album of nursery rhymes.

Meanwhile, Hardin had become a decades-long fixture in Manhattan streets, appearing in a modification of the dress he debuted in north-central Arkansas—homemade Viking chic. He used an army blanket as a tunic and had a horned helmet, staff, and long beard. Hardin lived on the street to finance his composing but also had a primitive cabin upstate. Few passersby knew he was a composer.

In 1974, Hardin moved to West Germany and eventually settled in Oer Erkenschwick. Many New Yorkers thought the street musician known as "the Viking of Sixth Avenue" had died. Instead, he became better known and was able to record more in Europe.

Hardin wrote the liner notes to *Big Band*, his

A selection of Moondog's albums.
Courtesy: Ian Moore

first release on his own Trimba label in 1995. For the song "You Have to Have Hope," he wrote: "Bill Clinton lived in Hope, I lived in Batesville, Arkansas. We never met. I heard he played the sax, for which I wrote the piece he hasn't heard, as yet. 'Back in Arkansas' are words that fit a falling bit of melody. I'm harking back sixty years to Batesville Bess and all she did for me," referring to his early Arkansas piano teacher, Bess Maxfield.

Jazz, classical, and rock musicians alike played Hardin's compositions. In the late 1960s, Big Brother and the Holding Company with Janis Joplin recorded Hardin's "All Is Loneliness," and Insect Trust, with Little Rock (Pulaski County) native Robert Palmer, covered Hardin's "Be a Hobo" in 1970. A Moondog song was in the 1972 film *Drive, He Said* with Jack Nicholson, and Hardin was interviewed on TV's *Today* and *The Tonight Show*.

In the 1980s and 1990s, musicians such as John Fahey, Kronos Quartet, and NRBQ recorded Hardin's songs. By then, with his lengthy

beard turned white, his reputation amongst musical tastemakers was indelible: he had invented several esoteric musical instruments (the oo, trimba, and ooo-ya-tsu), played with everyone from Charles Mingus to Philip Glass, and influenced the likes of Tom Waits. In 1997, Atlantic issued *Sax Pax for a Sax*, his first major U.S. release in more than twenty-five years—and his last.

Hardin died on September 8, 1999, in Munster, Germany. Hardin's death was noted internationally, although his Arkansas roots were seldom mentioned. A few years later, a sampled version of his song "Bird's Lament" was used in auto commercials.

For additional information:

Hyde, Gene. "Iconoclastic New York Musician Had Arkansas Roots." *Arkansas Democrat-Gazette*, March 17, 2000, p. 1E. Online at http://www.radford.edu/~wehyde/moondog.html (accessed February 26, 2013).

Koch, Stephen. "'Moondog' Hardin." *Arkansas Times*, July 15, 2004, p. 20.

"Louis (Moondog) Hardin, 83, Musician, Dies." *New York Times*, September 15, 1999. Online at http://www.nytimes.com/1999/09/12/nyregion/louis-moondog-hardin-83-musician-dies.html (accessed February 26, 2013).

Obituary of Louis (Moondog) Hardin. *London Times*, September 15, 1999.

Scotto, Robert. *Moondog: The Viking of 6th Avenue*. Los Angeles: PROCESS, 2007.

Stephen Koch

CLASSICAL / OPERA CHARLOTTE MOORMAN (1933–1991)

Charlotte Moorman was a cellist, avant-garde performance artist, and founder of the New York Avant Garde Festival.

Madeline Charlotte Moorman was born on November 18, 1933, in Little Rock (Pulaski County) to J. R. and Vernan Moorman; her father was a sales manager. Moorman began playing the cello at the age of ten, going on to perform with local symphonies while enrolled at Central High School. A member of the National Honor Society and a Central High debutante group called the Southernaires, Moorman graduated in 1951 and attended Centenary College in Shreveport, Louisiana, on a music scholarship. After receiving a BA in 1955, Moorman earned a master's degree in 1957, studying under illustrious concert cellist Horace Britt at the University of Texas at Austin. She then enrolled at the Juil-

liard School in New York City, studying there for the next two years.

While at Juilliard, Moorman performed in classical concert hall orchestras, including the American Symphony Orchestra, of which she continued to be a member through 1967. Yoko Ono, Moorman's friend and one-time roommate, encouraged her participation in the avant-garde scene.

Moorman founded the New York Avant Garde Festival in 1963 at the age of twenty-nine, overseeing all fifteen festivals until its end in 1982. French composer Edgard Varèse, who died two years after the festival was founded, famously designated Moorman as the "Jeanne d'Arc of New Music." In interviews, she repeatedly asserted that she disliked the term "avant-garde," insisting that her work was "of its time," not *avant-garde*, as in "ahead of its time."

The first festival featured works from a broad swath of cutting-edge luminaries such as Allen Ginsberg, John Cage, David Behrman, and Nam June Paik, a Korean artist considered the first practitioner of "video art"—as well as Moorman's future close collaborator.

Paik's pieces, performed by Moorman, conflated technology and cultural controversies with the female form. A few notable examples include *Cello Sonata no. 1 for Adults Only* (1965), in which Moorman shed clothes while performing Bach's C Major Sonata; *TV Bra for Living Sculpture* (1969), in which two miniature televisions were attached to the cups of a clear vinyl bra worn by Moorman; and *Opera Sextronique* (1967), during which Moorman was arrested while performing nude, as dictated by the score.

Moorman and Paik also collaborated on a number of multi-media cellos, most notably the "TV Cello" in which the instrument's body is constructed out of three televisions.

In spite of being diagnosed with cancer in 1979, Moorman continued performing through the 1980s. In September 1982, during the Sky Art Conference in Linz, Austria, she performed *Sky Kiss* by Otto Piene, in which Moorman and her cello, strapped to a number of helium-inflated balloons, were lifted into the sky. At the same festival, Moorman performed Yoko Ono's famous *Cut Piece*, in which members of the audience were requested to cut off pieces of the artist's dress.

Moorman died on November 8, 1991, ten days before her fifty-ninth birthday, at Roosevelt Hospital in Manhattan after a twelve-year battle with breast cancer. She was survived by her second husband, Frank Pileggi. Her archival and manuscript collections are held as part of the Dick Higgins Archive at Northwestern University in Evanston, Illinois.

For additional information:
Charlotte Moorman Collection. Dick Higgins Archive. Northwestern University Library, Evanston, Illinois.

Collins, Glenn. "Charlotte Moorman, 58, Is Dead; A Cellist in Avant-Garde Works." *New York Times*, November 9, 1991. Online at http://www.nytimes.com/1991/11/09/arts/charlotte-moorman-58-is-dead-a-cellist-in-avant-garde-works.html (accessed March 26, 2013).

John Tarpley

JAZZ — "SNUB" MOSLEY (1905–1981)

Lawrence Leo "Snub" Mosley was a jazz trombonist, composer, and band leader originally from Little Rock (Pulaski County). Nicknamed "Snub," Mosley had a career that spanned more than fifty years, which included stints in the 1930s with Claude Hopkins, Fats Waller, and Louis Armstrong. Mosley is probably best remembered today as creator of his own unique instrument—the slide saxophone—which combined an upright saxophone and mouthpiece with a trombone mouthpiece and slide.

Snub Mosley was born on December 29, 1905, in Little Rock. Encouraged by his grandfather, he took an interest in the trombone and played in the band at M. W. Gibbs High School in Little Rock. His tendency to improvise on sheet music and (as Mosley put it) "swing" drew the ire of his band director but did bring him to the attention of Syncho Six members Eugene Crooke and Alphonso Trent, who witnessed Mosley's trombone skills during a parade. Mosley accompanied the Syncho Six to a gig in Helena (Phillips County) and some subsequent shows, but at his mother's insistence, he came home to graduate from high school before leaving for good. The Syncho Six— renamed the Alphonso Trent Orchestra—went on to make history in 1925 as an attraction at the Adolphus Hotel in Dallas, Texas; the band's performances at a white hotel in an era of segregation and the band's radio broadcasts on WFAA were firsts for an African-American band in the South.

After the Alphonso Trent Orchestra broke up in 1933, Mosley played with numerous musicians, including Claude Hopkins, Louis Armstrong, and Fats Waller before settling in New York City in 1938 and forming his own band. He achieved his greatest professional success when he performed in Ken Murray's *Blackouts* variety show from 1943 to 1944, while continuing to lead his own group. On and off from 1943 through 1946, Mosley and his band toured Europe and the South Pacific with the United Service Organizations (USO), entertaining Allied troops. Mosley's band went on a USO tour once again from 1952 to 1953, visiting Europe and the Far East.

As live bands gave way to television as America's entertainment medium, Mosley and his fellow musicians found work harder to come by.

"Snub" Mosley and his band; circa 1940. Mosley is holding his slide saxophone. Courtesy: Adam Miller

According to music producer Frank Driggs, Mosley "was always working and was much too proud to take any type of day job. It meant though that the quality of the jobs often left a lot to be desired." Regardless, Mosley made a living in music and split his performances between New York City and hotels in upstate New York.

As a band leader, Mosley's biggest hit was his "The Man with the Funny Horn," recorded with Decca in 1940, which featured his performance on the ghostly sounding slide saxophone. Following his final recording with Decca in 1942, he went on to record sessions with Sonora (1946), National (circa 1946), Avalon (also circa 1946), Penguin (1949), and Columbia (1959), as well as an entire album with United Kingdom–based Pizza in 1978, titled *Live at the Pizza Express*. A joyful Mosley briefly went back to Europe, this time touring as a featured artist for the Pizza label.

Toward the end of his life, Mosley suffered two debilitating strokes, one of which was further complicated by pneumonia in January 1981. He consequently moved into a nursing home in upstate New York, where he spent most of his remaining days being visited by well-wishers. Mosley died suddenly on July 21, 1981, just a few days after moving back into his apartment in New York City.

For additional information:

Carr, Ian, et al. *The Rough Guide to Jazz*. London: Rough Guides Ltd., 2004.

Driggs, Frank. "The Man with the Funny Little Horn...Snub Mosley." *Whiskey, Women, And...* 12/13 (December 1983).

Feather, Leonard, et al. *The Biographical Encyclopedia of Jazz*. New York: Oxford University Press, 2007.

Manskleid, Felix. "Snub Mosley." *Jazz Monthly* (March 1960).

Rinne, Henry. "A Short History of the Alphonso Trent Orchestra." *Arkansas Historical Quarterly* 45 (Autumn 1986): 228–249.

Wright, Laurie. "(Very) Young Man With A Horn." *Storyville* 97 (October/November 1981).

Adam Miller

CLASSICAL / OPERA | # CONLON NANCARROW (1912–1997)

Samuel Conlon Nancarrow composed innovative music and produced a body of work largely for player piano. According to musicologist Kyle Gann, who has published a study of Nancarrow's compositions, they are the most rhythmically complex ever written by anyone anywhere, featuring up to twelve different tempos at the same time. Gann describes "whirlwinds of notes... joyously physical in their energy." The wealth of ideas in Nancarrow's works has had a lasting impact on other composers.

Conlon Nancarrow was born in Texarkana (Miller County) on October 27, 1912. His father, Samuel Charles Nancarrow, was a businessman and mayor of Texarkana from 1927 to 1930. His mother was Myra Brady Nancarrow, and he had one brother, Charles.

At the insistence of his father, Nancarrow attended Western Military Academy in Alton, Illinois. While there, his interest in music blossomed, and he attended the National Music Camp in Interlochen, Michigan, the following summer. He began listening to jazz and composing. Nancarrow's father sent him at age fifteen to Vanderbilt University to study engineering, but he stayed just one semester. Already proficient on the trumpet, he was still a teenager when he left Texarkana in 1929 to study at the Cincinnati College-Conservatory. He played jazz there in a German beer hall.

In 1932, he married Helen Rigby, a singer and contrabass player, in Cincinnati, Ohio. She divorced him in 1940. Later marriages were to Annette Margolis, a painter, from 1948 until their divorce in 1953, and Yoko Seguira, an anthropologist, in 1970, with whom he had a son, David Makoto, in 1971.

In 1934, Nancarrow moved to Boston, Massachusetts, where he studied composition privately with Walter Piston, Roger Sessions, and Nicolas Slonimsky and conducted a Works Progress Administration (WPA) orchestra.

Like many artists in that period, he joined the Communist Party in 1934 and went to Spain in 1937 with the Abraham Lincoln Brigade to fight against Francisco Franco's fascist army. He was wounded and escaped in 1939 after Franco's victory.

Upon his return to the United States in 1939, he discovered that Slonimsky had arranged for publication of two of his compositions. He settled in New York City, where he associated with other composers, including Aaron Copland and Elliott Carter.

Describing Nancarrow as an "undesirable" because of his Spanish experience, the State Department refused to issue him the passport he applied for after learning that his friends in the Abraham Lincoln Brigade were denied permission to travel. In protest, he moved to Mexico City in 1940, Mexico being the only country other than Canada where he could go without a passport. He lived there the rest of his life, becoming a Mexican citizen in 1956. His only return visit to Arkansas after moving to Mexico was in 1992, when he dealt with family matters.

As he continued composing, he realized that the complex rhythms he envisioned could be cut on a player piano roll. In 1947, he bought a player piano and punching machine and began composing his *Studies for Player Piano*, which captured the attention of the musical world. In 1960, Merce Cunningham choreographed several of Nancarrow's compositions and presented them on a world tour in 1964. It was not until 1977, however, that scores of his *Studies* were published and recordings of all the *Studies* began.

Beginning in 1981, Nancarrow made trips to the United States and Europe for performances of his music, and he received commissions from major artists. In 1982, he received a $300,000 MacArthur Fellowship "given in recognition of… major accomplishments in music which demonstrate…originality, dedication to creative pursuits, and capacity for self-direction." In 1990, the New England Conservatory of Music awarded him an honorary doctorate, and the University of Mexico City presented two days of performances of his music, including his works for player piano. Significant works include approximately fifty *Studies for Player Piano* (1952–1992), *String Quartet no. 1* (1945), *String Quartet no. 3* (1987), and *Piece for Small Orchestra no. 2* (1985).

Nancarrow died on August 10, 1997, apparently from heart failure, at his home in Mexico City.

In 2012, a documentary called *Conlon Nancarrow: Virtuoso of the Player Piano*, written and directed by James Greeson, premiered in Little Rock (Pulaski County).

For additional information:

Carlsen, Philip Caldwell. "The Player Piano Music of Conlon Nancarrow: An Analysis of Selected Studies." PhD diss., City University of New York, 1986.

Gann, Kyle. *The Music of Conlon Nancarrow*. Cambridge, MA: Cambridge University Press, 1995.

Greeson, James R., and Gretchen B. Gearhart. "Conlon Nancarrow: An Arkansas Original." *Arkansas Historical Quarterly* 54 (Winter 1995): 457–469.

Hocker, Jürgen. *Encounters with Conlon Nancarrow*. Lanham, MD: Lexington Books, 2012.

———. "My Soul Is in the Machine—Conlon Nancarrow—Composer for Player Piano—Precursor of Computer Music." In *Music and Technology in the Twentieth Century*, edited by Hans Joachim Braun. Baltimore: Johns Hopkins University Press, 2002.

Scrivener, Julie A. "Representations of Time and Space in the Player Piano Studies of Conlon Nancarrow." PhD diss., Michigan State University, 2002.

Williams, Nancy A., ed. *Arkansas Biography: A Collection of Notable Lives*. Fayetteville: University of Arkansas Press, 2000.

Gretchen B. Gearhart

This entry, originally published in *Arkansas Biography: A Collection of Notable Lives*, appears in the *Encyclopedia of Arkansas Music* in an altered form. *Arkansas Biography* is available from the University of Arkansas Press in Fayetteville.

BLUES / R&B · NE-YO (1982–)

Ne-Yo is one of the most prominent and active Arkansas-born recording artists and songwriters performing in the early twenty-first century. Initially known for songs he wrote for other artists, Ne-Yo has released five solo rhythm and blues (R&B) albums.

Shaffer Chimere "Ne-Yo" Smith Jr. was born on October 18, 1982, in Camden (Ouachita County) to Lorraine and Shaffer Smith. Smith displayed his songwriting acumen at a young age, writing his first song at the age of five. After his parents separated, he relocated with his mother to Las Vegas, Nevada, where he spent the remainder of his formative years. His mother worked in a variety of jobs before becoming a bank manager, though music was a constant

Ne-Yo and Jennifer Hudson at the Nobel Peace Prize Concert in Oslo, Norway; 2012.
Photo: Bjoertvedt

presence in the Smith household. While still in high school, Smith began performing with local R&B group Envy and later moved with the group to Los Angeles, California. After the group disbanded, he worked as a staff writer at a production company, which eventually led to a record deal with Columbia Records in 2000.

Smith recorded a full-length album for Columbia Records under the performing name of Shaffer, but it was never released. Soured by the experience, he focused on songwriting instead. The nickname Ne-Yo was given to him by producer Deon "Big D" Evans due to his songwriting prowess, as Big D felt that Smith saw music the same way that the character Neo saw the intricacies of the matrix in the movie *The Matrix*. Smith quickly adapted it, with a change of spelling due to copyright reasons, as his stage name. He garnered attention after the song "That Girl" from his Columbia Records album was re-recorded by Marques Houston in 2003. Ne-Yo's acclaim as a songwriter grew even more after he co-wrote Mario's 2004 single "Let Me Love You," which reached number one on the *Billboard* pop and R&B singles charts.

While Ne-Yo continued to focus on writing songs, during a visit to Def Jam Recordings, he was persuaded to perform for label executives. This led to a recording contract and his return as a performing artist. Ne-Yo's first released solo album, *In My Own Words*, came out in 2006 on the Def Jam label and debuted at number one on the *Billboard* albums chart. The album also featured three singles that reached the top ten on the singles chart, including "So Sick" which reached number one. His second album, *Because*

of You (2007), also debuted at number one and won the 2008 Grammy Award for Best Contemporary R&B Album. His two subsequent albums, *Year of the Gentleman* (2008) and *Libra Scale* (2010), have also been top sellers, and Ne-Yo received two additional Grammy Awards in 2009 for the song "Miss Independent." His fifth studio album, *R.E.D.*, was released in 2012.

While Ne-Yo's prominence as a performer grew, he continued to stay active as a songwriter. In addition to Mario's "Let Me Love You," Ne-Yo has written songs for Beyoncé ("Irreplaceable") and Rihanna ("Take a Bow") that have reached number one on the *Billboard* Hot 100 chart. He has also written songs for Chris Brown, Mary J. Blige, Whitney Houston, and Celine Dion, among others. Ne-Yo also works with young artists and producers through his production company, Compound Entertainment, which he founded in 2004. He opened his own recording studio, Carrington House, in Atlanta, Georgia, in 2007. Ne-Yo left Def Jam in 2012 to take a position as a senior vice president of artists and repertoire at Motown Records.

In addition to his career in music, Ne-Yo has acted in movies and television. He appeared in the movies *Save the Last Dance 2* (2006), *Stomp the Yard* (2007), *Battle: Los Angeles* (2011), and *Red Tails* (2012) and guest-starred on the television show *CSI*.

He has two children with his long-time girlfriend, Monyetta Shaw.

For additional information:

Crosley, Hillary. "Ne-Yo Compositions." *Billboard* (March 24, 2007): 26–28.

Ford, Tracey, "Ne-Yo Releases His 'Own Words.'" RollingStone.com, February 26, 2006.

Gwynn, John. "Ne-Yo Talks 'Battle: Los Angeles.'" *ASU State Press*, March 10, 2011.

Jones, Steve. "Ne-Yo Keeps the Tunes Coming." *USA Today*, May 16, 2007, p. 8D.

Mitchell, Gail, and Joy Mitchell. "'Word' is Spreading About Ne-Yo." *Billboard* (March 4, 2006): 39–40.

Matthew Mihalka

BLUES / R&B — ROBERT NIGHTHAWK (1909–1967)

Robert Nighthawk was among the most remarkable slide guitarists in blues history, widely admired among his peers and the southern audiences he spent his life entertaining. Nighthawk influenced a generation of bluesmen such as Muddy Waters, B. B. King, Earl Hooker, and

supposedly Elmore James. He was the archetype of the rambling bluesman, roaming all over the South with frequent trips to the North, though he chose Helena—present-day Helena-West Helena (Phillips County)—as his home base. This rambling nature and his decision to remain in the South likely explain why Nighthawk never achieved greater fame.

Robert Nighthawk was born Robert Lee McCollum in Helena on November 30, 1909, to Ned and Mattie McCollum. He was one of three children. His was a musical family that performed at dances, parties, and picnics. His first instrument was the harmonica, which he recalled picking up in 1924. Nighthawk married for the first time in 1928 to Mary Griffen in Friars Point, and they had two children. He was married a second time in 1947 to Hazel Momon, whom he met in 1945. They stayed together until 1953 and had three children.

Houston Stackhouse, who claimed to be Nighthawk's cousin, taught him guitar in 1931. The two became lifelong friends and partners. Nighthawk soon began traveling around the Delta, where he met many fellow blues musicians. Between 1932 and 1935, he roamed farther afield, playing in the orchestra of the Dan Hildrege Show, traveling with singer Laura Dukes, and fronting a jug band in Memphis, Tennessee. During this period, he met and played with musicians such as Sleepy John Estes, Yank Rachell, Sonny Boy Williamson, Big Joe Williams, Hammie Nixon, "Big Bill" Broonzy, Memphis Slim, and John Lee Hooker.

After a run-in with the law in 1935, he moved to St. Louis, Missouri, where he remained through 1939. Nighthawk first surfaced on record in 1936, for Vocalion playing guitar on a four-song session with Jack Newman. A year later, pianist Walter Davis got Nighthawk signed to the Bluebird label. On May 5, 1937, Nighthawk made his debut as part of a historic recording session cutting six songs under his own name backed by Sonny Boy Williamson and Big Joe Williams. One of the songs was "Prowling Night-Hawk," and it was this song's popularity that was the basis for his name change in the early 1940s.

Nighthawk returned to the Bluebird studios in 1937 and 1938, cutting sixteen songs under his own name; he was also an in-demand session musician. In 1940, he returned to the studio, recording four songs for Decca including "Friars Point Blues," his most polished slide work to date, a trademark he would become famous for in the postwar era.

Nighthawk was in Chicago, Illinois, around 1940–41 fronting his own band, but he was back in Helena by 1941. During this period, Nighthawk began playing electric guitar and refined his slide technique, drawing much inspiration from Tampa Red. In 1942, he got a spot on KFFA radio in Helena advertising Bright Star Flour.

In 1948, Nighthawk landed his next recording contract with Aristocrat Records (soon to change its name to Chess) through the help of Muddy Waters, who was a star on the fledgling label. The following year, he cut five songs, including his most enduring record, the double-sided hit "Annie Lee Blues" backed with "Black Angel Blues." In 1950, he recorded his final session for Chess. The following year, he moved over to the newly formed United label and its subsidiary, States. United recorded him on its very first day of sessions, and two of the label's first five releases were listed as performed by "Robert Nighthawk & His Nighthawks Band."

After his United recordings, Nighthawk returned to the South, staying mainly in the Helena/Friar's Point area working with CeDell Davis, Sam Carr, harmonica player Frank Frost, and later Jack Johnson—the latter three backing him as the Nighthawks. A return to Chicago in 1964 resulted in several recordings; he cut songs for Chess, Testament, and Swedish Radio, who were in Chicago documenting blues, as well as two songs for a United Kingdom compilation album. He was also recorded and filmed live on Maxwell Street in conjunction with the filming of a 1964 documentary *And This is Free*. In 1965, he made an appearance in Toronto, Canada, where he recorded five songs in a small Toronto studio; these did not surface until 2006. In 1967, George Mitchell recorded Nighthawk for the final time in Houston Stackhouse's combo, mostly playing bass due to ailing health.

Two months after these recordings, Nighthawk died of congestive heart failure on November 5, 1967, at the Helena Hospital. He is buried in Helena's Magnolia Cemetery. "He loved Helena," said Sam Carr. "That's the reason I buried him there."

For additional information:

Harris, Jeff. CD liner notes for *Prowling with the Nighthawk*. Document Records, 2004.

Johnson, Greg, "Robert Nighthawk." *BluesNotes* (November 2000). Online at http://www.cascadeblues.org/History/RobertNighthawk.htm (accessed February 26, 2013).

Trail of the Hellhound: Robert Nighthawk. http://www.nps.gov/history/DelTA/BlueS/people/robert_nighthawk.htm (accessed February 26, 2013).

Jeff Harris

SMOKIE NORFUL (1975–)

Smokie Norful—a popular pastor in Chicago, Illinois, and a Grammy Award–winning gospel singer—spent most of his developing years in Pine Bluff (Jefferson County) and is one of the most commercially successful gospel recording artists to have emerged from Arkansas.

Born Willie Ray Norful Jr. in Little Rock (Pulaski County) on October 31, 1975, to the Reverend W. R. Norful and Teresa Norful, Norful is the oldest of three boys. Like so many other African-American gospel singers, he found church to be a nurturing environment in which his musical skills could be honed. At a 2012 taping of the Trinity Broadcast Network's flagship program, *Praise the Lord*, Norful joked before a studio audience about growing up as a "P. K." (preacher's kid) and expressed gratitude for his minister father and no-nonsense mother. Norful remarked, "Most of the family sermons came from the other end of her belt."

Having spent his earliest years in Muskogee and Tulsa, Oklahoma, Norful relocated with his family to Pine Bluff, where he attended junior high and high school. Earning a bachelor's degree in history at the University of Arkansas at Pine Bluff (UAPB), Norful also prepared for the ministry by attending Trinity International Seminary in Deerfield, Illinois, and Garrett-Evangelical Theological Seminary in Evanston, Illinois, earning a Master of Divinity degree. Thereafter, Norful taught history for several years at the schools of his youth, Jack Robey Junior High School and Pine Bluff High School, before securing a position at Evanston Township High School in Illinois.

While in Arkansas, Norful served as educational director for the Pine Bluff Housing Authority's after-school program, historian for the National Park Service, and congressional aide for the Fourth Congressional District. In Pine Bluff, Norful was also ordained a church elder and became a licensed minister in 1997. Serving as minister of music, youth pastor, and associate pastor under his father at Pine Bluff's St. John African Methodist Episcopal (AME) Church, Norful was heavily involved in ministry by the time he launched his music career.

Norful's debut album, *I Need You Now* (2002), received gold certification from the Recording Industry Association of America (RIAA). The title track, enhanced by Norful's mastery of the piano, became the song for which he is perhaps best known. Another gold record, *Nothing without You* (2004), garnered the Grammy Award for Contemporary Soul Gospel Album of the Year. Other albums have included: *Life Changing* (2006); *Smokie Norful Live* (2009), which features Tony Award winner Heather Headley on "Jesus Is Love"; *How I Got Over: Songs That Carried Us* (2011), a project on which Norful returned to his traditional gospel roots by recording with the Twelfth District AME Mass Choir and gospel veterans Melvin Williams, Myron Butler, and Sheri Jones-Moffett, as well as his greatest musical influence, Vanessa Bell Armstrong; and *Once in a Lifetime* (2012), an album that includes his popular compositions "No One Else," "Justified," and "God Is Able." In addition to his Grammy, Norful has won multiple Dove Awards from the Gospel Music Association as well as several Stellar Awards. He has also been nominated for an NAACP Image Award, a Soul Train Award, and two BET awards for gospel music.

Norful resides in the Chicago area, where he ministers at Victory Cathedral Worship Center, the church he founded in Bolingbrook, Illinois, and its satellite location on Chicago's South Side. He also serves on the Board of Regents for Trinity International University. With his wife, Carla, Norful has two sons and an adopted daughter. Norful and his wife are entrepreneurs, with business interests in real estate, entertainment, and publishing.

For additional information:
"Smokie Norful." EMI Gospel. http://smokienorful.emigospel.com/ (accessed January 29, 2013).
Victory Cathedral Worship Center. http://www.getthevictory.org/index.aspx (accessed January 29, 2013).

Greg Freeman

WALTER NORRIS (1931–2011)

Walter Norris created an amalgamation of jazz improvisation with classical music in a style that no other pianist has duplicated. His varied career includes eight years as a pianist, musical director, and entertainment manager for New York's Playboy Club. In addition, he authored noted books on the piano.

Walter Norris was born on December 27, 1931, in Little Rock (Pulaski County). His father, Lucian Norris, was an accountant for the Federal Reserve Bank. Walter Norris began studying classical piano at the age of five, was playing "boogie woogie" by eight, and was playing in local bands by twelve. After graduation from Central High School, he began playing with Mose Allison on a southern tour. From 1950 to 1952, he served in the U.S. Air Force. He played the El Morocco in Las Vegas, Nevada, in 1953 and 1954 and then moved to Los Angeles, California, to play the Haig and Tiffany clubs for two years with such famous jazz musicians as Frank Rosolino, Stan Getz, and Dexter Gordon. He later toured with Nat King Cole.

In 1963, he was hired as house pianist, musical director, and entertainment manager of New York City's Playboy Club. During the day, he studied as a piano-major and conductor at the Manhattan School of Music. He then toured with the Thad Jones and Mel Lewis Band, playing in Europe, Japan, and the United States. He joined with Red Mitchell to play a Scandinavian tour and then worked with Charles Mingus's quintet in New York. He moved to Berlin, Germany, where he became a professor of piano improvisation at Hochschule der Kunste (1984–1994), during which time he recorded five CDs for the Concord Jazz label and gave seminars and concerts in Europe, South America, and the United States, including one given at the University of Arkansas (UA) in Fayetteville (Washington County).

In 1995, Norris was inducted into the Arkansas Jazz Hall of Fame and was also named a Steinway Artist. In 2003, he was inducted into the Arkansas Entertainers Hall of Fame. Norris was acknowledged by many jazz critics as one of the world's greatest living jazz pianists.

Norris married three times and had two daughters from his first marriage. He resided in Berlin, Germany, until his death on October 29, 2011.

For additional information:

Kernfield, Barry. *The New Grove Dictionary of Jazz.* New York: Grove's Dictionaries, 2002.

Walter Norris. http://www.walter-norris.de/ (accessed February 8, 2013).

"Walter Norris." *All About Jazz.* http://www.allaboutjazz.com/php/musician.php?id=9910# (accessed February 8, 2013).

Jim Porter

OFFICIAL STATE MUSICAL INSTRUMENT

On February 28, 1985, the Arkansas legislature approved Act 277, designating the fiddle as the official musical instrument of the State of Arkansas. The designation, which originated as House Bill 749 sponsored by Representative Bob Watts of Harrison (Boone County), asserted that the instrument was "most commonly associated with the musical education and entertainment of the pioneer families of Arkansas and… continues as a dominant musical instrument in the culture…of the people of Arkansas." Watts's measure was supported in the chamber by Representative Napoleon Bonaparte "Nap" Murphy of Hamburg (Ashley County), who delivered a brief oration on the floor of the House on the history of the fiddle from medieval times to its modern form.

This official designation is a tangible acknowledgment of the primacy of the vernacular violin in early American musical life. The words "fiddle" and "violin" describe the same instrument, the highest-pitched of the viol family of unfretted stringed instruments. The fiddle's design was effectively standardized by the mid-eighteenth century: a body shaped like an hourglass with a pronounced waist, an ovoid arched fingerboard, four strings usually tuned in intervals of perfect fifths, an arched bridge or string support, and a wooden tailpiece or string anchor. Any violin, when used for playing vernacular or "folk" music, is apt to be termed a fiddle, but some folk performers have modified their instruments by flattening the bridge, making it easier to play double notes or chords.

Arkansas man playing the fiddle; circa 1910.
Courtesy: Shiloh Museum of Ozark History/Bob Besom Collection (S-92-139-1)

The art of fiddling is promoted in Arkansas by local folk music societies, a handful of luthiers (violin-makers), and the state's annual Old-Time Fiddling Championship, a competition and reunion of vernacular violinists held each autumn at the Ozark Folk Center in Mountain View (Stone County).

The violin, or fiddle, was perhaps the most commonly encountered musical instrument in the years of the United States' westward expansion. The fiddle's convenient size, relative robustness, high volume, and the ease of rudimentary apprehension made it well suited for carrying on long trips; even the musically challenged could manage to scrape out the rhythms of sacred and secular melodies for family, community, and congregational gatherings.

The fiddle's association with Arkansas was made manifest in the humorous tale and song "The Arkansas Traveler." Popularized by—and possibly originating with—Arkansas politician and raconteur Sandy Faulkner, the story turned on a "city slicker" proving his mettle to a rural squatter by demonstrating skill on the fiddle; the result is an overwhelming outpouring of hospitality. The tale was the subject of a painting by Edward Payson Washbourne that, in the form of chromolithographs published by both Grozelier and Currier & Ives, hung in thousands of American households in the mid-nineteenth century.

For additional information:

Goerzen, Chris. "George Cecil McLeod, Mississippi's Fiddling Senator and the Modern History of American Fiddling." *American Music* 22 (Fall 2004): 339–379.

Randolph, Vance, and Frances Emberson. "The Collection of Folk Music in the Ozarks." *Journal of American Folklore* 60 (April 1947): 115–125.

David Ware

OFFICIAL STATE SONGS

Forty-eight of the fifty states have designated one or more songs as official "state songs." Arkansas has so designated no less than four compositions. (Only three states—Massachusetts, New Hampshire, and Tennessee—have adopted more.) Their styles include devotional anthem, sprightly folk melody, and 1980s vintage country-pop. The earliest was adopted contemporaneously with the flowering of progressivism in Arkansas and marked a popular appreciation of the state's natural beauty and agricultural bounties, turning away from the "hillbilly" Arkansas of early twentieth-century popular humor. Subsequent state song adoptions largely followed in this vein.

Arkansas's first unofficial song was likely the fiddle tune known popularly as "The Arkansas Traveler." It appeared under this title by the mid-nineteenth century and became associated with a popular comic monologue, doing much to establish a popular image of Arkansas as a place populated by rural eccentrics. The first officially recognized state song, however, owed nothing to the folk fiddling tradition. In 1916, Eva Ware Barnett, a classically trained composer and sometime professor of music at Ouachita Baptist College (now Ouachita Baptist University) in Arkadelphia (Clark County), published "Arkansas," an anthem that substituted a genteel characterization of the state for the older "hillbilly" image. Barnett's lyrics evoked visions of a bucolic, be-flowered, and fertile state always providing a warm welcome and safe shelter for "her children." It was so well received that the 1917 legislature designated it the official state song. Barnett retained the copyright for the song, which apparently sold steadily through the next two decades.

In 1939, the office of Secretary of State C. G. "Crip" Hall prepared a pamphlet of information about the state, including the words and the music to "Arkansas." According to later testimony by secretary of state employees, Barnett offered no objection to this free publication. The pamphlet, bearing Hall's name, was issued in 1940, an election year; 60,000 copies were distributed. In June 1940, Barnett filed a claim against the state for $3,000 in damages, asserting that the free distribution (characterized as having been done for political purposes) had injured sales of her sheet music, on which she collected about six cents per copy. The case was argued on June 24, 1941, in U.S. District Court. On June 25, Barnett's lawyers opted for a "no suit" action, effectively withdrawing the charge while retaining the option of reopening the case within a year. The reason remains murky, but journalism of the day suggests that inexperience with copyright law and a plausible suggestion that Barnett had granted informal permission for the song to be published in the pamphlet made her case weak.

The next episode in the case began on June 20, 1943; newspapers reported that Governor Homer Adkins had appointed a committee to choose a new state song. On June 27, Barnett placed an advertisement in the *Arkansas Gazette* indicating that she withdrew her song from consideration as the next official state song. The committee's actions after that are undocumented, but a mid-September newspaper article indicated that several songs had been submitted.

Over the next five years, little progress was made, but by September 1948, the *Arkansas Democrat* asked in an editorial squib, "What's Wrong with the Travelers?" The *Democrat* editorial writer suggested that the old fiddle tune "The Arkansas Traveler" would be a fine state song. On November 10, 1947, the state committee adopted "The Arkansas Traveler" as the title and melody of the official song, with lyrics to be added after submissions from the public. In 1949, the State Song Commission published lyrics to the old fiddle tune with no indication of authorship. Two verses offered a nostalgic look at the traditional tale of the Arkansas Traveler, while the chorus offered sentiments worthy of any progressive booster:

> *For the wonder state we'll sing a song,*
> *And lift our voices loud and long.*
> *For the wonder state we'll shout hurrah!*
> *And praise the opportunities we find in*
> *Arkansas.*

The legislature did not ratify the commission's choice, but this updated version of the "Traveler" was the state's de facto official song from 1949 to 1963. Despite its traditional roots, it was not popular, perhaps because of its somewhat awkward lyrics (particularly the rhyming of "Hurrah" with "Arkansas"). "Arkansas" remained popular, particularly with school choirs, and eventually Barnett's unhappiness moderated. The legislature acknowledged the unpopularity of the replacement state song in its 1963 session, when it approved a resolution by Roscoe Brown of Craighead County asserting that the words to "The Arkansas Traveler" did little to develop pride in or respect for the state and that, moreover, doubt existed as to whether it ever had been officially adopted as the state song. Claiming that Barnett's anthem best described Arkansas's "attractions, traditions and loyal-

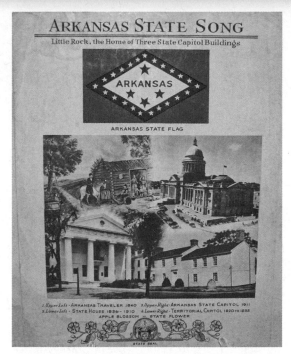

Courtesy: Old State House Museum Collection

ties," the resolution proclaimed "Arkansas" the official song, provided that Barnett would assign its copyright to the secretary of state.

Governor Orval Faubus signed the resolution on March 4, 1963, restoring "Arkansas" to its former status. On October 5, 1963, Secretary of State Kelly Bryant hosted a reception for Barnett at the capitol, at which the songwriter autographed copies of the sheet music, which would be distributed free to the public upon request.

No serious challenge to the status of "Arkansas" was mounted until 1971, when the state Senate voted to designate "Arkansas Waltz" by Bill Urfer of Heber Springs (Cleburne County) and Cletus Jones of Benton (Saline County) as the official state waltz. The song extolled Arkansas's scenery, its agriculture, and even the athletic prowess of its flagship college teams:

> *Your teams win almost every game*
> *Those Hogs and Indians are hard to tame*
> *When you hear the call they've got the ball*
> *That's Arkansas.*

The House did not follow suit in endorsing the song, and the Senate passed a solo resolution, which served as an expression of sentiment with no legal standing.

In 1985, another challenge to Barnett's anthem was mounted. In February, state Representative Robert "Sody" Arnold of Arkadelphia introduced House Bill 824, which would replace Barnett's song with another composition, also titled "Arkansas," written by Billie Francis Taylor and Keith Hays. Arnold claimed that few Arkansans knew the words to Barnett's "obscure but official" anthem; he noted that the only time he remembered hearing it was during an impromptu performance in the House chamber by the late Representative William Thompson of Marked Tree (Poinsett County). Ultimately, Arnold took steps to end the consideration of his bill after learning that Barnett's daughter, Martha Fors of Little Rock (Pulaski County), had cried upon learning that her mother's song might be scrapped.

Arkansas celebrated its sesquicentennial throughout 1986, and several songs honoring the state debuted; two attracted general popularity: "Oh, Arkansas," written by Little Rock musician Terry Rose and veteran Chicago-based songwriters Gary Klaff and Mark Weinstein, and "Arkansas (You Run Deep in Me)," by Nashville, Tennessee, songwriter and Mallet Town (Conway County) native Wayland Holyfield. Arkansas Power and Light Company (AP&L) commissioned Holyfield to write and perform the song. He termed the assignment "the toughest challenge I think I've ever had," adding that he did not want it to be a travelogue or an anthem; to record it, he assembled a group of musicians with Arkansas roots. AP&L presented the song to the state in a ceremony on the capitol steps on January 24, 1986. "Oh, Arkansas" was widely performed throughout the sesquicentennial year by Rose, a regionally popular performer; it was also performed and championed by Little Rock television personality Ned Perme.

The popularity of the two songs, which rested in some respects upon their modernity, encouraged state Representative Bill Stephens of Conway (Faulkner County) to introduce a resolution in the 1987 legislative session designating both compositions official state songs while reserving for Barnett's "Arkansas" the honorific of official state anthem. An additional measure designated the revamped "The Arkansas Traveler" the official historic song. The resolution's sponsor, Bob Fairchild of Fayetteville (Washington County), declined to sing the song, claiming tone deafness; the *Arkansas Gazette* reported that Representative Pat Flanagin of Forrest City (St. Francis County) voted against the measure, claiming that the state "was loaded up with songs."

Today, the Secretary of State's Office offers the lyrics to all four official state songs on its website, as well as in packets of materials distributed annually to grade school classes across the state. The office receives fifty to 100 requests per year for copies of the printed music to one or all of the songs, usually from school choirs or civic groups.

For additional information:
Bristow, Michael James, ed. *State Songs of America*. Westport, CT: Greenwood Press, 2000.
Hladczuk, John, and Sharon Schneider Hladczuk. *State Songs: Anthems and Their Origins*. Lanham, MD: Scarecrow Press, 2000.
Shearer, Benjamin F., and Barbara S. Shearer. *State Names, Seals, Flags, and Symbols: An Historical Guide*. Westport, CT: Greenwood Press, 2002.

David Ware

GOSPEL / CONTEMPORARY CHRISTIAN — OLD FOLKS' SINGING

What became known as Old Folks' Singing started on May 17, 1885, with the dedication of a new Methodist church and cemetery in Tull (Grant County). The event was multi-denominational, with the entire community participating in the singing and midday dinner. The annual event, which celebrated its 125-year anniversary in 2010, is held in Tull at the Ebenezer United Methodist Church on the third Sunday in May. It is believed to be the oldest continuous singing day held west of the Mississippi River. While the shape-note system of learning music is no longer part of Old Folks' Singing, the musical heritage of the event can be traced back to the shape-note singing popular in New England and moving to rural southern and western states in the mid-1800s.

The origin of the name "Old Folks' Singing" is unknown (the earliest surviving record book is from 1921 and calls the event "Old Folks' Singing Convention"), but an apocryphal story holds that the singing from the old *Christian Harmony* songbooks was done in the morning to please the elder residents. The afternoon singing consists of songs from the newer *Cokesbury Worship Hymnal*.

The singing is held in a morning and then an afternoon session, with a meal in between. Since at least 1921, the morning session has hosted a welcome address and a response. After the first song in the afternoon session, a memorial service is held in which a list of those who have died during the past year is read. "Happy Land" is the favorite song of the morning session, while the afternoon session's favorite is "Awakening Chorus."

While the singing is done inside the church, much activity takes place throughout the day on the church grounds, especially for young children who are too active to sit inside and sing all day. Although the practice ended by the 1950s when the owner of the land around the spring let the underbrush become overgrown, young people traditionally walked to (and courted by) the Ebenezer Spring a short walk from the church. A tradition that survives into the twenty-first century is walking around the Ebenezer Cemetery, which has graves dating from the early 1800s.

An important part of the day is "dinner on the ground," a meal enjoyed between the morning and afternoon singing. In the early years of the event, people packed their own meals for the dinner, but during the Depression, large crowds showed up in hopes of being fed. The stress of about 2,000 people arriving for a meal nearly killed the tradition, but George DuVall, the first president of Old Folks' Singing, saved the yearly event by suggesting that each woman "bring enough food for your own family and multiply it by two." The dinner was originally served and eaten on quilts and tablecloths spread on the ground, but an incident in the 1940s involving a pig running into a five-layer coconut cake resulted in the dinner being moved onto tables ever after.

One of the earliest known photographs of Old Folks' Singing, 1913.
Courtesy: Butler Center for Arkansas Studies, Central Arkansas Library System

In 1936, guests began "signing the book" when they attended the event, which has created a record of who has attended over the years. KBBA radio station in Benton (Saline County) recorded portions of Old Folks' Singing in 1955 and 1956.

Famous professor and folklorist John Quincy Wolf attended the event in 1963, remarking, "As the old folks die the interest in the old style decreases. The prospects for survival are not good, but it is difficult to kill a seventy-seven-year-old tradition." However, the event has persisted. It today serves as a kind of reunion for people who have moved away from the area or who have relatives there. Although this may not have been the tradition in earlier years, the welcome address is given by a Tull resident and the response address is given by someone who has moved away.

Old Folks' Singing is governed by a president, vice president, secretary, treasurer, and chaplain. A planning committee arranges the details of the day, including inviting people to deliver the welcome and response addresses.

For additional information:
Old Folks' Singing Planning Committee. *Blest Be the Tie that Binds: 125 Years of Old Folks' Singing in Tull, Arkansas: 1885–2010*. Benton, AR: 2010

Ali Welky

OPERA IN THE OZARKS AT INSPIRATION POINT

Opera in the Ozarks at Inspiration Point is a summer program that trains opera singers and stages performances at Inspiration Point, overlooking the White River seven miles west of Eureka Springs (Carroll County). The company has always performed in repertory style, with each student learning several roles over the season. Generally, three operas make up the summer season, with at least one being performed in the original language.

Charles Mowers, a German-born engineer and inventor, came from Texas to the Ozark Mountains around 1900 to hunt wild game. He bought the land known as the Big Rock Candy Mountain in 1928 and began construction of a "castle" based on his memories of buildings along the Rhine River. Using stone quarried on the property, he incorporated an unusual building method he called Egyptian Rock Work.

After the stock market crash of 1929, Mowers abandoned his castle and returned to Texas. The castle was finished in 1932 by the Reverend Charles Scoville (1869–1938), a renowned preacher of the Disciples of Christ, who planned to use it as a retreat from his evangelistic labors. He named the site "Inspiration Point." After his death, his widow gave the property to Phillips University in Enid, Oklahoma, for a conference and retreat center. Ten years later, however, this project was abandoned, and Henry Hobart, formerly dean of fine arts at Phillips, joined with Gertrude Stockard, director of music at Eureka Springs High School, to organize a music camp, Inspiration Point Fine Arts Colony (IPFAC), which held its first session in the summer of 1950. Hobart and his wife financed extensive repairs to the buildings with loans and donations from Eureka Springs businesses. Some furnishings were obtained from government surplus stores. Practice pianos were donated by area churches and schools.

The Oklahoma, Arkansas, Kansas, and Missouri Federations of Music Clubs provided financial support beginning in the 1950s. In 1959, the enterprise was incorporated as a nonprofit organization, with a ninety-nine-year lease on the property. In the early 1970s, Dr. Vernon Baker purchased the property and donated it to IPFAC. As the school outgrew the original "castle," the physical plant was more like a children's camp than an opera workshop, with simple dormitory housing, small faculty apartments, and a barn for storage and rehearsals.

But the quality of the performances belied their surroundings. Hobart hired outstanding teachers and coaches, who often remained on the staff for many summers. Dr. Isaac Van Grove (1892–1979) was artistic director from 1955 to 1977. In addition, he composed six operas on biblical themes suited to the voices of the younger singers. IPFAC's motto was "The students are the stars"—that is, they would sing all the roles without relying on guest performers.

Early on, performances were held in Eureka Springs' auditorium, until an open-air pavilion with stage lighting was built in the early 1960s. Traffic noise and the flutter of nocturnal birds and insects were frequently part of a production, and rain occasionally dampened the audience. Carroll Freeman, a scholarship student in 1975, returned for three years afterward as assistant

director to Van Grove. Then, from 1987 to 2001, Freeman was artistic director of Opera in the Ozarks, a name chosen to reflect the Fine Arts Colony's evolving emphasis on a single art form. Freeman and music director Frank Hube capped the enrollment at fifty participants. The directors also began to focus on more mature singers, a group not well served in other "young artist" programs. Freeman and Hube reasoned that these singers would come to Inspiration Point already trained in the essentials of music performance. The faculty could then work with students more capable of meeting the musical and physical demands of singing challenging repertoire in an outdoor Arkansas theater every night for a month.

During the last fifteen years of the twentieth century, Opera in the Ozarks experienced renewed growth and popularity. In 1985, the governing board adopted a long-range plan for a new, modern campus and purchased 200 acres adjoining the property. In 1989, Jim Swiggart, an Inspiration Point alumnus and music teacher in Oklahoma's public schools, became the general director. Under his leadership, both the musical and administrative aspects of Opera in the Ozarks have experienced dramatic improvements. Swiggart and Freeman, the artistic director, steadily expanded and improved the instructional program. Equally important, Swiggart paid off the company's debts and began upgrading the housing and work areas. The performance pavilion was partially enclosed, the stage was expanded, and a small pit was built to accommodate the orchestra. After the construction of the Walton Arts Center in Fayetteville (Washington County), the company performed once each season there and also in Bella Vista (Benton County).

Around the turn of the century, the organization sold a substantial part of the undeveloped property to finance extensive future improvements. As part of a five- to six-year development plan, the organization commissioned David McKee of Core Architects in Rogers (Benton County) to create a preliminary design for a 750-seat auditorium, enclosed and climate-controlled. This project is expected to cost approximately $10–12 million and would enable a much longer performance schedule than is possible in the present open pavilion. Other goals of the development plan include building restoration, program preservation and support, and an increase of the endowment. In about 2007, the institution employed a publicity agent, Vantage Point Communications, to increase its visibility in the region. In 2010, an alumni association was formed to build support for the institution. A new artistic director, Thomas Cockrell, was hired in 2010, and a studio artists program was inaugurated for undergraduate students. The performance schedule in the twenty-first century has included "A Taste of Opera" outreach events in Bentonville (Benton County), Bella Vista, and Fayetteville. In 2010, the organization was awarded a $25,000 Arkansas Heritage Resource Grant to support renovations of the auxiliary buildings at the site.

In the 2011 season, from late June to late July, the company included students from twenty states. It gave twenty-three performances of three operas, and at the beginning of the performance season, the company hosted "Family Day at the Opera," an educational and recreational effort to engage young people's interest in opera. In addition, the company toured the region in eleven performances of a one-hour version of *The Pirates of Penzance* by Gilbert and Sullivan. Despite the oppressive heat in the open-air pavilion, about 6,500 people from more than twenty-five states attended these performances.

For additional information:

Horton, Ray F. *Inspiration Point...and Its Personalities*. St. Louis: The Bethany Press, 1961.

"Inspiration Point Fine Arts Colony: History." A one-page unsigned account printed in the annual programs of Opera in the Ozarks, beginning circa 2000.

Martin, Becca Bacon. "Opera in the Ozarks." *Morning News of Northwest Arkansas*, June 24, 2005, p. 1E.

Opera in the Ozarks at Inspiration Point. http://opera.org/ (accessed February 26, 2013).

Polikoff, Rich. "Officials Seek New Venue to Extend Opera Season." *Northwest Arkansas Newspapers*, September 5, 2011, p. 9.

Ethel C. Simpson

COUNTRY K. T. OSLIN (1942–)

Kay Toinette (K. T.) Oslin is a country music singer who skyrocketed to fame in her mid-forties with the hit album *80's Ladies* (1987). Her work is known for its humor and mature perspective, as she achieved success much later in life than most popular musicians.

K. T. Oslin was born in Crossett (Ashley County) on May 15, 1942. Soon after her birth, her family moved to Memphis, Tennessee, and then to Houston, Texas. Oslin considers Houston her hometown.

Oslin initially performed as a folk singer with Guy Clark in the 1960s and then moved to New York, where she performed as a chorus girl on and off Broadway. She soon began doing advertising jingles, which led to appearances in a number of television commercials. She also wrote songs that were performed by Dottie West, Gail Davies, Sissy Spacek, and the Judds.

In 1987, after a brief run with Elektra Records, during which she released two singles, she landed a contract with RCA Records, which released Oslin's debut *80's Ladies*. The album debuted at No. 15 on the *Billboard* charts and soon went platinum, with two No. 1 hits. Oslin became the first female songwriter to win the Country Music Association Song of the Year award for her title song, "80's Ladies," and also earned the Female Vocalist of the Year honors and a Grammy Award for the song. Oslin was honored with two Academy of Country Music awards and a Grammy for best female country vocal performance in 1987. Her follow-up album, *This Woman* (1988), shot to platinum and spawned five singles, including "Hold Me," "Hey Bobby," and "Money." It also netted her two Grammy Awards, one for Best Country Female Vocal Performance and one for Best Country Song; two Academy of Country Music awards; and a Country Music Association award.

K. T. Oslin Albums
80's Ladies (1987)
This Woman (1988)
My Roots Are Showing (1996)
Live Close By, Visit Often (2001)

After releasing several more well-received songs, Oslin branched out into acting. She took one-time guest roles on the television shows *Paradise* and *Evening Shade*. On the big screen, she co-starred in *The Thing Called Love* (1993) with Sandra Bullock and River Phoenix.

In 1995, Oslin had coronary bypass surgery. She recovered and released the acclaimed album *My Roots Are Showing* (1996) and, more recently, *Live Close By, Visit Often* (2001). Oslin has never married.

For additional information:

"The Best Interviews with Country Music Legends." *CNN Larry King Weekend*. May 20, 2001. http://transcripts.cnn.com/TRANSCRIPTS/0105/20/lklw.00.html (accessed February 8, 2013).

C. L. Bledsoe

ROBERT PALMER (1945–1997)

Robert Franklin (Bob) Palmer Jr. was an author, music critic, musician, ethnomusicologist, lecturer, record producer, and documentary filmmaker, not to be confused with the British rock singer of the same name. Critic Greil Marcus called Palmer "one of the few distinguished pop music critics to come out of the South."

Bob Palmer was born on June 19, 1945, in Little Rock (Pulaski County) to teacher/pianist Robert F. Palmer Sr. and award-winning poet and freelance writer Marguerite Bowers Palmer. He grew up in the lower Pulaski Heights area of Little Rock. He had one sister, a half brother, and a half sister.

From an early age, Palmer had his ear to the radio. Unbeknownst to his parents, the teenaged Palmer sometimes climbed out his bedroom window at night and snuck off to some of the clubs and dives dotting Little Rock's 9th Street to soak up the live music.

Palmer played clarinet in the Hall High School marching band and attended Little Rock University, now the University of Arkansas at Little Rock (UALR), where he was active in journalism and in the civil rights and peace movements of the 1960s. After receiving a BA in 1967, he moved to New York City. Later, he moved to Hoboken, New Jersey, where he was in an eclectic rock/folk/jazz band, the Insect Trust. The group cut two albums, both cult favorites, *Insect Trust* and *Hoboken Saturday Night.*

While continuing to play professionally, Palmer made his foray into music writing by writing freelance articles for *Crawdaddy* and other publications. In the early 1970s, he began writing for *Rolling Stone* magazine and became one of its contributing editors.

Palmer's ability to climb inside a piece of music and describe it in passionate and visceral terms, along with his ability to trace a type of music to its roots, helped establish him as the *New York Times*'s first full-time popular music critic. He was the paper's chief pop critic from 1981 to 1988. His abilities also led to many freelance articles for *Penthouse, Atlantic Monthly,* the *Journal of American Folklore,* and other publications.

Trips to Morocco, India, and Cuba deepened Palmer's interest in world music. Never one to stay behind a desk, he played clarinet with musicians in Jajouka, Morocco, and immersed himself in their culture. During visits home from New York City, Palmer played with Little Rock jazzmen Walter Henderson and the late John Stubblefield and with blues guitarist CeDell Davis of Helena-West Helena (Phillips County). Blues music was always central to Palmer's career, and in the 1990s, he began producing albums for blues label Fat Possum Records. Palmer said he preferred the live sounds of juke joints in the Delta to polished recordings made in studios. He also liked helping musicians gain fame and was instrumental in getting Davis and other musicians gigs and exposure to larger audiences.

One of Palmer's best-known books is *Deep Blues.* Published in 1981, it has been used as a textbook in college classrooms and traces the blues from its African roots to the Delta to post–World War II Chicago, Illinois. It is considered a definitive work on the subject. Palmer was screenwriter, narrator, and musical director for the documentary film by the same name and co-directed a documentary film, *The World According to John Coltrane.* Another of Palmer's well-known books is *Rock & Roll: An Unruly History* (1995), a companion to a ten-part miniseries on rock by the British Broadcasting Corporation and the Public Broadcasting Service for which he was the primary consultant. He also authored *A Tale of Two Cities: Memphis Rock and New Orleans Roll, Jerry Lee Lewis Rocks,* the text for a coffee table book on the Rolling Stones, *Baby, That Was Rock and Roll: The Legendary Leiber and Stoller,* and collected works from his writings in *Rolling Stone* magazine. Palmer also wrote many scholarly liner notes for such artists as Ray Charles, Albert King, Charles Mingus, Miles Davis, Yoko Ono, John Lee Hooker, and Ornette Coleman. He lectured at Yale University, Carnegie Mellon University, Bowdoin College, and the University of Mississippi, among other schools. He was the first senior research fellow of the Institute for Studies in American Music while teaching at Brooklyn College in the early 1970s.

Palmer died on November 20, 1997, in the Westchester County Medical Center in Valhalla, New York, of complications from liver disease.

He was survived by his fourth wife, JoBeth Briton, and a daughter by a previous marriage. He was cremated in New York, and his remains rest at Roselawn Cemetery in Little Rock. At UALR's seventy-fifth-anniversary celebration in 2003, fellow musicians paid tribute to Palmer as someone who cared more about advancing others' careers than his own. In November 2009, Scribner released a 480-page anthology of Palmer's writing about music.

For additional information:

DeCurtis, Anthony, ed. *Blues & Chaos: The Music Writings of Robert Palmer*. New York: Scribner, 2009.

Lensing, Eric G. "Robert Palmer: An Unruly Writer." *Pulaski County Historical Review* 47 (Spring 1999): 2–11.

Palmer, Robert. *Deep Blues*. New York: Viking Press, 1981.

"Robert Palmer." The Arkansongs Music Festival: Roots Music and a Tribute to Robert Palmer. http://www.ualr.edu/arkansongs/bios/palmer.html (accessed February 8, 2013).

Dorothy Palmer Cox

GOSPEL / CONTEMPORARY CHRISTIAN — TWILA PARIS (1958–)

Twila Paris, one of the most successful artists in the field of contemporary Christian music.
Courtesy: Twila Paris

Twila Inez Paris Wright is a prolific contemporary Christian singer, songwriter, pianist, and author who lives in Fayetteville (Washington County). She is the winner of ten Gospel Music Association (GMA) Dove Awards and three American Songwriter Awards and has hundreds of published and recorded songs to her credit. Hymns and choruses she has composed have appeared in such widely varying hymn collections as the *United Methodist Hymnal* and the *Baptist Hymnal*, as well as those of various Pentecostal and non-denominational churches.

Twila Paris was born on December 28, 1958, in Fort Worth, Texas, one of four children of Oren Paris II, the founder of Youth With A Mission ministries and Ecclesia College in Springdale (Washington and Benton counties), and Rachel Inez Paris, a writer of Christian songs. She was raised in Elm Springs (Washington and Benton counties).

Paris was involved in church music since her childhood (having reportedly composed lyrics and melodies for songs since age two and studied piano since age six), but her career as a singer/songwriter and public figure essentially began in 1981 with the release of her first full-length album, *Knowin' You're Around*. In the 1980s and 1990s, she was at the forefront of the praise and worship movement among church musicians and Christian artists. In 1992, her album *Sanctuary* won the GMA Praise and Worship Album of the Year. Her Dove Awards include Female Vocalist of the Year for 1993 and 1994. In 1995, she won the GMA Song of the Year award for "God Is in Control"; she also made a popular music video for the song. Originally associated with Star Song Communications, her parent company EMI switched her to Sparrow Records in 1996. Her contract expired in 2003, and she then signed with the praise and worship label Integrity Music. Her first project for Integrity was *He Is Exalted: Live Worship* (2005).

Among Paris's better-known compositions are "He Is Exalted," "We Bow Down," "Lamb of God," and "We Will Glorify." In December 2007, she released *Small Sacrifice*, which was made available only through her website and Lifeway Christian Stores. This album collects a number of her own favorite worship standards and presents them in a more typical style of live worship music, including a version of "He Is Exalted" in Portuguese as used by Christians in Brazil.

Paris has produced more than fifteen albums and has had over thirty number-one hit songs on the Christian Contemporary charts. She has worked with such well-known contemporary Christian artists as Amy Grant and Michael W. Smith. In addition, she is a published author with several books to her credit that (as with her music) deal with personal worship and praise in devotional life, among them *In this Sanctuary: An Invitation to Worship the Savior* (1992, co-authored with Dr. Robert Webber) and *Perennial: Meditations for Seasons of Life* (1998).

A firm believer that Christian music should be accessible to all kinds of Christians, Paris

Twila Paris Hit Songs

"Lamb of God" (1985)

"We Bow Down" (1991)

"We Will Glorify" (1991)

"God Is in Control" (1994)

"He Is Exalted" (1998)

works to cross over between the traditional hymnody of the denominational churches and the freer, more emotional praise and worship of the Charismatic/Pentecostal renewal. Although offered a full music scholarship to the University of Arkansas (UA) in Fayetteville, she believed that she was called by God for ministry and attended Youth With A Mission discipleship training instead.

Paris is married to Jack Wright of Fayetteville and has one son. The couple has worked with Youth With A Mission and various other church and para-church ministries. She has been a spokesperson for World Vision for several years and has performed a number of benefit concerts for that charity.

For additional information:
"The Sanctuaries of Twila Paris." *Contemporary Christian Music Magazine* (November 1991).
"Twila Paris: Home for the Holidays." *Today's Christian Woman* (December 1994).
Twila Paris. http://www.twilaparis.com (accessed February 8, 2013).

David O. Bowen

FOLK MARY CELESTIA PARLER (1904–1981)

Mary Celestia Parler was responsible for developing and implementing the most extensive folklore research project in Arkansas history. She was a professor of English and folklore at the University of Arkansas (UA) in Fayetteville (Washington County) and the wife of noted Ozark folklore collector Vance Randolph. Through her vast knowledge and appreciation of Arkansas culture, she enabled many future generations to glimpse the state's cultural history, much of which remains only in the stories, songs, and images she collected with the help of her students and assistants.

Mary Parler was born on October 6, 1904, in Wedgefield, South Carolina, the daughter of a country doctor and farmer, Marvin Lamar Parler, and a local historian, writer, and teacher, Josie Platt Parler. Mary had one brother, Marvin Lamar Jr., and a sister, Francis Lott, who was actually a cousin adopted by the family at an early age. The family's three farms grew mainly cotton.

Parler was schooled in Wedgefield until the tenth grade, when she took an early placement exam and was admitted to Winthrop College in Rock Hill, South Carolina. She graduated in 1924 with a BA in English literature and went on to the University of Wisconsin, where she began a lifelong study of Geoffrey Chaucer and earned an MA in English in 1925. She did more graduate work at the University of South Carolina, the University of North Carolina, and at Brown and Columbia universities.

Parler arrived at UA in 1948 while working on a dissertation for the University of Wisconsin on southern dialects, based on the works of William Gilmore Simms. She had a strong background in English literature and had begun dialect work as part of a graduate minor in comparative linguistics while at the University of Wisconsin. She began teaching folklore and Chaucer in the UA English department, where she became known to her students as "Miss Chaucer." When asked how a Chaucer scholar came to be so interested in Arkansas folklore, Parler commented "It is perhaps in exploring the intricacies of human behavior that Chaucer and Arkansas folklore are relatable," and that "there's a good deal of folklore in Chaucer."

During her first year in Fayetteville, she was asked to help found the Arkansas Folklore Society, and she served as its secretary-treasurer from 1950 to 1960 and later as the society's archivist and as a member of its Council of Members. She recommended the creation of a society newsletter, and much of the folklore collected and reported by the group appeared there, making up a large part of the University of Arkansas Folklore Collection.

In 1949, she developed UA's first folklore course, became director of the University of Arkansas Folklore Research Project, and began compiling the archival material with the help of her field assistant, Merlin Mitchell. The collection of folksongs includes 442 reels (137,400 feet) of audiotape with full transcriptions, making it one of the largest collections of its kind.

Collected over fifteen years, these recordings include many "event" ballads native to Arkansas, a Cherokee choir singing Baptist hymns, songs collected from immigrants, fiddle tunes, jokes, and tales. The collection of English language ballads includes both those written in this country as well as those that came over from the British Isles, the written forms of which can be traced to the thirteenth century.

As a folklorist, Parler understood the cyclical nature of folklore but also believed that traditional culture was threatened by the rapid expansion of towns and cities, and from developing technologies such as radio and television. She was unusual in having the foresight to look beyond strictly traditional forms and preserve "original" songs written by her informants (those who supplied cultural information to her), as well as Ozark versions of early commercial country music adapted from tradition by performers such as the Carter Family. This was innovative collecting, perhaps influenced by her future husband and collaborator, the preeminent Ozark folklorist Vance Randolph.

Many at the time believed she would have a hard time collecting anything, even suggesting she would come up empty handed. She just laughed. She returned from her first trip in September 1953 with eighteen songs recorded from Virgil Lance of Mountain Home (Baxter County). Ultimately, her collection comprised 3,640 songs.

She collected more than just folksongs. Stored in the University Libraries' Special Collections department is an unprocessed collection of 60,000 handwritten note cards of "Ozarkisms" collected by Parler, her assistants, and her students. They include eighteen volumes of typescript citations composed of eleven volumes of folk beliefs and superstitions, four of proverbs, two of riddles, and one of ballads and songs.

In 1954, CBS television made Parler's collecting the focus of an episode of the program *The Search*. The episode centered on her search for "the great-great-grandchild" of an Elizabethan ballad, "The Two Sisters."

The first collaboration between Vance Randolph and Parler took place in 1953, when they worked together on Randolph's dialect book, *Down in the Holler: A Gallery of Ozark Folk Speech*. She also assisted Randolph with his later books, *The Talking Turtle* (1957) and *Hot Springs and Hell* (1965). A flirtation that had begun at Arkansas Folklore Society meetings in

1950 led to their wedding in the spring of 1962. The marriage certificate is dated March 27, 1962, but there is no account of a ceremony. They had no children. Though Parler legally assumed the last name of her husband, she continued professionally under her maiden name.

Mary Celestia Parler; circa 1950s.

Courtesy: Special Collections, University of Arkansas Libraries, Fayetteville

In 1963, Parler published her only book, *Arkansas Ballet Book*, a compilation of Ozark ballads she had collected from informants over the years. In 1972, she was made professor emerita, and she retired from UA in 1975, having taught half-time for the previous three years. She returned to South Carolina shortly after Randolph died in 1980, and she died there less than a year later on September 15, 1981. She is buried at the Church of the Holy Cross in Stateburg, South Carolina, alongside her mother and father.

The work of Parler was revisited in 2005 when the University Libraries' Special Collections department hosted a two-day conference, "A Collector in Her Own Right: Reassessing Mary Celestia Parler's Contribution to Ozark Folklore." The conference brought together collectors, scholars, and former students of Parler to discuss her life and work.

For additional information:
Mary Celestia Parler Research Materials. Special Collections. University of Arkansas Libraries, Fayetteville, Arkansas.
Mary Celestia Parler Vertical File. Special Collections. University of Arkansas Libraries, Fayetteville, Arkansas.
Reynolds, Rachel. "Mary Celestia Parler Randolph: 'Gladley Wolde She Lerne and Gladley Teche.'" *Overland Review* 31 (2003).

Rachel Reynolds Luster

BLUES / R&B   "SUNSHINE" SONNY PAYNE (1925–)

"Sunshine" Sonny Payne is the longtime host of *King Biscuit Time*, the radio program broadcast on KFFA 1360 AM in Helena (Phillips County) that has done much to popularize blues music. As blues journalist Don Wilcock wrote, "Sunshine Sonny Payne exists totally outside

the boundaries that define and confine most of society. That he loves blues music and the people… all people…who make it and that he has a vehicle for expressing that love to thousands who then in turn influence millions makes the contribution of his cherub wisdom and good hu-

"Sunshine" Sonny Payne at the KFFA studio in Helena-West Helena.
Courtesy: Delta Cultural Center

mor of incalculable value."

Sonny Payne was born John William Payne on November 29, 1925, to Gladys Swope Payne and William G. Payne, in Helena, now Helena-West Helena (Phillips County). After the death of his mother in 1938, his sisters Rebecca (Becky) and Fosteen (Teen) left home to get married, and Payne lived first with his father and then with Becky. In 1940, he went out on his own and lived in a rooming house in Helena. At that time, his father worked at a gas station in town, and Payne often spent time there during breaks from his work as a paper boy. The gas station is where he met Robert Lockwood Jr., leading to their lifelong friendship.

KFFA 1360 AM radio station was built in Helena and became operational in 1941. Having watched the building's progress, Payne applied for a job as soon as it was completed and started work as a janitor and errand boy at the station two days before broadcasts began. His curiosity about electronics earned him lessons after hours every Monday, Wednesday, and Friday from one of the engineers, after which he was required to clean the old 78 rpm records for the next day's broadcast.

In July 1942, during the fifteen-minute time slot sponsored by King Biscuit Flour, the show's announcer, Sam Anderson (also the general manager and owner), stepped out of the control room and returned too late to broadcast the next commercial script. Seeing that Payne was in the control room, he banged on the control room's glass wall and gestured for Payne to read the copy over the air. Flustered, Payne glibly ad-libbed his way through the commercial. Despite the flubs, later that day Payne was allowed to read a few Sonny Boy cornmeal commercials, and he performed the scripts perfectly. Meanwhile, he began learning to play the upright bass from a local band, the Copeland Cowboys, who often played live in the studio.

In December 1942, tired of being hungry making $12.50 a week, Payne lied about his age and joined the U.S. Army. He served in the Seventy-Fifth Signal Battalion until December 1948. He attained the rank of "buck" sergeant and left the service as a corporal. He served in the Aleutian Islands and New Guinea, where he fought alongside the infantry to dig in behind their lines to set up communications. While in the army, he often went to United Service Organizations (USO) clubs to get music lessons from band members.

When he got out of the service in December 1948, he was released in San Antonio, Texas. A guitarist friend, Bud Davis, had a gig at the time with Tex Ritter in Austin, Texas, and Davis suggested that Payne join them, since they needed a bass player for the remaining three weeks of their tour. Payne agreed to join that tour and signed up with the musicians' union so that he could continue touring as a side man with Harry James, Ted Williams, and numerous others until 1951.

Tiring of road tours, he returned in 1951 to Helena and asked KFFA's Sam Anderson to hire him back as an announcer. That year, he began hosting the *King Biscuit Time* blues music radio show, which has become the longest-running blues show in the world, with Payne its longest-running blues show host. *King Biscuit Time* is still broadcasting as of 2013.

Payne acquired the nickname "Sunshine" because of his attitude one day while assigned to host a live, remote-location, all-day broadcast in Marianna (Lee County) called "Marianna Calling." It was a cold, miserable, rainy day, and Helena disc jockey Bill Fury "threw" the live broadcast over to Payne in Marianna. When Fury announced Payne's name to switch the broadcast over to him, Payne did not answer right away. After Fury's second attempt to rouse him, Payne grumpily returned the hail over the air, and Fury asked Payne, "What's wrong with you?" "Nothing wrong with me," Payne replied. "But it's cold and rainy here, with ice and snow." "Well, boy you're just a ray of sunshine, aren't you?" said Fury. The next morning, when Payne walked into the Helena station, everyone greeted him saying, "Hey, Sunshine." It might not have stuck except that Robert Lockwood Jr. kept it going to get a rise out of Payne.

Payne is an inductee of the Arkansas Tourism Hall of Fame, and he received the George Foster Peabody Award in 1992 for outstanding achievement in the field of radio and broadcast journalism. He has twice received the Blues Foundation's Keeping the Blues Alive Award and is the recipient of the Arkansas Broadcasters Association's Pioneer Award. In 2010, he was inducted into the Blues Hall of Fame.

Payne was married twice but has outlived both his wives. He had one daughter, now deceased, from his first marriage.

For additional information:

Clancy, Sean. "John William 'Sonny' Payne." *Arkansas Democrat-Gazette*, December 12, 2010, pp. 1D, 7D.

Khatchadourian, Sonia. "A Ray of Sunshine in the Blues." *Living Blues* (May–June 1991).

King Biscuit Time. http://www.kingbiscuittime.com/ (accessed February 26, 2013).

Neal, Amy. *King Biscuit Time Magazine* (Summer 1971).

Palmer, Robert. *Deep Blues*. New York: Viking Press, 1981.

Liz Lottmann

GOSPEL / CONTEMPORARY CHRISTIAN — POINT OF GRACE

Point of Grace, which originated in Arkadelphia (Clark County) in 1990, is a female vocal trio—formerly a quartet—that sings contemporary Christian music.

Three of the singers in Point of Grace—Denise Jones, Heather Floyd, and Terry Lang—were life-long friends from Norman, Oklahoma. They had sung together in their church choir and school musicals. The trio enrolled at Ouachita Baptist University (OBU) in Arkadelphia in 1988. While singing in the "Ouachitones," an OBU-sponsored group, they met fellow student Shelley Phillips from North Little Rock (Pulaski County), and in 1991, they formed a quartet.

Originally, the four named themselves Sayso from a biblical verse in Psalms: "Let the Redeemed of the Lord say so." The quartet began singing at local churches, retreats, and other faith-based institutions. From 1991 to 1993, while still enrolled full time at OBU, they went on tour, part time during school and full time during the summer break. They used recorded music and sometimes sang a cappella. They built a large base of fans throughout the South. At the urging of their fans, the young women made a self-produced tape, titled *Sayso*, which they sold at their concerts.

At the Christian Arts Seminar in Estes Park, Colorado, in 1992, Sayso won the Overall Grand Prize group competition. Record companies, both Christian and non-Christian, offered recording contracts. The group was determined to maintain the religious theme of their music. One stipulation of theirs was that the word "Jesus" be used in every song, rather than vague references to "him," so as to eliminate doubt that the song was religious. In 1993, Sayso decided to sign with Word Recording, based on the pledge that they would have input in the selection and treatment of the albums. They found there was another group with the same name, so they changed their name to Point of Grace from the C. S. Lewis quotation, "We as Christians live every day at the point of God's grace."

Their first album was titled *Point of Grace* (1993) and went gold. Between 1993 and 2005, Point of Grace produced five gold albums, including *The Whole Truth* (1995), and two platinum, *Life, Love and Other Mysteries* (1996) and *Steady On* (1998). Their number-one singles included "I'll Be Believing," "The Great Divide," "Gather at the River," and "Circle of Friends." Gospel Music Association (GMA) in 1994 voted them New Artist of the Year. GMA also awarded the group the Dove Award, its highest award, eight times.

Despite their hectic schedules, all the young women graduated from OBU with degrees in vocal music. Shelley (Phillips) Breen graduated in 1991, Terry Lang and Heather (Floyd) Payne in 1992, and Denise Jones in 2000. Terry Lang married and continued to sing with the group, but after the birth of her third child, she became a full-time wife and mother, leaving the group in November 2003. Her successor was Leigh Cappillino, a singer with

Point of Grace (clockwise from top): Heather Payne, Denise Jones, Shelley Breen, and Leigh Cappillino.

Courtesy: The Breen Agency

Truth and wife of Point of Grace's guitarist and bandleader, Dana Cappillino. The new foursome made their first album together, *I Choose You*, in 2004. Heather Payne left the group in 2008 and has not been replaced, changing the quartet into a trio.

By the end of 2011, Point of Grace had recorded more than fifteen albums, including a few Christmas albums. The group released the album *A Thousand Little Things* in 2012.

On April 18, 2005, they were inducted into the Arkansas Walk of Fame in Hot Springs (Garland County). The members of the group live in Nashville, Tennessee.

For additional information:
Jones, Rebecca. "Point of Grace." *Ouachita Circle* 1 (Summer 2004): 1–3.
"Point of Grace." *Ouachita Circle* 1 (Summer 2000): 1–3.
Point of Grace. http://www.pointofgrace.net/ (accessed February 25, 2013).

Billie Francis Taylor

BLUES / R&B — ANITA POINTER (1948–)

Anita Marie Pointer is an original member of the singing group the Pointer Sisters. She started singing gospel in her father's church in West Oakland, California, and went on to attain pop/R&B stardom. The group's top-ten hits include the songs "Fire," "Slow Hand," "He's So Shy," "Jump (For My Love)," "Automatic," "Neutron Dance," and "I'm So Excited."

Rhythm and blues/soul singer Anita Pointer.
Courtesy: Sterling/Winters Company

Anita Pointer was born on January 23, 1948, in Oakland, California, the fourth of six children (four of them daughters) of Elton Pointer and Sarah Elizabeth Silas Pointer. Her parents were Arkansas natives, and Pointer's two older brothers, Fritz and Aaron, were born in Little Rock (Pulaski County). Shortly thereafter, their parents moved the family to Oakland. The family traveled by car almost yearly from California to Arkansas to visit Pointer's grandparents. Usually, the trip was related to her father's ministry.

As a child, Pointer loved Arkansas so much that she did not want to leave one year, so her mother allowed her to stay in Prescott (Nevada County) with her grandparents to attend fifth grade. She went back to Arkansas again for seventh grade and tenth grade. Pointer still owns the land on which sat the two-story house her grandfather built.

Pointer noticed the differences between Oakland and racially segregated Prescott: "Going to school in the segregated South is an experience that will bring history to life. The 'colored only' and 'white only' signs, I never saw in Oakland, even though there were places we knew not to go just because. Only being allowed to sit in the balcony of the movie theatre, picking up food from the back door of the restaurant because you can't go inside, picking cotton, I did all that and then some."

Pointer attended McRae Elementary, McRae Jr. High, and McRae High School, which were all-black schools at the time. She was a member of the McRae High School Band, playing alto sax. She did not get to listen to much radio, but she was able to listen to broadcasts from the Grand Ole Opry and sneak to juke joints a few times.

Pointer and her sisters began singing gospel in their father's church, the West Oakland Church of God. Before long, their interest in music expanded and proved too strong for their parents to corral. Bonnie and June Pointer began performing as a duo in the Bay Area, calling themselves Pointers—A Pair. Shortly thereafter, Anita Pointer quit her job at a law office to join the fold, and the Pointer Sisters were officially born. The group started singing back-up in clubs and in studio sessions for such acts as Taj Mahal, Grace Slick, Boz Scaggs, Elvin Bishop, and others. Ruth Pointer later joined the group, and they released their debut album in 1973. Critics called the Pointer Sisters "the most exciting thing to hit show business in years." The Pointer Sisters were the first black female group ever to perform at the Grand Ole Opry, and their song "Fairytale," written by Anita and Bonnie Pointer, won the sisters their first Grammy Award in 1975 for Best Country Performance by a Duo or Group; Elvis Presley later did his own recording of "Fairytale."

With her sisters, Pointer has performed in front of millions around the world and recorded eighteen albums and one solo album. She has performed in diverse settings from Disneyland and the San Francisco Opera House to Roseland Ballroom, Carnegie Hall, and the White House. She has also performed on television shows such as *American Bandstand*, *Soul Train*, *The Flip Wilson Show*, *The Carol Burnett Show*, *The Tonight Show*, and *Arsenio Hall*. The Pointer Sisters were one of the first black acts to be played in heavy rotation on MTV. Pointer also participated in the recording of "We Are the World," the 1985 charity single that raised funds to help famine-relief efforts in Africa. Her acting roles have included the movie *Car Wash* (1976) with Richard Pryor, as well as *The Love Boat*, *Gimme a Break*, and the Pointer Sisters' NBC Special *Up All Night*.

In 1998, Anita Pointer was inducted into the Arkansas Black Hall of Fame. The Pointer Sisters are the recipients of many music awards, including three Grammys and three American Music Awards. They have five gold records, one platinum record, and one multi-platinum record. They were presented with a star on the Hollywood Walk of Fame in 1994. That same day, it was announced that Pointer and her sisters would embark on a national tour of the Tony-winning musical *Ain't Misbehavin'*.

Pointer, who had married at age seventeen, is divorced; she had one daughter, who was born in 1966 and died in 2003. She has said of Arkansas: "I do feel like home is where the heart is, and my heart feels at home in Arkansas. I love the South."

For additional information:
Arkansas Black Hall of Fame. http://www.arblackhalloffame. org/honorees/profile.aspx?year=1998 (accessed February 11, 2013).
The Pointer Sisters Official Website. http://www. thepointersisters.com (accessed February 11, 2013).

Paul Ciulla

JAZZ · ART PORTER JR. (1961–1996)

Arthur Lee (Art) Porter Jr. was an extremely talented musician proficient on saxophone, drums, and piano. He was an energetic, engaging entertainer and a creative composer whose work ranged across jazz, rhythm and blues, funk, and ballads. The son of legendary jazz musician Art Porter Sr., he released four albums through Polygram/Verve Records before his accidental death in 1996.

Art Porter Jr. was born on August 3, 1961, in Little Rock (Pulaski County) to Thelma Pauline Porter and Arthur Porter Sr.; he had four siblings. Porter played alto saxophone in the Benkenarteg, Inc., sound group, which was composed of the five siblings. Porter was awarded the title of most talented young jazz artist in America by the Music Educators of America at age sixteen; this honor included the chance to perform as a soloist with the U.S. Marine Band and with trumpet player Dizzy Gillespie in Dallas, Texas, at the group's annual convention in 1977. For three years consecutively, he was first-chair saxophonist in All-State Band. He also won commendations for classical solos in regional and all-state competitions before graduating from Parkview Performing Arts High School in 1979.

During Porter's youth, his playing while underage in venues where liquor was sold proved controversial. Bill Clinton, then attorney general, researched and established a framework for the legislature that would allow minors to work in such venues with parental supervision. State senator Jerry Jewell and state representative Townsend authored and shepherded the "Art Porter Bill" into Arkansas law.

Porter graduated from Northeastern University in Chicago, Illinois, in 1986 with a BA in music education and performance. While in college, he won two certificates for excellence in jazz at the Notre Dame Festival of

Jazz musician Art Porter Jr.
Courtesy: Dotty Oliver/*Little Rock Free Press*

Music in South Bend, Indiana. He later earned a few graduate hours at Roosevelt University, studying music education, and attended Virginia Commonwealth University for one semester, also studying music education and performance.

Porter married Barbi Lynn Howlett on October 15, 1988; they went on to have two sons. They moved to Murfreesboro, Tennessee, in 1994. That same year, he performed at Carnegie Hall for the Polygram Anniversary Celebration.

Porter's first album, *Pocket City* (1992), featured "LA" and "Little People," both inspired by his son Arthur Porter III. His second album was *Straight to the Point* (1993). In 1994, his third album, *Undercover*, was a great success, placing Porter solidly on the "wave" radio charts with R&B artists as well as "cool jazz" artists. His final album, *Lay Your Hands on Me* (1996), contained the radio favorite "Lake Shore Drive." Many of his compositions were expressions of his spirituality, such as the song "Lay Your Hands on Me." During an inaugural prayer service for President Bill Clinton in 1993, he performed solo renditions of "Amazing Grace" and "My Tribute."

Porter died on November 23, 1996, in a boating accident in Thailand. He had just completed a performance at the Thailand International Golden Jubilee Jazz Festival commemorating the fiftieth anniversary of King Bhumibol Adulyadej's reign.

In 1998, Verve Records released the memorial album *For Art's Sake*, featuring Porter's unrecorded music, songs of tribute to him from other artists, and favorites from his previous albums. Porter received posthumous awards from the recording industry, media and production companies, and the educational community of Gary, Indiana. He was also inducted into the Arkansas Jazz Hall of Fame and the Arkansas Entertainers Hall of Fame.

For additional information:

Alford, Andy. "Jazz Player to President Drowns at 35." *Arkansas Democrat-Gazette*, November 25, 1996, pp. 1B–2B.

Kernfield, Barry. *The New Grove Dictionary of Jazz*. Vol. 3. 2nd ed. New York: Grove, 2002.

Lawson, Felley. "Arthur Lee Porter Jr." *Arkansas Democrat-Gazette*, April 30, 1995, pp. 1D, 6D.

Eugene Porter

Art Porter Sr. (1934–1993)

Arthur Lee (Art) Porter Sr., referred to as an "Arkansas treasure," was a pianist, composer, conductor, and music teacher. Though best known as a jazz musician, he also performed classical compositions and spirituals. Some of his more memorable performances include two gubernatorial inaugurations for Governor Bill Clinton. Joined by Art Porter Jr. on saxophone, he performed at President Clinton's Inaugural Interfaith Prayer Service in January 1993 at one of the inaugural receptions in Washington DC. Porter was also responsible for entertaining many heads of state who visited Arkansas during the tenure of governors Dale Bumpers, David Pryor, and Jim Guy Tucker.

Art Porter was born on February 8, 1934, in Little Rock (Pulaski County) to Eugene Porter Sr., a stonemason, and Lillie Mae Porter. He was the younger of two children. Porter began his music education at home with his mother. He played in church at age eight; played his first recital at twelve; and, by fourteen, hosted a half-hour classical music radio program on KLRA-AM. He earned a bachelor's degree in music from Arkansas AM&N College (now the University of Arkansas at Pine Bluff) in May 1954. He married Thelma Pauline Minton on June 10, 1955. They spent their honeymoon in graduate study at the University of Illinois in Urbana in 1955. Porter continued his graduate study at the University of Texas at Austin in 1974 and earned a master's degree in music from Henderson State University (HSU) in Arkadelphia (Clark County) in 1975.

Porter began his teaching career at Mississippi Valley State University in Itta Bena, Mississippi, in 1954 immediately after college graduation. After two years, he was drafted into the U.S. Army. His extraordinary musical talent on the organ and piano, along with his extensive repertoire of church music, was immediately recognized during his basic training. Consequently, he spent the next two years as a chaplain's assistant in Fort Niagara, New York.

Porter returned to Little Rock in the late 1950s and spent the next twelve years teaching vocal music at Horace Mann High School, Parkview High School, and Philander Smith College. Porter supplemented his income by playing piano jazz in the evenings, sometimes as a single but most of the time with his group, the Art Porter Trio. The trio was in great demand, especially for weddings, country club affairs, and city and state social affairs. Porter entertained all over the state and in surrounding states. He was once asked to play for the dedication of the ship *Arkansas* in Virginia Beach, Virginia. Singer Tony Bennett, during a two-week stay in Hot Springs (Garland County), sat in with the Art Porter Trio and performed every night. Other entertainers, such as Liberace, Julius La Rosa, and Art Van Dam, often dropped by to join in and enjoy the trio's music.

By 1971, Porter's popularity was soaring. From 1971 to 1981, he hosted *The Minor Key*, a musical talent showcase on the Arkansas Educational Television Network (AETN), and *Porterhouse Cuts*, a syndicated series featuring the Art Porter Trio that was shown in a thirteen-state area in the South. Porter was approached many times to tour, but he declined. As he once said, "I don't like to travel, especially all the time." He made a couple of exceptions to travel in 1977 to the World Black and African Festival of Arts and Culture in Lagos, Nigeria, and in 1991 with his son, jazz saxophonist Art Porter Jr., to jazz festivals in Germany, Belgium, and the Netherlands.

Despite Porter's popularity as a jazz pianist, he found time to pursue his interest in classical music. He was featured as a guest artist on piano as he performed with both the Arkansas Symphony Orchestra in Little Rock and the Northwestern Symphony Orchestra in Fort Smith (Sebastian County). In 1976, Porter organized his former vocal music students as the Art Porter Singers to perform Handel's *Messiah* at the Bethel AME Church in Little Rock. The Art Porter Singers remain together and are dedicated to continuing the legacy of Porter's service by performing throughout the years whenever they are invited to do so; they perform the *Messiah* each Christmas season.

Porter's music found continued expression in the performances of four of his children in their group Benkenartreg, Inc. The name is composed of the first three letters of each of the members' names: Benita, Kenneth, Art Jr., and Reginald. A fifth child, Sean Porter also inherited his father's talent on organ and piano. Porter's musical legacy was passed on to Art Jr., whose career, expressed in four albums, ended with his accidental death on November 23, 1996.

Portrait of Art Porter Sr.; circa 1980s.

Courtesy: Butler Center for Arkansas Studies, Central Arkansas Library System

Though Porter received many honors and awards, he found particular satisfaction in the "Art Porter Bill" enacted by the state legislature, which allowed minors to perform in clubs while under adult supervision. Porter's children thus were able to perform with him throughout the state. Governor Bill Clinton, at the time a huge fan and friend of Porter, often joined Porter's group on his saxophone.

Porter died on July 22, 1993, of lung cancer. He was eulogized at Bethel AME Church, where he was the organist for thirty-five years. He is buried in the National Cemetery in Little Rock. A newspaper article noted that Porter's "natural gifts" were "polished by intelligence, flawless phrasing and good taste...with modesty."

For additional information:

"Art Porter." Arkansas Jazz Hall of Fame. http://www.arjazz.org/artists/hof/1994/94_art_porter.html (accessed February 23, 2013).

Art Porter Collection. Center for Arkansas History and Culture. University of Arkansas at Little Rock, Little Rock, Arkansas.

Eugene Porter

JAZZ · JIM PORTER JR. (1932–)

In the early 1960s, Jim Skillern Porter Jr. was a leader in integrating the music venues in Little Rock (Pulaski County), and he produced Arkansas's first integrated-seating concert. Later that decade, he operated Arkansas's first integrated country club, the Riverdale Club, offering golf, tennis, swimming, dining, and dancing. (The name is not to be confused with Riverdale Country Club, whose members had previously moved west and formed Pleasant Valley Country Club.) During the two years the club was open (1968–1970), integrated groups played jazz nightly to full houses. Porter continued his work as a booking agent, trying to interest other venues in hiring integrated groups.

Jim Porter Jr. was born on September 1, 1932, in Little Rock to James Skillern Porter and Verla Menard. He had one sister. His father owned several businesses, including warehousing, moving and storage, and food distribution. Porter's childhood was primarily spent with his grandparents. He attended public schools, graduating from Little Rock Senior High School (now known as Central High School) in 1950. He graduated from the University of Arkansas (UA) in Fayetteville (Washington County) in 1954, with a BS in business administration. He married Jo Ann Wilbourn on August 24, 1952. His second marriage was to Lillian Turner on May 4, 1976. Porter has three children from his first marriage, as well as one stepdaughter and an adopted daughter.

Porter's early career was working in the family businesses, in charge of sales and public relations, and doing volunteer work, such as serving as chairman of the United Way of Pulaski County and serving on the boards of the Donaghey Foundation, the Little Rock Chamber of Commerce, and the Little Rock Boys Club. Porter also served on the board of Union National Bank, which became part of Bank of America.

Jim Porter Jr.; circa 1975. In the early 1960s, Porter was a leader in integrating music venues in Little Rock.
Courtesy: Jim Porter

However, Porter was called to the music business—not as a performer, but as an agent and manager, and as a promoter of famous jazz artists. In 1957, he was starting his own production business when the desegregation of Central High began. Black artists refused to play in Little Rock due to concern for their safety, causing Porter to postpone his promoting plans and concentrate on building Arkansas's only full-time booking and management agency, Consolidated Talent Corporation.

By 1960, Porter renewed his promoting efforts, going on to present such artists as Count Basie, Lionel Hampton, Dizzy Gillespie, Erroll Garner, Ramsey Lewis, Pete Fountain, Al Hirt, Stan Kenton, George Shearing, Harry James, the Four Freshmen, Woody Herman, Dave Brubeck, and Buddy Rich, in addition to Ray Charles and Louis Armstrong. At a Ray Charles concert in 1961 held at Robinson Auditorium, Porter was arrested for entering the "colored" section

and was charged with "attempting to incite a riot." Another disturbance was Duke Ellington's cancellation on August 26, 1961, with only five days notice, due to pressure from the National Association for the Advancement of Colored People (NAACP) and the auditorium's refusal to allow integrated seating. By the time of the Louis Armstrong concert in September 1966, the auditorium had abandoned its unwritten segregation policy, and Armstrong played before a fully integrated sellout crowd.

From the late 1950s until his retirement in 2001, Porter was the foremost booking agent in Arkansas. From nightclubs to hotel lounges, from private affairs and society galas to festivals and fairs, Porter was the man to call for live entertainment. He represented bands playing every style of music: rock and roll, jazz, pop, country and western, big band, and more.

Porter not only brought a high level of professionalism to the music scene but worked in other aspects of entertainment as well. He started MusAd Recording Studio in 1970, which specialized in commercial jingles and provided space for bands to record demo tapes to send prospective buyers. Porter also ran the Hot Air Balloon Theatre, in what had been the Center Theater, located at 4th and Main in downtown Little Rock. This theater for children, running only G-rated films, also had a stage where live entertainment was provided between films.

Porter not only fought for equal rights for African Americans but also fought prejudice against those of Jewish faith. While serving as chairman of the United Way, he spoke against the exclusion of Jewish women from membership in the Junior League of Little Rock, resulting in the resignation of numerous members who agreed with him. The following year, a Jewish woman was invited to join.

Porter's entertainment career was not just in music. In the mid-1980s, he hosted two TV shows. The *After Five* show ran on local Channel 18, featuring Porter in various restaurants and bars, interviewing happy hour customers, managers, bartenders, waiters, and waitresses. *Scene Around* ran on KLRT, Channel 16, and featured Porter attending various charity balls and society functions, interviewing chairmen of the events. He also wrote two columns under the same names for the *Arkansas Democrat* during most of the 1980s, along with an award-winning supplement titled "Arkansas Dining & Entertainment Guide." Porter was also featured on a weekly radio program, also called *After Five*, describing various places to go for dining and entertainment.

Porter's honors include appointment to the Arkansas Entertainers Hall of Fame Board in 1996, induction into the Entertainers Hall of Fame in 2005, appointment to the Martin Luther King Commission in 2005, and induction into the Arkansas Jazz Hall of Fame in 2006. Porter also served four terms as a member of the Quorum Court of Pulaski County (1998–2006). Porter has lived in Little Rock all his life.

For additional information:
"Arkansas Jazz Hall of Fame 2006 Inductees." Arkansas Jazz Heritage Foundation. http://www.arjazz.org/artists/hof/2006/2006_jim_porter.html (accessed February 26, 2013).

Porter, Jim S. "The Musical Integration of Little Rock." *Pulaski County Historical Review* 53 (Fall 2005): 82–88.

Harry Snider
Tim Jones

GOSPEL / CONTEMPORARY CHRISTIAN — LUTHER PRESLEY (1887–1974)

Luther G. Presley was a music teacher, song director, and prolific writer of gospel songs who has been credited with writing more than 1,100 hymns. His best-known song is most likely "When the Saints Go Marching In," for which he wrote the lyrics in 1937 (the melody was written by Virgil O. Stamps).

Luther Presley was born in Faulkner County on March 6, 1887, to James Thomas Presley and Nancy Ann Brooks Presley. He was educated in Faulkner County's public schools. Presley attended his first singing school at the age of fourteen, under the direction of M. W. Beckett, and taught at his first singing school at the age of eighteen.

Presley continued his musical education, and according to a 2005 article in the *White County Record*, "he studied harmony under L. B. Leister, a graduate of the music department at the University of Arkansas and namesake for Luther's son. He also studied under W. W. Combs, head voice teacher for the Stamps-Baxter Schools, and Dr. J. H. Ruebush, dean of Shenandoah College in Dayton, Virginia." According to the *Arkansas Democrat*, he also studied harmony with Dr. J. B. Herbert. His first published song was in the Showalter-Patton Company songbook in 1907.

Presley was married first to Julia Magdaline "Maggie" Yingling of the Clay community in White County. The couple married on October 1, 1911, and had two children before Maggie and their third child, an infant son, both died on February 16, 1922, during childbirth. Presley married Rena Henderson, a native of Faulkner County on December 30, 1923. She was also a songwriter and wrote approximately forty songs, as well as several children's stories. The couple had one child together.

Starting as a young adult, Presley was immersed in the world of writing music, teaching music, and editing the works of other songwriters. In some of his works, he wrote only the lyrics or words, and in others just the melody. However, in other songs, he wrote both the lyrics and the melody. His oldest son, Leister Presley, credited his father with writing the words and music to 649 songs, writing the lyrics only to 429 songs, and writing the melody only to another twenty-five songs.

Beginning in 1928 and ending in early 1930, Presley was associated with the Hartford Music Company, where he edited songbooks and was in charge of the mailing department. He also worked for fourteen years for the Central Music Company, which was originally located in Hartford (Sebastian County) and later moved to Little Rock (Pulaski County). However, the majority of his professional life, from 1930 until his death in 1974, was spent with the Stamps-Baxter Music and Printing Company of Chattanooga, Tennessee, and Dallas, Texas. During his career with Stamps-Baxter, he composed hymns and also ran a music supply store out of his home in Pangburn (White County).

Presley told his friends that his best song was "I'd Rather Have Jesus," which has been translated into several languages. Other songs that he wrote and thought had merit included "God's Wonderful Book Divine," "Getting Ready to Leave This World," "In Mother's Way," "I'll Have a New Body," and "He Wills It So."

Leister Presley said that the motivation for many of his father's songs came from actual events. In one case, his song "He Wills It So" came from the comments made at a funeral. According to an article in the December 3, 1944, *Arkansas Democrat*, "'He Wills It So' was written after a funeral for a young man. His mother in her deep agony kept repeating 'Lord, why did he have to go? Why didn't you take me and let him stay?' Her agonizing words kept ringing in his mind until he wrote this song."

In another incident that inspired a gospel song, Presley was involved in a car accident during a rainstorm that resulted in a head-on collision with another automobile. Fortunately, no one suffered serious injury in either vehicle. The next day, while reflecting back on the accident, Presley wrote the lyrics to "The Lord Is with Me."

At the time of his death on December 6, 1974, Presley, then eighty-seven, was still employed by the Stamps-Baxter Music and Printing Company. He is buried at St. Mary's Cemetery near Rose Bud (White County). His wife continued to operate the Stamps-Baxter Music store out of her home for the next ten years.

Many of Presley's songs are preserved at the University of Central Arkansas (UCA) archives in the Luther G. Presley Papers. Leister Presley donated 195 songbooks to UCA's archives; each songbook contains at least one song written by his father.

For additional information:
Allard, C. C. "Arkansan Writes and Sings Hymns: Gospel Song Poems Come Easy to State's Most Prolific Author and Composer." *Arkansas Democrat Sunday Magazine*, December 3, 1944, p. 1.
Cloie Smith Presley Papers. Torreyson Library Special Collections. University of Central Arkansas, Conway, Arkansas.
Luther G. Presley Papers. Torreyson Library Special Collections. University of Central Arkansas, Conway, Arkansas.
Sallee, Bob. "Pangburn Songwriter Remembered with 'Saints.'" *Arkansas Democrat-Gazette*, April 21, 1998, p. 4E.
"Songs by Native Arkansan Donated to Conway Archives." *Arkansas Democrat-Gazette*, July 7, 2005, p. 6R.
"White County Songwriter's Works Donated to UCA." *White County Record*, July 7, 2005, p. 5.

Jimmy Bryant

CLASSICAL / OPERA FLORENCE PRICE (1887–1953)

Florence Beatrice Smith Price was the first African-American female composer to have a symphonic composition performed by a major American symphony orchestra. The Chicago Symphony Orchestra performed her *Symphony in E Minor* on June 15, 1933, under the direction of Frederick Stock. The work was later performed at the Chicago World's Fair as part of the Century of Progress Exhibition.

Florence Smith was born in Little Rock (Pulaski County) on April 9, 1887, to James H. Smith and Florence Gulliver Smith. Her father was a dentist in Little Rock, while her mother taught piano and worked as a schoolteacher and a businesswoman.

As a child, Smith received musical instruction from her mother, and she published musical pieces while in high school. She attended Capitol Hill School in Little Rock, graduating as valedictorian in 1903. Smith then studied at the New England Conservatory of Music in Boston, Massachusetts, which was a notable achievement for a black woman at that time. In 1907, she received degrees as an organist and as a piano teacher.

After graduation, Smith returned to Arkansas to teach music at the Cotton Plant–Arkadelphia Academy in Cotton Plant (Woodruff County). She left Cotton Plant after only one year, however, to teach at Shorter College in North Little Rock (Pulaski County), where she remained until 1910. In that year, however, Smith moved to Atlanta, Georgia, where she was head of the music department at Clark University until 1912.

Smith returned to Little Rock in 1912 to marry attorney Thomas Jewell Price on September 25, 1912. The couple had two daughters and one son, who died in infancy. Her husband worked with Scipio Jones, a noted attorney who successfully defended the appeals of twelve black men sentenced to death in the aftermath of the Elaine Massacre of 1919 in Phillips County.

While in Little Rock, Price established a music studio, taught piano lessons, and wrote short pieces for piano. Despite her credentials, she was denied membership into the Arkansas State Music Teachers Association because of her race.

Worsening racial tensions in Arkansas in the 1920s convinced the Prices to move to Chicago, Illinois, in 1927. There, Price seemed to have more professional opportunity for growth despite the breakdown and eventual dissolution of her marriage. She pursued further musical studies at the American Conservatory of Music and Chicago Musical College and established herself in the Chicago area as a teacher, pianist, and organist. In 1928, G. Schirmer, a major publishing firm, accepted for publication Price's *At the Cotton Gin*. In 1932, Price won multiple awards in competitions sponsored by the Rodman Wanamaker Foundation for her *Piano Sonata in E Minor*, a large-scale work in four movements, and her more important work, *Symphony in E Minor*.

The latter work premiered with the Chicago Symphony Orchestra on June 15, 1933, and the orchestras of Detroit, Michigan; Pittsburgh, Pennsylvania; and Brooklyn, New York, performed subsequent symphonic works by Price. This was the first time a black woman had presented her work on such a stage. In this regard, Price shared similar accomplishments with fellow black composers William Grant Still and William Dawson, whose works were performed by leading orchestras in the 1930s and 1940s. Price's art songs and spiritual arrangements were frequently performed by well-known artists of the day. For example, contralto Marian Anderson featured Price's spiritual arrangement *My Soul's Been Anchored in de Lord* in her famous performance on the steps of the Lincoln Memorial in Washington DC on Easter Sunday, April 9, 1939. European orchestras later played Price's works.

This national and international recognition made her more popular back home, and in 1935, the Alumni Association of Philander Smith College in Little Rock sponsored Price's return to Arkansas, billing her as "noted musician of Chicago" and presenting her in a concert of her own compositions at Dunbar High School.

In her lifetime, Price composed more than 300 works, ranging from small teaching pieces for piano to large-scale compositions such as symphonies and concertos, as well as instrumental chamber music, vocal compositions, and music for radio. Her musical style is a mixture of classical European music and the sounds of black spirituals, especially the rhythms associated with African heritage, such as the juba dance.

Price's southern heritage had an obvious impact on her work, as the titles for some of her shorter works suggest: *Arkansas Jitter, Bayou Dance*, and *Dance of the Cotton Blossoms*.

Price died in Chicago on June 3, 1953, while planning a trip to Europe. In 1964, a Chicago elementary school took her name as its own in recognition of her legacy as both a Chicago musician and an important black composer.

Florence Price; circa 1930.
Courtesy: Special Collections, University of Arkansas Libraries, Fayetteville

For additional information:

Brown, Rae Linda. "Florence B. Price, 1887–1953." In *Women Composers: Music through the Ages, Vol. 7: Composers Born 1800–1899, Vocal Music*, edited by Sylvia Glickman and Martha Furman Schleifer. New Haven, CT: G. K. Hall, 2003.

———. "Florence B. Price's Negro Symphony." In *Temples for Tomorrow: Looking Back at the Harlem Renaissance*, edited by Geneviève Fabre and Michel Feith. Bloomington: Indiana University Press, 2001.

———. "Selected Orchestral Music of Florence B. Price (1888–1953) in the Context of Her Life and Work." PhD diss., Yale University, 1987.

Farrah, Scott David. "Signifyin(g): A Semiotic Analysis of Symphonic Worlds by William Grant Still, William Levi Dawson, and Florence B. Price." PhD diss., Florida State University, 2007.

Florence Beatrice Smith Price Papers. Special Collections. University of Arkansas Libraries, Fayetteville, Arkansas.

Hudgins, Mary D. "Chicago School Named for State Composer." *Arkansas Gazette*, June 30, 1968, p. 5E.

Peebles, Sarah Louise. "The Use of the Spiritual in the Piano Works of Two African-American Women Composers—Florence B. Price and Margaret Bonds." PhD diss., University of Mississippi, 2008.

Smith, Bethany Jo. "Song to the Dark Virgin: Race and Gender in Five Art Songs of Florence B. Price." PhD diss., University of Cincinnati, 2007.

Dan Dykema

R

FOLK   RACKENSACK FOLKLORE SOCIETY

The Rackensack Folklore Society was organized for the purpose of perpetuating the traditional folk music of the people of Arkansas, particularly in the mountainous area of the north-central part of the state. Stone County, located in the area, was unique in having music-making families throughout its boundaries who founded the base of the organization.

The society was begun by Lloyd Hollister, a doctor, and his wife, Martha. They came from the Little Rock (Pulaski County) area in 1962 and settled in the Fox (Stone County) community. Hollister set up his medical practice in Mountain View (Stone County) with Howard Monroe, a noted surgeon in the area. The Hollisters attended various musical sessions in the Fox community and joined in the music-making.

In February 1963, Hollister held a meeting

Singers at a Rackensack meeting, Little Rock; 1965.

Courtesy: Arkansas History Commission

with six others at the Monroe Clinic to form an organization that would reach out to the people of the area and provide an opportunity for them to share their music with the public. Before adjourning, it was decided to meet again that week and organize the new folklore society, elect officers, and solicit membership. The seven charter members of the new organization were Hollister, Eddie A. Walker, William (Willie) P. Morrison, Glenn D. Morrison, Lloyd Westbrook, Otis Johnson, and Gerald Cain. Musician Jimmy Driftwood attended the second meeting, where Hollister was elected president, with Driftwood as vice president. Driftwood suggested naming the organization the Rackensack Folklore Society.

In the next few weeks, several meetings were called to address the different issues. Walker informed the membership that John Opitz had told him that a plan to have a large public gathering of musicians would be beneficial because it would promote Mountain View as it tried to bid for a water system and possibly justify an investment in a cultural center. The Rackensack Folklore Society was scheduled to be part of a folk festival for the third weekend in April, the Arkansas Folk Festival. By this time, Rackensack membership had grown to more than sixty.

The group acquired permission from the county to use the courtroom in the courthouse for practice sessions for the upcoming festival program. These Friday night sessions became a weekly attraction to the public and were contin-

ued until the Ozark Folk Center was built. Turnout for the April folk festival was phenomenal, with local, state, and national media covering the event. In response, the Rackensack Folklore Society established itself as a permanent organization. Rackensack continued to have an annual folk festival the third weekend in April until the early 1970s, at which time the city of Mountain View, with its newly formed Chamber of Commerce, assumed the responsibility of having the festival at the same time each year.

During the mid-1960s, a branch organization of the Rackensack was created by George Fisher in Little Rock. This branch chapter assembled a large membership in the Little Rock area and followed the traditional guidelines of the Rackensack Society in perpetuating the folk music of the area. Their meetings and concerts were held at the Arkansas Arts Center.

In 1968, the Rackensack Society sponsored a Young Rackensack Club. This was developed and directed by Coleman Gammill, Sue Gammill, and Lester Passmore, teachers in a Mountain View school. The membership of the junior society was made up of elementary and high school students from the three schools in Stone County. These students participated jointly with Rackensack members in concert and also had an annual program consisting only of the Young Rackensack members.

In the spring of 1973, the Ozark Folk Center had its grand opening, with the Rackensack members providing the music. Music programs were scheduled weekly with Jimmy Driftwood as the principal entertainer and emcee. Driftwood was appointed to the State Publicity and Parks Commission and immediately pursued his quest of getting the folk center made a state park. After the folk center became a state park, officers of the Rackensack received notice from the State of Arkansas that Rackensack would have to enter into a contract with the state if they were to provide the music, but the state could not contract Rackensack since it was a nonprofit organization. A general meeting was called, and Josephine Linker Hart, attorney for Rackensack, reported that the state had recommended that the name Rackensack Folklore Society be changed to Rackensack Incorporated and that members be allowed to buy shares at a fee of twenty dollars each. The membership, by a large majority, voted to go with the state recommendation. This would allow the Rackensack to provide the musical programs, and the performers would receive a small remuneration for their performances.

Driftwood objected and told the membership that Rackensack Incorporation would not be formed, no contract would be made with the State of Arkansas, and the members would not be paid to perform. Governor David Pryor's office was following the developments and consulted with Driftwood and asked him to reconsider. Driftwood would not change his thinking, and it became necessary for Pryor to remove him from his position at the folk center. Rackensack contracted with the state and provided the musical programs that first season of 1973.

After leaving the folk center, Driftwood, with a small following of original Rackensack members, erected a building north of Mountain View and named it the Jimmy Driftwood Barn. The Jimmy Driftwood Barn is still active with weekly musical programs portraying the folk music of the area.

The Rackensack Folklore Society continues to work at bringing together people in the area and providing them with the opportunity to display their music. The Little Rock branch also continues to hold monthly meetings.

For additional information:

"The Creation and Development of the Arkansas Folk Festival and the Ozark Folk Center: An Oral History Project." Regional Studies Center, Lyon College. http://web.lyon.edu/groups/mslibrary/rcol/oralhistory.htm (accessed March 1, 2013).

The Faces of Rackensack. Mountain View, AR: Stone County Leader, 1972.

Glenn D. Morrison

COUNTRY WAYNE RANEY (1921–1993)

Wayne Raney was an American country singer and harmonica player best known for his hit song "Why Don't You Haul Off and Love Me." Raney, along with fellow Arkansan Lonnie Glosson, played a major role in making the harmonica a popular instrument through their musical performances as well as through their mail-order harmonica business. Raney was inducted into the Country Music Disc Jockey Hall of Fame after his death.

Wayne Raney was born on August 17, 1921, on a farm near Wolf Bayou (Cleburne County), the youngest of five children of William Franklin (Frank) Raney and Bonnie Davis Raney. Due to a foot deformity, he could not do heavy labor. Instead, he pursued an interest in music, learning to play harmonica at an early age. He was drawn to the harmonica after hearing a street performer play. At the age of thirteen, he hitchhiked to Eagle Pass, Texas, to record transcription records for radio station XEPN, of which he had been a longtime listener. In 1936, he met fellow Arkansan Lonnie Glosson, a hero of Raney's who would become his longtime musical associate. The pair found work at radio station KARK in

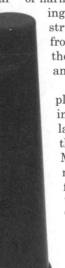

Wayne Raney's Meg-O-Harp harmonica.
Courtesy: Old State House Museum Collection

Little Rock (Pulaski County) in 1938 and later worked for WCKY out of Cincinnati, Ohio, and played on syndicated radio. They also established a harmonica mail-order business that became enormously successful; they sold millions of harmonicas and played a major role in turning the harmonica into a widely popular instrument. Raney married Loys Southerland from Drasco (Cleburne County) in 1941; they had three children—Wanda, Zyndall, and Norma.

In the years after World War II, Raney played with the Delmore Brothers, releasing several records with them on the King label between 1946 and 1952, including the Delmores' hit "Blues Stay Away from Me" (which he co-wrote with the Delmores), as well as releasing solo work. His first two singles, "Lost John Boogie" and "Jack and Jill Boogie," both reached the Top 15 on the U.S. country charts. His 1949 single "Why Don't You Haul Off and Love Me," produced by Hot Springs (Garland County) native Henry Glover (who also produced "Blues Stay Away from Me"), was a number-one country hit and also appeared in the Top 40 of the pop charts. Raney co-wrote "Why Don't You Haul Off and Love Me" with Glosson. Raney also recorded novelty songs such as "Pardon My Whiskers" and "I Love My Little Yo Yo."

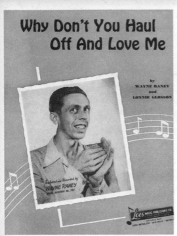

Why Don't You Haul Off And Love Me

by
WAYNE RANEY
and
LONNIE GLOSSON

Sheet music for song recorded by Wayne Raney.

Courtesy: Old State House Museum Collection

Raney played at the Grand Ole Opry in 1949. That year, he also toured briefly with "Lefty" Frizzell and also worked on the *California Hayride* and the *WWVA Jamboree*. Late in the 1950s, he worked as a disc jockey, record producer, and label owner (starting Rimrock Records, a bluegrass-oriented label), as well as experimenting with rock and roll, as with his Decca Records version of "Shake Baby Shake." In 1958, the King label collected many of his singles on the *Songs of the Hills* record. In the late 1950s, he wrote the Christian revival song "We Need a Whole Lot More of Jesus (And a Lot Less Rock and Roll)," which has been covered by numerous artists in a variety of styles, among them the Greenbriar Boys and Linda Ronstadt. He recorded country music into the early 1960s, including for his own label, and ceased the mail-order harmonica business in 1961.

After returning to Arkansas, he recorded a gospel album titled *Don't Try to Be What You Ain't* in 1963 for Starday Records. Eventually, he went into semi-retirement, running his own chicken farm and performing only occasionally in the late 1960s and 1970s. He appeared sporadically on *Hee Haw* in the 1970s. He was diagnosed with a form of muscular dystrophy in 1974 and lost his voice in the 1980s and ceased performing. In 1990, he published his autobiography, *Life Has Not Been a Bed of Roses*.

Raney died of cancer at Batesville (Independence County) on January 23, 1993, and is buried in Cleburne County at Pleasant Ridge Cemetery. He was posthumously inducted into the Country Music Disc Jockey Hall of Fame and the Western Swing Society Hall of Fame in 1994, and the George D. Hay Country Music Hall of Fame in 2000. He received the Ozark Pioneer Music Award in 1999.

For additional information:

Barger, Carl J. *Cleburne County and Its People*. 2 vols. Bloomington, IN: AuthorHouse, 2008.

Kingsbury, Paul, ed. *The Encyclopedia of Country Music*. New York: Oxford University Press, 1998.

Larkin, Colin. *The Encyclopedia of Popular Music*. Washington DC: Grove's Dictionaries, 1998.

Manheim, James. "Wayne Raney" Allmusic.com. http://www.allmusic.com/cg/amg.dll?p=amg&sql=11:j9fixqtgldte~T1 (accessed February 26, 2013).

C. L. Bledsoe

COUNTRY | # COLLIN RAYE (1960–)

With five platinum records and fifteen number-one singles to his credit, country star Collin Raye is one of the most successful recording artists to ever have emerged from Arkansas. Joining the ranks of acclaimed country performers Johnny Cash, Conway Twitty, and K. T. Oslin, Raye has proven to be a versatile performer, turning out diverse hits ranging from tender ballads to socially relevant tunes.

Collin Raye was born Floyd Elliott Wray on August 22, 1960, in De Queen (Sevier County). His mother, Lois Wray, had achieved notoriety in the 1950s as a regional musician, opening shows for Elvis Presley, Jerry Lee Lewis, and Carl Perkins. Later in her solo career, Raye's mother had Raye and his older brother accompany her on stage to perform harmony vocals.

When Raye was a young boy, his family relocated to Texas. He and his brother, Scott, formed the Wray Brothers Band when he was thirteen. Using the stage name Bubba Wray, Raye eventually began performing with his brother in the Pacific Northwest before moving to Reno, Nevada, where they played in casinos and nightclubs.

Raye married Connie Parker in 1980, and they had two children. They later divorced.

The Wrays recorded a number of singles which subsequently attracted the attention of Mercury Records in Nashville, Tennessee. Mercury released two of their singles in 1986 and 1987. Around that time, Scott Wray opted to stop touring. Raye also considered giving up touring. But he persevered, eventually landing a recording deal with Epic Records.

His debut album, *All I Can Be* (1991), contained the number-one hit "Love, Me," as well as "Every Second," a tune that reached number two on the country music charts. The title cut of

In This Life (1992) was a number-one hit, while "Somebody Else's Moon" and "That Was a River" were top-five singles. The critically acclaimed *Extremes* (1994) featured another number one, "My Kind of Girl," as well as the up-tempo hit "That's My Story" and the poignant "Little Rock." Raye's fourth album, *I Think about You* (1995), was also his fourth consecutive platinum record. It was noted for the top-five hits, "One Boy, One Girl," and "I Think about You," and "What If Jesus Comes Back Like That." A 1998 Christmas project containing the single "The Gift" won a Dove Award from the Nashville-based Gospel Music Association. Raye's other releases include *Live at Billy Bob's Texas* (a DVD), *Twenty Years and Change* (2004), and *Fearless* (2006) for independent labels. In 2007, Raye's *Selected Hits* was released on his own label, StarPointe. In 2009, he released *Never Going Back*. Late in 2011, he released the album *His Love Remains*, consisting of spiritual and inspirational music.

Noted for a number of issue-related songs, Raye has been recognized for his humanitarian work with organizations ranging from Al-Anon, Special Olympics, Boys Town, and Easter Seals to Country Cares About AIDS, Childhelp USA, and the Tennessee Task Force Against Domestic Violence. Though reluctant to endorse companies or particular products, in 2005 Raye sang a humorous commercial jingle, "You Can't Over-Love Your Underwear," for Fruit of the Loom.

Raye received nominations for male vocalist of the year by the Academy of Country Music in 1998 and the Country Music Association (CMA) in 1996 and 1997. His singles, "Love, Me" and "Little Rock" were CMA song of the year nominees in 1992 and 1994, respectively.

For additional information:

Carlin, Richard. *Country Music: A Biographical Dictionary*. New York: Routledge, 2003.

"Collin: A Real Hero." *Country Weekly*, March 5, 2001.

Collin Raye. http://www.collinraye.com/ (accessed February 26, 2013).

"Collinfest at De Queen." *Arkansas Democrat-Gazette*, June 24, 2005, p. 2W.

Hornaday, Sarah. "Country Balladeer Puts Life, a Little Rock, into Lyrics for Austin Livestock and Rodeo." *Austin American-Statesman*, March 19, 1996.

McCloud, Barry, ed. *Definitive Country: The Ultimate Encyclopedia of Country Music and Its Performers*. New York: Berkley Publishing Group, 1995.

Greg Freeman

COUNTRY CHARLIE RICH (1932–1995)

Charlie Rich was a gospel, blues, and country singer and songwriter, and was probably the most musically gifted of the first generation of rockabilly stars.

Charlie Rich was born on December 14, 1932, in Colt (St. Francis County), the only son (he had two sisters) of devout Missionary Baptist parents who sang in a church quartet; his mother also played piano. He grew up immersed in the whole range of southern music—along with the church music, there was the country music on the radio and the blues he learned from a sharecropper named C. J., who taught him piano.

Rich played in his high school band in Forrest City (St. Francis County), where he was already known as Charlie Kenton for his love of jazz (especially the music of Stan Kenton, George Gershwin, and Oscar Peterson). He met his future wife, Margaret Ann, in high school—they married in 1952 and raised two sons and two daughters. After a single year at the University of Arkansas (UA) in Fayetteville (Washington County), where he was a member of the marching band, Rich spent four years (1953–1956) in the air force, based in Enid, Oklahoma, where he played with a blues and jazz group called the Velvetones. Margaret Ann was their vocalist.

In 1956, he moved to the West Memphis (Crittenden County) area, where he farmed (with little success), played local bars, and co-wrote songs with his wife. In 1957, he signed with Sun Records, initially as a songwriter and studio musician; by 1958, he was on records himself, with the 1960 "Lonely Weekends" hitting No. 22 on the pop charts. In 1965, he scored again with "Mohair Sam," which made it to No. 3 on the pop charts, but sustained success eluded him until 1973, when two blockbuster hits, "Behind Closed Doors" (No. 1 on the country charts) and "The Most Beautiful Girl" (No. 1 on both pop and country charts), earned him a Grammy and the Country Music Association's Male Vocalist of the Year award.

Rich's attitude toward this material was often ambivalent at best, but it brought him money and fame; he was the "Silver Fox," a huge star of the lush "countrypolitan" sound that took country to Las Vegas and other big-city outlets. He often handled this fame and fortune poorly, drinking heavily and misbehaving in high-visibility settings. When announcing the Entertainer of the Year at the 1975 Country Music Association awards show, he startled a national television audience and outraged industry moguls by opening the envelope and, seeing John Denver's name, whipping out his lighter and setting the offending card ablaze.

Rich lived much of his later years in Benton (Saline County). In the early 1980s, he took time out to get off alcohol, reappearing in 1992 with the jazz- and blues-laced *Pictures and Paintings*, his first new album in a decade. Sales were modest, but reviewers loved it, calling it the album he had waited his whole life to make.

Rich died on July 25, 1995. His music still sells, but even after his death, the broad scope of his talent has been an obstacle to his recognition. Country music had few if any bigger stars in the mid-1970s, but Rich has not yet been inducted into the Country Music Hall of Fame.

For additional information:
Guralnick, Peter. *Feel Like Going Home: Portraits in Blues and Rock and Roll*. New York: Outerbridge and Dienstfrey, 1971.
———. *Lost Highway: Journeys and Arrivals of American Musicians*. Boston: David Godine, 1979.
Official Website of Charlie Rich. http://www.charlierich.com/charlierich.htm (accessed February 26, 2013).

Robert B. Cochran

FOLK

ALMEDA RIDDLE (1898–1986)

Discovered by a ballad collector in the 1950s, Almeda James Riddle of Greers Ferry (Cleburne County) became a prominent figure in America's folk music revival. Her memory of ballads, hymns, and children's songs was one of the largest single repertories documented by folksong scholars. After two decades of concerts and recordings, she received the National Heritage Award from the National Endowment for the Arts for her contributions to the preservation of Ozark folksong traditions.

Almeda James was born on November 21, 1898, in the community of West Pangburn (Cleburne County). She was the fifth of eight children of J. L. James, a timber worker, and Martha Frances Wilkerson. In 1916, she married H. Price Riddle and started family life near Heber Springs (Cleburne County). Three of their four children survived to adulthood: Clinton, Milbry, and John Lloyd. A tornado on November 25, 1926, took the life of both her husband and their young baby.

Riddle was a widow caring for her mother and living near her grown children in Greers Ferry when John Quincy Wolf, the first "ballad hunter" in the area, found her in 1952. Wolf, a Batesville (Independence County) native teaching English at what is now Rhodes College in Memphis, Tennessee, realized that many of Riddle's songs dated back to seventeenth-century Scotland, England, and Ireland. In his chance meeting with Riddle, Wolf had found a prolific tradition bearer. Thirty years later, the National Endowment for the Arts would pay tribute to Riddle as "the great lady of Ozark balladry," noting that "she once listed a hundred songs she could call to mind right then, and later added she could name another hundred if she had the time."

Recordings in 1959 by another folklorist, Alan Lomax, brought Riddle the first of many invitations to sing on college campuses around the country. At the age of sixty-two, after her mother's death, Almeda found herself starting on her new career "of getting out the old songs," as she put it, in person, in print, and on tape.

By the early 1960s, America's folk music revival was picking up momentum. Riddle and other traditional singers and musicians were appearing at festivals literally coast to coast. She traveled by bus to Washington DC, Philadelphia, New York, and the Newport Jazz and Folk Festival, on to Yale University and Harvard University, to Montreal and Quebec in Canada, to Chicago and Minneapolis, and to the West Coast at UCLA and Berkeley. She frequently shared the stage with Doc Watson and Pete and Mike Seeger, as well as Joan Baez, Bob Dylan, and other dynamic new performers.

Young audiences heralded both the traditional songs and plain singing style of Riddle, an authentic contrast to formula lyrics, packaged sounds, and exaggerated performances from the contemporary music industry and entertainers. Asked when she herself first noticed the sea change in American music since her childhood, Riddle pointed to the popularity—and popularizing—of Elvis Presley. "Elvis was a good boy, and I liked him alright," she admitted, "but he and others got to performing. They got out in front of the music. And performance took over music."

With the help of folklore scholar Roger Abrahams, Riddle recorded more than 200 of her childhood favorites, fifty of which were transcribed in the book *A Singer and Her Songs: Almeda Riddle's Book of Ballads*. Abraham's book challenged the stereotype of traditional singers as uneducated hill people. To the contrary, their "high, lonesome" style was learned, and many could read music. Riddle's own father taught at singing schools held in summers between planting and harvest. "He made us learn the round note, but the shape notes are quicker read," Riddle said of her father. "We learned both the four and the eight note system. And anything I know the tune to," she told Abrahams matter-of-factly, "I can put the notes to."

Her extensive repertory included American variants of the ballads collected by Harvard folklorist Francis Child in his traverse of the Scottish and English countryside in the 1880s. Riddle also sang the songs about railroaders and cowboys that had spread through her part of the Ozarks—as well as the rest of turn-of-century rural America—often via newspapers first, before entering into oral tradition. Her versions of children's songs like "Go Tell Aunt Rhody" and "La La Chicka-la-leo," the latter a rare English nursery song, were frequent requests at concerts.

While the source and lyrics of these American variants held primary interest for early folksong scholars, later generations of folklorists like Abrahams became equally focused on questions of the meaning and function of a song in the life of the singer. Among the hundreds Riddle could sing on request, she told Abrahams it was the older narrative ballads and the shape-note hymns that she preferred and sang most often. "I never really cared too much for a song that didn't tell a story or teach a lesson," she remarked.

As folk music became newsworthy and folk festivals became big business, reporters and promoters gave Riddle bigger and longer titles. Headlines shifted from simply "Mrs. Almeda Riddle" to "Granny Riddle" to "balladeer" to "folk artist of the Arkansas Ozarks." Though the publicizing made her uncomfortable, Riddle turned the concerts and coverage into a grandmother's duty and kept on traveling. "Well, the kids kept begging for the old songs," she told a younger

Almeda Riddle with "Uncle Abbie" Morrison (playing fiddle) at the annual Arkansas Folk Festival in Mountain View; April 16, 1965.
Courtesy: Arkansas History Commission

musician. "If you had a child standing there hungry with a hand out for bread, and you had the bread, you'd hand out the bread as long as you had bread. And God gave me the strength to go, and I went," she added.

Riddle's final in-state performance came in 1984 at the Ozark Folk Center in Mountain View (Stone County). Joined there by Mike Seeger, she sang "From Jerusalem to Jericho," a camp meeting song about the parable of the Good Samaritan—which she promptly turned into another lesson for herself. "I've often thought about that myself, and I'm as guilty as the next," she admitted to the audience. "But in my 85 years, I've seen a lot of it—people who are like the letter 'p': they're first in pity and the last in help."

This appearance closed out Riddle's twenty-two years of getting out the old songs. In December 1984, she moved into a nursing home in Heber Springs where she died on June 30, 1986. She is buried next to her husband at Shiloh Cross Roads Cemetery.

A final album of Riddle's favorite and previously unrecorded hymns and semi-sacred songs, *How Firm a Foundation*, was released in 1985. The revised edition of *A Singer and Her Songs* was started the same year. A half-hour television documentary, *"Now Let's Talk About Singing":* *Almeda Riddle, Ozark Singer*, was produced in 1986 and aired on the Arkansas Educational Television Network.

For additional information:

Abrahams, Roger, and George Foss, eds. *A Singer and Her Songs: Almeda Riddle's Book of Ballads.* Baton Rouge: Louisiana State University Press, 1970.

How Firm a Foundation: Favorite Hymns and Other Sacred Songs of Almeda Riddle. Mountain View: Arkansas Traditions, 1985.

John Quincy Wolf Folklore Collection. Regional Studies Center. Lyon College, Batesville, Arkansas. Online at http://web.lyon.edu/wolfcollection/ (accessed February 13, 2013).

Randolph, Vance. *Ozark Folk Songs.* 4 vols. Columbia: State Historical Society of Missouri, 1947–1950.

Stark, Merrelyn. "Interview with Almeda Riddle." *Cleburne County Historical Society Journal* 16 (Fall 1990): 81–102.

George West

ROCKABILLY

BILLY LEE RILEY (1933–2009)

Billy Lee Riley was a rockabilly musician whose career began in the Arkansas Delta and peaked in the 1950s after he signed a record deal with Sun Records in Memphis, Tennessee. He recorded many songs during his life, alternating between the rockabilly style that made him famous and the blues music that he loved.

Billy Lee Riley was born in Pocahontas (Randolph County) on October 5, 1933, to Amos and Mae Riley; he was one of nine children. Although his father was a house painter by trade, the economic disparities of the time led the family into sharecropping. As a result, the Riley family moved frequently to different towns in Arkansas, at times living

Billy Lee Riley playing harmonica.   Photo: Ken King

in intense poverty. Through this lifestyle, Riley found a taste for the blues. At age six, he learned to play the harmonica and was introduced to the blues for the first time by his African-American playmates, who took him to their side of town to listen to music. Many Saturdays he could be found sitting on the back steps of honkytonks listening to the jukebox.

Riley received only three years of formal education, quitting school to help earn money for the family by picking cotton. In 1943, during a small period of prosperity, Riley's father bought Riley's first guitar, a Silvertone, from a family friend. Riley began to learn to play it after moving to Forrest City (St. Francis County) and meeting a couple of young guitar players.

In 1949, at age fifteen, Riley joined the army and served until 1953, during which time he further improved his guitar skills. Upon his honorable discharge from the army, he returned to Arkansas and started a hillbilly band that played shows at high schools and appeared on local radio shows. In 1954, he married his first wife, with whom he had one child. In 1955, after a failed attempt at running a restaurant in Memphis, Riley met Jack Clement and his partner Slim Wallace, who gave him a opening in the music business. They were both established in Nashville, Tennessee, and invited him to join their band and sing at Wallace's club in Paragould (Greene County). In March 1956, Riley recorded his first two songs at Fernwood Studios, owned by Clement and Wallace. The two tracks found their way into the hands of Sam Phillips at Sun Records. After hearing one of the songs, Phillips insisted on having another, to which Riley obliged by writing and singing, "Rock with Me Baby." He then signed a record deal with Sun Records that lasted from 1956 to 1960.

Riley's fickle career hit its high in the late 1950s while he was recording for Sun Records. In 1957, he released his two most popular songs, "Flying Saucer Rock and Roll," a track that encouraged him to call his band the Little Green Men, and "Red Hot." It was during this period that he met Jerry Lee Lewis, who played in his band for a short while, although Sam Phillips insisted there was no need for a piano player in a rockabilly band. A takeoff in Lewis's career later greatly affected Riley's. In 1958, Riley was set to go on tour to promote his single "Red Hot," which was becoming recognized around the country. However, the track was abandoned by Phillips, who chose to endorse Lewis's "Great Balls of Fire" instead.

Riley then left Sun Records, though he returned to record three more songs before leaving again in 1960. He and a former band member established Rita Records after his break with Sun, but it disintegrated quickly. He founded another label, Mojo Records, but after producing Willie Cobb's "You Don't Love Me," he abandoned the failing venture.

In 1962, Riley moved to Los Angeles, California, where he began working as a studio musician for artists such as Glen Campbell and Leon Russell. He was a featured harmonica player on recordings for the Beach Boys, Sammy Davis Jr., Rick Nelson, and Dean Martin, among others. He appeared on several television shows and recorded six albums before leaving California in 1966. For the next nine years, he dabbled in music, recording for several different studios and even reviving his own Mojo label for a while, all without significant commercial success.

In the early 1970s, Riley divorced his second wife, with whom he had two children. In 1975, he married Joyce Riley, with whom he had one daughter. Around the time of their marriage, he abandoned music and started decorating houses, but he was unable to stray from the music business for long. After a performance at the Memphis in May music festival in 1979, he toured in Europe throughout the 1980s, performing his popular songs from the 1950s as well as many blues numbers. He recorded his first all-blues album in 1991 and afterward was rediscovered by Bob Dylan, perhaps his most well-known fan. In 1997, his blues album *Hot Damn* was considered for a Grammy. His last recording was in March 2009, on which he sang on several tracks for Pocahontas native Gary Gazaway's album *Arkansas Traveler: A Cross-Cultural Excursion Into the Historical Music Heritage of the Americas.*

On August 2, 2009, Riley died of colon cancer in Jonesboro (Craighead County). He is buried at Walnut Grove Cemetery in Newport (Jackson County). He had lived in Newport with his wife for many years.

For additional information:

"Billy Lee Riley." Delta Boogie. http://www.deltaboogie.com/deltamusicians/rileyb/ (accessed February 8, 2013).

Burke, Ken. "The Billy Lee Riley Interview!" *Rocktober*, September 1999. Online at www.rockabilly.net/billyleeriley/interview.shtml (accessed February 9, 2013).

Obituary of Billy Lee Riley. *Arkansas Democrat-Gazette*, August 4, 2009, p. 4B.

Whayne, Jeannie. "Interview with Billy Lee Riley." *Arkansas Historical Quarterly* 55 (Autumn 1996): 297–318.

Kayla Kesterson

MISCELLANEA RIVERFEST ARTS AND MUSIC FESTIVAL

Riverfest Arts and Music Festival is Arkansas's premier summer event, offering three days of music, arts, food, and children's activities over Memorial Day weekend. The festival is held on the banks of the Arkansas River in downtown Little Rock (Pulaski County) and North Little Rock (Pulaski County). Operated by Riverfest Inc., a nonprofit organization overseen by a board of directors, Riverfest attracted more than 250,000 people in 2013, creating an economic impact of more than $30 million in the local community.

Founded by the Junior League of Little Rock as the Summer Arts Festival in July 1978, the first Riverfest presented the American Wind Symphony and other activities at Murray Park. Following the event's initial success, the date of the Summer Arts Festival was moved the next year to its current Memorial Day weekend slot, and the event was renamed Riverfest Arts and Music Festival. Riverfest was moved from Murray Park in 1982 to the Convention Center Plaza and then in 1983 to its current home in Julius Breckling Riverfront Park, adding activities at North Little Rock's North Shore Riverwalk in 2002. The event was free for its first twelve years, but as the quality and quantity of the entertainment rose, admission prices were introduced. The gate price for Riverfest 2013 was $35.

The Arkansas Symphony Orchestra presents an annual performance, and past nationally recognized musical acts include Willie Nelson, Al Green, ZZ Top, B. B. King, Hank Williams Jr., James Brown, Run DMC, the Black Crowes, LL Cool J, and Carrie Underwood. An Arkansas-only musical tent was added to the festival in 2008, showcasing the state's best live musical acts.

Beyond the annual economic impact of the event, Riverfest has played a part in the redevelopment of the riverfront and downtown areas of

Crowd at the Riverfest Arts and Music Festival in Little Rock.
Courtesy: Little Rock Convention and Visitors Bureau

Little Rock and North Little Rock through more than $700,000 in donations to a myriad of projects. Riverfest Inc.'s first financial contribution to the community was a $50,000 contribution in 1983 to construct the East Fountain in Riverfront Park. Since then, Riverfest Inc. has contributed to the construction of Riverfest Amphitheatre and the East Pavilion in the River Market, along with a 2008 pledge of $100,000 toward the Le Petite Roche project in Riverfront Park. Riverfest Amphitheatre was renamed First Security Amphitheater in 2013.

Riverfest Inc. is operated by an executive director and four full- and part-time staff members, along with a board of directors with standing positions from the Junior League of Little Rock, the Little Rock Regional Chamber of Commerce, the City of Little Rock Department of Parks and Recreation, the Little Rock Convention and Visitors Bureau, the Downtown Partnership, the North Little Rock Advertising and Promotion Commission, and the North Little Rock Chamber of Commerce. The nonprofit organization is supported by a network of benefactors—both corporate and private—who sponsor the event's large fireworks show, children's craft activities, and more. Local government agencies such as police, fire, and city departments donate worker hours to support the event. An army of volunteers works year-round planning and then working the three-day event.

For additional information:
Hill, Jack W. "Take Me To The River." *Arkansas Democrat-Gazette*, May 23, 2008, pp. 6W, 8W.
Lewis, Bill. "Centerpiece at Arts Festival's 1st Day Offers a Sort of Civilized Surrealism." *Arkansas Gazette*, July 30, 1978, p. 3A.
Marymount, Mark. "Riverfest." *Arkansas Gazette*, May 24, 1991, Weekend edition, p. 1.
Riverfest Arkansas. http://www.riverfestarkansas.com (accessed February 23, 2013).

Shea Stewart

ROBINSON CENTER MUSIC HALL

Built in downtown Little Rock (Pulaski County) during the Great Depression as a Public Works Administration (PWA) project, the Joseph Taylor Robinson Memorial Auditorium—known since 1973 as the Robinson Center Music Hall—frequently hosts touring performances, including Broadway musicals, and is home to the Arkansas Symphony Orchestra. Named for Lonoke County native Joseph Taylor Robinson, who was governor of Arkansas and a U.S. senator, the Art Deco building on Markham Avenue near Broadway Street is a major Little Rock landmark.

Prior to the construction of the Robinson Center, Little Rock's largest auditorium for concerts and other public events was at Little Rock High School (now called Central High School). Senator Robinson, a strong supporter of President Franklin Roosevelt's New Deal, helped to bring several major projects to Arkansas, including a new civic auditorium. Unlike other New Deal programs, the PWA required local funding to accompany federal dollars. On January 26, 1937, Little Rock voters approved a bond referendum to help fund the auditorium, as well as additions to the public library and a city park for African Americans.

Construction of the auditorium began on December 27 of that year and was largely completed by December 8, 1939. The structure was received by the City of Little Rock on January 24, 1940, and formally dedicated on February 16, 1940. The building was named for Robinson, who had supported its creation; he had died in 1937. The total cost of construction was $855,000, more than $200,000 over the initial budget. In addition to the main stage and arena, including mezzanine and balcony seating, the building also holds lecture/exhibit halls and meeting rooms. As originally designed and built, the auditorium had two separate performance venues on an upper and lower level. Its team of architects included the firm of George Wittenberg and Lawson Delony, as well as associate architect Eugene Stern, all of whom had designed many other prominent buildings in Little Rock and around Arkansas.

The first use of the auditorium was as a basketball court for high school games, but orchestral performances, ballet, and traveling theater rapidly came to the impressive new building. During the 1940s, the building also was used as a community center, offering ping pong, shuffleboard, bridge, checkers, and domino tournaments. Among the many famous performers and speakers to appear at the Robinson Memorial Auditorium in the 1940s were Louis Armstrong, Katharine Hepburn, Ella Fitzgerald, Mae West, Gene Autry, Bob Hope, Ethel Barrymore, Duke Ellington, Guy Lombardo, Eleanor Roosevelt, and Dwight D. Eisenhower. Some performers would offer two shows on the same day to different audiences, one upstairs and one downstairs. Elvis Presley performed at the auditorium in 1955 and 1956; for the first appearance, he was paid $150, but he grossed $9,000 when he returned a year later.

During the 1940s and 1950s, seating in the auditorium was often segregated by race. Music manager and promoter Jim Porter Jr. sought to overturn this policy in the wake of the desegregation of Little Rock's school system. In 1961, he was arrested during a Ray Charles concert for sitting among black audience members; other concerts by black performers such as Duke Ellington were canceled because of the segregated seating. By the time Louis Armstrong performed there in September 1966, this policy had ended.

Robinson Center Music Hall in Little Rock.   Photo: Mike Keckhaver

In 1966, the Arkansas Symphony Orchestra made the Robinson Memorial Auditorium its home. The building underwent extensive renovation in 1973, with underground parking added in the place of the lower performance hall. An attached hotel was erected to the east. That same year, the name was formally changed to the Robinson Center Music Hall. Famous acts continue to appear at the Robinson Center, including traveling Broadway shows such as *Les Miserables*, *Riverdance*, and *Wicked*. Since its renovation, the auditorium seats 2,609.

The building was added to the National Register of Historic Places on February 21, 2007. In 2012, the Little Rock Convention and Visitors Bureau announced plans for an extensive upgrade of the center's facilities, including an expanded lobby and stage, as well as acoustical and technological improvements. Work is expected to begin in 2014 and be completed in 2016.

For additional information:

"Joseph Taylor Robinson Memorial Auditorium." National Register of Historic Places nomination form. On file at Arkansas Historic Preservation Program, Little Rock, Arkansas. http://www.arkansaspreservation.com/historic-properties/_search_nomination_popup.aspx?id=2319 (accessed February 27, 2012).

Roy, F. Hampton, Sr., and Charles Witsell Jr. *How We Lived: Little Rock as an American City*. Little Rock: August House, 1984.

Steven Teske

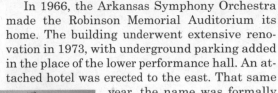

ROCK   ROCK 'N' ROLL HIGHWAY 67

Rock 'n' Roll Highway 67 is a segment of U.S. Highway 67 running approximately 111 miles through Jackson, Lawrence, Randolph, and Clay counties in northeastern Arkansas, with a portion in Miller County in southwestern Arkansas.

Its name is derived from the rockabilly music performed at nightclubs and other venues located on the highway by legendary progenitors of the genre. The designation by Act 497 of the Eighty-seventh Arkansas General Assembly in 2009 has since spawned music festivals, museum exhibits, and plaques in communities situated along the highway.

The term "rockabilly"—a portmanteau of "rock 'n' roll" and "hillbilly"—is defined as a mixture of blues, country and western, and rhythm and blues music that saw its biggest popularity beginning in the post–World War II era and lasting until around the time of the so-called British Invasion of the early 1960s. Original rockabilly artists included Elvis Presley, Roy Orbison, and Jerry Lee Lewis, along with noted Arkansans Johnny Cash, Conway Twitty, Sonny Burgess, and Billy Lee Riley. These same musicians are cited as influences by later musical legends—ranging from the Beatles to Bob Dylan—who credit rockabilly as an inspiration for their own distinctive styles of music. Establishments locat-

Highway 67, near Tuckerman. A stretch of Highway 67 was designated the "Rock 'n' Roll Highway" by the Arkansas legislature in 2009.

Photo: Mike Polston

ed on U.S. 67 that hosted these acts included Bob King's King of Clubs in Swifton (Jackson County), the Silver Moon Club in Newport (Jackson County), and the rooftop of the Skylark Drive-In Theater in Pocahontas (Randolph County). Some were still hosting live music as recently as 2010.

The idea to honor the road originated in 2005 with noted Pocahontas musician Gary Gazaway (who has performed and recorded with the likes of Stevie Ray Vaughan, Steve Winwood, Joe Cocker, and Phish). As a lifelong resident of the area, Gazaway had long recognized the significance of the highway as a musical artery. He suggested the idea to director of the Arkansas Folklife Program at Arkansas State University (ASU) Michael Luster and to music historian Stephen Koch, co-founder and host of the radio program *Arkansongs*. All three concluded that it was a worthy project and agreed that the highway should be called the "Rockabilly Highway." Gazaway advanced his idea for the designation during the three-week Pocahontas Sesquicentennial celebration in 2006—the highlight of which was a performance by Billy Lee Riley and Sonny Burgess.

The original idea was for the highway to run from Bald Knob (White County) to the Missouri state line north of Corning (Clay County). A committee was formed that included representatives from the counties through which the highway would pass, as well as others such as Michael Luster of ASU, state representative J. R. Rogers of Walnut Ridge (Lawrence County), and Little Rock (Pulaski County) author Marvin Schwartz, the committee's director.

The committee was soon divided over the name. Gazaway and the historians favored the "Rockabilly Highway" designation, while the pol-

iticians and civic boosters did not want any association with the perceived pejorative term "hillbilly," proposing instead the name "Rock 'n' Roll Highway 67." The committee ultimately voted 8–5 in favor of naming it Rock 'n' Roll Highway 67. Gazaway disagreed with the decision, saying that the name dishonors the historical aspect of the road: "Rockabilly was the kind of music they played there," he said. "The hillbilly culture is what made the music. To call it anything else is to go against the historical aspect of it." Giving a nod to the naming controversy, the legislation reads, "While academics and historians have indicated that a change in the name of this music to 'rockabilly' should be made, everyone who lived, breathed, and rocked during this time called the music rock 'n' roll."

After Governor Mike Beebe signed legislation for the highway designation on March 20, 2009, there was growing effort to capitalize on the designation by civic boosters eager to attract tourists to their communities. For example, Walnut Ridge—where the rockabilly-influenced Beatles stopped briefly at the municipal airport in 1964 en route to a vacation destination in Missouri—started a Beatles-themed music festival called Beatles at the Ridge (tag line: "Where Abbey Road Meets the Rock 'n' Roll Highway!"), erected a life-sized sculpture depicting the Beatles from the cover of their landmark album *Abbey Road*, and created the Walnut Ridge Guitar Walk—a colored concrete walkway in the shape of an Epiphone Casino electric guitar popular with musicians of the era. Also, highway signs reading ROCK 'N' ROLL HIGHWAY 67 can be seen lining the route.

In October 2011, signs were dedicated marking a portion of Highway 67 through Texarkana (Miller County) as part of the Rock 'n' Roll Highway. Early rock and roll performers sometimes played at Arkansas Municipal Auditorium when they traveled through Texarkana on Highway 67.

For additional information:

Act 497 of 2009. http://www.arkleg.state.ar.us/assembly/2009/R/Acts/Act497.pdf (accessed August 26, 2012).

DeMillo, Andrew. "Arkansas Hopes 'Rock 'n' Roll Highway' Will Boost Tourism." *USA Today*, March 24, 2009. Online at http://www.usatoday.com/travel/destinations/2009-03-24-arkansas-rock-n-roll-highway_N.htm (accessed August 26, 2012).

Heard, Kenneth. "Group Hoping to Make U.S. 67 A

Rocking Road." *Arkansas Democrat-Gazette*, December 28, 2007, pp. 1B, 8B.

———. "Legendary Musicians Stepped Out on U.S. 67." *Arkansas Democrat-Gazette*, January 13, 2008, p. 17B.

———. "Rock 'N' Roll Highway 67." *Arkansas Democrat-Gazette*, April 13, 2009, pp. 1A, 2A.

———. "Rock 'N' ROLL Highway." *Arkansas Life* (May 2012): 44–45.

———. "U.S. 67 Gets Rock 'N' Roll Christening." *Arkansas Democrat-Gazette*, January 25, 2008, pp. 1B, 5B.

Rock 67. http://www.rock67.com/ (accessed August 26, 2012).

Keith Merckx

FOLK   "THE ROCK ISLAND LINE"

"The Rock Island Line" is a world-famous song—recorded by the likes of Johnny Cash, Harry Belafonte, and Grandpa Jones—the earliest known performances of which are two 1934 recordings made in Arkansas prisons. A tall tale in rhyme, the song's subject is a train so fast that it arrives at its destination in Little Rock (at 8:49) before its departure from Memphis (at "half past nine").

The collectors responsible for the first recordings were an unlikely pair. John Lomax was a white, Mississippi-born college teacher already well known as a folksong collector, while Huddie Ledbetter was a black, Louisiana-born singer and guitar player just released from prison and soon to be even better known as "Leadbelly." Arriving in Arkansas in late September and working first in Little Rock (Pulaski County) and then at the Tucker and Cummins prison farms to the south, they recorded two versions of "The Rock Island Line." Both versions were dominated by the chorus, in call-and-response form. "I say the Rock Island Line," the leader sings, answered by, "Is a mighty good road" from the group. Three repeats of this are then closed off by the verse's final lines, sung by all: "If you want to ride, you got to ride it like you're flyin' / Buy your ticket at the station on the Rock Island Line." It was from the beginning a celebration of speed, a hymn to motion itself raised by men who could go nowhere.

In recording the second version, Lomax and Ledbetter encountered, as the song's leader, their most outstanding Arkansas prison singer, Kelly Pace, a petty criminal from Camden (Ouachita County) who eventually contributed more than thirty performances to the Library of Congress archives. Lomax made additional recording trips to Arkansas prisons in 1939 and 1942, unaccompanied by Ledbetter. Pace was a free man at the time of the 1939 visit, but Lomax collected a third version of "The Rock Island Line," this time in Cummins Prison. By 1942, Pace was back in prison, sent up for forty-two years for stealing a car, and once again he was the star, performing some twenty-six songs as a soloist or member of a larger group. One of these is a fourth performance of "The Rock Island Line," the last version collected in Arkansas by Lomax.

Ledbetter was the one who made "The Rock Island Line" famous. He remembered the song from the two 1934 sessions and eventually recorded it many times, first for folksong collectors at the Library of Congress in 1937 and later for commercial labels (RCA Victor in 1940 and Capitol in 1944, among others). Ledbetter's fame carried several songs into the nation's folksong repertoire—"Goodnight Irene" and "The Midnight Special" are two other examples—but "The Rock Island Line" became as famous as any.

The train itself shifted its destination to New Orleans, Louisiana, in these later versions, losing its Arkansas references in the process. Then, in 1956, "The Rock Island Line" became a pop music hit when Scottish singer Lonnie Donegan's version spent twenty-two weeks on the British charts, reaching the No. 8 spot in February. The same version also did well in the United States, spending several weeks in the top twenty and topping out at the No. 9 spot in April.

"The Rock Island Line" remains a staple of the American folk music repertoire, available in scores of performances across a wide range of musical genres. Its Arkansas roots have mostly been forgotten, but Johnny Cash, who had earlier recorded the song for Sun and other labels, performed it at Cummins in 1969, bringing the state's most famous train back home.

For additional information:

Cochran, Robert. "Ride It Like You're Flyin': The Story of 'The Rock Island Line.'" *Arkansas Historical Quarterly* 56 (Summer 1997): 201–229.

Cohen, Norm. *Long Steel Rail: The Railroad in American Folk Song.* Urbana: University of Illinois Press, 1981.

Robert B. Cochran

The July 5, 1975, lunch stop and subsequent arrest of Rolling Stones guitarists Ron Wood and Keith Richards in Fordyce (Dallas County) is fabled in the town, and the incident became a footnote in the police record of the English rock and roll band. The quintet had cultivated an outlaw image since its early 1960s inception. According to Arkansas native Bill Carter, the Rolling Stones' attorney from 1973 to 1990, everywhere the Stones went in 1975, it was a challenge for authorities. Riot squads and narcotics units were common during the group's twenty-eight-city, $13 million-grossing tour.

On July 4, the Stones played Memphis, Tennessee. Richards and new member Wood decided to sightsee and drive with two others to their July 6 concert in Dallas, Texas. Hours later, driving a rented yellow 1975 Chevy Impala, they stopped for lunch at the 4-Dice Restaurant and Station. Paul Holt, whose family owned the restaurant, was in Memphis, however-

The Rolling Stones on tour in 1975.
Photo: Tony Morelli

er, hoping to see one of the Rolling Stones. "Who could have thought for a second they'd be here?" he later said. Wood hit the buffet, going back for seconds on the fried chicken. Richards ordered the sixteen-ounce T-bone and tried brown gravy over his French fries on the recommendation of waitress Wanda Parnell. They left a $1.65 tip and autographs.

Soon after 3:00 p.m., the Richards-driven Impala, with Tennessee license plate IKR 160, was cited for reckless driving. Stories differ by a few miles concerning where the car was pulled over. Fordyce police officers Joe Taylor and Eddie Childers thought that they smelled marijuana, and the Impala was impounded. After getting a search warrant, police did not find marijuana but discovered less than two grams of cocaine in a briefcase said to belong to passenger Fred Sessler. Though he passed a sobriety test, Richards was cited for carrying an illegal weapon—a hunting knife.

Hundreds of people gathered outside city hall as word spread. British Embassy officials were called. Inside, the group drank soda, and Wood rode a confiscated bicycle around the halls. No one spent time behind bars. Before midnight, with Carter's help, the group was released. Richards posted $162.50; he was scheduled to appear in court August 1 but forfeited bond. The Stones also covered Sessler.

All left by a plane waiting at the local airport. Former Stones bassist Bill Wyman mentions the incident briefly in his 1990 autobiography, calling it a "tough baptism" for Wood. Richards reputedly swore the Stones would never play Arkansas, but the band performed on November 11, 1994, in Little Rock (Pulaski County) and returned on March 9, 2006. In November 2006, thirty-one years after the incident, Governor Mike Huckabee issued a pardon to Richards for his reckless driving conviction. Keith Richards opened his 2010 memoir, *Life*, by recalling his arrest in Fordyce.

The Stones have other Arkansas connections. Little Rock native Jim Dickinson plays piano on "Wild Horses," Little Rock native Robert Palmer wrote a book about the Stones, their song "Rip This Joint" references Little Rock, and many Arkansas-related bluesmen—such as Howlin' Wolf—influenced the band.

For additional information:

Koch, Stephen. "Stones Tumble in Fordyce." *Arkansas Times*, October 21, 2004, p. 32. Online at http://www.arktimes.com/arkansas/stones-tumble-in-fordyce/Content?oid=949362 (accessed February 14, 2013).

Matthews, Gerard. "Fact-Checking Keef." *Arkansas Times*, March 30, 2011, pp. 10–13. Online at http://www.arktimes.com/arkansas/fact-checking-keef/Content?oid=1614881 (accessed February 8, 2013).

Richards, Keith. *Life*. New York: Little, Brown, and Company, 2010.

Steed, Stephen. "Jumpin' Jack Flash(back)." *Little Rock Free Press*, June 9–22, 1994, pp. 8–10.

Stewart, Shea. "Chasing Keith Richards in Fordyce." *Arkansas Life* (March 2011): 34–39.

Wood, Ronnie. *Ronnie: The Autobiography*. New York: St. Martin's Press, 2007.

Wyman, Bill. *Stone Alone: The Story of a Rock 'n' Roll Band*. New York: Penguin Books, 1990.

Stephen Koch

BOBBY RUSH (1935–)

Bobby Rush, known as the "King of the Chitlin' Circuit," is an award-winning blues artist whose music also parlays elements of southern soul, funk, and rap into a genre he calls "folk-funk."

Bobby Rush was born Emmett Ellis Jr. on November 10, 1935, near Homer, Louisiana, to Emmett and Mattie Ellis; however, the 1940 census lists him as three years old. The son of a minister, Rush was influenced by his father's guitar and harmonica playing, and he first experimented with music by tapping on a sugar-cane syrup bucket and playing a broom-and-wire diddley bow. In 1947, his family moved to Pine Bluff (Jefferson County), where his music career began. He headed a band at a local juke joint behind a sawmill, donning a fake mustache so he would look older. It was also in Pine Bluff that he formed key associations with area blues artists such as Elmore James, "Moose" Walker, Boyd Gilmore, and others. It is unclear why he chose the stage name Bobby Rush, though perhaps he changed his name out of respect to his minister father, with whom he shared a name.

After moving to Chicago, Illinois, in the early 1950s, Rush made additional associations with legends such as Howlin' Wolf, Muddy Waters, Little Walter, Albert King, and others. By the early 1970s, he had his first *Billboard* R&B hit with the song "Chicken Heads," which reached No. 34. Rush later made his first full album, *Rush Hour*, in 1979, with another hit, "I Wanna Do the Do."

Since the late 1970s, Rush has made dozens of albums and has built both a national and international fan base. Interestingly, his awards and acclaim have come in his later years, as he received his first major recognition after the release of *Raw*, his twenty-second album, when he received the Soul Blues Male Artist of the Year award at the Blues Music Awards in 2007. His album *Hoochie Momma* received a Grammy nomination in the blues category in 2001. In 2006, Rush was inducted into the Blues Foundation's Blues Hall of Fame.

Rush has been married at least twice. His first wife and three children all died from sickle-cell anemia.

Sexually suggestive, edgy, and humorous, Rush has always had a high-energy performance show that is as entertaining as his music. He touts his desire to keep these shows an integral part of his performances, especially for smaller "Chitlin' Circuit" clubs, which have limited means to attract big stars. His fans have thusly dubbed him "King of the Chitlin' Circuit."

Rush has also become an ambassador for blues, representing the genre in cultural venues worldwide, and has also been noted as a humanitarian. In 2007, he became the first blues artist to perform in China, earning him the title "International Dean of the Blues." He was later named Friendship Ambassador to the Great Wall of China after performing the largest concert ever held at that site. Rush has also performed for troops in Iraq and supported projects for prisons and at-risk youth.

For additional information:

Booth, Stanley. "Bobby Rush: A Blues Access Interview." *Blues Access* 34 (Summer 1998). http://www.bluesaccess.com/No_34/rush.html (accessed May 13, 2013).

Gordon, Keith A. "Bobby Rush Profile." About.com. http://blues.about.com/od/artistprofi3/p/BobbyRushProf.htm (accessed May 13, 2013).

Hight, Jewly. "Interview with Bobby Rush." *Oxford American* (April 9, 2013). http://www.oxfordamerican.org/articles/2013/apr/09/interview-bobby-rush/ (accessed May 15, 2013).

Komara, Edward, ed. *Encyclopedia of the Blues*. Vol. 2. New York: Routledge, 2006.

Mullins, Terry. "Bobby Rush Interview." *Blues Blast Magazine* (March 24, 2011). http://www.thebluesblast.com/Archive/BluesBlasts/2011/BluesBlast3_24_11.htm (accessed May 13, 2013).

Jimmy Cunningham Jr.

RWAKE

Rwake is a sludge/doom/experimental metal band based in Little Rock (Pulaski County). The band, originally called Wake, formed in 1996 and consisted of Kris Graves on guitar, Jeff Morgan on drums, Chris (C. T.) Terry on vocals, and Aaron Mills on bass. The band added the R to its name when it realized that another band had already claimed the name Wake. The original line-up played its first show on March 15, 1997, in Batesville (Independence County).

Rwake melds elements of a number of metal subgenres including sludge, doom, hardcore, and

Central Arkansas sludge metal band Rwake. Courtesy: Relapse Records

death metal. Due to the band members' fondness for many styles of music, especially southern music, subtle influences from artists such as Charlie Daniels, Hank Williams (as well as Williams's son and grandson), and Lynyrd Skynyrd find their way into the band's compositions, resulting in sounds that are often difficult to categorize. Adding to the diversity, and unusual for the genre, Rwake often includes acoustic interludes in its recordings. Another source of the band's unique sound is the presence of two vocalists, one male and one female.

After releasing several demos, Rwake recorded and self-released its first full-length album, *Absence Due to Projection*. After the independent releases of *Hell Is a Door to the Sun* (2002) and *If You Walk Before You Crawl, You Crawl Before You Die* (2004), and inclusion in two metal compilation albums, the band signed to major metal label Relapse in 2006 and appeared that year at the South by Southwest (SXSW) music festival in Austin, Texas. *Voices of Omens*, released in 2007, was Rwake's first release for Relapse. In 2011, Relapse released *Rest*, an album of longer, more exploratory songs.

Rwake embarked on its first major tour, in support of *Hell Is a Door to the Sun*, in 2002 with headliner Alabama Thunderpussy. In addition to touring extensively in the United States and performing at many American metal festivals, Rwake has performed at two prestigious European metal festivals: Hellfest in France (2010) and Roadburn in the Netherlands (2011).

As of 2013, Rwake is a seven-piece band consisting of Graves (guitar), Morgan (drums, guitar), Terry (vocals), Britney Fugate (moog, vocals, samples), Kiffin Rodgers (guitar), John Judkins (bass, lap steel), and Chris Newman (guitar). Previous members of Rwake have formed or joined other significant Arkansas metal bands such as Deadbird and Shitfire.

Voices of Omens by Rwake. Courtesy: Relapse Records

For additional information:
"Rwake." Encyclopaedia Metallum. http://www.metal-archives.com/bands/Rwake/9299 (accessed May 17, 2013).
"Rwake." Relapse Records. http://www.relapse.com/label/artist/rwake.html (accessed May 17, 2013).

Mike Keckhaver

S

JAZZ   PHAROAH SANDERS (1940–)

Pharoah Sanders is a noted jazz saxophonist who is recognized as a pioneer of the "free jazz" movement. Collaborations with artists such as Sun Ra and John Coltrane remain his most noted work, but his solo efforts stretch over four decades from 1964 to the present.

Pharoah Sanders was born Ferrell Sanders on October 10, 1940, in Little Rock (Pulaski County). His mother worked as a cook in a school cafeteria, and his father worked for the City of Little Rock. An only child, Sanders began his musical career accompanying church hymns on clarinet. His initial artistic accomplishments were in art, and it was not until he was at Scipio Jones High School in North Little Rock (Pulaski County) that Sanders discovered the tenor saxophone. The band director, Jimmy Cannon, was also a saxophone player and introduced Sanders to jazz. When Cannon left Scipio Jones High School, Sanders—still a student—took over as the band director until a permanent director could be found.

During the late 1950s, Sanders sneaked into African-American clubs in downtown Little Rock to play with acts that were passing through. At the time, Little Rock was part of the touring route through Memphis, Tennessee, and Hot Springs (Garland County) for rhythm and blues (R&B)

and jazz musicians, including Junior Parker. Sanders found himself limited by the state's segregation and the R&B and jazz standards that dominated the Little Rock music scene.

After finishing high school in 1959, Sanders moved to Oakland, California, and lived with relatives. He briefly attended Oakland Junior College and studied art and music. Once outside the Jim Crow South, Sanders could play in both black and white clubs. Sanders's Arkansas connection stuck with him in the Bay Area with the nickname of "Little Rock." It was also during this time that he met and befriended John Coltrane.

Sanders transplanted himself again in 1961, this time to New York City. Sanders often found himself financially destitute and on more than one occasion had to sell his saxophone for money. A year after moving to New York City, Sanders joined Sun Ra's Arkestra and received another nickname, "Pharoah," which proved to have more staying power than "Little Rock."

Jazz saxophonist Pharoah Sanders in Little Rock; 2013.
Photo: Mike Keckhaver

Sanders formed his first band in 1963 while still collaborating and making appearances on records with Don Cherry and Sun Ra. Beginning in 1964, Sanders and Coltrane began to work together on a regular basis. Critics have often claimed that Sanders pushed Coltrane into a more radical and experimental direction, but it is a claim that Sanders denies. Sanders continued to play with Coltrane and his "free" group until Coltrane's death in 1967.

The same year that Sanders began playing with Coltrane, Sanders's first album, *Pharoah's First*, was released on the Calibre label. Along with other experimental musicians, Sanders began to restructure and re-conceptualize the boundaries of jazz compositions. This movement was called "free jazz" and earned both acclaim and ridicule from critics. In 1966, Sanders released the first of a string of albums with Impulse! Records. Among these was his most critically acclaimed, *Karma* (1969), containing his most recognized recording, "The Creator Has a Master Plan."

Sanders left Impulse! in 1973 and redirected his compositions back to earlier jazz conventions. He continued to explore the music of different cultures and refine his compositions. However, he found himself floating from label to label. He found a permanent home with a small label called Theresa in 1987, which was sold to Evidence in 1991. Frustration with record labels continued to plague Sanders for most of the 1990s. Also during this time, he went to Africa for a cultural exchange program for the U.S. State Department.

Sanders's major-label debut would finally come in 1995 when Verve Records released *Message from Home*, followed by *Save Our Children* (1998). But again, Sanders's disgust with the recording business prompted him to leave the label. In 2000, Sanders released *Spirits* and, in 2003, a live album titled *The Creator Has a Master Plan.*

Sanders lives in the Bay Area. He continues to compose music, including ballets, and tours in Europe and the United States.

For additional information:
Jung, Fred. "A Fireside Chat with Pharoah Sanders." *All About Jazz*, March 21, 2003. Online at http://www.allaboutjazz.com/php/article.php?id=224 (accessed February 8, 2013).
Odell, Jennifer. "Legend of the Pharoah." *All About Jazz*, December 8, 2004. Online at http://www.allaboutjazz.com/php/article.php?id=15624 (accessed February 8, 2013).

David Prater

BLUES / R&B — "SON" SEALS (1942–2004)

Frank "Son" Seals was a singer who became a driving force behind a brief but stormy rejuvenation of the blues throughout the mid- to late 1970s. For three decades, he dominated the Chicago blues as no one has since.

Son Seals was born on August 13, 1942, in Osceola (Mississippi County). His father was musician Jim "Son" Seals. He acquired the nickname "Son" while a child in Osceola.

Seals came to the blues early. He grew up in a

juke joint operated by his father, who had been a member of the Rabbit Foot Minstrels. Juke joint the Dipsy Doodle featured some of the greatest of all blues performers, including Albert King, Robert Nighthawk, and Sonny Boy Williamson. The Dipsy Doodle also presented touring acts, so Seals routinely heard not only rustic innovators but traveling stars. Nevertheless, he maintained that his chief inspiration was his father, who played piano, guitar, trombone, and drums and began teaching him when he was twelve.

"Son" Seals performing; 1977.
Photo: Lionel Decoster

At first, Seals joined the traveling musicians for informal jam sessions. Before long, he was touring as a drummer with Chicago, Illinois, guitarist Earl Hooker. At eighteen, he played drums on Albert King's seminal "concert" album, *Live Wire/Blues Power* (1968), for the Stax label in Memphis, Tennessee.

Seals moved to Chicago in 1971 and immersed himself in the music of Hound Dog Taylor, Buddy Guy, James Cotton, and others. Taylor soon had a modest hit album with a young label known as Alligator, and Seals inherited Taylor's weekend shows at Chicago's Expressway Lounge.

Alligator proprietor Bruce Iglauer released Seals's first solo album, *The Son Seals Blues Band* (1973), and Seals was suddenly a star. He toured extensively after that, garnering critical praise wherever he went, including notices in *Rolling Stone* magazine and the *New York Times*. But the good times did not last. Even though Seals followed his debut recording with one powerful album after another (*Bad Axe*, which Alligator released in 1985, won a W. C. Handy Award for Best Contemporary Blues Album) and was acclaimed as a genuine blues artist—a real genius—things began to go wrong in the 1990s.

Seals was diabetic, and in 1999, his left leg was amputated below the knee because of the disease. Two years before that, his ex-wife had shot him in the face while he slept, resulting in months of reconstructive surgery. Finally, fire destroyed his motor home, and someone stole his custom-made guitar.

Seals died on December 20, 2004, in Richton Park, Illinois, from complications of diabetes. He was survived by fourteen children from his one marriage and various long-term relationships over the years.

For additional information:

Emery, Mike. "Son Seals: Dues-Paying Bluesman Perseveres." *Blues Access* 45 (2001). Online at http://www.bluesaccess.com/No_45/sonseals.html (accessed February 13, 2013).

Moon, D. T. "Son Seals: Intensity Is the Key." *Living Blues* 153 (September/October 2000): 14–25.

Jim Kelton

ROCK

LOUIE SHELTON (1941–)

Millions of people have heard Louie Shelton's smooth guitar-playing on hit records and albums without knowing who he was. Since the 1960s, he has worked as a session guitarist or a producer for Barbra Streisand, Whitney Houston, John Lennon, Lionel Richie, Boz Scaggs, Stevie Wonder, the Jackson Five, Seals and Crofts, Marvin Gaye, and many other famous pop, rock, and jazz musicians.

William Louis Shelton was born on April 6, 1941, in Little Rock (Pulaski County) but grew up in the Levy neighborhood of North Little Rock (Pulaski County). He was the youngest child and only son of five children born to William Lewis Shelton and Carrie Lois Middleton Shelton. His mother was a housewife, and his father was in law enforcement, serving as chief of the North Little Rock Police Department around the time Louie Shelton was born. Shelton grew up in poverty but spent his early years teaching himself to play the guitar. He dreamed of playing professionally, often spending his nights listening to the radio and learning to duplicate intricate guitar pieces made famous by Chet Atkins and Jimmy Bryant. He was also heavily influenced by jazz greats Johnny Smith and Wes Montgomery.

By the time he was twelve, Shelton's talent caught the attention of Shelby Cooper and the

Dixie Mountaineers, who invited him to join their band. The foursome played regularly on the *Barnyard Frolics*, a Grand Ole Opry–style program broadcast live on KLRA from Robinson Auditorium in Little Rock. As a result of the media coverage, the Dixie Mountaineers started performing five days a week on the radio and had a regular television show on local ABC affiliate KATV. Seeing Elvis Presley perform in Pine Bluff (Jefferson County) in the early 1950s intensified his interest in rock and roll, and Shelton joined a band that played regularly at Club 70 in North Little Rock.

Shelton left Little Rock in 1958 and moved to Albuquerque and Santa Fe, New Mexico, where he started a band. He also met Glen Campbell, a fellow musician and native Arkansan, there. Later that year, he decided to follow Campbell to Los Angeles, California, hoping his friend could help him break into lucrative session playing. However, his hopes for a quick transition into studio work did not materialize. Over almost a decade, Shelton joined or formed several bands. He teamed up with Jimmy Seals and Dash Crofts in a group called the Dawnbreakers in Los Angeles in 1966. Through that association, he also met musical entrepreneur Marcia Day and her five daughters.

Shelton married Betty Deaguero on May 29, 1959, in Santa Fe; they had three daughters during their nine years of marriage. Shelton later married Marcia Day's daughter Donadell (Donnie) Feinberg on August 9, 1969; they have two children. During this era, Shelton converted to the Baha'i Faith, which influenced the rest of his life and his music, especially his work with Seals and Crofts.

By the middle 1960s, another opportunity came through a demo session with songwriters/producers Tommy Boyce and Bobby Hart. One of the duo's first projects was the creation and marketing of the band the Monkees, as well as the television show of the same name. They were looking for a signature sound to enhance what they hoped would be a hit record on the Monkees' first album. They asked Shelton to come up with some opening chords. What resulted was the now-famed guitar riff that opens the song "Last Train to Clarksville."

As a result of playing on that hit pop tune, Shelton became highly sought after as a session musician, going on to work with famous music producers Phil Spector, Quincy Jones, and oth-

Louie Shelton (center), with Seals and Crofts on the Midnight Special *television show; 1973.*

Courtesy: Louie Shelton

ers. By the late 1960s, he had created music behind the scenes for the Jackson Five hits "I Want You Back," "ABC," and "I'll Be There." Simultaneous to some of his busiest years as a session guitarist, he was playing music for several television shows, including *The Glen Campbell Goodtime Hour*.

Shelton had also been introduced to production work through Herb Alpert of A&M Records. He decided to turn his talents to producing records and began churning out hit songs with former band mates and friends Jimmy Seals and Dash Crofts. Under Shelton's direction, Seals and Crofts produced five gold-selling albums, including *Summer Breeze* (Warner Bros., 1972), which spent eighteen weeks on the pop music charts. In 1977, *Billboard* magazine wrote of Shelton that he "has played on perhaps more 'hits' than any other guitar player in the industry."

However, by 1984, Shelton and his family had had enough of the fast-paced life in Los Angeles, and after a vacation to Australia, the family decided to relocate to that country. There, he produced several Australian musicians, including Peter Cupples and Noiseworks, among others.

Shelton remained in Australia until 1996, when a desire to be closer to aging family members prompted a return to the United States. He settled in Nashville, Tennessee, where he produced several albums, including one for Jimmy Seals's brother, Dan Seals. His first solo album compilation was *Guitar* (Lightyear, 1996), followed by *Hot and Spicy* (1998), *Urban Culture* (1999), and *Something Live* (2000).

In 2005, Shelton returned to Australia but

continues to make trips back to the United States. He was inducted into the Musicians Hall of Fame in Nashville in October 2009 and the Arkansas Entertainers Hall of Fame in 2013.

For additional information:
Bryson, Alan. "Louie Shelton: In Session." *All About Jazz.* http://www.allaboutjazz.com/php/article.php?id=35286

(accessed February 26, 2013).
Louie Shelton. http://www.louieshelton.com (accessed February 26, 2013).
Shelton, Louie. "Interview with Louie Shelton." October 19, 2010. Audio online at Butler Center AV/AR Audio Video Collection.
Special insert, *Billboard* (February 26, 1977).

Lisa H. Armstrong

"ARKIE" SHIBLEY (1914–1975)

Jesse Lee "Arkie" Shibley was a country singer best known for recording the original version of "Hot Rod Race" in 1950. The song is included in the book *What Was the First Rock 'n' Roll Record?* as one of fifty recordings that were influential in the origination of rock and roll. According to authors Jim Dawson and Steve Propes, its importance lies in the fact that "it introduced automobile racing into popular music and underscored the car's relevance to American culture, particularly youth culture."

Jesse Lee Shibley was born on September 21, 1914, in Van Buren (Crawford County) to David M. and Prudie Shibley, both farmers. He was a cattle farmer himself and, on November 25, 1935, married Evelyn Marie Breeden; they had three children. The following year, he relocated to Bremerton, Washington, where he helped build the Illahee State Park by day and played swing country by night. Self-taught on guitar, Shibley assembled a group of musicians in the mid-1940s who would stay with him for almost a full decade: Leon Kelley (lead guitar), Phil Fregon (fiddle), Jackie Hayes (bass and banjo), and "Docie" Dean Manuel (piano). Calling themselves the Mountain Dew Boys, they made their first recordings for the obscure MaeMae label on the West Coast in the late 1940s. By that time, Shibley had moved to California, where "Arkie" was a common nickname for immigrants from Arkansas.

In 1950, Shibley was offered a song called "Hot Rod Race," written by George Wilson (not a pseudonym for Shibley, as has been suggested elsewhere). He took it to Bill McCall, owner of 4 Star Records in Pasadena, California, who turned him down. The experience was later related in Shibley's recording "Arkie's Talking Blues": "So I went to 4 Star with a smile on my face / I had a little tune called Hot Rod Race / Bill McCall he said it was no good / I'd be better off cutting hard wood."

Shibley then decided to form his own label, Mountain Dew Records, and released "Hot Rod Race" in November 1950. Sensing a potential hit, McCall had second thoughts about the song. He purchased the master and reissued "Hot Rod Race" on his own Gilt-Edge label. With McCall's promotional machine behind the record, it sold spectacularly, peaking at number five on *Billboard*'s country charts in February 1951. However, there was strong competition from several cover versions on major labels by Ramblin' Jimmie Dolan (Capitol), Red Foley (Decca), and Tiny Hill (Mercury). These were more polished than the original, with its occasional odd tempos and awkward verses. All three cover versions peaked at number seven on the country charts, with the Tiny Hill version also crossing over to the pop charts at number twenty-nine.

Shibley recorded four sequels to his hit, all in 1951 and all performed in a Woody Guthrie–like talking blues style. A variation on "Hot Rod Race" called "Hot Rod Lincoln" was a pop hit in versions by Charlie Ryan (rising to number thirty-three in 1960), Johnny Bond (number twenty-six, 1960), and Commander Cody and His Lost Planet Airmen (number nine, 1972).

Though Shibley has been ignored by most country music encyclopedias, his place in country and early rock and roll history is assured on the strength of "Hot Rod Race." Its influence was immense, not only on rock and roll car songs like "Maybellene" by Chuck Berry and "Race With the Devil" by Gene Vincent, but also on the hot rod music from the early 1960s (the Beach Boys, Jan and Dean, the Hondells, etc.).

Shibley died on September 9, 1975, in Van Buren.

For additional information:
"Arkie Shibley." *BlackCat Rockabilly Europe.* http://www.rockabillyeurope.com/references/messages/arkie_shibley.htm (accessed February 26, 2013).
Dawson, Jim, and Steve Propes. *What Was the First Rock 'n' Roll Record?* Boston: Faber and Faber, 1992.

Dik de Heer

HOUSTON STACKHOUSE (1910–1983)

Houston Stackhouse never achieved much in the way of success, yet he was a pivotal figure on the southern blues scene from the 1930s through the 1960s, having worked with numerous significant blues musicians during that period, mentoring more than a few. He was a familiar figure in the small country juke joints, mainly in Arkansas and Memphis, Tennessee, and was highly respected among his fellow musicians. He also achieved a measure of regional fame as a member of the King Biscuit Boys who played on station KFFA out of Helena, present-day Helena-West Helena (Phillips County). When he finally made his first recordings in 1967, he was still a working musician, taking jobs within a 150-mile radius of his home base in Helena.

Houston Stackhouse was born Houston Goff on September 28, 1910, the son of Garfield Goff from Wesson, Mississippi. He only learned of his parentage and name at birth in the 1970s while trying to obtain a passport. He was raised on the Randall Ford Plantation by James Wade Stackhouse. As a youngster, he heard music from fiddler Lace Powell, who lived on the plantation, and two visiting uncles. His musical education began when the family moved a few miles north to Crystal Springs around 1925 and encountered the brothers Tommy, Mager, and Clarence Johnson. In addition to learning from the Johnson brothers, he was inspired by local musicians, as well as the records of Blind Lemon Jefferson, Lonnie Johnson, and Blind Blake. He launched his own career in the mid-to-late 1930s playing all over Mississippi, Arkansas, and Louisiana and working with musicians such as the Chatmon brothers (who performed as the Mississippi Sheiks), Robert Johnson, Charlie McCoy, Walter Vinson, and others. His two most enduring partnerships from this period were with Carey "Ditty" Mason and his cousin Robert McCollum—better known as Robert Nighthawk, whom he taught how to play guitar.

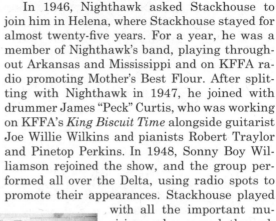

King Biscuit Time, *a blues radio show broadcast from station KFFA in Helena; 1942. Shown here are (left to right) Joe Willie Wilkins, Pinetop Perkins, Sonny Boy Williamson, announcer Hugh Smith, James "Peck" Curtis, and Houston Stackhouse.*
Courtesy: Arkansas History Commission

In 1946, Nighthawk asked Stackhouse to join him in Helena, where Stackhouse stayed for almost twenty-five years. For a year, he was a member of Nighthawk's band, playing throughout Arkansas and Mississippi and on KFFA radio promoting Mother's Best Flour. After splitting with Nighthawk in 1947, he joined with drummer James "Peck" Curtis, who was working on KFFA's *King Biscuit Time* alongside guitarist Joe Willie Wilkins and pianists Robert Traylor and Pinetop Perkins. In 1948, Sonny Boy Williamson rejoined the show, and the group performed all over the Delta, using radio spots to promote their appearances. Stackhouse played with all the important musicians who passed through Helena, including Jimmy Rogers and Sammy Lawhorn, both of whom he tutored on guitar, as well as Elmore James, Earl Hooker, Willie Love, Ernest Lane, and Roosevelt Sykes. While he was an active blues musician at night, he worked days at the Chrysler plant in West Memphis (Crittenden County) between 1948 and 1954.

Unlike many of his fellow bluesmen, Stackhouse remained in the South, continuing to perform locally as well as working regular jobs through the 1950s. He continued to play with notable musicians through the 1960s, including Boyd Gilmore, Houston Boines, Frank Frost, and Baby Face Turner. In 1965, Sonny Boy Williamson returned to Helena and enlisted Stackhouse to join him once again on *King Biscuit Time*. That May, the group was recorded live by Chris Strachwitz of Arhoolie Records, a recording subsequently released under Williamson's name as *King Biscuit Time*. Williamson died shortly after that recording, and Stackhouse continued briefly on the program with former partner Robert Nighthawk.

In 1967, field researcher George Mitchell recorded Stackhouse in Dundee, Mississippi. The group, calling themselves the Blues Rhythm Boys, consisted of Peck Curtis and Nighthawk. These were the final recordings of Nighthawk, who died a few months later. A week later, field researcher David Evans recorded Stackhouse in Crystal Springs with longtime partner Ditty Mason. With the death of Mason in 1969 and Curtis the following year, Stackhouse moved to Memphis in 1970, where he lived with Joe Willie Wilkins and Wilkins's wife, Carrie. He began taking part in the blues revival, touring with Wilkins throughout the decade as the King Biscuit Boys, traveling with the Memphis Blues Caravan, playing various festivals, and making a lone trip overseas to Vienna, Austria, in 1976. He recorded for Adelphi in 1972, with various live tracks appearing on compilations. Outside of playing the first two Delta Blues Festivals in Greenville, Mississippi, he largely retired from music after his European tour and moved to Crystal Springs.

Stackhouse returned to Helena, where he died on September 23, 1980, at the Helena Hospital, having outlived most of his peers. A son, Houston Stackhouse Jr., survived him. On September 26, 2012, Stackhouse was honored with a Mississippi Blues Trail marker.

For additional information:

Evans, David. CD liner notes for *Big Road Blues*. Wolf Records, 1999.

"Houston Stackhouse." Mississippi Blues Trail. http://www.msbluestrail.org/blues-trail-markers/houston-stackhouse (accessed February 27, 2013).

O'Neal, Jim, and Amy van Singel, eds. *The Voice of the Blues—Classic Interviews from Living Blues Magazine*. New York: Routledge, 2002.

Jeff Harris

FOLK "THE STATE OF ARKANSAW"

The ballad, or narrative folksong, usually titled "The State of Arkansaw" has been a principal exhibit in Arkansas's recurrent laments about its disreputable image. It is a clear example of the expressive culture of the late nineteenth century that depicted Arkansas pejoratively.

The story, which the ballad relates in first person, has its protagonist—known by several names, including "Sanford Barnes" and "John Johanna"—leave his home, most frequently "Buffalo town" or "Nobleville town," to seek employment. He hears of job opportunities in Arkansas, sets out by railway, and arrives in an Arkansas community, variously identified as Fort Smith (Sebastian County), Van Buren (Crawford County), Little Rock (Pulaski County), or Hot Springs (Garland County). There he meets a "walking skeleton" who conducts the narrator to the state's finest hotel. One night in these accommodations convinces him to leave Arkansas immediately. His host, though, persuades him to take a job draining some land. Several weeks of hard labor in an ague-producing climate subsisting on the poorest rations ("corndodgers" and "sassafras tea") have the narrator claiming, "I never knew what misery was till I came to Arkansas," a refrain for several of the ballad's stanzas. In some versions, he prefers marriage to a "squaw" in Indian Territory to life in Arkansas.

The earliest printed text of this song may be that which E. C. Perrow published in *Journal of American Folklore* in 1913. The earliest sound recording is probably the one by Kelly Harrell and the Virginia String Band, done in a studio in Camden, New Jersey, in 1927. One of Vance Randolph's Ozark consultants, however, suggested that he knew the song from the 1890s. Writing in *Arkansas Historical Quarterly*, Robert Morris proposed an earlier origin date, in the 1870s. Several commentators, including Library of Congress folksong researcher Alan Lomax, hypothesized that the song was of Irish-American origin. It does bear some resemblance to "The Spalpeen's Complaint to the Cranbally Farmer," which Patrick Weston Joyce published in 1909. Ballad scholar D. K. Wilgus reported a text of the song from Ireland and proposed that it had originated there and was imported to the United States in the late nineteenth century.

When G. Malcolm Laws created his catalogue of what he called "native American ballads," he included "The State of Arkansaw" as the first entry in his chapter "Ballads on Various Topics." He also contributed to some confusion about the song by titling it "The Arkansas Traveler." Though it has been reported under that name—along with "The Arkansas Navvy," "A Hobo in Arkansas," and "The Arkansas Emigrant," among others—"The State of Arkansaw" has no connection with the skit and fiddle tune to which Laws's title usually refers. It more likely derives from the tradition of complaint songs popular in the nineteenth century, which responded to the failure of westward migration to meet media-generated expectations. "The State of Arkansaw" joins "Michigan-I-O," "The Dreary

Black Hills," "Nebraska Land," and "The Lane County Bachelor" in a category of "folk dystopias," hyperbolic descriptions of frontier disappointments.

For additional information:

Clements, William M. "'The State of Arkansaw': A Folk Dystopia." *Southern Folklore* 46 (1989): 3–14.

Joyce, P. W. *Old Irish Folk Music and Songs: A Collection of 842 Irish Airs and Songs Hitherto Unpublished*. London: Longmans, Green, 1909.

Laws, G. Malcolm. *Native American Balladry: A Classification and Bibliographic Syllabus*. Philadelphia: American Folklore Society, 1964.

Lomax, Alan. *The Folk Songs of North America in the English Language*. Garden City, NY: Doubleday, 1960.

Masterson, James R. *Tall Tales of Arkansaw*. Boston: Chapman and Grimes, 1942.

Morris, Robert L. "The Arkansan in American Folklore." *Arkansas Historical Quarterly* 9 (1950): 99–107.

Perrow, E. C. "Songs and Rhymes from the South." *Journal of American Folklore* 26 (1913): 123–173.

Randolph, Vance. *Ozark Folksongs*. Volume III: Humorous and Play-Party Songs. Rev. ed. Columbia: University of Missouri Press, 1980.

Wilgus, D. K. "The Early American Influence on Narrative Songs in Ireland." *In Folklore Studies in Honour of Herbert Halpert:* A Festschrift, edited by Kenneth S. Goldstein and Neil V. Rosenberg. St. John's: Memorial University of Newfoundland, 1980.

William M. Clements

ROCK — *STEVE'S SHOW*

Steve's Show was a popular television program in the 1960s hosted by communications pioneer Steve Stephens of Newport (Jackson County).

Stephens's entry into radio coincided with the beginnings of rock and roll, and he soon became a proponent of this new type of music. In 1957, a trip to Little Rock (Pulaski County) television station KTHV with rock and roll band Sonny Burgess and the Pacers resulted in his being offered a position as a booth announcer for the station.

Stephens was soon asked to host a television "dance party," six months prior to the national launching of the ABC television program *American Bandstand*. The first show aired on a Saturday afternoon in March 1957, initially called *Your Party*. By May, the program had become so popular that it was expanded to six days a week and renamed *Steve's Show*.

Attendance at *Steve's Show* soon became so high that, in order to comply with the city's fire code, ticket reservations were required to limit the busloads of teenagers arriving from all over the state. The show helped launch the careers of Conway Twitty, Charlie Rich, Johnny Cash,

Steve Stephens (center) with Steve's Show *guests.*
Courtesy: Steve Stephens

Brenda Lee, Sonny Burgess, Fabian, and many others who appeared on the program, which ended in 1964.

For additional information:

Danielson, Kay. "Dancing the Past Today: Steverenos." *Arkansas Democrat-Gazette*, February 3, 1994, p. G1.

Hubbard, Sandra. *Steve's Show*. Documentary film. Little Rock: Morning Star Studio, 2003.

Adapted from Steve Stephens entry by Charles William Cunning

CLASSICAL / OPERA — WILLIAM GRANT STILL (1895–1978)

William Grant Still grew up in Little Rock (Pulaski County) and achieved national and international acclaim as a composer of symphonic and popular music. As an African American, he broke race barriers and opened opportunities for other minorities. He was strong advocate for the performance of works by American composers.

William Grant Still was born on May 11, 1895, in Woodville, Mississippi, the only son of William Grant Still Sr. and Carrie Lena Fambro Still. Still's mother moved to Little Rock with her infant son shortly after the death of her husband in 1895. Still and his mother lived with his grandmother, and his mother worked as a teach-

Classical composer William Grant Still of Little Rock at his piano; circa 1945.

er. In 1904, Still's mother married a railway postal clerk, Charles Benjamin Shepperson, whose own interest in music influenced the young Still. With Shepperson's support, he studied violin in 1908 with American violinist William Price, who lived for a short time in Little Rock.

Still attended M. W. Gibbs High School in Little Rock and graduated in 1911 as class valedictorian. That fall, he enrolled at Wilberforce University in Ohio (which was supported by the African Methodist Episcopal Church), where his mother hoped he would pursue studies in medicine. His interest in music, however, led him to leave Wilberforce in early 1915 without graduating in order to play in bands and orchestras in Ohio.

On October 4, 1915, he married Grace Bundy. The couple had four children, but the marriage ended in divorce in 1939.

In 1916, Still was in Memphis, Tennessee, where he met blues musician W. C. Handy, who provided Still with the opportunity to arrange and perform with his band. The next year, he entered the Oberlin Conservatory of Music in Ohio to pursue a formal education in music. Still's education was interrupted by World War I, when he served in the U.S. Navy. He served as a mess hall attendant and violinist for officers' meals. He returned to Oberlin after his discharge but did not receive a degree. Instead, in 1919, he moved to Harlem in New York City, where he worked for the Pace and Handy Music Publishing Company and performed with bands and orchestras. He also studied music with George Whitefield Chadwick, director of the New England Conser-

vatory of Music, and Edgard Varèse, the French modernist. These diverse experiences provided Still with professional contacts and valuable insight to performing, arranging, orchestrating, and composing popular and symphonic music.

From the Black Belt (1926), *From the Land of Dreams* (1924), *Darker America* (1924–1925), *From the Journal of a Wanderer* (1924), *La Guiablesse* (1926–1927), and *Levee Land* (1925) are among the noteworthy works Still composed during his developmental period. The *Afro-American Symphony*, completed in 1930 and first performed in 1931 by the Rochester Philharmonic Orchestra under conductor Howard Hanson, is Still's most well-known composition. It was the first symphony composed by an African American that was performed by a major orchestra, and it is still performed today. Hanson later conducted many of Still's compositions as part of Hanson's American Composers' Concerts in Rochester and also in Europe, where he conducted programs of American music.

While living in New York, Still met Paul Whiteman, who hired him to arrange music. When Whiteman took his orchestra to Hollywood, California, in May 1929, Still went, too. During the course of a year, Still completed more than 100 arrangements for Whiteman. Whiteman later commissioned Still to create original compositions, including *A Deserted Plantation* (1933), *Beyond Tomorrow* (1936), *Land of Superstition* (1933), *Ebon Chronicle* (1934), *Down Yonder* (circa 1935), and *Blues from Lennox Avenue* (circa 1937). Still moved permanently to Los Angeles, California, in 1934.

The 1930s and 1940s proved to be quite successful for Still, as major orchestras increasingly performed his compositions. The Chicago Symphony Orchestra performed *La Guiablesse*, written for the ballet, on June 16, 1933. On November 20, 1935, the New York Philharmonic performed Still's *Afro-American Symphony* at Carnegie Hall. Leopold Stokowski and the Philadelphia Symphony premiered his *Symphony in G Minor* on December 10, 1937. Still wrote the theme music for the 1939–1940 New York World's Fair. *Song of a City*, once recorded, was played 31,857 times at the fair, according to *New Yorker* magazine. The New York Philharmonic first performed *And They Lynched Him on a Tree* on June 24, 1940, at Lewisohn Stadium. The New York Philharmonic also premiered *Plain-Chant for America* on October 23, 1941, and *The Colored Soldiers Who Died for Democracy* on January 5, 1944, both at Carnegie Hall. The Cleveland Orchestra premiered *Poem for Orchestra* on December 7, 1944, and the Cincinnati Symphony Orchestra premiered *Festive Overture* on January 19, 1945. The opera *Troubled Island*, with a libretto by poet Langston Hughes, was premiered by the New York City Opera Company on March 31, 1949.

Two days after his divorce from Grace Bundy on February 6, 1939, he married Verna Arvey in Mexico where interracial marriages were legal. Arvey was an accomplished pianist and excellent writer, talents that served her husband well for over forty years. They had two children.

Still's compositions include symphonies, ballets, operas, chamber music, and works for solo instruments. Together, they number almost 200 pieces. His lengthy list of honors and awards includes: the William E. Harmon Award for Distinguished Achievement among Negroes in Music

Carrie Lena Fambro Still Shepperson, mother of William Grant Still; circa 1910.

Courtesy: Special Collections, University of Arkansas Libraries, Fayetteville

in 1928; the Guggenheim Fellowship in 1934, 1935, and 1938; the Julius Rosenwald Foundation Fellowship in 1939 and 1940; and a Freedoms Foundation Award in 1953. He received honorary degrees from the following institutions: Wilberforce University in 1936; Howard University in 1941; Oberlin College in 1947; Bates College in 1954; University of Arkansas in 1971; Pepperdine University in 1973; Peabody Conservatory of Music in 1974; and the University of Southern California in 1975.

Still's health began to decline in 1970. He spent his last years in a convalescent home and died in Los Angeles on December 3, 1978. His ashes were scattered over the Pacific Ocean.

For additional information:

Arvey, Verna. *In One Lifetime*. Fayetteville: University of Arkansas Press, 1984.

———. *Studies of Contemporary American Composers: William Grant Still*. New York: J. Fischer, 1939.

Edwards, Benjamin Griffin. "The Life of William Grant Still." PhD diss., Harvard University, 1987.

Farrah, Scott David. "Signifyin(g): A Semiotic Analysis of Symphonic Worlds by William Grant Still, William Levi Dawson, and Florence B. Price." PhD diss., Florida State University, 2007.

Hudgins, Mary D. "An Outstanding Arkansas Composer, William Grant Still." *Arkansas Historical Quarterly* 24 (Winter 1965): 308–314.

Murchison, Gayle. "'Dean of Afro-American Composers' or 'Harlem Renaissance Man': The New Negro and the Musical Poetics of William Grant Still." *Arkansas Historical Quarterly* 53 (Spring 1994): 42–74.

Smith, Catherine Parsons. *William Grant Still*. Champaign: University of Illinois Press, 2008.

———. *William Grant Still: A Study in Contradictions*. Berkeley: University of California Press, 2000.

Still, Judith Anne, Celeste Anne Headlee, and Lisa M. Headlee-Huffman, eds. *William Grant Still and the Fusion of Cultures in American Music*. 2nd ed. Flagstaff, AZ: The Master-Player Library, 1995.

Still, Judith Anne, Michael J. Dabrishus, and Carolyn L. Quinn. *William Grant Still: A Bio-Bibliography*. Westport, CT: Greenwood Press, 1996.

Still, William Grant. *My Life, My Words: The Autobiography of William Grant Still*. Flagstaff, AZ: The Master-Player Library, 2011.

William Grant Still and Verna Arvey Papers. Special Collections. University of Arkansas Libraries, Fayetteville, Arkansas.

Williams, Nancy A., ed. *Arkansas Biography: A Collection of Notable Lives*. Fayetteville: University of Arkansas Press, 2000.

Michael J. Dabrishus

This entry, originally published in *Arkansas Biography: A Collection of Notable Lives*, appears in the *Encyclopedia of Arkansas Music* in an altered form. *Arkansas Biography* is available from the University of Arkansas Press in Fayetteville.

William Grant Still Noteworthy Works
From the Black Belt (1926)
From the Land of Dreams (1924)
Darker America (1924–1925)
From the Journal of a Wanderer (1924)
La Guiablesse (1926–1927)
Levee Land (1925)
Afro-American Symphony (1930–1931)
A Deserted Plantation (1933)
Land of Superstition (1933)
Ebon Chronicle (1934)
Down Yonder (circa 1935)
Beyond Tomorrow (1936)
Blues from Lennox Avenue (circa 1937)
Symphony in G Minor (performed 1937)
New York World's Fair *Song of a City* (1939–1940)
And They Lynched Him on a Tree (performed 1940)
Plain-Chant for America (performed 1941)
The Colored Soldiers Who Died for Democracy (performed 1944)
Poem for Orchestra (performed 1944)
Festive Overture (performed 1945)
Troubled Island (performed 1949)

SUNDOWN TO SUNUP GOSPEL SING

The Sundown to Sunup Gospel Sing, an outdoor gospel music event, was held on the first weekend in August in Springdale (Washington and Benton counties) starting in 1969. During that time, the event was billed as the "largest outdoor gospel sing." It was later named for its founder, gospel songwriter Albert Edward Brumley of Powell, Missouri, who penned such well-known songs as "I'll Fly Away" and "Turn Your Radio On."

The idea for the Sundown to Sunup Gospel Sing was conceived after a gospel singing event in Bentonville (Benton County) in 1968. Brumley and his sons, Bill and Bob, worked with Springdale Chamber of Commerce president Lee Zachary to bring the event to Springdale's Parsons Stadium in 1969. That first year, the singing was a one-night event. A flat-bed truck served as the stage for performers, with stacked chicken crates as steps leading to the stage. About 1,000 people attended, netting about $100 profit, which was split between the Brumleys and the event's sponsoring organization, the Springdale Chamber of Commerce.

In 1972, a second night was added to the singing. A third night was added in 1977. In 1993 the event was expanded to four nights. Several nationally known gospel groups sang each evening.

The list of performers over the years includes the Oak Ridge Boys, Bill Gaither, the Blackwood Brothers, and the Kingsmen.

The Saturday session lived up to the event's name, with groups literally performing all night long. The popularity of the Sundown to Sunup Gospel Sing peaked in the early 1990s, when attendance over the four days averaged 30,000. By that time, the event had expanded to include a golf tournament, a talent contest, and an old-fashioned singing school.

In 2002, the event moved to an air-conditioned indoor venue on the campus of the University of Arkansas (UA) in Fayetteville (Washington County). In 2006, the event moved to Lebanon, Missouri, where it is known as the Albert E. Brumley Memorial Gospel Sing.

For additional information:

Albert E. Brumley & Sons Inc. http://www.brumleymusic. com (accessed February 14, 2013).

Fredrick, Leon. "25th Brumley Gospel Sing Becomes Four-Day Event at Springdale." *Ozark Mountaineer* 41 (July/August 1993): 38–39.

Hall, Kay. "Gospel Sing Had Shaky Start." *Springdale Morning News*, July 13, 1996, p. 6A.

Hively, Kay, and Albert E. Brumley Jr. *I'll Fly Away: The Life Story of Albert E. Brumley.* Branson, MO: Mountaineer Books, 1990.

Susan Young

ROOSEVELT "THE HONEYDRIPPER" SYKES (1906–1983)

Roosevelt Sykes was a leading blues pianist in the 1930s and is considered by many in the music world to be the father of the modern blues piano style. Sykes's early musical experiences in Arkansas provided the blues background that served as the foundation for his later recording successes. He was a professional bluesman for more than sixty years, recorded on a dozen different labels, and played in St. Louis, Missouri; Chicago, Illinois; Memphis, Tennessee; New Orleans, Louisiana; and Europe.

Roosevelt Sykes was born the son of a musician on January 31, 1906, in the sawmill town of Elmar (Phillips County). By 1909, the Sykes family had moved to St. Louis. However, Sykes often visited his grandfather's farm near West Helena (Phillips County), where he began playing the church organ around the age of ten. By 1918, Sykes was also playing blues piano.

Around the age of fifteen, Sykes began playing

piano in barrelhouses and juke joints in Helena (Phillips County). Later in his life, Sykes commented: "When I did get started, I wouldn't do nothing else, just play piano....If I didn't play, I didn't eat." Sykes developed his technique while listening to Helena's piano players of the 1920s. In 1925, Sykes met Leothus Lee "Pork Chops" Green while Green was playing piano in West Helena. Green mentored Sykes in a style known as "The Forty-four Blues," which was characterized by separate bass and treble rhythms.

Although Sykes moved to St. Louis and began recording tunes such as his version of "Forty-four Blues" in 1929, he was no stranger to the Arkansas blues scene. By the mid-1930s, Helena was the blues capital of the Delta, and Sykes, along with Green, played in gambling dens along Walnut Street and the side streets closer to the river. Sykes also played in Memphis, St. Louis, and Chicago during the 1930s and, at this time, became known as the "Honeydripper," a nickname given to him by a female blues singer because of his outgoing personality. Sykes recorded hits such as his 1936 "Driving Wheel Blues" and his 1937 "Night Time is the Right Time" during this period.

In 1941, Sykes moved to Chicago and recorded for several labels, including sessions with fellow Arkansan Robert "Washboard Sam" Brown. While in Chicago in 1943, Sykes formed his own band, the Honeydrippers. The band had as many as a dozen members, including many horn players, and this significantly altered Sykes's playing style. As the popularity of the blues declined in the 1950s, Sykes moved to New Orleans in 1954 and played in small clubs. After moving back to Chicago in 1960 amidst a folk music revival, Sykes toured Europe and played the American Folk Blues Festival in the 1960s. Sykes moved back to New Orleans in the late 1960s and played in clubs such as the Court of the Two Sisters.

Sykes continued to play blues piano until he died of a heart attack in New Orleans on July 17, 1983. He was inducted into the Blues Foundation's Blues Hall of Fame in 1999.

For additional information:
Cohn, Lawrence, ed. *Nothing But the Blues: The Music and the Musicians*. New York: Abbeville Press, 1993.
Palmer, Robert. *Deep Blues*. New York: Viking Press, 1981.

Jamie Metrailer

T-U

GOSPEL / CONTEMPORARY CHRISTIAN JOHN MICHAEL TALBOT (1954–)

John Michael Talbot—the founder and leader of the Brothers and Sisters of Charity at the Little Portion Hermitage near Eureka Springs (Carroll County)—is one of the preeminent Catholic musicians in the world, with more than fifty albums to his name. He is also the founder of the Catholic Association of Musicians and the author of more than a dozen books on Christian meditations and music.

John Michael Talbot was born in Oklahoma City, Oklahoma, on May 8, 1954, to Jamie Margaret Cochran Talbot and Richard Talbot. The family moved to Little Rock (Pulaski County) when Talbot was seven years old and then to Indianapolis, Indiana, two years later. Struggling to make friends in Indianapolis, the family started playing music as a way to be a part of the community. Talbot and his two siblings formed a band with two others, calling themselves the Quinchords with Talbot playing guitar, banjo, dobro, and several kinds of drums.

With changes to the lineup, the Quinchords became Four Score and then Sounds Unlimited, with Talbot on rhythm guitar and vocals. Talbot's sister Tanni eventually dropped out, but Talbot and brother Terry remained band mates, eventually forming Mason Proffit around 1968. The folk-rock-country band performed with major bands, including Pink Floyd, the Grateful Dead, Iron Butterfly, and Fleetwood Mac, and had hits such as "Two Hangmen" and "A Thousand and Two."

Talbot, at age seventeen, married a woman named Nancy in Indianapolis in 1971; their daughter, Amy Noel, was born in 1974. The couple divorced a few years later.

Becoming disillusioned with rock and roll and believing that he had seen a vision of Christ holding out tattered monk's robes to him, Talbot had his final tour with Mason Proffit in 1973. During that tour, the band played at the Ozark Mountain Folk Fair near Eureka Springs, and

John Michael Talbot at St. Paul Church in Pocahontas at the end of his "The Living Water 50th Recording Tour"; 2008.
Courtesy: Arkansas Catholic

Talbot bought a parcel of land in the Ozark Mountains.

After recording an album with Terry as the Talbot Brothers for Warner Bros., Talbot began his career as a Christian recording artist with the newly formed Sparrow Records in 1976, recording his first solo album, *John Michael Talbot*. His second solo album was *New Earth*.

Following his divorce, Talbot's religious study and spiritual searching eventually led him to Franciscan priest Martin Wolter at Alverna, a Franciscan retreat center near Indianapolis, where Talbot was living with his parents. In 1978, he became a Roman Catholic in the Third Order of St. Francis (this order of "Secular Franciscans" includes vowed and non-vowed members, as well as married couples). After recording one of his bestselling albums, *The Lord's Supper* (1979), Talbot built a hermitage in the woods near Alverna, where he spent the winter of 1978–79, and he then went on a pilgrimage to the Middle East. Subsequent albums released on the Sparrow/Birdwing label were *Come to the Quiet*, *The Painter*, *For the Bride*, *Troubadour of the Great King*, *Light Eternal*, and *No Longer Strangers*. After a trip to Ireland in 1982, he recorded *God of Life* (1984), which featured Celtic-influenced music.

Wanting to build and lead a community, Talbot started a community called Charity, which was later renamed the Little Portion House of Prayer, at Alverna. In 1982, construction began on the land he owned in the Ozarks of what would become the Little Portion Hermitage and the Motherhouse of the community called the Brothers and Sisters of Charity. The Little Portion community moved to Eureka Springs the same year. The property was designed by noted Arkansas architect E. Fay Jones. Initial construction and landscaping were completed in 1983. The community is mostly self supporting, but Talbot's music career is one of its main sources of income. Little Portion has a unique status in the U.S. Catholic Church, being a Church-approved community of celibate men, celibate women, and married couples.

Talbot's first digital album, *The Heart of the Shepherd*, was released in 1987. *Quiet Reflections* (1987), *The Regathering* (1988), and *Hiding Place* (1990) followed.

After the annulment of his first marriage, and despite some controversy in the Catholic community, Talbot married former nun Viola Pratka on February 17, 1989; the marriage was blessed by Bishop Andrew McDonald of Little Rock (Pulaski County). The state of their Franciscan vows was such that there was no religious reason the couple could not marry. Talbot's biographer Dan O'Neill called Talbot and Pratka "examples of radical monastic living in Catholic marriage as well."

Talbot continued to tour and release albums, including a series called *Come Worship the Lord* and a Christmas album recorded in London, England, with an orchestra and boys' choir. In 1990, Talbot left Sparrow Records because he felt that money, rather than God, was too much the focus of contemporary Christian music. He started his own label, Troubadour For The Lord, in 1990, recording *Master Musician* (1992), *Meditations in the Spirit* (1993), and *Meditations from Solitude* (1994). In 1995, he embarked on a bus tour of the United States, and he subsequently recorded the six-disc *Pathways* (1998) instrumental project and *Table of Plenty* (1997), which included world music.

Around this time, Talbot instituted "Itinerant Prayer Walks," the first being from the Little Portion Hermitage to Little Rock (about 200 miles). The walks are often done in conjunction with Talbot's concerts. Talbot and the Little Portion Hermitage are supporters of Mercy Corps International, which provides emergency and humanitarian aid around the world. Talbot founded the Catholic Association of Musicians (CAM) in 1996; CAM's annual conference is held at Little Portion Hermitage.

In addition to his work as a recording artist, Talbot has published more than a dozen books, including *The Joy of Music Ministry* (2001), *The World Is My Cloister* (2010), and *The Universal Monk: The Way of the New Monastics* (2011). In 2011, he released an album called *Worship and Bow Down*.

In 2001, EMI Records gave Talbot an award to recognize his twenty-five years of Christian

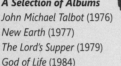

music ministry. In 2005, Talbot was inducted into the Arkansas Entertainers Hall of Fame.

For additional information:
John Michael Talbot. http://www.johnmichaeltalbot.com/
(accessed March 9, 2013).
O'Neill, Dan. *Signatures: The Story of John Michael Talbot.* Revised ed. Berryville, AR: Troubadour For The Lord Publishing, 2003.

Ali Welky

BLUES / R&B	# JOHNNIE TAYLOR (1934–2000)

Johnnie Harrison Taylor was a popular gospel and rhythm and blues singer, known as the "Philosopher of Soul," whose recording career spanned forty-six years. His single, "Disco Lady," was the first single ever to be certified platinum.

Johnnie Taylor was born in Crawfordsville (Crittenden County) on May 5, 1934. The official date of his birth was not revealed until after his death; he had long claimed to be four years younger. The youngest of three siblings, he was raised by his grandmother in West Memphis (Crittenden County). She was religious and made sure he attended church regularly. He made his church singing debut at age six, and inspired by both gospel and the blues, he decided at a young age that he wanted to make a living by singing.

Taylor moved to Kansas City, Missouri, at age ten with his grandmother, and during his teen years, sang with a gospel quartet, the Melody Kings. They occasionally opened for the famous, highly influential gospel group, the Soul Stirrers, whose young lead singer, Sam Cooke, befriended Taylor.

By 1953, Taylor had moved to Chicago, Illinois, and was singing with the doo-wop group the Five Echoes, with whom he made his first recordings on the VeeJay label. Shortly afterward, he also began singing with the Highway QCs, a long-running, popular gospel quartet in which Cooke and Lou Rawls had previously been members. The QCs made their recording debut in 1955 with Taylor singing lead on "Somewhere to Lay My Head," which made the group a nationwide gospel attraction.

When Cooke left the Soul Stirrers, Taylor was chosen to be his replacement in 1957. While a member of the group, he became an ordained minister and preached his first sermon at Fellowship Baptist Church in Chicago.

After a wreck in which he ran over a little girl in 1960, Taylor was booted from the Soul Stirrers and went to Los Angeles, California, intending to preach full time. In 1963, however, Cooke signed him as the first artist on his new SAR label, and Taylor, still stinging from being kicked out of the Soul Stirrers and determined to find his place in the music marketplace, began recording secular music. His first solo single was "A Whole Lot of Woman" in 1961. Other notable early R&B recordings were "Rome (Wasn't Built in a Day)" (1962) and "Baby We've Got Love" (1963), which was his first song to appear on *Billboard* magazine's Top 100 chart. The label folded after Cooke's death in 1964.

In 1966, Taylor signed with Stax Records in Memphis, Tennessee, where Stax executive and native Arkansan Al Bell of North Little Rock (Pulaski County), dubbed him the "Philosopher of Soul." At Stax, Taylor polished his musical style, which combined gospel, R&B, and blues, as well as his flamboyant appearance, and he proceeded to become one of the label's top-selling performers, outselling such big stars as Otis Redding and Carla Thomas. He had a prolific run on the R&B charts, beginning with "I Had A Dream" (1966). His first song on the Stax label to break the pop Top 100 was "Somebody's Sleeping in My Bed" (1967).

In 1968, Taylor had his first major crossover pop and R&B hit in "Who's Making Love," a funk/soul song that went to number one on the R&B charts and hit number five on the pop charts. The success of "Who's Making Love" enabled Taylor to hire a superb, permanent touring band for the first time in his career, and he became a major performer on the "Chitlin' Circuit" all across the South. Subsequent hits included "Take Care of Your Homework" (1969), "Jody's Got Your Girl and Gone" (1971), "I Believe in You (You Believe in Me)" (1972), and "Cheaper to Keep Her" (1973). By this time, he had perfected his style of smooth, soulful crooning, which incorporated gospel, blues, and soul.

When Stax Records went bankrupt in 1975, Taylor signed with CBS/Columbia. In 1976, he released his first CBS album, titled *Eargasm*, which contained his biggest hit, "Disco Lady," which went to number one on both the R&B and pop charts and became the first single ever to be certified platinum, selling more than two million copies. CBS pushed him to record more tunes in the disco genre, not taking advantage of the full range of his talent. His record sales slipped, and he began to look for another label.

In 1982, Taylor signed with Beverly Glen Records and got back on the R&B charts with "What About My Love." In 1984, he signed with Malaco Records and became one of its most popular artists. He released a succession of hit R&B albums for the label, beginning with *This Is Your Night*. His 1996 album, *Good Love*, topped *Billboard*'s blues charts on the strength of the single "Last Two Dollars," and the album became the biggest seller in Malaco history. Taylor released his final album, *Gotta Get the Groove Back*, in 1999. In that same year, he was given a Pioneer Award by the Rhythm and Blues Foundation.

While living in Duncanville, Texas, a suburb of Dallas, Taylor suffered a heart attack, and on May 31, 2000, he died at Charleton Methodist Hospital in Dallas.

He is buried at Forest Hill Cemetery in Kansas City, Missouri.

For additional information:

George-Warren, Holly, and Patricia Romanowski, eds. *The Rolling Stone Encyclopedia of Rock & Roll*. New York: Rolling Stone Press, 2001.

Hildebrand, Lee. "J. T." From the liner notes to *Johnnie Taylor—Lifetime: A Retrospective of Soul, Blues & Gospel, 1956–1999*. Stax Records, 2000.

"Johnnie Taylor." AllMusic.com. http://www.allmusic.com/artist/johnnie-taylor-mn0000198162 (accessed February 26, 2013).

Obituary of Johnnie Taylor. *Dallas Morning News*, June 2, 2000.

"The Philosopher of Soul, Johnnie Taylor, Dies at 62." BluesMusicNow.com. http://www.bluesmusicnow.com/taylor60.html (accessed February 8, 2013).

Bryan Rogers

GOSPEL / CONTEMPORARY CHRISTIAN — "SISTER ROSETTA" THARPE (1915–1973)

Arkansas native Rosetta Nubin Tharpe was one of gospel music's first superstars, the first gospel performer to record for a major record label (Decca), and an early crossover from gospel to secular music. Tharpe has been cited as an influence by numerous musicians, including Bob Dylan, Little Richard, Elvis Presley, and Arkansan Johnny Cash.

Rosetta Nubin was born in Cotton Plant (Woodruff County) on March 20, 1915, to Katie Bell Nubin, an evangelist, singer, and mandolin player for the Church of God in Christ (COGIC). No mention is found of her father. Nubin began performing at age four, playing guitar and singing "Jesus Is on the Main Line." By age six, Nubin appeared regularly with her mother, performing a mix of gospel and secular music styles that would eventually make her famous. As a youth, she could sing and keep on pitch and hold a melody. Her vocal qualities, however, paled beside her abilities on the guitar—she played individual tones, melodies, and riffs instead of just strumming chords. This talent was all the more remarkable because, at the time, few African-American women played guitar.

Nubin's guitar style was influenced by her mother's mandolin playing, pianist Arizona Dranes, and composer Florence Price, with whom Rosetta studied in Cotton Plant. She also sang the popular hymns of the day, including the compositions of bluesman turned gospel musician Thomas A. Dorsey. Indeed, elements of the blues are readily apparent in Nubin's guitar styling. Later, Nubin's music would be influenced by her work with jazz greats Lucky Milliner and Cab Calloway.

Billed as the "singing and guitar-playing miracle," Nubin was an added attraction at her mother's church services. Both mother and daughter worked as members of an evangelistic troupe that worked throughout the South before arriving in Chicago, Illinois, in the late 1920s. There they became part of the growing Holiness movement, a late nineteenth-century offshoot of the Pentecostal denomination which, in the 1890s, led to the formation of COGIC and other new religious groups.

After several years of working with her mother and on the advice of several Chicago promoters, Nubin moved to New York in the mid-1930s. She married minister Thomas A. Thorpe in 1934. The marriage was short-lived; after their divorce, Rosetta kept the last name, changing the spelling to "Tharpe" for use as her stage name. Later, in the 1940s, Tharpe was married

"Sister Rosetta" Tharpe Hit Songs

"This Train" (1938)

"Hide Me in Thy Bosom" released as "Rock Me" (1938)

"Trouble in Mind" (1941/1942)

"Shout, Sister, Shout" (1941/1942)

"Strange Things Happening Every Day" (1944)

"That's All" (1941/1942)

"Didn't It Rain" (1947)

"Up Above My Head" (1947)

a second time, to promoter Fosh Allen.

Tharpe was signed to Decca Records in 1938 and was successful immediately. Versions of Thomas A. Dorsey's "This Train" and "Hide Me in Thy Bosom," released as "Rock Me," were smash hits featuring Tharpe on guitar and Lucky Millinder's jazz orchestra as accompaniment. These releases started a trend for Tharpe, who recorded both traditional numbers for her gospel fan base and up-tempo, secular-influenced tunes for her growing white audience.

The popularity of her singles led to Tharpe's inclusion in John Hammond's black music extravaganza, "From Spirituals to Swing," held in Carnegie Hall in New York City on December 23, 1938. After this well-publicized event, Tharpe went on a concert tour throughout the northeast. She also recorded with Cab Calloway to some success but fared better with "Trouble in Mind," "Shout, Sister, Shout," and "That's All"—all recorded with Lucius "Lucky" Millinder's jazz orchestra in 1941 and 1942. Tharpe's popularity was so great that she was only one of two black gospel acts—the other was the Dixie Hummingbirds—to record "V-Discs" for U.S. troops overseas. In the late 1940s, Tharpe returned to more strictly religious songs, recording "Didn't It Rain" (1947) and "Up Above My Head" (1947) with Marie Knight. From 1944 to 1951, her main accompanist was Samuel "Sammy" Blythe Price, a boogie-woogie pianist from Texas. His trio backed her on "Strange Things Happening Every Day," a top ten "race record."

Tharpe continued her success in the religious market. Such was Tharpe's popularity that on July 3, 1951, 25,000 people paid to witness Tharpe's third marriage to Russell Morrison, her manager, in a ceremony held at Washington DC's Griffith Stadium.

Tharpe and Marie Knight parted ways after unsuccessfully trying to enter the blues music market. As a result of the foray into the pop music market, Tharpe's popularity waned; soon her concert dates dropped off, and she lost her recording contract with Decca. Tharpe kept working and had signed with Mercury Records by the late 1950s. She first toured Europe in 1957 and made return trips in the 1960s, making several live recordings while overseas. Although she never realized

her comeback, Tharpe continued to perform. A stroke in 1970 necessitated a leg amputation and caused speech difficulties, but it merely slowed her down. Tharpe continued to tour and perform until her death in Philadelphia, Pennsylvania, on October 9, 1973.

Tharpe's music and influence continue years after her death. Her songs have been recorded by Elvis Presley, and Johnny Cash spoke of her impact on his music. In 1998, the U.S. Postal Service issued a Rosetta Tharpe postage stamp. In 2003, the album *Shout, Sister Shout: A Tribute to Sister Rosetta Tharpe* was released, with versions of Tharpe's songs performed by female artists including Maria Muldaur, Odetta, and Marcia Ball.

In 2013, the PBS series *American Masters* featured an episode on Tharpe, and she was inducted into the Arkansas Entertainers Hall of Fame.

For additional information:

Boyer, Horace Clarence. *The Golden Age of Gospel*. Urbana: University of Illinois Press, 2000.

Jackson, Jerma. *Singing in My Soul: Black Gospel Music in a Secular Age*. Chapel Hill: University of North Carolina Press, 2000.

Wald, Gayle F. *Shout, Sister, Shout!: The Untold Story of Rock-and-Roll Trailblazer Sister Rosetta Tharpe*. Boston: Beacon Press, 2007.

———. "Sister Rosetta Tharpe: Remembering Rosetta." *Living Blues* 34 (November–December 2003): 106–113.

William K. McNeil
Terry Buckalew

This entry, originally published in *Arkansas Biography: A Collection of Notable Lives*, appears in the *Encyclopedia of Arkansas Music* in an altered form. *Arkansas Biography* is available from the University of Arkansas Press in Fayetteville.

Gospel performer and recording artist "Sister Rosetta" Tharpe.
Artists: Patterson and Barnes / From the Old State House Museum Collection

TOP OF THE ROCK CHORUS

The Top of the Rock Chorus is the Little Rock (Pulaski County) chapter of Sweet Adelines International, the female barbershop singing group. The chorus was formed on February 7, 1961, and two original members sang with Top of the Rock until 2005. The group was originally called Little Rock Chorus and was renamed Top of the Rock Chorus in the 1980s. It is composed of about sixty women—ages thirteen to eighty-six—who rehearse weekly and compete annually against other female choruses and quartets in Region 25 (Arkansas, Louisiana, Missouri, Oklahoma, and Texas), the Heart of America Region.

Sweet Adelines International was formed on July 13, 1945, in Tulsa, Oklahoma. A few women wanted to participate in the "chord-ringing, fun-filled harmony" that their husbands—members of the relatively new Society for the Preservation and Encouragement of Barber Shop Quartet Singing in America—were singing.

In addition to the main chorus, a smaller group is called Piece of the Rock. This group has lower performance fees and often can fit in venues where the full chorus cannot. The chorus also has several quartets. All groups perform for a wide variety of events, from the capitol lighting ceremonies in Little Rock during the winter holidays to convention banquets and birthday parties.

Among the ways the chorus raises money are annual dues, paid performances, and two annual shows: Hot August Night and Jingle Jam. The chorus cooperates with the men's barbershop chorus—the Diamond State Chorus—by selling "singing Valentines" in February.

Top of the Rock Chorus at the Region 25 competition in 2006. Courtesy: Ellen E. Withers

At competition, choruses are judged in the categories of sound, music, showmanship, and expression. The chorus has won the region's chorus competition five times and the Harmony Achievement Award for best small chorus at the international convention in 2000. Over the past fifty years, the group has consistently ranked in the top five choruses in Region 25. As either a regional champion or wildcard selection, Top of the Rock Chorus has represented its region internationally eight times. Quartets from the chorus have won many awards, including regional honors. Director Peggy Gram's quartet, Rumors, won the international quartet championship in 1999.

Gram became director in 1972, when she was twenty-two. Kelly Causey replaced her as director in 2006.

The chorus has produced three recordings of its songs—in 1995, 2001, and a Christmas album in 2002.

For additional information:

Top of the Rock Chorus. http://www.topoftherockchorus.com (accessed February 23, 2013).

Withers, Ellen. "Directing to Success: Two Women from Maumelle Conduct Top of the Rock Chorus to International Competition." *Arkansas Democrat-Gazette*, River Valley and Ozark Edition, May 1, 2005, p. 1.

C. Dennis Schick

ALPHONSO "PHONNIE" TRENT (1902–1959)

Alphonso E. "Phonnie" Trent was a nationally renowned jazz pianist and "territory" band leader from Fort Smith (Sebastian County). ("Territory" bands were those that traveled outside the large eastern markets, such as New York City.) He led the Alphonso Trent Orchestra, a group of young African-American musicians who toured the country, made several recordings, and had a lengthy engagement at the Adolphus Hotel in Dallas, Texas. During that engagement, the band became the first group of black musicians to be featured on regional broadcasts over WFAA radio in Dallas.

Alphonso Trent was born in Fort Smith on October 24, 1902, the son of E. O. Trent and Hattie S. Smith. Trent's father was one of the first African-American graduates of Ohio State University. He settled in Arkansas, eventually becoming principal of Fort Smith's Lincoln High School in 1886.

Trent began his musical education at an early age, studying piano with local musician Professor W. O. Wiley. While still in his teens, Trent gained valuable experience as a pianist working around western Arkansas and eastern Oklahoma in Sterling Todd's Rose City Orchestra and the Quinn Band. Because his father was a prominent educator, Trent received a strong classroom education and, in the fall of 1923, moved to Little Rock (Pulaski County) to attend Shorter College in North Little Rock (Pulaski County).

Shortly after arriving in the capital city, he began working with a group led by Eugene Crooke, called the Syncho Six. The group featured pianist Trent, Crooke playing banjo, trumpeter Edwin Swayzee, saxophonist James Jeter, vocalist John Fielding, and drummer A. G. Godley. Legendary jazz trombonist Leo "Snub" Mosley, then only fifteen years old, joined the band for a show in Helena (Phillips County). Because of Trent's strong musical leadership and his skill at booking engagements, the band's name was changed to the Alphonso Trent Orchestra.

In the spring of 1925, the band set out for Texas, playing street corners for nickels and dimes and an occasional dance engagement. They arrived in Dallas and played numerous low-paying dance jobs. A bellman from the Adolphus Hotel heard Trent's orchestra at a dance. On his recommendation, the manager of the hotel booked the group for a two-week engagement in the hotel's second ballroom. The two weeks stretched into eighteen months, a record length of time unequaled by any other African-American band in the region.

As a result of the Adolphus engagement, Trent and his orchestra received exposure through broadcasts over the 50,000-watt radio station, WFAA. Trent's broadcasts from the Adolphus were the first for an African-American orchestra and reached an audience throughout the central United States and Canada.

The long engagement at the Adolphus provided the musicians a chance to rehearse and refine their musical identity. The band, which had grown to eleven musicians, had been founded as a co-op unit, a practice that was common with bands in the Southwest. All members received the same pay and were expected to contribute ideas to the development of the musical arrangements.

Under Trent's musical direction, the band emphasized good tone quality (actual tone or timbre of the instruments), intonation (tuning of notes and chords), and showmanship. During the Adolphus engagement, Trent married Dallas native Essie Mae Grissom, whom he had met at a party held in the band's honor. The couple never had children, but Trent had a son, Alphonso B. Trent, born in 1922 to a woman in Fort Smith.

Alphonso "Phonnie" Trent, a jazz pianist who led a band in the 1920s that became one of the most respected in the pre-swing era.
Courtesy: Arkansas History Commission

In the summer of 1926, Trent's orchestra left the Adolphus and toured major hotels throughout the state of Texas. The orchestra performed at the opening of a new hotel in San Antonio, the Plaza, and also performed at the inaugural ball of Texas's first woman governor, Miriam A. Ferguson, in 1925.

Trent's orchestra toured Texas, Arkansas, Louisiana, and Mississippi until October 1927. For the next two years, the Alphonso Trent Orchestra played in Cincinnati, Ohio; Louisville, Kentucky; Lexington, Kentucky; Buffalo, New York; and other cities. During this time, the band made its first recordings, four songs for the Gennett Company in Richmond, Indiana. The band's publicity materials often mention recordings for the Brunswick label, but neither recordings nor information concerning the sessions have ever been located.

In the summer of 1929, the Alphonso Trent Orchestra performed at a resort in Port Stanley, Ontario. At the close of the engagement, the band headed for its one and only date in New York City, a two-week stint at the Savoy Ballroom. At the end of the two weeks, Meyer Davis offered Trent an extended run at the Arcadia Ballroom, but he refused, opting instead for a higher-paying job at the Plantation Club in Cleveland, Ohio. Trent was also fearful that other bands would steal away his musicians, a practice common among band leaders of the era.

During the engagement in early 1930 at the Plantation Club, a fire of suspicious origins

Advertisement for the Alphonso Trent Orchestra, highlighting recordings, compositions, members, and engagements.
Courtesy: Henry Q. Rinne

consumed the establishment and destroyed the orchestra's instruments and library. According to accounts by members of the band, a fight between rival gangs had led to an altercation between Trent and one of the gang members. As retaliation, the gang had set fire to the club.

The disastrous fire, combined with the onset of the Great Depression, caused severe hardship and contributed to the band's ultimate demise. After the fire, the band was stranded in Cleveland without instruments. Trent's family came to the rescue, purchasing new instruments for the group so that they could resume their careers. Jobs during these times were scarce, and the band hobbled back to Fort Smith. Trent kept his musicians busy, however, using his hometown as a base of operations.

The Alphonso Trent Orchestra made one last road trip in the winter of 1932–33, but Trent did not accompany them. It was not long, however, before Trent had another band on the road, a small group touring the Dakotas, Wyoming, Colorado, and Texas during the 1930s and early 1940s. He continued to promote young musical talent, including pioneering jazz guitarist Charlie Christian.

After World War II, Trent settled permanently in Fort Smith to manage the family's real estate holdings and, beginning in 1953, the city's first housing project, Elm Grove Homes. He remained active in the music business but restricted his performances to local nightclubs.

Alphonso Trent died of a heart attack in Fort Smith on October 14, 1959. He is buried in the city's Oak Cemetery.

For additional information:

"Alphonso Trent and His Orchestra." Red Hot Jazz Archive. http://www.redhotjazz.com/trent.html (accessed February 6, 2013).

Fitzgerald, Sarah. "Alphonso Trent—One of the Best." *Journal of the Fort Smith Historical Society* 8 (April 1984): 3–6. Online at http://library.uafortsmith.edu/fshsj/08-01_Complete_Issue.pdf (accessed February 6, 2013).

Rice, Marc. "Frompin' in the Great Plains: Listening and Dancing to the Jazz Orchestras of Alphonso Trent, 1925–44." *Great Plains Quarterly* 16 (Spring 1996): 107–115.

Rinne, Henry. "A Short History of the Alphonso Trent Orchestra." *Arkansas Historical Quarterly* 45 (Autumn 1986): 228–249.

Henry Q. Rinne

This entry, originally published in *Arkansas Biography: A Collection of Notable Lives*, appears in the *Encyclopedia of Arkansas Music* in an altered form. *Arkansas Biography* is available from the University of Arkansas Press in Fayetteville.

FOLK | # TROUT FISHING IN AMERICA

Trout Fishing in America (TFIA), based in northwestern Arkansas, is a musical performance duo consisting of Keith Grimwood, who plays bass and sings, and Ezra Idlet, who sings and plays acoustic guitar and banjo. The name of the duo comes from the seminal 1960s experimental novella by Richard Brautigan. Trout Fishing in America has been nominated for four

Grammys and has released more than twenty albums.

Grimwood has been a bass player since the age of eleven. He earned a degree in music from the University of Houston and performed with the Houston Symphony. Idlet, a guitarist since the age of fourteen, performed as a strolling musician at a Houston dinner theater. The two met as members of the Houston-based folk/rock band St. Elmo's Fire, which Grimwood joined after the Houston Symphony went on strike in 1976. In 1979, the group disbanded after a disastrous tour of California, and Grimwood and Idlet began playing on the streets of Santa Cruz in order to feed themselves. In an interview with *Acoustic Guitar*, Idlet says about this time, "We learned a valuable lesson. People will stop if they're entertained, but if you're singing these sad introspective songs, people will walk away as fast as they can." The duo soon formed Trout Fishing in America, which was originally located in Houston but moved to the Prairie Grove (Washington County) area of Arkansas in 1992.

When the compact disc (CD) revolution took place, TFIA formed Trout Records and began to record and market its own music successfully. The band's style is eclectic, mixing folk/pop and family music with reggae, blues, jazz, Latin, and classical influences. Many of the songs focus on children's themes, featuring catchy tunes with lyrics on topics as broad as the importance of family to a humorous song about a booger monster. The song "When I Was a Dinosaur" became a favorite of radio disc jockey Dr. Demento, who played it frequently on his radio program.

TFIA has received four Grammy Award nominations in the Best Musical Album for Children category for *inFINity* (2001), *Merry Fishes to All* (2004), the 2006 live performance release *My Best Day*, and *Big Round World* (2008). In addition, TFIA recordings have garnered three National Indie Awards: one in 1992 for *Over the Limit*, which helped the band achieve national distribution for its label, Trout Records; one in 1995 for *Mine!*; and one in 1997 for *My World*. The band has also won several Parents' Choice Gold and American Library Association Awards. In June 2008, TFIA was chosen by *Performing Songwriter Magazine* as one of the top 100 most influential independent artists in the past fifteen years. TFIA was also inducted into the Kerrville Folk Festival Hall of Fame.

The duo tours extensively to more than forty states and several Canadian provinces. In addition to touring, TFIA also conducts song-writing workshops for teachers and students in schools. In an interview with National Public Radio, the duo described its music as for kids and adults. About the eclectic nature of the band's music, Grimwood said, "You can do that if you call it children's music. If you're playing adults' music you're not allowed to play...different styles." The two have said that they try to avoid writing songs that tell kids what to do or think. Instead, they take a lighter tone with songs, including: "It's Mine," "Why I Pack My Lunch," and "My Hair Had a Party Last Night." These songs are meant to appeal to adults as well as children, but the duo writes music for adults as well. In an interview with Shelton Clark for *Bassics Magazine*, Grimwood stated that, "Adults recognize similar things that they've experienced. I think that's why we appeal to a lot of generations."

For additional information:

Hill, Jack W. "State Duo Gets Grammy Nod." *Arkansas Democrat-Gazette*, February 8, 2009, p. 4E.

Hill, Jack W. "Singing Duo Now Writers with Chicken Book, CD." *Arkansas Democrat-Gazette*, May 17, 2009, pp. 1E, 3E.

Trout Fishing in America. http://www.troutmusic.com/ (accessed February 26, 2013).

C. L. Bledsoe

Trout Fishing in America's Ezra Idlet (left) on guitar and Keith Grimwood on bass.   Courtesy: Trout Records.

CONWAY TWITTY (1933–1993)

A member of the Country Music Hall of Fame, Conway Twitty has sold over 50 million records. Twitty had anywhere from forty-one to fifty-three No. 1 singles on the country and rock charts, depending upon the industry source used. He recorded 110 albums.

Harold Lloyd Jenkins was born on September 1, 1933, in Friars Point, Mississippi, and was named after the famous silent film actor, Harold Lloyd. Jenkins had an older brother and sister. He was given his first guitar at age four. The family moved to Helena (Phillips County)—now Helena-West Helena—when Jenkins was ten, and soon thereafter, he formed his first band, the Phillips County Ramblers. His father worked off and on as a Mississippi riverboat captain, though his mother was the real breadwinner. Jenkins worked as a carhop and later had a weekly radio show. Jenkins also played baseball and was drafted by the Philadelphia Phillies after high school; he was also drafted by the military.

While stationed in Japan, Jenkins played baseball and performed with a band called the Cimmarons. After the war, Jenkins went to Memphis, Tennessee, and recorded at Sun Studios. At this point, he took the stage name of Conway Twitty, combining the names of two cities—Conway (Faulkner County) and Twitty, Texas. Twitty garnered a record deal with MGM that led to his first No. 1 hit in 1958, a rock and roll song titled "It's Only Make Believe."

Twitty also had a short-lived career in film, appearing in such films as *Sex Kittens Go to College* (1960) alongside Mamie Van Doren and *Platinum High School* (1960) with Mickey Rooney.

Though Twitty was very successful as a rock and roll performer, he preferred country music and eventually switched genres. In 1965, Twitty signed to MCA and released several singles. In 1968, "Next in Line" became his first No. 1 country single. Twitty went on to perform duets with Loretta Lynn. In 1971, they recorded *After*

Country singer Conway Twitty.
Courtesy: Old State House Museum Collection

the Fire Is Gone and went on to release several hit records.

In 1982, Twitty opened Twitty City, a tourist attraction located in Hendersonville, Tennessee. Dedicated to Twitty's work, the park included views of his mansion and the homes of his family members. Another enterprise, a fast-food restaurant named Twitty Burger, went bankrupt.

Twitty was married three times. His first marriage, to Ellen Matthews, began in 1953 and ended a year later in divorce in 1954. His second wife was Temple Maxine Jaco. They were married in 1955 and divorced in 1985. They had three children. Twitty married his third wife, Dolores Virginia Henry, in 1987.

Twitty became ill while performing a show in Branson, Missouri, and died on June 5, 1993, from an abdominal aneurysm. He was survived by his wife and four adult children. He was inducted into the Country Music Hall of Fame in 1999.

For additional information:

Cross, Wilbur, and Michael Kosser. *The Conway Twitty Story*. New York: Doubleday, 1986.
Conway Twitty. http://www.conwaytwitty.com/ (accessed

Conway Twitty:

Top of the Charts

"It's Only Make Believe," No. 1 on rock and roll charts (1958)

"Next in Line," No. 1 on country charts (1968)

Trivia

- Sold more than 50 million records
- Recorded 110 albums
- Member of the Country Music Hall of Fame
- Made his stage name by combining Conway, Arkansas, and Twitty, Texas

---

February 6, 2013).

"Conway Twitty." Country Music Hall of Fame. http://countrymusichalloffame.org/full-list-of-inductees/view/conway-twitty (accessed February 6, 2013).

"Conway Twitty." Country Music Television. http://www.cmt.com/artists/az/twitty_conway/bio.jhtml (accessed

February 6, 2013).

"Conway Twitty." Internet Movie Database. http://www.imdb.com/name/nm0878617/#actor1950 (accessed February 6, 2013).

C. L. Bledsoe

COUNTRY · T. TEXAS TYLER (1916–1972)

T. Texas Tyler, the charismatic Arkansas native with a growling voice, initiated a distinctive country and western musical style that made him a success in the recording industry and on stage in the 1940s, 1950s, and into the 1960s. He pioneered a storytelling style in which the performer spoke some or all of the lyrics, later employed by other country stars such as "Red" Sovine, Jimmy Dean, "Whispering" Bill Anderson, and others. Tex Ritter, one of Tyler's contemporaries, often referred to the influence Tyler's style had on him.

Tyler was born David Luke Myrick in Mena (Polk County) on June 20, 1916. His parents were James E. Myrick and Ida Bell Cagle Myrick. He was the youngest of three brothers. His childhood years were difficult, as the Myrick household had no electricity, no indoor plumbing, and very little furniture. His parents did menial jobs and sold eggs, butter, and vegetables on the side. The children were expected to help. His mother worked as a housekeeper, took in laundry from local families, and cared for other people's children.

Myrick never finished the eighth grade, and his teachers recalled he was often truant, either from disinterest or from having to help with family chores. During these years, he developed an interest in music. Teaching himself on a Sears Roebuck guitar (he often commented that it cost $3.98, including postage), he soon became good enough to perform in local talent shows and at dances. He left home in 1932 at age sixteen, going to Newport, Rhode Island, to live with a brother who was stationed there with the navy.

While living with his brother in the early 1930s, he obtained a non-paying program on WMBA in Newport. For the next four or five years, he traveled around the country, spending short periods at a variety of radio stations. Myrick appeared on the popular *Major Bowes Amateur Hour* radio program in 1935 while in West Virginia, and his rendition of "Silver Haired Daddy" won first place in that week's contest, jump-starting his entertainment career. He toured with one of Major Bowes's units for the next several weeks. Myrick had been using "Ozark Mountain Dave" as a stage name, but Bowes convinced him to change it to "Texas Tyler," combining the names of cowboy singers Tex Ritter and Tom Tyler. A few years later, Tyler sang a song called "I Was Only Teasing You," and an announcer introduced him as the "Teasing singer T. Texas Tyler"; the T became part of his stage name from that point on.

In early 1939, Tyler went to WCHS Charleston, West Virginia, where he entered into a partnership with a young fiddler named Clarence "Slim" Clere. The duo of Slim and Tex worked together for three years in Charleston and in Huntington, West Virginia. While in Huntington, he met and married Claudia Foster in 1942.

Tyler and Clere soon split up, and Tyler went to WMMN in Fairmont, West Virginia, where he worked individually and also with Little Jimmy Dickens. Soon thereafter, he won a spot on KWKH in Shreveport, Louisiana. He was at WIBC in Indianapolis, Indiana, when World War II interrupted his fledgling career; he served in the army until the war ended.

After his discharge in 1946, Tyler went to southern California and organized a band. He signed a contract with a small but growing Pasadena record label, Four Star. With his distinctive growl accompanied by brash honky-tonk instrumentation, he soon had some moderate hits with covers of "Filipino Baby," "Remember Me," and "Oklahoma Hills." His 1948 "Deck of Cards" topped the charts, and its recitative style was widely imitated. His next hit was "Dad Gave My Dog Away." By 1949, he had his own Los Angeles television show, *The Range Roundup*.

Tyler was soon voted by disc jockeys as one of

T. Texas Tyler Hit Songs

"Filipino Baby" (1946)
"Remember Me" (1946)
"Oklahoma Hills" (1946)
"Divorce Me C. O. D." (1947)
"Deck of Cards" (1948)
"Dad Gave My Dog Away" (1948)
"My Bucket's Got a Hole in It" (1949)
"Courtin' in the Rain" (1953)

the top country performers in the United States. In 1950, *Country Song Roundup* magazine voted his television program the best country music show of the year. He performed at Carnegie Hall in New York City and was cast in two western movies—the 1949 "Durango Kid" (Charles Starrett) Columbia production *Horsemen of the Sierras*, and the 1950 Roy Rogers Republic production *Twilight in the Sierras*. He appeared often at the Grand Ole Opry and on the *Louisiana Hayride* and *Country Jamboree* radio programs. His hits "Divorce Me C. O. D." and "My Bucket's Got a Hole in It" (a cover of the Hank Williams song) perpetuated his fame.

The advent of rock and roll sent his personal and professional life into a slump. He was arrested in Texas on marijuana possession in the mid-1950s, and alcohol abuse added to his many problems. His last hit was in 1953 with "Courtin' in the Rain." In 1958, Tyler had a religious experience when he attended the Foursquare Gospel Church in Long Beach, California, and turned to evangelism and gospel music, becoming a licensed Assembly of God minister. He made gospel albums which he sold at revivals and at other church services. In April 1968, his wife, Claudia, died, and one year later, his mother died at age ninety-five. Two years later, Tyler married Doria, a Canadian he often described as "a wonderful Christian lady." They soon settled in Springfield Missouri, where he continued to speak in churches.

In 1971, radio personality Paul Harvey announced to his listeners that T. Texas Tyler had cancer of the stomach and had only a short time to live. Later, from Cox Medical Center in Springfield, Tyler confirmed the report in letters sent to churches, in which he encouraged them to buy his records so that he could pay his mounting medical bills.

"The man with a million friends," who had held services in churches across America and in Canada, died on January 23, 1972, in Springfield. He is buried in Huntington, West Virginia.

For additional information:

Coogan, Harold. "T. Texas Tyler: Singer, Guitarist, Band Leader & Song Writer." *The Looking Glass* 15 (February 1990): 9–13.

Obituary of T. Texas Tyler. *Mena Evening Star*, January 24, 1972, p. 4

Shestack, Melvin. *The Country Music Encyclopedia*. New York: T. Y. Crowell Printers, 1977.

Stamble, Irwin, and Grelun Landon. *The Encyclopedia of Folk, Country and Western Music*. New York: St. Martin's Press, 1983.

Harold Coogan

This entry, originally published in *Arkansas Biography: A Collection of Notable Lives*, appears in the *Encyclopedia of Arkansas Music* in an altered form. *Arkansas Biography* is available from the University of Arkansas Press in Fayetteville.

ROCK VADEN RECORDS

Vaden Records, based in Trumann (Poinsett County), started as a mail-order company featuring gospel music. It soon grew into a regional studio that released music by such blues and early rock and roll artists as Bobby Brown, Teddy Riedell, Larry Donn, and many others who went on to regional and national fame.

In the early 1950s, husband and wife Arlen and Jackie Vaden of Trumann were singing gospel music all over northeastern Arkansas in a group called the Southern Gospel Singers. They also started singing on local radio stations in Osceola (Mississippi County) and Blytheville (Mississippi County) and soon branched out to stations in other states, such as XREF in Del Rio, Texas, and XEG Radio in Fort Worth, Texas; XREF and XEG broadcast out of Mexico and were much more powerful than U.S. stations. The Vadens taped their shows in Trumann each week and mailed them to radio stations. On the shows, they would offer records of their music for sale, as well as those of other gospel singers featured on the show. The mail-order company that became Vaden Records was a big business for the post office in Trumann, receiving orders every day.

With the advent of rock and roll, Arlen Vaden decided to branch out and release some other types of music. He met a young singer, Bobby Brown, from the Newport (Jackson County) area, who had just moved back to Arkansas and, with his band the Curios, had been playing the clubs in northeastern Arkansas. Vaden took the band to KLCN radio station in Blytheville, and they recorded "Down at Big Mary's House/I Get the Blues at Midnight" (1958). As this started playing locally, Vaden began to book shows across northeastern Arkansas, finding other Arkansas artists wanting to release records.

Vaden released songs by Jerri Patterson and Ray Baker, as well as Teddy Riedel from Rose Bud (White County), who recorded "Knocking on the Backside/Before it Began" (1958). Riedel eventually had five releases through Vaden, with "Judy" (1960) being his most popular song; he later leased the song to Elvis Presley and put it on an LP with RCA. Other artists Vaden recorded were the Jimmy Haggett band featuring Johnny Moore from the Blytheville area and Joyce Green from the Searcy (White County) area, who had a release titled "Black Cadillac" (1959), which later became a big hit with collectors. Vaden also worked with Larry Donn in Bono (Craighead County), who had a record titled "HoneyBun/That's What I Call a Ball" (1959). This would also become a collector's item and got Donn some work in Europe in the 1980s and 1990s. Vaden released a single by Vena Townsend, "I Walked the Soles off My Shoes/Too-Lonesome" (1959). A young disc jockey, Chuck Comer, in Newport recorded "Shall We Dance/Little More Lovin'" (1960) with Vaden.

Most of the recording took place at local radio stations, but Bobby Crafford of Cotton Plant (Woodruff County)—the drummer for the Pacers who had never before recorded a vocal—recorded "It's a Sin/Wee Wee Hours" (1961) at Hi Studio in Memphis, Tennessee. Next, a young artist from Jonesboro (Craighead County), Bobby Lee Trammell, who had been living in California and had a popular record on the West Coast, moved back home and recorded "Hi Ho Silver/Been a Walkin'" (1961). Later, Vaden would release records from Bill Duniven, Onie Wheeler, Ray Baker, the Stewart Family, Hank Locklin, William Moore, Maddox Brothers, and Rose.

Jackie Vaden remained with the company until the couple divorced in the early 1960s. In 1962, Vaden Records stopped releasing records due to poor sales. Many of the artists had migrated to other companies. After the closing of Vaden Records, Arlen Vaden took a job with a radio station, though he returned to Trumann later with his new wife and opened a video store.

In 2010, a Vaden reunion took place in Trumann; performing were Chuck Comer, Joyce Green, Teddy Riedel, Bobby Brown, Larry Donn, and Bobby Crafford, as well as Sonny Burgess and the Pacers. A film crew from Europe filmed the sold-out show. This was released on DVD in 2011 by Collector Records in the Netherlands.

For additional information:

Randall, Mark. "Trumann Record Label Produced Early Rock N Roll Hits." *Poinsett County Democrat-Tribune*, September 17, 2009. Online at http://www.democrattribune.com/story/1571333.html (accessed July 9, 2012).

Remaklus, Miranda. "Rockabilly Returns to Trumann as Vaden Records is Honored." *Poinsett County Democrat-Tribune*, February 12, 2010. Online at http://www.democrattribune.com/story/1610433.html (accessed July 9, 2012).

Bobby Crafford

THE VAPORS

The Vapors was a nightclub in Hot Springs (Garland County) during the last era of illegal gambling in the city. Upscale entertainment in the style of Las Vegas, Nevada—featuring well-known acts like Edgar Bergen, the Smothers Brothers, and Tony Bennett—distinguished it from many of the rival clubs in the area.

Dane Harris, who had been a World War II pilot, accumulated money from a stake he had in the Belvedere Country Club and casino during the 1950s and used that money to build the Vapors nightclub. Harris partnered with Owen Vincent "Owney" Madden, owner of the Cotton Club in New York and a noted gangster, to build the nightclub at a site at 315 Park Avenue formerly occupied by the Phillips Drive-In. The club was built in the summer of 1959 and opened in 1960, offering the Vapors' Coffee Shop; the Monte Carlo Room for

Former location of the Vapors in Hot Springs; 2010.

Photo: Mike Keckhaver

meetings, events, and luncheons; a large lobby; a dance floor; a theater restaurant with tiered seating and a retractable stage big enough for an orchestra; and a casino that opened late in the evening. Entertainment included two shows every night featuring some of the most popular entertainers in the country.

Tony Bennett notes in his autobiography that he first sang his signature hit "I Left My Heart in San Francisco" at the Vapors. While rehearsing the song there for a later appearance at the Fairmont Hotel in San Francisco, California, Bennett sang the song through once and was told by the only audience member, a bartender setting up for the evening, "If you guys record that song, I'll buy the first copy."

In the late morning of January 4, 1963, an explosion rocked the Vapors, causing extensive damage. Twelve injuries were reported, and three people required hospitalization. Speculation about who was responsible ranged from outside crime syndicates attempting a takeover to local small club owners lashing out in response to raids against their own facilities. Such raids were intended to take the public pressure off authorities while leaving more prominent clubs like the Vapors alone. As a result of the bombing, a wall separating the casino from the lobby was demolished, exposing the club's gaming tables and slot machines to the street. Reporters covering the bombing for the *Arkansas Gazette* managed to snap a photograph of the slot machines and craps tables against the orders of police officers securing the area. The photo appeared on the front page of the next day's edition, providing clear proof of illegal gambling in Hot Springs, but illegal gambling would not be completely curtailed in the city until 1967, six months into the first term of reformist Governor Winthrop Rockefeller.

Unlike many former casinos in Hot Springs, the Vapors continued to operate as a nightclub and restaurant after its casino was closed. In 1977, responding to changing tastes in entertainment, Dane Harris began renovations to the club, which would see the addition of the Cockeyed Cowboy and Apollo Disco, as well as an additional showroom completed in 1980.

Harris died in 1981. The Vapors continued to operate as a nightclub into the 1990s but only as a lackluster shadow of its former self. The building was sold in October 1998 to Tower of Strength Ministries for use as a church and is still in use by that organization.

For additional information:

Allbritton, Orval E. *Leo and Verne: The Spa's Heyday*. Hot Springs, AR: Garland County Historical Society, 2003.

Bennett, Tony. *The Good Life*. New York: Pocket Books, 1998.

Brown, Dee. *The American Spa: Hot Springs, Arkansas*. Little Rock: Rose Publishing Company, 1982.

"Dane Harris Dies at 62; Rose to Prominence in Hot Springs Heydays." *Arkansas Gazette*, June 11, 1981, p. 2A.

Davis, Lynn A. *They Said It Couldn't Be Done: Closing Down the Biggest Illegal Casino Operation in America, Hot Springs, Arkansas, 1967, in 120 Days*. Little Rock: Days Creek Press, 2009.

"Home-Owned? 'No,' Chicago Official Says of Hot Springs Clubs." *Arkansas Gazette*, January 8, 1963, pp. 1, 8A.

Ramsey, Patsy Hawthorn. "A Place at the Table: Hot Springs and the G.I. Revolt." *Arkansas Historical Quarterly* 59 (Winter 2000): 407–428.

Scully, Francis J. *Hot Springs, Arkansas and Hot Springs National Park: The Story of a City and the Nation's Health Resort*. Little Rock, AR: Hanson Co., 1966.

Shaw, Robert. "Mysterious Blast Rips Vapors Club; At Least 12 Hurt." *Arkansas Gazette*, January 5, 1963, p. 1A.

Michael Hodge

W

COUNTRY JIMMY WAKELY (1914–1982)

Jimmy Wakely, an American country and western singer and actor from the 1930s through the 1950s, made several recordings and appeared in B-western movies with most major studios as a "singing cowboy." Wakely was one of the last singing cowboys after World War II and also appeared on radio and television; he even had his own series of comic books. He has a star on the Hollywood Walk of Fame at 1680 Vine Street.

Jimmy Wakely was born James Clarence Wakeley on February 16, 1914, in Mineola (Howard County) to Major Anderson Wakeley, a farmer, and Caroline (or Carolin) "Cali" Burgess Wakeley. As a teenager, he changed "James" to "Jimmy" and dropped the second "e" in his last name, making it Wakely.

Wakely married Dora Inez Miser on December 13, 1935. They had four children.

In 1937 in Oklahoma City, Oklahoma, Wakely formed a country singing group named the Bell Boys after their Bell Clothing sponsor. The group performed locally and made recordings and frequent radio broadcasts on Oklahoma City's WKY. The name of the band changed over time, becoming the Jimmy Wakely Trio.

Wakely was discovered by western movie star Gene Autry while Autry was on a tour through Oklahoma. Autry invited Wakely to play on his new *Melody Ranch* radio show, which debuted on CBS in January 1940. The Jimmy Wakely Trio joined the show in mid-1940. After a couple of years, Wakely left to pursue movie work and a recording contract with Decca Records that ran from 1941 through 1947.

Wakely made his screen debut with the Jimmy Wakely Trio in a 1939 Roy Rogers western called *Saga at Death Valley*. In the 1940s, he provided songs and musical support for many B-westerns and appeared alongside many notable performers, including Hopalong Cassidy, Johnny Mack Brown, and Tex Ritter. He appeared in one Autry film, *Heart of the Rio Grande*, in 1942. Wakely also appeared in non-westerns, including *I'm from Arkansas* (1944), a showcase for country performers. He also had his own comic book series from 1949 to 1952, published by DC Comics and titled *Hollywood's Sensational Cowboy Star!*

Wakely was sometimes referred to as a "low-budget Gene Autry." In response, he declared that, "Everybody reminds somebody of someone else until they are somebody. And I had rather be compared to Gene Autry than anyone else. Through the grace of God and Gene Autry, I got a career."

Wakely recorded several country and western albums throughout his career, but some crossed over to the pop charts, notably collaborations with singers Margaret Whiting and Karen Chandler, as well as the Christmas song "Silver Bells."

In addition to appearing on Autry's radio program, Wakely had his own radio show on CBS, *The Jimmy Wakely Show* (1952–1958), and he co-hosted others. He appeared on several television variety shows including hosting the NBC-

Jimmy Wakely starred in the 1945 Monogram Pictures film *Riders of the Dawn.*
Courtesy: Old State House Museum Collection

Jimmy Wakely trading card.
Courtesy: Old State House Museum Collection

TV program *Five Star Jubilee.* Wakely developed Shasta records in the 1960s and owned two music publishing companies. Working from a studio converted from part of his California ranch, he produced recordings for himself as well as for other notable country performers, including Tex Williams, Merle Travis, Eddie Dean, Tex Ritter, and Rex Allen.

In his later years, Wakely performed at the Grand Ole Opry and on the *National Barn Dance.* His nightclub act visited Las Vegas, Nevada; Reno, Nevada; and elsewhere. He did a Christmas USO tour with Bob Hope. He also made appearances at western film nostalgia conventions and continued with personal appearances and stage shows, often performing with his daughter Linda and son Johnny.

After contracting emphysema, Wakely died on September 23, 1982, in Mission Hills, California. He was inducted into the Nashville Songwriters Hall of Fame in 1971 and the Western Music Association Hall of Fame in 1991.

For additional information:
"Jimmy Wakely." B-Westerns. http://www.b-westerns.com/wakely0.htm (accessed February 8, 2013).
"Jimmy Wakely." Internet Movie Database. http://www.imdb.com/name/nm0906843/ (accessed February 8, 2013).
"The Jimmy Wakely Trio." Western Music Association Hall of Fame. http://www.westernmusic.com/performers/hof-wakely-trio.html (accessed February 26, 2013).
Kingsbury, Paul, ed. *The Encyclopedia of Country Music.* New York: Oxford University Press, 1988.

C. L. Bledsoe

WILLIAM WARFIELD (1920–2002)

William Caesar Warfield was a noted African-American bass-baritone concert artist who had an extensive career that included major roles in two Hollywood films as well as stints on stage and on television. Probably no one ever performed "Ol' Man River" from Jerome Kern's *Show Boat* more times than Warfield, who performed it in several languages.

William Warfield was born on January 22, 1920, to Robert Warfield and Bertha McCamery Warfield in West Helena (Phillips County). He spent only a few years in Arkansas; however, because of a strong family background in Arkansas and Mississippi, he described himself as "an Arkansas boy from tip to toe." His multi-racial ancestry included a paternal grandfather who appeared in photographs to be a white man and Native American ancestry on both sides of his family.

Warfield's family moved to St. Joseph, Missouri, in 1922, where his father worked in a meat-packing plant. In 1925, the family moved to Rochester, New York, where Warfield's father entered the Baptist ministry. Warfield attended the public schools in Rochester and took piano lessons. After winning the National Music Educators League's singing competition in 1938, he entered the University of Rochester's Eastman School of Music. He was drafted into the army in 1942 but received his degree from Eastman. Because his college education included language classes in French, German, and Italian, Warfield was transferred to military intelligence and never saw active service.

In 1946, he was hired as the lead in a touring company performing Harold Rome's musical *Call Me Mister*. After the show's run, he found work singing and playing piano in clubs and landed parts in other shows. He was working in a club in Toronto, Canada, when a patron, Walter Carr, decided to finance Warfield's Town Hall debut in New York City on March 19, 1950. Warfield impressed the critics and immediately snagged an extended tour of Australia. This, too, proved to be a great success and was followed by his first film, a remake of *Show Boat*, in which Warfield sang "Ol' Man River" for the first time commercially.

Porgy and Bess was his next theatrical endeavor. The Bess in the cast was soprano Leontyne Price, whom Warfield married in 1952. The marriage did not survive the stresses of their musical careers—they separated in 1958 but did not divorce until 1972. Price's career as a Metropolitan Opera star began with her debut in 1957, while Warfield, despite his strong theatrical abilities, was limited largely by his gender to a concert career.

Warfield undertook six tours for the U.S. Department of State. His stage appearances were highlighted by *Porgy and Bess* in New York in 1961. He performed *Porgy and Bess* in Vienna from 1965 to 1974, as well as a German-language touring version of *Show Boat*, although audiences requested that he sing "Ol' Man River" in English.

Television also enlisted Warfield. He played De Lawd in Marc Connelly's *Green Pastures*, a Hallmark Hall of Fame production done "live" in 1957 and again in 1959. He narrated Aaron Copland's *A Lincoln Portrait*, for which he won a Grammy in 1984. During a European tour with

William Warfield, concert baritone singer; circa 1965. Warfield sang in a production of Porgy and Bess *that toured Europe in 1952.*

Courtesy: Butler Center for Arkansas Studies, Central Arkansas Library System

Leonard Bernstein and the New York Philharmonic in 1976, he narrated the text in French in Paris and in German in Vienna.

Warfield began teaching in 1975 at the University of Illinois in Urbana-Champaign and, after 1994, at Northwestern University in Chicago. He was active in concerts and dramatic readings, occasionally sharing the stage with fellow Arkansan Robert McFerrin. He served on the boards of the National Association of Negro Musicians (NANM) and the Schiller Institute.

Warfield's first records were made in 1950 for Columbia and consisted of "Five Sea Chanties." He sang bass on recordings of George Frideric Handel's *Messiah* with the Philadelphia Orchestra, conducted by Eugene Ormandy, and Wolfgang Amadeus Mozart's *Requiem Mass* with the New York Philharmonic, conducted by Bruno Walter. He gave the world premieres of both sets of Aaron Copland's "Old American Songs" in 1952 and 1958. His last works consisted of a jazz and spirituals album released in 2004, *Something Within Me*, and narration for *Dreamer: A Portrait of Langston Hughes*, made up of songs set to Hughes's texts, released in 2002.

Warfield received an honorary Doctor of Laws degree from the University of Arkansas (UA) in Fayetteville (Washington County) in 1972. He performed in Helena (Phillips County) on October 23, 1987, in the Warfield Concerts, a community concert series, and gave a poetry and song program at Arkansas State University (ASU) in Jonesboro (Craighead County) on October 14, 1999. Warfield remained an active performer until his death from a fall at his home on August 25, 2002. Had Warfield been born a half century later, he likely would have become a major operatic star. Instead, as he observed in his memoir, *My Music & My Life* (1991), "Opera wasn't ready for me, or any black male."

For additional information:

Baker's Biographical Dictionary of Musicians. Vol. 6. New York: Schimer Publishing, 2001.

Southern, Eileen. *Biographical Dictionary of Afro-American and African Musicians*. Westport, CT: Greenwood Press, 1982.

Warfield, William, with Alton Miller. *William Warfield: My Music & My Life*. Champaign, IL: Sagamore Publishing Inc., 1991.

Michael B. Dougan

BLUES / R&B | # PEETIE WHEATSTRAW (1902–1941)

William Bunch, known as "Peetie Wheatstraw," was raised in Cotton Plant (Woodruff County) and became one of the most popular and widely imitated bluesman of the 1930s and 1940s. He was an incredibly successful pianist, recording more than 160 songs between 1930 and his death in 1941.

William Bunch was born on December 21, 1902, in Ripley, Tennessee, although some accounts list Bunch's birthplace as Arkansas. Bluesman Big Joe Williams, who recorded with Bunch, stated: "Peetie come from Cotton Plant, Arkansas." Bunch's family was living in Cotton Plant soon after his birth. Cotton Plant was a local cultural center in the early 1900s, and Bunch began playing both piano and guitar there at a young age. Around 1920, all members of the Bunch family were farm laborers. This family included the head of the household, Jim; his wife, Mary; and their four sons and three daughters. In 1927, Bunch left Cotton Plant to travel throughout the Deep South as a musician.

In 1929, Bunch moved north to play venues in East St. Louis, Illinois, and across the river in St. Louis, Missouri. At this time, he was a capable musician with a new name, Peetie Wheatstraw. The name was derived from African-American folklore and referred to the evil half of a twin personality. He also used "the High Sheriff of Hell" and "the Devil's Son-in-Law" as nicknames during his recording career. According to ethnomusicologist Robert Palmer, Bunch's music was characterized by his "two-fisted barrelhouse piano work" and his "falsetto cry, 'Ooh, well, well,' that he tended to insert at the end of almost every verse." Bunch began recording in Chicago in 1930 and recorded more than 160 songs for the Vocalion, Decca, and Bluebird labels, including such tunes as "Tennessee Peaches Blues" (1930), "Six Weeks Old Blues" (1931), and "Peetie Wheatstraw Stomp" (1937).

Bunch lived in East St. Louis starting in 1929, where he frequently played piano in local clubs and bars. He died on his thirty-ninth birthday, December 21, 1941, when the car he was riding in failed to make a curve and struck a standing freight train. He was less than a block from his home. The other two passengers, both of whom died, were a packing house worker and a steel plant worker. His body was shipped to

Cotton Plant for burial.

Bunch was tremendously popular on the national blues scene and had a profound influence on many bluesmen playing in Arkansas during the 1930s and 1940s. Robert Johnson borrowed many lyrical ideas from him, and Bunch's influence could later be heard in the music of "Big Bill" Broonzy and Muddy Waters.

On June 4, 2011, the Bunch family, the Sonny Boy Blues Society, and the National Trust for Historic Preservation dedicated a Delta Music Trail Marker in Cotton Plant for Bunch. A grave marker was also dedicated, and Governor Mike Beebe proclaimed the day Peetie Wheatstraw Day.

For additional information:

Garon, Paul. *The Devil's Son-in-Law: The Story of Peetie Wheatstraw and His Songs*. Revised ed. Chicago: Charles H. Kerr, 2003.

Palmer, Robert. *Deep Blues*. New York: Viking Press, 1981.

Jamie Metrailer

FOLK — ELTON AND BETTY WHITE

In the mid- to late 1980s, Elton and Betty White were highly visible Little Rock (Pulaski County) street musicians and eccentrics, recognized for their sexually explicit ukulele songs and their flamboyant wardrobe of sombreros and skimpy swimwear.

Betty White was born Betty Crandall in 1927 in Mabelvale (Pulaski County), one of seven children of the town's postmaster and his wife. In 1946, after graduating as valedictorian of Mabelvale High School, she married air force sergeant Scotty White, with whom she had a son, Sammy. Together, they traveled the nation and the world. After returning to Arkansas, she found secretarial work with the law firm of Wright, Lindsey & Jennings, for whom Bill Clinton was then practicing. Following a diagnosis of schizophrenia, though, Betty divorced her husband and lost her job.

Elton White was born in 1958 in Dumas (Desha County). A high school basketball star, he played four years of college ball at Westark Community College (now the University of Arkansas at Fort Smith) and the University of the Ozarks. He tried out with the Atlanta Hawks, but his professional prospects were eradicated by a knee injury. He moved to Little Rock, finding work as a day laborer, until the night someone "put something in his drink," as he often told the story, and he fell on hard times.

Elton and Betty met in 1984 at Little Rock's Union Rescue Mission, and despite the thirty-year age difference between the white woman and the black man, "It was love at first sight," Betty later recalled, adding, "There was a real magnetism." The two of them began delivering newspapers and writing music together, renting an apartment at the Albert Pike Residence Hotel. They married in 1989.

From 1986 to 1989, with the assistance of producer Jerry Colburn, they released three albums—*The Best of Elton and Betty*, *Sex Beyond the Door*, and *Hard Deep Sex Explosion*—and recorded some 250 songs, many of them frank celebrations of their sex life, both raunchy and tender, with titles such as "A Jelly Behind Woman Blows My Mind," "Lady, Your Breast, I Love to Caress(t)," "My Three-Feet Red-Hot Tongue Is Sweet as Sugar," "Menopause Mama," "Tight Blue Jeans Shows Your Thing," and "America, We Are Sexy." During these years, they also dabbled in politics, with Elton running for Congress and Betty for governor in 1986, and Elton for governor and Betty for the U.S. Senate in 1990.

In 1991, *The Arsenio Hall Show* aired a recording of the couple performing Elton's "I'm in Love with Your Behind" in the aisles of Little Rock's RAO Video. That same year, the couple moved to Venice Beach, California, where they began performing on the boardwalk as "The Married Couple" and launched a public-access television show, *Husband and Wife Time*. Their jubilant outlandishness led to television appearances on *Sally Jessy Raphael*, *Maury Povich*, and

Elton and Betty White.
Courtesy: Jerry Colburn

The Daily Show, as well as articles in periodicals such as *Variety*, *LA Weekly*, and the French *Agence de Presse Photographique*. The *Philadelphia Inquirer* said of Betty, "She's 72, a former coworker of Bill Clinton's, wears a beaded bikini, plays the ukulele, and freely offers advice on love, marriage and sex," and of Elton, "He's 41, a onetime NBA prospect, wears a Speedo stuffed with socks, plays a toy keyboard, and holds the umbrella they perform behind."

Betty White died on August 20, 2003, at the age of seventy-six. Elton White continues to reside in the beachfront apartment the couple once shared on Venice Beach.

Elton and Betty White are the subject of a forthcoming documentary produced by Jerry Colburn and Donavan Suitt. While much of their music has become scarce, their album *Hard Deep Sex Explosion* is available on iTunes through Rural War Room Records.

For additional information:

Brockmeier, Kevin. "Elton & Betty White: Bouncing Back Like Basketballs." *Oxford American* 63 (2008): 64–70.

Hill, Jack W. "Bicycling to the Big Time." *Arkansas Democrat-Gazette*, December 8, 1995, p. 8E.

Leveritt, Mara. "Little Rock's X-Rated Hit Parade." *Arkansas Times*, October 1988, p. 22.

Scudder, James. "Downtown LR Couple Ejected During Gala. Asked to Leave Despite Tickets." *Arkansas Gazette*, October 14, 1987, p. 13A.

Woestendiek, John. "An Act Too Big for Arkansas (Not the Clintons) Finds Mecca. The Married Couple Does All Together (Nearly in the Altogether, At Times)—And Dreams." *Philadelphia Inquirer*, October 4, 1998, p. 3A.

Kevin Brockmeier

COUNTRY   THE WILBURN BROTHERS

The Wilburn Brothers were among the most successful and influential sibling duos in the country music industry during the 1950s, 1960s, and early 1970s. Brothers Virgil Doyle ("Doyle") Wilburn (1930–1982) and Thurman Theodore ("Teddy") Wilburn (1931–2003), who hailed from Hardy (Sharp County), were stars of the Grand Ole Opry, recording artists with over thirty albums, recipients of the only "Lifetime Recording Contract" ever given by Decca Records, and hosts of their own nationally syndicated country music show for eleven years. In addition, they were talent agents who helped launch the careers of many other legendary country music stars, including Loretta Lynn, Patty Loveless, and the Osborne Brothers. Their Surefire Music, formed in 1957, is the only remaining family-owned music-publishing house in Nashville, Tennessee.

Teddy and Doyle Wilburn were the youngest two children of Benjamin (B. E.) "Pop" Wilburn and Katie "Mom" Wilburn. Pop Wilburn was a disabled World War I veteran struggling through the hard times of the 1930s, taking odd jobs to feed his family. One day, he saw a family of performers whose car had broken down; the family paid for the repairs by performing for tips. He subsequently ordered instruments from the Sears and Roebuck catalogue and taught his children to become performers. On December 24, 1937, the Wilburn family children made their first public performance on a street corner in Thayer, Missouri. Teddy and Doyle, along with older brothers Lester Lloyd and Leslie Floyd and sister Geraldine, played and sang with their guitars, mandolin, ukulele, and fiddle for the people who gathered around.

Pop Wilburn took his children to a talent contest in Birmingham, Alabama, being held by the "King of Country Music," Roy Acuff. They arrived too late for the contest, but Pop placed his children at the stage door exit and waited for Acuff to come out between shows. The children performed one of Acuff's favorite hymns, leaving him so impressed that he arranged an invitation to the Grand Ole Opry in Nashville. In 1940, after performing as Opry members for six months, the Wilburns were forced to leave due to the child labor laws.

Geraldine Wilburn left the group to marry, but the four brothers continued performing and eventually became cast members of the *Louisiana Hayride* as well as having their own morning radio show on KWKH. Though the brothers had broken up by the time Doyle and Teddy Wilburn were called to serve in the military during the Korean War, they had been lucky enough to befriend a regionally popular singer named Webb Pierce while working on the *Hayride*. Pierce eventually became a huge star in Nashville and, after the war, invited Doyle and Teddy Wilburn to join him. The Wilburns realized that a duo act would work better for them than a family group. They honed their skills as a duo while working with future legends Webb Pierce, Faron Young, and Ernest Tubb.

Soon, the Wilburn Brothers were gaining popularity through their records and performances. Some of their best-known songs are "Sparkling Brown Eyes," "Trouble's Back in Town," "Roll Muddy River," and "Somebody's Back in Town." Eventually, they branched out into music publishing and talent management along with partner Don Helms (member of the Steel Guitar Hall of Fame and one of Hank Williams Sr.'s Drifting Cowboys). Brothers Lester and Leslie Wilburn were brought in to help run the many businesses.

In 1964, *The Wilburn Brothers* show debuted as a nationally syndicated program. On this show, they were able to give mass exposure to a then-little-known singer named Loretta Lynn. When Lynn first came to Nashville, she had sought out the Wilburns to obtain their autographs and to ask if they would listen to her record produced by an independent West Coast label. The Wilburns added Lynn to their road shows, negotiated a deal with Decca Records for her, and later added her as a regular cast member to their show. During the eleven-year run of the show, guests ranged from country music legends to talented, newer artists. Crystal Gayle, Barbara Mandrell, and the Oak Ridge Boys were just some of the young artists that benefited from the exposure early in their careers.

Doyle Wilburn died from lung cancer on October 16, 1982. Teddy Wilburn continued to perform on his own into the early 1990s, when his health forced him to give it up. He died of congestive heart failure on November 24, 2003. In 2008, the Wilburn Brothers were inducted posthumously into the Arkansas Entertainers Hall of Fame.

For additional information:
Ankeny, Jason. "Wilburn Brothers." *Country Music Television.* http://www.cmt.com/artists/az/wilburn_brothers/bio.jhtml (accessed February 26, 2013).
Dahl, Bill. Liner notes for the *Wilburn Brothers' Greatest Hits.* Varese Sarabande, 2005.
Kitsinger, Otto. Liner notes for the *Wilburn Brothers' Trouble's Back in Town—The Hits of the Wilburn Brothers.* Edsel Records, 1998.
"Wilburn Brothers." AllMusic.com. http://www.allmusic.com/artist/the-wilburn-brothers-mn0000820999 (accessed February 27, 2013).
Wilburn Brothers Tribute Site. http://www.wilburnbrotherstribute.com/ (accessed February 26, 2013).

Susan H. Brant

J. MAYO "INK" WILLIAMS (1894–1980)

J. Mayo "Ink" Williams was the first African-American producer at a major record label and the most successful record producer of music by black performers, particularly blues and jazz, from the 1920s through the 1940s.

The son of Daniel and Millie Williams, J. Mayo Williams was born in Pine Bluff (Jefferson County) on September 25, 1894. He left Pine Bluff with his mother at age seven after his father was murdered in a shooting at the local railway station. After moving to Monmouth, Illinois, he attended public schools, where he excelled in academics and football. In 1916, he enrolled at Brown University, where he became a star athlete.

In the early 1920s, Williams became one of the first black players in the National Football League (NFL), which was in its infancy. He played for the Indiana-based Hammond Pros, ending his career in 1926.

Williams's interest in music overshadowed his athletic exploits even before his football career was over. In the early 1920s, Paramount Records, recognizing the interest among African Americans in regional jazz and blues, introduced their "race records" series featuring black jazz and blues artists. When the company looked for a manager for the Chicago, Illinois, "Race Division" to tap the talent in the rapidly growing black population in the city, it found blues enthusiast Williams, who later said that he may have overstated his experience to get the position. Nonetheless, he was hired by Paramount (who never discovered his side career as an NFL player) to recruit talent and produce artists, becoming the first black executive at a major record label.

Williams identified incredible southern talent in the local clubs and juke joints of Chicago, discovering the great blues singer Mamie Smith, who would become Paramount's best-selling artist of the 1920s. He also discovered blues legend Papa Charlie Jackson. He went on to assemble and produce other major artists while at Paramount, such as Ida Cox, Trixie Smith, Blind Lemon Jefferson, Tampa Red, Thomas A. Dorsey (a.k.a. Georgia Tom), Jimmy Blythe, Jelly Roll Morton, King Oliver, and Freddy Keppard.

Williams decided to start his own company under the Black Patti label in 1927. This was only the second independent black record label in the United States, but it did not fare well, as competition with the major record labels was stiff.

At the onset of the Great Depression, Williams got out of the music business for a time and turned to coaching football at Morehouse College in Atlanta, Georgia. At the end of the 1934 season, he was hired by Decca Records as the manager of the race record division of the company. At Decca, he produced, wrote for, and discovered a remarkable array of artists, including Mahalia Jackson, Alberta Hunter, Blind Boy Fuller, Roosevelt Sykes, Sleepy John Estes, Kokomo Arnold, Peetie Wheatstraw, Bill Gaither, Bumble Bee Slim, Georgia White, Trixie Smith, Monette Moore, Sister Rosetta Tharpe, Marie Knight, and Tab Smith. His work with small blues/jazz ensembles such as the Harlem Hamfats and Louis Jordan's early bands laid the groundwork for the wildly popular jump blues trend among young African Americans in the 1940s and early 1950s. This genre is credited by many music historians with being the progenitor of rock and roll.

The subject of criticism by some artists in the industry, Williams was called "Ink" because he had an ability to talk artists into signing contracts. However, some of those artists who lacked education or business savvy were unhappy with the small profits they made from their recordings. Under each record label he worked for, Williams would negotiate rights to the music or writing credits with artists to provide himself with additional sources of revenue, since his label salary was so meager.

Upon retiring from Decca in 1946, Williams started the Chicago, Southern, and Ebony labels, working with artists such as Muddy Waters, Lil Hardin Armstrong, Bonnie Lee, Oscar Brown, and others. William Kenney observed in *Recorded Music in American Life* that Williams "built the longest running and most productive career of any African American in the phonograph business before World War II."

Williams died on January 2, 1980, just as plans were being developed to conduct extensive interviews for his biography. In 2004, he was posthumously inducted into the Blues Foundation's Blues Hall of Fame.

For additional information:

Kenney, William Howland. *Recorded Music in American Life: The Phonograph and Popular Memory, 1890–1945.* New York: Oxford University Press, 1999.

Komara, Edward, ed. *Encyclopedia of the Blues.* Vol. 2. New York: Routledge, 2006.

Lentz, Eddy. "J. Mayo Williams." Ivy League Black History. http://ivy50.com/blackhistory/story.aspx?sid=12/26/2006 (accessed May 13, 2013).

Jimmy Cunningham Jr.

GOSPEL / CONTEMPORARY CHRISTIAN — J. PAUL WILLIAMS (1937–2010)

J. Paul Williams made notable contributions to the field of church music. His catalog of published lyrics exceeds 925 songs, running the gamut of sacred and secular texts. A leader of choral clinics and composer symposiums, he was also a member of the American Society of Composers and Publishers (ASCAP).

James Paul Williams was born in Oklahoma City, Oklahoma, on December 29, 1937. He was the only child of Ferris Woodrow Williams (a taxi driver) and Violet Simonton Williams (a bank supervisor). He was a member of Capitol Hill Baptist Church in Oklahoma City until he left for college. Williams admired the church's minister of music, and he decided to pursue that career, even though he had never had a music lesson of any kind before attending college.

He entered Oklahoma Baptist University (OBU) in Shawnee, Oklahoma, in 1956, where he was selected to sing in the Bison Glee Club. He was also in an elite men's quartet called the Fallen Angells (named for his choral director, Dr. Warren M. Angell). At OBU, he met Donna Liane Shiplet and married her on June 5, 1959; they had two children. Williams completed his voice major in the spring of 1964. During college, he worked part time at West 10th Street Baptist Church in Oklahoma City as choir director.

He began his career as a minister of music full time at Highland Hills Baptist Church in San Antonio, Texas, serving from 1962 to 1966. There, he initiated a program of graded choirs. After writing music for use in his choir program for several years, he began to be published in 1963.

Williams received his master's degree in composition and theory at Southwestern Baptist Theological Seminary in Fort Worth, Texas, in 1969; during his degree program, he served part time at First Baptist Church in Quanah, Texas.

After graduating from seminary, he spent two years working as a salesman for Thermacor Pipe Company before returning to church work, serving as music and youth minister at Southcrest Baptist Church in Lubbock, Texas. After serving that church for four years, the family moved to Little Rock (Pulaski County) to serve Calvary Baptist Church. Williams's tenure stretched from October 1975 through May 1992, when he resigned from the church to write lyrics on a freelance basis.

He maintained his home and church affiliation in Little Rock as he wrote lyrics and oversaw choir clinics and composer symposiums, collaborating with more than sixty people who wrote the music. Williams had more than 900 published songs at the time of his death, and twenty-five more of his songs have been published posthumously.

Some of his best-known lyrics are for the songs "Who Are the Brave?," "With Wings as Eagles," "Creation Will Be at Peace," "Because of Love," "Brushstrokes," "Goliath," "I Am His Lamb," "No Night There," "Sometimes I Hear God's Music," "Talitha Kum!," "Our God is God," "Walk Worthy," "God Made the World," "Heroes of the Faith," "Waterfall," and "He Chose to Die." His works have been published with Broadman Press, Shawnee Press, Lorenz Publishing, Alfred Publishing, Beckenhorst, Lillenas, Hal Leonard, Hope Publishing Company, Warner Bros., and Fred Bock Music Company. Most recently, two of his lyrics were set to music and included in the *Celebrating Grace* hymnal. The Houston Children's Chorus has released an album of his songs.

Williams died on February 17, 2010, and is buried in Pinecrest Cemetery at Alexander (Pulaski and Saline counties).

For additional information:

J. Paul Williams. http://jpaulyrics.com/ (accessed February 26, 2013).

Outstanding Young Men of America. Chicago: Outstanding Young Men of America, 1971.

Donna Liane Williams

FOLK | LUCINDA WILLIAMS (1953–)

Lucinda Williams is one of America's most critically acclaimed songwriters and recording artists, as well as the daughter of poet Miller Williams. She has won three Grammy Awards and is considered a leading light of the so-called "alt-country" movement. Her songs, with their simple chord structures and gorgeous melodies, incorporate elements of rural blues, traditional country, and rock and roll. They are distinguished by evocative, plain-spoken lyrics that investigate the human mystery. In 2002, *Time* magazine called her "America's best songwriter."

Lucinda Williams was born on January 26, 1953, in Lake Charles, Louisiana. Her mother was Miller Williams's first wife, Lucille Day. With her peripatetic professor father moving from job to job, Williams grew up in southern towns such as Vicksburg, Mississippi; Jackson, Mississippi; Baton Rouge, Louisiana; and New Orleans, Louisiana. She also lived for a time in Mexico and Santiago, Chile.

Lucinda Williams Albums

Ramblin' on My Mind (1979)
Happy Woman Blues (1980)
Lucinda Williams (1988)
Sweet Old World (1992)
Car Wheels on a Gravel Road (1998)
Essence (2001)
World Without Tears (2003)
Live @ the Fillmore (2005)
West (2007)
Little Honey (2008)
Blessed (2011)

As a child, she met many of her father's writer friends, including Eudora Welty and Flannery O'Connor, who famously allowed the five-year-old Lucinda to chase her peacocks. By the time she was twelve years old, she was writing her own songs on guitar and performing for her parents' guests.

Her family moved to Arkansas in 1971 when her father took a teaching position at the University of Arkansas (UA) in Fayetteville (Washington County). After a brief stint at UA herself, she began the career of an itinerant musician, playing in bars and coffeehouses in Austin, Texas; Nashville, Tennessee; Houston, Texas; and Greenwich Village, New York. In 1979, calling herself simply "Lucinda," she recorded *Ramblin' on My Mind* for Smithsonian/Folkways. It was a minimalist album of old blues and country songs by the likes of Robert Johnson, the Carter Family, and Memphis Minnie. Williams sang and played twelve-string guitar; her only accompaniment was John Grimaudo on six-string guitar. The sole original song was Williams's own "Disgusted." Her second album, 1980's *Happy Woman Blues*, credited to "Lucinda Williams," was recorded with a full band and consisted mainly of Williams's original pop country material. Neither album received much attention.

Williams moved to Los Angeles, California, in the early 1980s, where she fronted rock bands and developed a cult following and a critical reputation. But it was not until 1988, with the release of *Lucinda Williams*, that she established herself as a singer/songwriter of the first rank. Sometimes referred to as "the white album" by fans and recorded for Rough Trade, a British label that specialized in punk and ska acts, the album was only a minor commercial success, though it earned her a small but intensely loyal following and a burgeoning reputation as a "musician's musician."

When Rough Trade abruptly folded after the album was released, RCA stepped in and signed Williams. But when they presented her with sugary, radio-ready mixes of her songs, she walked out. She eventually landed at Chameleon, another tiny independent label, and the RCA songs showed up—mixed her way—on her 1992 album *Sweet Old World*, a collection of trenchant songs about longing, love, death, and survival. (The song "Pineola" was a fictionalized account of the suicide of a family friend, poet Frank Stanford.) *Sweet Old World* was voted the eleventh best album of 1992 by the *Village Voice*'s prestigious "Pazz and Jop Poll" of critics.

In 1993, Mary Chapin Carpenter had a hit with "Passionate Kisses," off *Lucinda Williams*, for which Williams won a songwriting Grammy. That same year, Patty Loveless recorded her "The Night's Too Long," and Tom Petty covered

Grammy Award–winning singer/songwriter Lucinda Williams.
Artists: Patterson and Barnes / From the Old State House Museum Collection

"Changed the Locks" off *Sweet Old World*. Williams toured with Bob Dylan, one of her primary influences, and on her own, in support of the album.

In 1998, she released what is often regarded as her masterpiece, *Car Wheels on a Gravel Road*, which went on to win a Grammy for Best Contemporary Folk Album. In *Rolling Stone* magazine, the venerable critic Robert Christgau called the album "perfect." Williams followed up the success of *Car Wheels* with the brooding, stripped-down *Essence* in 2001 and the musically adventurous *World Without Tears* in 2003. In 2005, she released an old-style double live album, *Live @ the Fillmore*. In part because of the relatively long time between album releases, Williams has developed a reputation as a perfectionist.

In recent years, Williams has done a number of low-key concerts with her father, trading acoustic versions of her songs with his poetry readings. She continues to tour and write songs. She released the album *West* in 2007 and followed that up the next year with *Little Honey*. In 2011, she released the album *Blessed*.

For additional information:
Cochran, Robert. *Our Own Sweet Sounds: A Celebration of Popular Music in Arkansas*. 2nd ed. Fayetteville: University of Arkansas Press, 2005.
Huey, Stephen. "Lucinda Williams." Allmusic.com. http://allmusic.com/cg/amg.dll?p=amg&sql=11:gifexqr5ldfe~T1 (accessed February 8, 2013).
Lucinda Williams. http://www.lucindawilliams.com/ (accessed February 8, 2013).

Philip Martin

Lucinda Williams; circa 2010.
Courtesy: Lucinda Williams

SONNY BOY WILLIAMSON (1912?–1965)

Blues harmonica great Sonny Boy Williamson.
Artists: Patterson and Barnes / From the Old State House Museum Collection

Sonny Boy Williamson first became famous as a blues harmonica player in 1941 on the groundbreaking *King Biscuit Time* radio program (often credited as the first regularly scheduled blues radio show) broadcast by station KFFA in Helena (Phillips County). Williamson's fame spread, particularly through Europe, in the 1960s and has continued to grow since his death. An annual blues festival in Helena-West Helena (Phillips County) still features his music.

Williamson went to great lengths to mislead would-be biographers, and facts about his life are difficult to verify. His real name was Aleck Miller; he was apparently sometimes called Rice, and he was most likely born in 1912 in Glendora, Mississippi, to Millie Ford. He took his stepfather Jim Miller's surname. As a very young child, he taught himself to play harmonica; by the age of six or seven, he was performing at church events and local parties, apparently billing himself at the latter as Reverend Blue.

For more than three decades, he was an itinerant musician, working as a solo act and in as-

sociation with a host of other now-famous bluesmen, especially Sunnyland Slim, Elmore James, Robert Johnson, Howlin' Wolf, and Robert Lockwood Jr. He traveled throughout the South, working carnivals and lumber camps as well as juke joints and street corners in Mississippi, Arkansas, and Tennessee. He probably played in New Orleans in the 1920s and almost certainly appeared on the radio in southern Illinois in the late 1930s, but his claim to a 1930s appearance on the Grand Ole Opry in Nashville has never been verified and is almost certainly apocryphal. During this period, he was known both as Willie Miller and as Willie Williamson, among other names and nicknames.

In November 1941, Williamson began playing with Robert Lockwood Jr. on *King Biscuit Time*, where he starred on and off for more than twenty years. It was on this show, apparently, that he first unveiled his "Sonny Boy Williamson" moniker, initiating enormous confusion among blues scholars since another Sonny Boy Williamson, a harmonica player from Tennessee named John Lee Williamson, had already established himself in Chicago. Williamson soon became *King Biscuit Time*'s most famous performer. The sponsor, the Interstate Grocery Company, was soon marketing Sonny Boy Corn Meal, with the harmonica-wielding blues musician displayed on every bag.

Despite these successes, Williamson did not record until 1951, when Lillian McMurry's newly established Trumpet label in Jackson, Mississippi, issued "Eyesight to the Blind," "Mighty Long Time," "Nine Below Zero," and "Mr. Down Child," among others. These first recordings, long since recognized as classics of the genre, show him at the very top of his form—a laconic, often mordant and sarcastic vocalist, as well as a masterful instrumentalist.

In 1954, the Chess label in Chicago purchased Williamson's contract, and he soon moved north, playing club dates in Detroit, St. Louis, Milwaukee, and Philadelphia. His several hits in the late 1950s and early 1960s ("Fattening Frogs for Snakes," "Don't Start Me to Talkin'," "Your Funeral and My Trial," "One Way Out," and "99") were followed by successful European tours in 1963 and 1964. The name game continued: on his passport, he was Sonny Boy Williams, and

Sonny Boy Williamson Hit Songs

"Eyesight to the Blind" (1951)
"Mr. Down Child" (1951)
"Mighty Long Time" (1952)
"Nine Below Zero" (1952)
"Don't Start Me to Talkin'" (1955)
"Fattening Frogs for Snakes" (1957)
"Your Funeral and My Trial" (1958)
"99" (1958)
"One Way Out" (1962)

he was often billed in Europe as Sonny Boy Williamson II.

He greatly enjoyed the appreciation of European blues fans, touring in Denmark, Germany, and Poland and performing in several concerts with the Animals and the Yardbirds. He seriously considered settling permanently in England, but he returned instead to Helena, where he again appeared on the *King Biscuit* show.

On May 25, 1965, he was found dead by drummer James "Peck" Curtis after Williamson had failed to arrive at the station for a performance. He is buried in Tutwiler, Mississippi, where the birth date on his tombstone is almost certainly incorrect and the death date wrong beyond any doubt. Several names are listed, but Aleck Miller is given precedence. In 2008, he was inducted into the Arkansas Entertainers Hall of Fame.

For additional information:

Donoghue, William E. *'Fessor Mojo's "Don't Start Me to Talkin'."* Seattle: Elliott & James, 1997.

Hay, Fred J. "The Sacred/Profane Dialectic in Delta Blues: The Life and Lyrics of Sonny Boy Williamson." *Phylon* 48 (Winter 1988): 317–326.

Oliver, Paul. Liner notes for *Sonny Boy Williams on King Biscuit Time.* Arhoolie, 1993.

Palmer, Robert. *Deep Blues.* New York: Viking Press, 1981.

"Sonny Boy Williamson." Mississippi Blues Trail http://www.msbluestrail.org/blues-trail-markers/sonny-boy-williamson (accessed March 15, 2013).

Robert Cochran

This entry, originally published in *Arkansas Biography: A Collection of Notable Lives,* appears in the *Encyclopedia of Arkansas Music* in an altered form. *Arkansas Biography* is available from the University of Arkansas Press in Fayetteville.

BLUES / R&B — JIMMY "SPOON" WITHERSPOON (1921?–1997)

James John (Jimmy) Witherspoon, also known by the nickname "Spoon," was a versatile singer who achieved commercial success and critical acclaim in the genres of blues, jazz, and rhythm and blues. His 1947 recording "Ain't Nobody's Business" was a hit in 1949 and became his signature song.

Jimmy Witherspoon was born in Gurdon (Clark County) to Leonard Witherspoon, a Missouri Pacific Railroad brakeman, and Eva Tatum Witherspoon, a church pianist. The family was devoutly religious. His parents were members of the choir at their Baptist church. His date of birth is usually given as August 8, 1923, but some sources give the birth year as 1920, and more than one source gives the birth date as August 18, 1921, attributing the information to his son. Since he may have run away from home to Los Angeles, California, as early as 1935, the earlier dates seem more plausible. In a 1996 interview, he gave his age as seventy-four, which also corresponds with the 1921 date.

His parents' religiosity, especially his mother's—his father died during his early childhood—was influential throughout his life. His mother strenuously objected to blues music, which she considered "dirty" and unsophisticated. Notwithstanding, at an early age Witherspoon listened to blues and other secular music locally on jukeboxes and the radio. Witherspoon's ambition to become a professional singer developed early in life, as did his talent. He joined the church choir at about age five and won a Clark County singing contest during the same time.

After arriving in Los Angeles in the mid-1930s, he worked as a dishwasher at a drugstore and patronized the blues and jazz clubs located in Los Angeles's Central Avenue District during his off hours. In these clubs, he met some of the leading West Coast blues and jazz performers, including his idol, blues singer Big Joe Turner. He also began sitting in with some of the local bands, quickly becoming an audience favorite.

In 1941, Witherspoon joined the U.S. Merchant Marines and served aboard ships transporting supplies to British forces in Asia. On shore leave in Calcutta, India, he sang with a big band led by American jazz pianist Teddy Weatherford, a performance broadcast by the U.S. Armed Forces Radio Service, a service the Department of War had created in 1942 to entertain and inform military personnel deployed overseas.

After being discharged from the Merchant Marines in 1943, Witherspoon returned to California and soon joined renowned blues and jazz pianist Jay

Jimmy Witherspoon in Paris, France; 1976.

Photo: Lionel Decoster

McShann's band. He was McShann's lead singer from 1944 until 1948. In 1949, the recording of their re-worked version of Bessie Smith's "Ain't Nobody's Business" reached the top of *Billboard* magazine's R&B chart. It stayed on the chart for an unprecedented run of thirty-four weeks.

Witherspoon's other hits with McShann, and as a solo artist, did not attain the extraordinary success of "Ain't Nobody's Business." His career soon began to founder, accelerated by the emergence of rock and roll music, resulting in serious financial and personal setbacks. In 1953, he declared bankruptcy and divorced his first wife, Rachel, whom he had married in 1951. (They had no children.) Witherspoon struggled through lean years in the 1950s, recorded for small labels, and staged a comeback at the 1959 Monterey Jazz Festival, headlining with the Count Basie Orchestra, Woody Herman, Sarah Vaughan, and others. Witherspoon's performance at the festival established his reputation as a formidable jazz singer; it also was the first time his mother attended one of his concerts.

From the early 1960s into the mid-1990s, Witherspoon performed regularly at concerts in the United States and abroad, maintained a sporadically successful solo recording career, and collaborated with dozens of artists, including admirers from the rock and roll world such as Dr. John, Eric Burdon, and Van Morrison. He also began acting occasionally, appearing in a few television shows and in the films *The Black Godfather* (1974), *To Sleep with Anger* (1990), and *Georgia* (1995).

Witherspoon's marital history is complicated. He reportedly reconciled briefly with his first wife in 1958. In mid-1962, however, he married Diana Williams, but by the end of the year he was reported to have initiated divorce proceedings. In the early 1970s, he was with a woman named Joyce. However, a 1978 news item announced his engagement to Sharon Rivera and reported that he had been a bachelor for twelve years. Finally, his 1997 obituary identifies his surviving spouse as Diana.

Witherspoon was diagnosed with throat cancer in the 1980s and survived, but the treatments damaged his vocal chords and harmed his singing voice. Rehabilitation enabled him to resume his career, albeit with a raspy vocal quality that was somewhat diminished from the resonant baritone of his glory years. The cancer returned in the 1990s, but he continued performing until shortly before his death in Los Angeles on September 18, 1997. He was survived by his wife, three children, and four grandchildren. His obituary listed two surviving siblings.

Witherspoon earned numerous accolades during his career, including inductions into several music halls of fame, most notably the *Ebony* magazine Blues Hall of Fame in 1976, Arkansas Jazz Heritage Foundation's Arkansas Jazz Hall of Fame and Arthur L. Porter Lifetime Achievement Award in 1996, the Blues Foundation's Blues Hall of Fame in 2008, and Grammy Award nominations in 1984, 1987, and 1996. He also was a recipient of the prestigious National Association for the Advancement of Colored People (NAACP) Image Award in 1975. His prolific recording output includes *Jimmy Witherspoon at the Monterey Jazz Festival* (1959), *Midnight Lady Called the Blues* (1986), and *Live at the Mint* (1996).

For additional information:

Clark, Donald, ed. *The Penguin Encyclopedia of Popular Music*. New York: Penguin Books, 1989.

Deffaa, Chip. *Blue Rhythms: Six Lives in Rhythm and Blues*. Urbana: University of Illinois Press, 1996.

Ratliff, Ben. "Jimmy Witherspoon, Singer of Blues and Jazz, Dies at 74." *New York Times*, September 22, 1997. Online at http://www.nytimes.com/1997/09/22/arts/jimmy-witherspoon-singer-of-blues-and-jazz-dies-at-74.html (accessed February 26, 2013).

Rowe, Monk. Interview with Jimmy Witherspoon, April 12, 1996. Hamilton College Jazz Archives. Hamilton College, Clinton, New York.

Greg A. Phelps

John Quincy Wolf Jr. (1901–1972)

A college professor and self-trained folklorist, John Quincy Wolf Jr. left a lasting legacy in the mid-South folk music world through his intrepid collecting and field recording and his broad-ranging scholarship.

Wolf was born in Batesville (Independence County) on May 14, 1901, the younger of the two children of John Quincy Wolf Sr. and Adele Crouch Wolf. Known as Quincy to distinguish him from his banker father, he spent the first twenty-one years of his life in Batesville, earning his bachelor's degree from Arkansas College (now Lyon College) in 1922. One year later, Wolf received an MA in English at Vanderbilt University and returned to his alma mater to teach English and history for much of the next decade, with occasional leaves of absence to pursue a doctorate at Johns Hopkins University. In 1931, he married former student and fellow Arkansas College employee Bess Millen of Malvern (Hot Spring County). After Wolf's brief teaching appointments at Goucher College and the University of Wisconsin, the couple settled in 1937 in Memphis, Tennessee, where he would spend the rest of his career on the faculty of Southwestern at Memphis (now Rhodes College) and where the couple would raise their two daughters. Wolf completed his PhD at Johns Hopkins in 1946.

At Southwestern, Wolf eventually became chairman of the English department, a post he held for more than twenty years. Although his academic expertise lay in Romantic poetry, Wolf is best remembered as a pioneer in the teaching and collecting of folklore and folk music. Wolf began collecting mountain ballads as a college student, but it was only in the early 1950s, on summer and Christmas vacations back home in Arkansas, that he and his wife began recording folk singers and musicians. Wolf recorded more than 1,000 songs in the rural Ozarks, primarily within a fifty-mile radius of Batesville. Among his most significant "discoveries" were Almeda Riddle, Ollie Gilbert, and folk music legend Jimmy Driftwood, who credited Wolf with convincing him to audition for the Nashville producers who eventually signed him to a contract.

When rheumatoid arthritis restricted his mobility in the early 1960s, Wolf increasingly turned his attention to shape-note congregational singing in northern Mississippi and Alabama and finally to the blues music of the Memphis area. He recorded bluesmen Gus Cannon, Furry Lewis, and Bukka White and invited them to perform for his folk music classes at Southwestern. Wolf's contemporaries recognized him as an authority on southern folk music. Alan Lomax consulted Wolf before making his 1959 recording trip to the Ozarks, and in the 1960s, promoters of the Newport Folk Festival in Rhode Island sought Wolf's assistance in identifying and scheduling blues, Ozarks, and shape-note performers.

John Quincy Wolf Jr.
Courtesy: Old Independence Regional Museum/Wolf Collection

At the time of his death on March 14, 1972, Wolf had been collecting his father's stories of growing up in the Ozarks in the years following the Civil War. Bess Wolf and Memphis State University (now University of Memphis) professor F. Jack Hurley shepherded those into publication as *Life in the Leatherwoods* in 1974. Nine years later, Bess Wolf, who had moved back to the Wolf family home in Batesville, donated Wolf's collection of almost 500 audio tapes to the Regional Studies Center at Arkansas College. This rich legacy of Wolf's passion for folk music is today available on the website of the Lyon College Regional Studies Center.

For additional information:

Hyde, Gene. "A Pioneer Ozark Folklorist: John Quincy Wolf, Jr." *Arkansas Democrat-Gazette*, April 3, 1998, 1E.

John Quincy Wolf Jr. Collection. Regional Studies Center. Lyon College, Batesville, Arkansas. Online at http://web.lyon.edu/wolfcollection/ (accessed February 19, 2013).

Lankford, George E. "John Quincy Wolf, Jr.: An Appreciation." *Mid-America Folklore* 13 (Winter/Spring 1985): 3–8.

Brooks Blevins

X-Y-Z

CLASSICAL / OPERA **FERDINAND ZELLNER** (1831–1919)

Ferdinand Frederick Zellner lived in Fayetteville (Washington County) from 1852 until 1863 and wrote a piece of music called the "Fayetteville Polka," which is believed to be the first Arkansas composition to be published as sheet music.

Ferdinand Zellner was born in Berlin, Prussia (now a part of Germany), in August 1831 and reportedly came to the United States in 1850 as part of the orchestra that toured with Jenny Lind, the "Swedish nightingale." After the tour ended and Lind returned to Europe, Zellner and his brother, Willhelm Emil Zellner, stayed in America and settled in Fayetteville.

Ferdinand Zellner filed paperwork with Washington County in 1852 to become an American citizen and was hired by Sophia Sawyer as a music teacher for the Fayetteville Female Seminary. Sawyer died in 1854, but the school continued under the ownership of two of the teachers, and Zellner continued as a music teacher.

The Balmer & Weber publishing house of St. Louis, Missouri, published Zellner's composition of the "Fayetteville Polka" in 1856, as well as a second song titled "Sunbeam Schottisch." Both the polka and the schottische styles of music originated in Bohemia and became popular in Germany during the early nineteenth century. By mid-century, they had become popular in America, too, and Zellner's two compositions were reprinted across the country.

Although Zellner was thirty years old at the outbreak of the Civil War, he does not appear to have served in either the Confederate army or the Union army. He purchased the property of the Fayetteville Female Seminary in 1862 and appeared intent on keeping the school in operation despite the destruction of much of Fayetteville during the early part of the war.

Cover for sheet music of "Sunbeam Schottisch," composed by Ferdinand Zellner; 1856.

Courtesy: Special Collections, University of Arkansas Libraries, Fayetteville

In 1863, the major buildings of the school were destroyed by fire, and Zellner left Fayetteville for St. Louis, Missouri, along with many other families sympathetic to the Union. "My desire is, like theirs, to find a place which we can call our home once more, a place of which we have been so ruthlessly deprived at the very outset of this unholy rebellion," Zellner wrote in 1864. He initially stayed with Matilda and Jonas Tebbetts, who had earlier left Fayetteville and purchased a farm, which they dubbed "Exilia." Zellner stayed for several months but moved into a boarding house in St. Louis in 1864 so that he could more easily offer music lessons and earn money. At the same time, the Tebbettses began planning a move to California with former Fayetteville residents Robert and Mariah Graham. Robert Graham had been offered presidency of a college at Woodland, California, and Zellner was invited to join the group.

On June 1, 1864, however, federal officials arrested Zellner and several other residents at his boarding house. They were taken to the Gratiot Street Military Prison and charged with being members of a secret society plotting the secession of Missouri.

Tebbetts, a lawyer and former Arkansas prosecutor and judge, and Charles Balmer, one of the principals of Balmer & Weber, came to Zellner's defense immediately. They were joined quickly by Judge Barton Bates of the Missouri Supreme Court, all arguing that Zellner could not have been involved. Zellner was released on $1,000 bond initially and then released from the bond in time for him to join the Tebbettses and Grahams on their trip to California.

Although his friends did not stay long in California, Zellner did, finding employment as a professor of music at Pacific Methodist College in Santa Rosa. He also married Penelope "Neppie" Cocke in 1866; she died two years later. In 1874, Zellner married Olive Jeanette "Jennie" Beam, and they had six children, five of whom lived to adulthood. In 1876, he left Pacific Methodist for a similar position at Mills College near Oakland, California, where he was one of many music professors in a college that made music as central to its curriculum as mathematics and literature.

Zellner worked there for ten years before moving the family back to Santa Rosa, where he once again taught at the reorganized Pacific Methodist College. He and his wife became estranged in about 1900, and she moved back to the Oakland area. He survived the 1906 California earthquake, which devastated San Francisco and most of Santa Rosa.

Zellner died of liver failure on July 2, 1919, at Santa Rosa. He is buried in Santa Rosa's Rural Cemetery. Zellner's brother, Emil Zellner, stayed in Washington County after the Civil War, and his descendants still live in northwestern Arkansas.

For additional information:

Allison, Charlie. "Ferdinand Zellner: Fayetteville's First Composer." *Flashback* 62 (Spring 2012): 3–26.

Banes, Marian Tebbetts. *The Journal of Marian Tebbetts Banes.* Fayetteville: Washington County Historical Society, 1977.

Zodrow, David. "Long Forgotten Song Surfaces." *Northwest Arkansas Times*, December 22, 1974, pp. 1D–2D.

Charlie Y. Alison

ACKNOWLEDGEMENTS

We are grateful to our parent organization, the Butler Center for Arkansas Studies at the Central Arkansas Library System, for providing all manner of support in this endeavor, particularly Jasmine Jobe, Anna Lancaster, Dr. Guy Lancaster, Rod Lorenzen, John Miller, Mike Polston, Bob Razer, Dr. Bobby Roberts, Brian Robertson, Nathania Sawyer, and Dr. David Stricklin. Over the years, the many authors who have written music-related entries for the Encyclopedia of Arkansas History & Culture (EOA) website have provided us with the material that is the backbone of this book. (See pp. 229–231 for a list of EOA authors and their entries.)

Many people have gone out of their way to help us gather materials and develop content for the book, including Keith Merckx of *Arkansongs*, Jo Ellen Maack at the Old State House Museum, Jimmy Bryant at the University of Central Arkansas Archives, Dr. William Clements at Arkansas State University, Dr. Michael Dougan, John Tarpley, intern extraordinaire Darby Burdine, Elizabeth Freeman and Jeff Lewellen at the Arkansas History Commission, Marie Demeroukas at the Shiloh Museum of Ozark History, Kimberly Kaczenski at the University of Arkansas at Little Rock Center for Arkansas History and Culture, Tim Nutt at Special Collections at the University of Arkansas in Fayetteville, Harold Ott at Psych of the South, Richard Davies at the Arkansas Department of Parks and Tourism, Ken King, Byron Werner, Ian Moore, Dotty Oliver, Sandra Hubbard, Matt Johnson, and Jerry Colburn.

And most of all, we thank the music makers and the music lovers who have made this book possible.

Author Index

Mamie Ruth Abernathy
Hot Springs, Arkansas
Marjorie Lawrence

Billie J. Abbott
Cabot, Arkansas
Dale Hawkins
Al Hibbler

Charlie Y. Alison
University of Arkansas, Fayetteville
Ferdinand Zellner

Lisa H. Armstrong
North Little Rock, Arkansas
Louie Shelton

Paula Harmon Barnett
McCrory, Arkansas
Sonny Burgess

C. L. Bledsoe
Sparks Glencoe, Maryland
Sarah Caldwell
K. T. Oslin
Wayne Raney
Trout Fishing in America
Conway Twitty
Jimmy Wakely

Brooks Blevins
Missouri State University
John Quincy Wolf Jr.

David O. Bowen
Little Rock, Arkansas
Twila Paris

Michael Bowman
Arkansas State University
Beatles—Stopover

Susan Brant
Hernando, Mississippi
Wilburn Brothers

Kevin Brockmeier
Little Rock, Arkansas
Elton and Betty White

Jimmy Bryant
University of Central Arkansas
Luther Presley

Terry Buckalew
Delta Cultural Center
Glen Campbell
CeDell Davis
"Sister Rosetta" Tharpe

Darby Burdine
University of Central Arkansas
Country
Barbara Fairchild
Tav Falco
Living Sacrifice
Melody Boys Quartet

Richard Allen Burns
Arkansas State University
King Biscuit Blues Festival

Chad Causey
Jonesboro, Arkansas
Hugh Ashley

Paul Ciulla
Everett, Massachusetts
Anita Pointer

William M. Clements
Arkansas State University
"The State of Arkansaw"

Robert B. Cochran
University of Arkansas, Fayetteville
Emma Dusenbury
Patsy Montana
Charlie Rich
"The Rock Island Line"
Sonny Boy Williamson

Thomas Cochran
Fayetteville, Arkansas
Ronnie Hawkins

Harold Coogan
Mena, Arkansas
Lee Hays
T. Texas Tyler

Zac Cothren
Arkansas Historic Preservation Program
Jimmy Driftwood

Dorothy Palmer Cox
Little Rock, Arkansas
Robert Palmer

Bobby Crafford
Maumelle, Arkansas
Vaden Records

Jimmy Cunningham Jr.
Hendersonville, Tennessee
Joshua Altheimer
Bobby Rush
J. Mayo "Ink" Williams

Michael J. Dabrishus
University of Pittsburgh
William Grant Still

Meredith Doster
Batesville, Arkansas
Jeffress/Phillips Music Company

Michael B. Dougan
Jonesboro, Arkansas
Classical/Opera
Fiddlin' Bob Larkan & His Music Makers
Marjorie Lawrence
Robert McFerrin Sr.
William Warfield

Dan Dykema
Southern Arkansas University
Florence Price

Greg Freeman
Southern Edition
E. M. Bartlett
Gospel/Contemporary Christian
Tracy Lawrence
Roberta Martin
Smokie Norful
Collin Raye

Lori Freeze
Stone County Leader
Arkansas Folk Festival

Robbie Fry
Florida State University
"Big Bill" Broonzy
King Biscuit Time

Gretchen B. Gearhart
Fayetteville, Arkansas
Conlon Nancarrow

T. J. (McClung) Gibson
Van Buren, Arkansas
Hartford Music Company and Institute

Brian Hallstoos
Cedar Rapids, Iowa
Willa Saunders Jones

Freda Cruse Hardison
Mountain View, Arkansas
Ollie Gilbert

Jeff Harris
Rochester, New York
Robert Nighthawk
Houston Stackhouse

Dik de Heer
University of Leiden – The Netherlands
"Arkie" Shibley

Nancy Hendricks
Arkansas State University
Dale Evans
"Fayetteville Polka"
Klipsch Audio Technologies
"Jim Dandy" Mangrum

Jack W. Hill
Arkansas Democrat-Gazette
Iris DeMent
Al Green

Michael Hodge
Butler Center for Arkansas Studies
Al Bell
The Vapors

Amber Hood
Little Rock, Arkansas
Carolina Cotton

Ed Hopkinson
Chester, Virginia
Dr. Smith's Champion Hoss Hair Pullers

Stephen Husarik
University of Arkansas at Fort Smith
Scott Joplin

Gene Hyde
Radford University
Fred Marshall

Esther Jennings
Little Rock Central High EAST Lab
Evanescence

William B. Jones Jr.
Bottle Imp Archives, Little Rock
E&M Recording Company and My
    Records
Garage Bands

George Keck
Ouachita Baptist University
Francis McBeth

Mike Keckhaver
Encyclopedia of Arkansas
Rwake

Kevin D. Kehrberg
University of Kentucky
Albert E. Brumley

Jim Kelton
University of Arkansas, Fayetteville
Luther Allison
Jim Ed Brown
The Browns
Cate Brothers Band
Floyd Cramer
"Lefty" Frizzell
Albert King
Robert Lockwood Jr.
"Son" Seals

Kayla Kesterson
Hot Springs, Arkansas
Billy Lee Riley

Stephen Koch
Arkansongs
Blues/R&B
Lonnie Glosson
"Little Willie" John
Louis Jordan
Moondog
Rolling Stones—Arrest

Eric Lensing
Memphis, Tennessee
Johnny Cash

Liz Lottmann
Bella Vista, Arkansas
"Sunshine" Sonny Payne

Rachel Reynolds Luster
Coalition for Ozarks Living Traditions
Mary Celestia Parler

Floyd W. Martin
University of Arkansas at Little Rock
Barbara Hendricks

Philip Martin
Arkansas Democrat-Gazette
Lucinda Williams

William K. McNeil
Ozark Folk Center
Elton Britt
"Sister Rosetta" Tharpe

Keith Merckx
Arkansongs
Narvel Felts
Dan Hicks
Music and Musicians (Introduction)
Rock 'n' Roll Highway 67

Jamie Metrailer
Little Rock, Arkansas
Roosevelt "The Honeydripper" Sykes
Peetie Wheatstraw

Matthew W. Mihalka
University of Arkansas, Fayetteville
Ne-Yo

Aaron Miller
Harding University
Bazooka

Adam Miller
Georgetown, Texas
"Snub" Mosley

Glenn D. Morrison
Rackensack Folklore Society
Rackensack Folklore Society

Bill Norman
Little Rock, Arkansas
Gretha Boston

Timothy G. Nutt
University of Arkansas Libraries
Bob Dorough

Greg A. Phelps
Lindsey Wilson College
Zilphia Horton
Jimmy "Spoon" Witherspoon

Eugene Porter
Little Rock, Arkansas
Art Porter Jr.
Art Porter Sr.

Jim Porter
Arkansas Entertainers Hall of Fame
Walter Norris

David Prater
Little Rock, Arkansas
Pharoah Sanders

Bob Purvis
Pine Bluff, Arkansas
Arkansas Entertainers Hall of Fame

Henry Q. Rinne
University of Arkansas at Fort Smith
Alphonso "Phonnie" Trent

Bryan Rogers
North Little Rock, Arkansas
Black Oak Arkansas
Roy Buchanan
Levon Helm
Howlin' Wolf

Johnnie Taylor

Laura Rosenberg
Hot Springs Music Festival
Hot Springs Music Festival

C. Dennis Schick
North Little Rock, Arkansas
Diamond State Chorus
Top of the Rock Chorus

Toney Butler Schlesinger
Granite Bay, California
Al Bennett

Marvin Schwartz
Little Rock, Arkansas
Rockabilly

Gwendolyn L. Shelton
Little Rock, Arkansas
Calvin "Slim" Leavy

Ethel C. Simpson
University of Arkansas, Fayetteville
Opera in the Ozarks at Inspiration Point

Harry Snider with Tim Jones
Little Rock, Arkansas
Jim Porter Jr.

Melvin "Bud" Stacey
Satsuma, Alabama
KAAY

Katherine Stanick
Little Rock, Arkansas
Arkansas Symphony Orchestra

Shea Stewart
Little Rock, Arkansas
Riverfest Arts and Music Festival

David Stricklin
Butler Center for Arkansas Studies
Brockwell Gospel Music School
King of Clubs

John Tarpley
Dallas, Texas
Jazz
Charlotte Moorman

Billie Francis Taylor
Arkadelphia, Arkansas
Point of Grace

Steven Teske
Butler Center for Arkansas Studies
Robinson Center Music Hall

David Ware
Arkansas Secretary of State's Office
Official State Musical Instrument
Official State Songs

John R. Way
Crossett, Arkansas
Hartford Music Company and Institute

Ali Welky
Encyclopedia of Arkansas
Wayland Holyfield
Sleepy LaBeef
Old Folks' Singing
John Michael Talbot

George West
Little Rock Central High School
Almeda Riddle

Elizabeth Whitaker
Little Rock, Arkansas
Ronnie Dunn
Rock

Donna Liane Williams
Little Rock, Arkansas
J. Paul Williams

Ann Phillips Worster
Yellville, Arkansas
Violet Brumley Hensley

Susan Young
Shiloh Museum of Ozark History
Sundown to Sunup Gospel Sing

Alice Zeman
Paw Paw, Illinois
Mary Lewis

Index

About the editors

Editors Ali Welky and Mike Keckhaver are both on the staff of the Encyclopedia of Arkansas History & Culture (EOA). Ali Welky, who lives in Conway, Arkansas, with her husband and two children, is the assistant editor of the EOA. As she is a lifelong lover of words and music, putting this book together has been a treat—like making a historical mix-tape. Mike Keckhaver, whose talents as media editor for the EOA are outstripped only by his vast musical skill and knowledge, lives in rural Pulaski County, Arkansas, where he can turn up his stereo (with Klipsch speakers, of course) as loud as he wants.